Mergers, Sell-Offs,
and Economic Efficiency

Mergers, Sell-Offs, and Economic Efficiency

DAVID J. RAVENSCRAFT

F. M. SCHERER

THE BROOKINGS INSTITUTION

Washington, D.C.

Library of Congress Cataloging-in-Publication data:
Ravenscraft, David J., 1952–
  Mergers, sell-offs, and economic efficiency.
  Includes index.
  1. Consolidation and merger of corporations—United
States. 2. Corporate divestiture—United States.
I. Scherer, F. M. (Frederic M.). II. Title.
HD2746.5.S34 1987   338.8′3′0973   87-14018
ISBN 0-8157-7348-X
ISBN 0-8157-7347-1 (pbk.)

9 8 7 6 5 4 3 2 1

THE BROOKINGS INSTITUTION is an independent organization devoted to nonpartisan research, education, and publication in economics, government, foreign policy, and the social sciences generally. Its principal purposes are to aid in the development of sound public policies and to promote public understanding of issues of national importance.

The Institution was founded on December 8, 1927, to merge the activities of the Institute for Government Research, founded in 1916, the Institute of Economics, founded in 1922, and the Robert Brookings Graduate School of Economics and Government, founded in 1924.

The Board of Trustees is responsible for the general administration of the Institution, while the immediate direction of the policies, program, and staff is vested in the President, assisted by an advisory committee of the officers and staff. The by-laws of the Institution state: "It is the function of the Trustees to make possible the conduct of scientific research, and publication, under the most favorable conditions, and to safeguard the independence of the research staff in the pursuit of their studies and in the publication of the results of such studies. It is not a part of their function to determine, control, or influence the conduct of particular investigations or the conclusions reached."

The President bears final responsibility for the decision to publish a manuscript as a Brookings book. In reaching his judgment on the competence, accuracy, and objectivity of each study, the President is advised by the director of the appropriate research program and weighs the views of a panel of expert outside readers who report to him in confidence on the quality of the work. Publication of a work signifies that it is deemed a competent treatment worthy of public consideration but does not imply endorsement of conclusions or recommendations.

The Institution maintains its position of neutrality on issues of public policy in order to safeguard the intellectual freedom of the staff. Hence interpretations or conclusions in Brookings publications should be understood to be solely those of the authors and should not be attributed to the Institution, to its trustees, officers, or other staff members, or to the organizations that support its research.

Foreword

THIS VOLUME ADDRESSES a set of questions on which there has been heated debate in industry, government, and academic circles: what are the consequences of mergers and takeovers for the subsequent performance of the companies involved and the productivity of the manufacturing sector more generally. Research using stock price data has produced equivocal results, while studies of profitability before and after mergers have suffered from diverse methodological problems. This study taps a rich data base that is well suited to illuminating the economic outcomes of mergers made during the 1960s and early 1970s. Its core is the Federal Trade Commission's Line of Business information on the financial performance of manufacturing operations in 471 U.S. corporations over the years 1975–77. The authors have linked to that data historical information on some 6,000 mergers and takeovers consummated between 1950 and 1976, pre-merger profitability statistics from several smaller samples, and the divisional sell-off records of the Line of Business companies from 1974 through 1981. These data permit a thorough analysis of the characteristics of acquired companies, the changes in profitability over the years following merger, and the survival history of acquired units.

The authors devote special attention to the high fraction of acquisitions that are subsequently sold off. In addition to a statistical analysis of the determinants of divestiture, the authors distill the results of 15 case studies, tracing the histories of units from their initial acquisition through the organizational and financial changes that followed divestiture. Using these data, the authors estimate the impact of mergers on productivity growth in the manufacturing sector during the 1970s and draw implications for business leaders and government policymakers.

For the research reported here, F. M. Scherer received a National Science Foundation grant, two Swarthmore College faculty research grants, and a sabbatical leave from Swarthmore in 1985–86, which he

vii

spent as a visiting fellow at Brookings. David J. Ravenscraft was a staff member of the Federal Trade Commission's Bureau of Economics through the project. The FTC's computer facilities were used to process the Line of Business data. The FTC's Disclosure Avoidance Officer has certified that the data in this volume do not identify data on individual companies in the Line of Business survey. Although the data on individual companies are confidential, data sets are available to researchers under FTC confidentiality rules.

Research assistance for the project was provided by Kevin Bespolka, John Caparusso, David Chapman, Susan Danzig, Geoffrey Hazard, and James Lamberth under Swarthmore College financing; by Nathaniel Levy of the Brookings Institution staff; and by Jonathan Broadnax, Ernest Cowan, Michael Dodman, Amie Ingber, Kenneth Ofori-Atta, Gloria Reyes, Diana Voss, Mike Warner, and Dorothy Wilson of the FTC's Line of Business program staff.

Valuable critical comments were received from Geoffrey Meeks, Dennis Mueller, Lawrence J. White, and Lee Sheppard, and from the participants in seminars at the National Bureau of Economic Research, the Econometric Society, the University of Maryland, the University of Massachusetts, the University of Chicago, Yale University, the U.S. Department of Justice, and the Federal Trade Commission. The authors are particularly grateful to the participants in 70 case study interviews, both for their openness and generosity in the interviews and for their responses to follow-up and verification inquiries.

The views expressed here are those of the authors and should not be ascribed to the trustees, officers, or staff members of the Brookings Institution, to the Federal Trade Commission or its operating divisions, or to any of the other institutions or persons acknowledged above.

BRUCE K. MAC LAURY
President

August 1987
Washington, D.C.

Contents

1. Introduction   1
   The Rationale of Mergers 2
   Research Methodology 17
   Plan of the Book 18

2. The Contours of Merger Activity Since 1950   20
   Merger Trends in Manufacturing and Mineral Industries 20
   The Sample Companies and Their Diversification 24
   The Conglomerates 36
   The Structural Correlates of Merger Activity 45
   Conclusion 54

3. The Profitability of Acquired Companies   56
   Prior Research 56
   New York Stock Exchange Listing Application Evidence 58
   Further Evidence 64
   Summary 73

4. Post-Merger Financial Performance   75
   The Line of Business Merger Data Link 75
   Asset Values and the Choice of Accounting Method 78
   Sample Composition 82
   Variables and Model Specification 83
   The Cross-Sectional Results 85
   Matched Pre- Versus Post-Merger Analysis 111
   Merged Unit Growth 117
   Expenditures on Research and Development 119
   Conclusion 122

5. The Economics of Sell-Off: Case Study Evidence   123
   Methodology 123

The Sample *127*
The Reasons for Merger *129*
What Went Wrong? *132*
The Sell-Off Decision *144*
Developments after Sell-Off *149*
Conclusion *157*

6. The Economics of Sell-Off: Statistical Evidence   159
The Frequency of Sell-Off *159*
The Determinants of Sell-Off *166*
Pre-Divestiture Investment Behavior *187*
Conclusion *190*

7. Pulling the Threads Together   192
The Efficiency Consequences *192*
Were Mergers Profitable for the Acquirers? *204*
Merger Performance and Merger Motives *210*

8. Broader Implications   216
The Importance of Understanding *216*
Is History Irrelevant? *218*
The Policy Instruments *221*

Appendixes
A. Predicting the Merger Accounting Method *229*
B. Narrative Summary of the Case Studies *239*
C. Mnemonics Used in the Principal Statistical Analyses *280*

Index   285

Tables
2-1. Distribution of Assets Acquired in Acquisitions of Large
Manufacturing and Mining Companies by FTC Merger Type
Classification, 1948–77   23
2-2. Distribution of Manufacturing Industry Assets Acquired, by
Experience-Oriented Merger Category, 1950–77   24
2-3. Manufacturing Sales and Line of Business Counts in 1950 and
1975 for the 471 Companies in the FTC's 1975 Line of Business
Survey   28
2-4. Diversification of Top 200 Companies of 1950 and 1975, Ranked
by Sales Quintile   30

2-5. Diversification of the 148 Top 200 Companies of 1950 Surviving in the 1975 Line of Business Survey, Ranked by 1950 Sales Quintile 32

2-6. Accounting for Changes in the Number of Lines of Business for the 148 Top 200 Companies of 1950 Surviving in the 1975 Line of Business Survey 34

2-7. Percentage of Added Lines of Business Attributed to Internal Growth Versus Acquisition for the 148 Top 200 Companies of 1950 Surviving in the 1975 Line of Business Survey, Ranked by 1950 Sales Quintile 36

2-8. The Leading Merger-Making Companies in the Line of Business Survey, Ranked by Number of Acquisitions, 1950–78 38

2-9. Cumulated Stock Market Value of $1,000 Investments in Thirteen Leading Conglomerates, 1965–83 and 1968–83 40

2-10. Value in 1983 of a $1,000 1965 Investment in Each of Thirteen Leading Conglomerates in the S&P Industrials Portfolio 43

2-11. Average Industry Characteristics of Newly Acquired and Original Lines of Business for Ninety Merger-Active Companies 50

2-12. Regression Equations Relating Measures of Industrywide Merger Activity to Industry Characteristics 54

3-1. Average Supranormal Profitability of Acquired Companies before Merger, by Year of Acquisition and Merger Accounting Method 61

3-2. Operating Income as a Percentage of Assets for All Manufacturing Companies in the FTC's Quarterly Financial Report, 1962–77 66

4-1. Distribution of Lines of Business by the Number of Nonequals Acquisitions Surviving into 1977 77

4-2. Basic Merger Effect Regressions 86

4-3. Merger Effect Regressions for 1977 with Continuous Industry Controls and Categorical Merger Activity Variables 90

4-4. Merger Effect Regressions Testing Additional Variables, with Fixed Industry Effects, 1977 Operating Income/Assets as Dependent Variable 96

4-5. Sensitivity Analyses Testing Additional Accounting Variables, *MERGSHR* Growth Variants, and Adjusted Sample Coverage, with 1977 Operating Income/Assets as Dependent Variable 104

4-6. Best-Fitting Time Lag Structure Regressions 109

4-7. Distribution of Asset Growth *MERGSHR:G* Values for Post-1950 Lines of Business with Acquisitions 119

4-8. Regressions with Ratios of 1977 Company-Financed R&D Outlays to Sales as Dependent Variable 121

5-1. Merger and Divestiture Highlights for Fifteen Case Study Units Sold Off between 1977 and 1984 128

5-2. Profitability of Eleven Case Study Companies in the Year before Their Acquisition 129

5-3. Characteristics of New Buyers in Fifteen Sell-Off Cases   150

6-1. Number of Manufacturing Lines of Business Sold Off per Year,
     1974–81   163

6-2. Average Operating Income as a Percentage of Assets for Lines
     of Business with Sell-Offs, by Interval between the Date of
     Profit Report and Initiation of Sell-Off, 1974–81   167

6-3. Deviations of Divested Lines' Profitability from the Average
     Operating Income/Assets Percentages of Nondivested Lines in
     the Same Industry, by Interval between the Date of Profit
     Report and Initiation of Sell-Off, 1974–81   168

6-4. Annual Turnover Rates for Chief Executive Officers of
     Companies in the Line of Business Sample, 1973–80   171

6-5. Recapitulation of Explanatory Variables Used in the Analysis of
     Full Sell-Offs   174

6-6. Availability (X) and Gaps (O) in Data for Estimating a Four-
     Year Lagged Relationship between Profitability and Line of
     Business Sell-Offs, 1970–80   175

6-7. Logit and Ordinary Least Squares (OLS) Regressions
     Explaining Full Sell-Offs   180

6-8. Changes in the Probability of Sell-Off Indicated by Logit
     Regression (1a) in Table 6-7 with a Four-Standard-Deviation
     Increase in Individual Variables, Other Variables Held at Their
     Mean Values   182

6-9. Multinomial Logit Results from Analysis of Partial and Full Sell-
     Offs for 2,683 Lines of Business   186

6-10. Average Deviations of the Ratios of R&D to Sales and
      Advertising to Sales from Industry Norms for Fully Divested
      Lines of Business, by Years before Sell-Off   189

7-1. Derivation of Asset-Weighted Deviations of Post-Merger from
     Pre-Merger Profitability of 634-Company Sample   198

7-2. Internal Rates of Return as of 1983 from Investments Financing
     the Leading Conglomerates' Acquisition Activity, 1962–78   210

A-1. Logit Regressions Predicting the Probability of Pooling
     Accounting for All Manufacturing Acquisitions, 1950–79   235

A-2. Logit Regressions Predicting the Probability of Pooling
     Accounting for Acquisitions with Both Asset and Consideration
     Paid Data, 1950–79   237

Figures

1-1. Normalized Weekly Stock Price Movements of Typical
     Acquiring and Acquired Firms in Time Period Surrounding the
     Merger Announcement   4

2-1. Constant-Dollar Volume of Manufacturing and Mineral Firm
     Acquisitions, 1895–1985   21

2-2. Stock Price Movements of a Portfolio of Thirteen Merger-Prone
     Conglomerates and the Standard & Poor's Industrials Portfolio,
     1964–83   41

4-1. Pooling Merger Effect Lag Structures from Regressions
     in Tables 4-2 and 4-6   110
4-2. Capital Allocation Decisions under Capital Rationing and Elastic
     Capital Market Conditions   112
6-1. Trends in Sell-Off and Merger Activity, 1965–85   161
7-1. Pre-Merger Profitability as a Function of Acquired Company
     Size   196

CHAPTER ONE

Introduction

THE MARKETPLACE of ideas concerning business enterprise mergers in the United States is curiously compartmentalized.

During the hiatus between the conglomerate merger wave of the 1960s and the record merger activity of the early 1980s, a vigorous school of thought emerged that sought to explain the causes and efficiency benefits of mergers through the study of stock price behavior. One of the first contributions found the pattern of stock price movements to support the hypothesis that "mergers are a mechanism by which the market system replaces incompetent management."[1] From the large number of studies that followed, the president's Council of Economic Advisers concluded in 1985 that "mergers and acquisitions . . . improve efficiency, transfer scarce resources to higher valued uses, and stimulate effective corporate management."[2]

Meanwhile another school, straddling parts of academia, the consulting profession, and the business press, focused with growing skepticism on the fruits of past mergers. *Fortune* magazine, for example, undertook a ten-year review of the ten largest conglomerate acquisitions made in 1971 and found that only two remained trouble-free. "Most of the acquirers," it concluded, "were lured into buying unstable companies, or into committing foolish mistakes that harmed stable ones."[3] Peter Drucker, gray eminence among students of managerial behavior, observed that two mergers out of five are "outright disasters," two "neither live nor die," and one "works."[4] In 1968 the journal *Mergers &*

1. Gershon Mandelker, "Risk and Return: The Case of Merging Firms," *Journal of Financial Economics*, vol. 1, no. 3 (1974), p. 324.
2. *Economic Report of the President, February 1985*, p. 196.
3. Arthur M. Louis, "The Bottom Line on Ten Big Mergers," *Fortune*, May 3, 1982, p. 89.
4. "Why Some Mergers Work and Many More Don't" (interview with Peter Drucker), *Forbes*, January 18, 1982, p. 36. See also Arthur Burck, "The Hidden Trauma of Merger Mania," *Business Week*, December 6, 1982, p. 14; and Thomas J. Murray, "Do Mergers Make Sense?" *Dun's Business Month*, October 1982, pp. 88–93.

Acquisitions began a regular column listing corporate sell-offs. At the time it predicted a "crush to unload . . . unprofitable operations, . . . some acquired businesses that just can't be made to fit, and . . . the poor earners that offer greater potential to someone else."[5] Statistical data published annually by the W. T. Grimm Company reveal that for every 100 acquisitions recorded between 1971 and 1980, there were 40 divestitures.[6] A substantial majority of those sell-offs, we shall see in chapter 6, involved previously acquired units.

How can one reconcile these conflicting views of the merger world, with one set of observers perceiving success and another widespread failure? The research reported in this book sought answers to the puzzle. It began from, and was sustained by, two fundamental premises. First, for a balanced assessment of mergers' consequences, the evidence had to be richer than, and escape the flaws of, data that had previously been used in merger studies. Second, it was necessary to probe the quantitatively large subset of cases in which mergers, once made, were subsequently undone through sell-off. These two premises set the framework for what follows.

The Rationale of Mergers

Why do mergers occur? In most mergers, there are more or less clearly identified sellers and buyers. The simplest explanation must be that both buyers and sellers consider themselves to be better off from the merger transaction than without it. But we must dig deeper. Why do the parties become better off?[7]

5. "Corporate Sell-Off," *Mergers & Acquisitions*, vol. 3 (May-June 1968), p. 84.

6. *Mergerstat Review: 1980* (Chicago: Grimm, 1981), and earlier issues. See also Leonard W. Weiss, "The Extent and Effects of Aggregate Concentration," *Journal of Law and Economics*, vol. 26 (June 1983), pp. 440–41, who found that 35 percent of the lines operated in 1950 by sizable corporations acquired during the 1950s and 1960s had disappeared by 1975.

7. The literature is huge, so we reference it only briefly. Seminal analyses of merger motives include Jesse W. Markham, "Survey of the Evidence and Findings on Mergers," in the National Bureau of Economic Research, *Business Concentration and Price Policy* (Princeton University Press, 1955), pp. 141–82; Robin Marris, "A Model of the 'Managerial' Enterprise," *Quarterly Journal of Economics*, vol. 77 (May 1963), pp. 185–209; Henry G. Manne, "Mergers and the Market for Corporate Control," *Journal of Political Economy*, vol. 73 (April 1965), pp. 110–20; Michael Gort, "An Economic Disturbance Theory of Mergers," *Quarterly Journal of Economics*, vol. 83 (November

Especially when small, closely held companies are acquired, common motives on the sellers' side include the desire of owners to diversify investment portfolios, to increase liquidity (often required to meet the demands of inheritance tax collectors), and to ensure that the enterprise they have worked hard to build will have a proper chain of managerial succession. For these and also for the sale of larger, more widely held companies, sellers sell because the buyer has made an offer too good to refuse.

Why should acquiring firms make such an offer? One possible reason is that there is a disparity of valuation judgments, given uncertainty about future business conditions: the buyer is for some reason more optimistic about the target firm's prospects than the seller. A second reason is that the buyer believes it can run the acquired entity more profitably as a part of its organization than the seller could by remaining independent. Such "synergies" from merger might include introducing superior management into the acquired entity, the realization of complementarities in production or marketing, the exploitation of scale economies and the elimination of duplicative functions, risk-spreading and its favorable consequences for the cost of acquiring new capital, a reduction of tax obligations through the pooling of losses and the internalization of capital transfers, and the enhancement of monopoly power by consolidating competing interests. A third possibility is that those who control the acquiring entity seek the prestige and monetary rewards associated with managing a large corporate empire, whether or not the consolidation adds to profits.

It is almost surely true that if one carefully investigates a large enough sample of mergers, all of these motives plus others will be found in varying proportions, often simultaneously and sometimes in conflict with one another. We would like, however, to know more than that the world is complex. In particular, it would be useful to know whether certain merger motives, or clusters of motives, predominate. Seeking such knowledge, usually with the added assumption that motives can be inferred from consequences, scholars have turned to statistical studies of merger behavior.

1969), pp. 624–42; and Dennis C. Mueller, "A Theory of Conglomerate Mergers," *Quarterly Journal of Economics*, vol. 83 (November 1969), pp. 643–59. For wider-sweeping surveys, see Peter O. Steiner, *Mergers: Motives, Effects, Policies* (University of Michigan Press, 1975), chaps. 2–5; and F. M. Scherer, *Industrial Market Structure and Economic Performance*, 2d ed. (Houghton Mifflin, 1980), pp. 118–41.

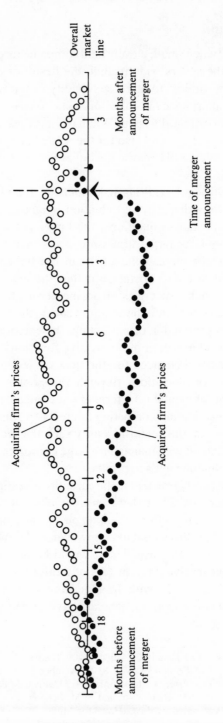

Figure 1-1. *Normalized Weekly Stock Price Movements of Typical Acquiring and Acquired Firms in Time Period Surrounding the Merger Announcement*

This statistical research has taken two main forms: the analysis of profit, sales, employment, and other data generated internally by one or both of the merging enterprises; and the analysis of external data, such as stock market reactions to events occurring at the time of merger or in its aftermath. Much of our research fits the first, more traditional, paradigm. The stock price approach is newer and has been widely adopted since 1974. Although, as we shall see, both methodologies have strengths and weaknesses, it is useful to begin with a critical survey of the newer stock price alternative.[8]

Stock Market "Event" Studies

Stock price analyses, commonly called "event" studies, view the announcement of a merger (or its ultimate consummation or abrogation) as an "event" in the stock price history of the merging companies. Using methods derived from the capital asset pricing model, each company's stock prices are normalized to take into account the price movements of all traded stocks bearing comparable risk. Cumulative deviations from the normal pattern ("abnormal returns") are computed for the acquired and acquiring enterprises. Figure 1-1 characterizes the pattern most commonly observed. For the firm acquired, stock prices trend downward relative to the norm from six months to two years before the merger announcement "event," so that cumulative abnormal returns are negative. Shortly before the merger announcement, the acquired firm's stock prices begin drifting upward, presumably because of leaked information about the impending event, but perhaps also because investors recognize that the firm is a prime candidate for acquisition. Usually, the acquiring company offers a sizable premium above the target firm's previous stock price to persuade the latter's management to accept the merger proposal and/or to induce shareholders to tender their shares. When the merger and its accompanying premium are announced, the target's stock prices

8. For a comprehensive survey, see Michael C. Jensen and Richard S. Ruback, "The Market for Corporate Control: The Scientific Evidence," *Journal of Financial Economics*, vol. 11, no. 1 (1983), pp. 5–50, and the articles that follow in an issue devoted almost entirely to mergers and related questions. For a somewhat more critical survey, see Paul Halpern, "Corporate Acquisitions: A Theory of Special Cases? A Review of Event Studies Applied to Acquisitions," *Journal of Finance*, vol. 38 (May 1983, *Papers and Proceedings, 1982)*, pp. 297–317. Still more critical is Robert L. Conn, "A Re-examination of Merger Studies That Use the Capital Asset Pricing Model Methodology," *Cambridge Journal of Economics*, vol. 9 (March 1985), pp. 43–56.

rise sharply so that, on average, acquired firm shareholders realize "abnormal returns" of from 10 to 50 percent relative to month-before-announcement date price levels (and rising on average since the 1950s).[9] If the merger occurs, of course, the acquired company's stock disappears; if the merger falls through, there is a tendency for the target's stock prices to drift downward again.

What happens to the acquiring corporation's stock during this period is less uniform and certain. Most commonly, as shown in figure 1-1, the acquirer's stock prices drift upward relative to the norm during the year or two prior to the merger, that is, positive abnormal returns are achieved. The weight of evidence suggests that acquiring firms realize no abnormal returns, positive or negative, between the month before the merger announcement and the month after consummation, after which a weak downward trend may materialize. But a minority of studies, especially those analyzing relatively large mergers, suggest that acquiring firm stockholders also realize modest positive abnormal returns at the time the merger event occurs.

These stock price movement patterns are interpreted as having important "real sector" behavioral counterparts. The combination of positive returns to acquired company shareholders and (at least in the short run) zero or mildly positive returns to acquiring firm shareholders is viewed as evidence that mergers are on average value-enhancing. The source of such value increases becomes a key question.

The sharp acquired firm stock price increases occurring when the merger is announced have two complementary explanations. For one, the stockholders who hold a company's stock at any moment in time are plainly those whose valuation of the stock exceeds the prevailing market price. If this were not true, they would sell. To induce a majority to sell, a premium, often sizable, must be offered. The more interesting question is why the acquiring firm is willing to pay that premium. An answer emphasized in the interpretation of event studies is that the acquirer expects the acquired firm to be more profitable after merger than it was before, justifying the stock price premium paid. Negative target firm abnormal returns in the pre-merger period are viewed as evidence of managerial inefficiency: either the target's management has lost its grip, or it had deliberately chosen to stray from the path of profit maximization. After merger, the sluggardly managers will be replaced by more effective leaders, or acquired firm policies will be modified in a profit-maximizing

9. Compare note 21 in chap. 7.

direction. Also, premiums may be warranted because "synergies" will be realized between the merger partners, reducing operating, financing, or tax costs and/or raising product prices.

Two tests of the price-raising (monopoly) hypothesis claim to have rejected it.[10] However, the evidence is in fact equivocal. It shows that the stock prices of *competitors* rise along with those of the merger partners when horizontal acquisitions are announced, suggesting that investors expect an ensuing increase in product prices. The further finding that competitors' stock prices did not *decline* when antitrust challenges were announced has numerous possible explanations, such as the well-known leak-proneness of antitrust enforcement agencies. The failure of event studies to rule out the monopoly price-raising explanation is important, since when enhanced monopoly power is plausible, it is less clear that the changes in company prospects for which acquirers pay premiums are rooted unambiguously in efficiency increases.

To the extent that acquiring companies realize no abnormal returns on average from their merger activity, it must be asked why they share so little in the resulting benefits. One possible answer is that to be the successful acquirer, one must bid up the target firm's stock price until the winner's curse—that is, the tendency for only the most eager competing bidder to win—has left the acquirer only a minor share of the added expected value.

Critique

One difficulty with the view that stock market value increases reflect efficiency increases is that an alternative set of hypotheses can also explain the stock price patterns associated with merger events. It says that at any moment in time some companies are undervalued by the stock market, while others are overvalued. Companies with undervalued stock—that is, inappropriately negative cumulative abnormal returns— are "bargains" and hence become prime targets for acquisition, perhaps (in stock-for-stock exchanges) by companies possessing the uniquely economical currency of overvalued stock. In other words, the depression of acquired firms' cumulative abnormal returns before the merger event is the result of mistakes *by the stock market*, not mistakes by managers

10. See B. Espen Eckbo, "Horizontal Mergers, Collusion, and Stockholder Wealth," and Robert Stillman, "Examining Antitrust Policy Toward Horizontal Mergers," *Journal of Financial Economics*, vol. 11, no. 1 (1983), pp. 241–73 and 225–40.

who have failed to maximize profits. The premium paid then reflects not the expectation of enhanced future operating efficiency, but the difference between the bargain price at which the target firm's stock is selling before merger and the price that would have to be paid in a competitive market recognizing the target's true value.

Event study adherents vigorously contest this interpretation, arguing that it is inconsistent with the assumption of "efficient" stock markets. An efficient market is one in which securities prices continually reflect all the information available on future earnings prospects and macroeconomic conditions.[11] If they do not, it is said, those who possess unaccounted-for information will be able to make profitable trades, driving prices to a level at which all relevant and available information is impounded.

To the assumption of stock market efficiency, a variety of objections have been raised. For one, even in its strongest form, it does not imply that stock market reactions are necessarily correct in their predictions of merger consequences, but only that the best available information is impounded. If that information is faulty, for example, because new merger strategies are being tried and investors have not been able to observe their effects sufficiently, the market's predictions may turn out after the fact to be erroneous.

Various anomalies inconsistent with the efficient markets assumption have come to light. For merger analysis, the most important are the tendency for the shares of companies with low stock price/earnings ratios to perform abnormally well, and evidence that acquiring company share values exhibit negative cumulative abnormal returns when postmerger periods of more than a few weeks are examined.[12] However, the reliability of the latter finding is questioned, since the statistical power

11. For various views on the degree of market efficiency, see Eugene F. Fama, "Efficient Capital Markets: A Review of Theory and Empirical Work," *Journal of Finance*, vol. 25 (May 1970), pp. 383–417; Fischer Black, "Noise," and Lawrence H. Summers, "Does the Stock Market Rationally Reflect Fundamental Values?" *Journal of Finance*, vol. 41 (July 1986, *Papers and Proceedings, 1985*), pp. 529–34 and 591–601.

12. See Ellen B. Magenheim and Dennis C. Mueller, "On Measuring the Effect of Acquisitions on Acquiring Firm Shareholders: Are Acquiring Firm Shareholders Better off After an Acquisition Than They Were Before?" in John C. Coffee, Jr., Louis Lowenstein, and Susan Rose-Ackerman, eds., *Knights, Raiders, and Targets: The Impact of the Hostile Takeover* (Oxford University Press, 1987); and Louis Lowenstein, "Pruning Deadwood in Hostile Takeovers," *Columbia Law Review*, vol. 83 (March 1983), pp. 268–306. Compare Jensen and Ruback, "The Market for Corporate Control," pp. 21–22.

of stock price analyses deteriorates as one- to three-year time frames are considered.[13]

Even if the assumption of stock market efficiency were true, which is singularly difficult to prove or disprove, its truth would not preclude the possibility that merger activity is driven by a (perhaps mistaken) belief that undervalued assets *do* exist and can be exploited. There is much evidence from interviews and "how to do it" tracts suggesting that merger-makers do actively seek undervalued targets.[14] There is also a

13. Thus, in a comment on the Magenheim and Mueller paper, "On Measuring the Effect of Acquisitions," Michael Bradley found a 16 percent negative cumulative abnormal return for acquiring corporations three years after merger events to be statistically insignificant, with a t-ratio of only 1.01 on the zero null hypothesis. What this t-ratio means is that there is one chance in three the 16 percent result could have emerged by chance when the "true" tendency was for acquirers' abnormal returns to be zero.

14. See, for example, "Some Candid Answers from James J. Ling," *Fortune*, August 1, 1969, p. 93 (Sperry Rand as a "fine and undervalued" acquisition candidate); Edward Ross Aranow and Herbert A. Einhorn, *Tender Offers for Corporate Control: A Treatise on the Legal and Practical Problems of the Offeror, the Offeree, and the Management of the Target Company in Cash Tenders and Exchange Offers* (Columbia University Press, 1973), p. 2 (companies with low price/earnings ratios are the choicest tender offer targets); "The Profit Potential in Spotting Takeovers," *Business Week*, October 24, 1977, p. 100 (corporate buyers and analysts look for companies in industries whose stock is out of favor); Robert Metz, "Babcock & Wilcox: A Battle That Shook Wall Street Notions," *New York Times*, September 19, 1977 (tender offer specialist says targets are "well-managed concerns . . . that are undervalued because of quirks in the stock market mechanism"); Richard Phalon, "Personal Investing: Getting in Before the Merger Bid," *New York Times*, October 8, 1977 (fund manager says merger makers are "always on the prowl for undervalued assets"); Alfred Rappaport, "Do You Know the Value of Your Company?" *Mergers & Acquisitions*, vol. 14 (Spring 1979), pp. 12–17 (using stock market value in merger decisions is "not economically sound and could be very costly to the acquiring company"); "Ira Harris: Chicago's Big Dealmaker," *Business Week*, June 25, 1979, p. 71 ("It has become cheaper to acquire companies than to build something from scratch. . . . It all comes back to low valuation put on the stock market"); Allan Sloan, *Three Plus One Equals Billions: The Bendix-Martin Marietta War* (Arbor House, 1983), p. 38 (ownership of Martin-Marietta valued by market at $1.4 billion, when it would take many years plus more than $2 billion to duplicate its businesses); Thomas A. Penn, "Premiums: What Do They Really Measure?" *Mergers & Acquisitions*, vol. 16 (Fall 1981), p. 34 ("forecast bargains" as one of the most plausible explanations for merger premiums); "The Raiders," *Business Week*, March 4, 1985, p. 83 (British tender offer maker sees "major bargains" among U.S. companies); "Companies Feel Underrated by the Street," *Business Week*, February 20, 1984, p. 14 (Harris poll shows 60 percent of surveyed executives believe stock market undervalues their companies' real value); "Is Steinberg Leading the Raiders Across the Atlantic?" *Business Week*, May 20, 1985, p. 76 (arbitrageur Ivan Boesky sees merger movement shifting to England because of "perceptions of undervalued opportunities"); Daniel F. Cuff, "Icahn Bids for Control of Uniroyal," *New York Times*,

paradox: if analysts and merger-makers did not allocate substantial resources to finding undervalued stocks, the quantity of information on the basis of which markets reach their "efficient" equilibrium would be much smaller. Thus, the undervaluation theory cannot be ruled out either logically or factually.

These difficulties demonstrate the need for research on the links between merger activity and efficiency gains outside the framework of efficient markets theory.[15] Developing evidence on the actual profitability consequences of merger was a major objective of the research reported here.

The Timing Problem

Suppose it is true that an important motive for merger is acquirers' expectation that, by changing the business policies of the acquired entity, they can increase its profits and hence its stock market value. What does it mean to increase profits? An important but often overlooked element of post-merger strategy is the selection of cash-flow timing patterns. When firms have well-established positions in their product markets, they may choose between "build" strategies, under which product prices are kept low and investments are made in R&D and marketing to achieve a market share that can sustain moderate profits indefinitely, and "harvest" or "cash cow" strategies, under which high prices and low levels of strategic investment encourage rival expansion and the eventual depletion of profit-making opportunities.[16]

April 11, 1985 (market analyst says Uniroyal, with "superb management," was "an underpriced equity"); "The Pied Piper of Arbitrage Draws More Followers," *Business Week*, October 21, 1985, p. 102 (investment banker expects merger "binge" to continue because "when you check your [computer] screens, there are still so many undervalued companies out there!"); "Paul Bilzerian: A Dwindling List of Takeover Targets," *Business Week*, December 30, 1985, pp. 101–02 (increased stock prices reduced the number of undervalued takeover candidates from "hundreds" to "about 50"); and Udayan Gupta, "Wesray and Chairman Simon Cancel Start-up of Leveraged Buyout Fund," *Wall Street Journal*, January 30, 1986 (with the boom in stock prices, "it's not easy to buy companies at or below value as we once did").

15. In this respect, we are following the metaphor of Gödel's theorem, which holds that the truth of a logical system cannot be proved self-referentially, that is, on the basis of its own internal axioms. Rather, one must "leap outside" the system and seek additional evidence governed by different axioms. See Douglas R. Hofstadter, *Gödel, Escher, Bach: An Eternal Golden Braid* (Vintage Books, 1980).

16. The Boston Consulting Group is well known for its work advising corporations on this strategy problem. See Bruce D. Henderson, *Henderson on Corporate Strategy*

That such choices exist suggests two questions. First, is the decision affected by mergers? Is there a tendency for policies to be shifted more in one direction than another—for example, toward more "cash cow" and less "building" behavior—after mergers impose a new organizational structure and inject new policymakers? And second, what is the "right" choice, from the perspective of both private decisionmakers and the broader public interest?

A key variable affecting the choice between build and harvest strategies (and variants in between) is the discount rate applied, which in turn depends upon the corporation's perceived cost of capital. High discount rates imply emphasizing near-in profits over those attainable in the more distant future. Low discount rates imply more farsighted policies. Mergers may change discount rates either by altering the cost of new capital or by changing the way corporate policymakers set applicable discount rates. At the level of the individual business firm, there may be considerable leeway for discount rate policy differences because firms face widely varying capital costs, both at any moment and over time.[17] Conflicts may exist between what is best for an individual firm and the broader public interest because income taxes and risks that cannot be diversified away by firms, but can be across the collection of all firms, drive wedges between privately and socially optimal discount rates.[18]

We cannot resolve here the persistently thorny question of what discount rate is right and hence how farsighted business decisionmakers should be, although we believe permanent industrial strength is more likely to be achieved through farsighted policies. What we will attempt

---

(Cambridge, Mass.: Abt, 1979), especially pp. 82–85 and 163–66. On the relevant price theory, see Scherer, *Industrial Market Structure and Economic Performance*, chap. 8.

17. On the movements of capital costs over time, see Robert J. Shiller, "Do Stock Prices Move Too Much To Be Justified by Subsequent Changes in Dividends?" *American Economic Review*, vol. 71 (June 1981), pp. 421–36; and "Stock Prices and Social Dynamics," *Brookings Papers on Economic Activity, 2:1984*, pp. 457–98; N. Gregory Mankiw, David Romer, and Matthew D. Shapiro, "An Unbiased Reexamination of Stock Market Volatility," *Journal of Finance*, vol. 40 (July 1985), pp. 677–87; and Louis O. Scott, "The Present Value Model of Stock Prices: Regression Tests and Monte Carlo Results," *Review of Economics and Statistics*, vol. 67 (November 1985), pp. 599–605. For a view critical of those contributions, see Terry A. Marsh and Robert C. Merton, "Dividend Variability and Variance Bounds Tests for the Rationality of Stock Market Prices," *American Economic Review*, vol. 76 (June 1986), pp. 483–98.

18. See Edward M. Gramlich, *Benefit-Cost Analysis of Government Programs* (Prentice-Hall, 1981), pp. 95–108; and Edgar K. Browning and Jacquelene M. Browning, *Public Finance and the Price System* (Macmillan, 1979), pp. 89–93.

to illuminate is whether such choices have in fact been significantly affected in one direction or the other by firms' merger experiences.

Using Financial Accounting Data

To sum up, our basic objective is to learn what actually happened after merger, both generally and in the substantial subset of cases where mergers ended in divestiture. We seek in particular to determine whether on average mergers were followed by profitability increases, as suggested by stock market event study interpretations. We proceed in part by questioning decisionmakers in the framework of historical case studies. In addition, we address the increased profits hypothesis quantitatively using profitability data for a large sample of merger-impacted business units. Specifically, we shall test whether acquired entities' profitability increased following merger either on a sustained basis or in the form of nonsustainable harvest strategies. To explore these questions thoroughly, we must also ascertain the profitability implications of sell-offs—that is, whether their profits differed systematically from those of retained units, how extensive any such differences were, and how they affected the observed profitability of merged and retained units.

Our profitability measures are drawn from company financial statements, and not from stock price records. In using accounting profit data to study merger effects, we follow a long tradition.[19] It is not, however, an uncontroversial tradition. Most, if not all, of the earlier merger profitability studies have labored under a number of difficulties.

One set of problems entails the counterfactual question: what would have happened to profits but for the merger? Such questions can never be answered with certainty, for history cannot be rerun. In the quantitative work on mergers, economists have tried to deal with the problem by comparing merged entities' profit performance with that of control groups. These have been of two main kinds: before-and-after comparisons, and comparisons with units that had no merger but were similar in size, industry orientation, and so forth.

---

19. For surveys of the literature, see Steiner, *Mergers,* chap. 8; Dennis C. Mueller, "The Effects of Conglomerate Mergers," *Journal of Banking and Finance*, vol. 1 (December 1977), pp. 315–47; and George J. Benston, *Conglomerate Mergers: Causes, Consequences, and Remedies* (Washington: American Enterprise Institute, 1980), chap. 2.

A serious impediment to before-and-after analyses is that, once merger occurs, the acquired entity disappears into the acquirer's accounts. Moreover, most acquired firms are quite small relative to the acquirer, with less than 5 percent of the acquirer's assets on average, so that whatever weighted average financial performance they contribute to the parent is likely to be "swamped" within the consolidated whole.[20] Confining the analysis to relatively large acquisitions is not a reliable solution for, as we shall see, there are systematic profitability differences associated with acquired entity size.

Analyses using "similar company" controls founder on a different reef. As we shall see in chapter 2, the typical large U.S. corporation of the 1970s operated in a multiplicity of industries. The most active merger-makers had by that time become particularly highly diversified. It is therefore difficult to establish a control group of companies with similar industrial roots but not involved in merger.

These problems can be avoided by analyzing post-merger perform-ance at the level of individual operating units, or "lines of business," rather than at the whole-company level. For individual operating units of diversified corporations, merged assets are likely to be sizable in proportion to total unit assets (sometimes comprising their entirety), and control group entities of similar industrial composition can be established with much greater precision. A focus on merger effects at the individual line of business level is a principal distinguishing charac-teristic of our statistical research. Our approach has precedents,[21] but it is by far the most comprehensive and carefully controlled effort of its genre.

Another set of problems comes from the way merger accounting is done. In the United States two quite different methods of accounting for acquired assets have been used with nearly equal historical frequency. Under *pooling-of-interests* accounting, the assets of the acquired firm are recorded at their pre-merger book value. If the acquirer pays more (or less) for the assets than their book value, the difference is debited (or credited) to the acquirer's stockholders' equity account. In contrast,

20. This is also a serious problem in stock market event studies. See Gregg A. Jarrell, "Do Acquirers Benefit from Corporate Acquisitions?" (University of Chicago, March 1983).

21. Federal Trade Commission, Bureau of Economics, *Conglomerate Merger Per-formance: An Empirical Analysis of Nine Corporations* (Washington: FTC, 1972); and Robert L. Conn, "Acquired Firm Performance After Conglomerate Merger," *Southern Economic Journal*, vol. 43 (October 1976), pp. 1170–73.

under *purchase* accounting, the acquired assets are entered at the effective price paid for them. If a premium is paid over the acquired entity's book value, as has been true on average, the acquired assets are "stepped up" relative to their pre-merger book values, and/or an addition may be made to the acquirer's "good will" (asset) account. Plant and equipment value increases attributable to purchase accounting premiums are always depreciated in subsequent years; good will amortization has been required on acquisitions made since 1970.

Because of these differences, the post-merger profit performance of purchase accounting acquisitions is likely to be systematically different from the performance of pooling acquisitions. To the extent that a purchase premium over book value has been paid, the denominator of any profit/assets ratio will be greater under purchase accounting than under pooling, all else equal. If purchase accounting premiums are amortized, the numerator of any post-merger profit ratio will be smaller than under pooling-of-interests accounting. Thus, again assuming that a premium above pre-merger book value was paid, both profit/assets and profit/sales ratios will be systematically lower under purchase accounting than under pooling accounting, although the deviation will be greater for asset-based than sales-based measures (since both numerator and denominator are affected in the former).

A related accounting choice bias is partly offsetting, but has similar analytic consequences. Purchase accounting depresses reported post-merger returns, the more so, the larger is the premium of the purchase price over pre-merger book values. Aware of this and anxious to show a favorable earnings record to the investing public, acquiring companies have tended to prefer pooling-of-interests accounting when they paid large acquisition premiums and use purchase accounting mainly for acquisitions with lower (or negative) premiums. Since premiums above book value tend to be positively correlated with acquired company profitability, and assuming some persistence of profitability over time, this bias again means that units treated under purchase accounting are likely to exhibit lower post-merger profitability than pooling-of-interests acquisitions.

In the profit analyses presented here, a major effort has been made to identify and control for such accounting biases.[22] The accounting method

22. The only other study attempting similar controls (in a different way) is Geoffrey Meeks, *Disappointing Marriage: A Study of the Gains from Merger* (Cambridge

for each sample merger has been identified so that the profitability consequences of pooling and purchase mergers can be analyzed separately and compared.

Despite these precautions, we cannot claim that the profitability data used here are free of error or bias. Accounting data (like stock price data) are imperfect. They have well-known deficiencies. With or without merger revaluations, what corporate financial reports say about profitability can be affected by the choice of depreciation policies.[23] Inflation has tended systematically to make book asset values understate market or replacement values, the more so, the more capital-intensive and slowly growing a business unit's operations are. Especially during inflationary or deflationary periods, profit figures are sensitive to the choice between LIFO and FIFO inventory accounting methods. Standard accounting practice is to write off as a current expense investments in research and development, exploratory oil well drilling, and advertising, whose time horizons can span more than a single accounting year. When the "true" profit rate exceeds the rate of growth of such outlays, this practice causes accounting profits to be biased upward, the more so, the larger the share of total costs the outlays represent.[24] When company financial accounts are disaggregated to the level of individual operating units, inaccuracies may arise if costs common to multiple units are allocated among the units, or if inter-unit transfers are made at non-market prices.[25]

That accounting data are imperfect and subject to error does not

---

University Press, 1977). See also G. Meeks and J. G. Meeks, "Profitability Measures as Indicators of Post-Merger Efficiency," *Journal of Industrial Economics*, vol. 29 (June 1981), pp. 335–44. Using British data, the Meeks study faced somewhat simpler problems because of the apparently ubiquitous use of purchase accounting. However, the fact that roughly half of all U.S. mergers were made under pooling-of-interests accounting provides an opportunity to analyze a large cohort of merged and control group activity free of merger-related asset revaluations.

23. See Franklin M. Fisher and John J. McGowan, "On the Misuse of Accounting Rates of Return To Infer Monopoly Profits," *American Economic Review*, vol. 73 (March 1983), pp. 82–97.

24. See, for example, Thomas R. Stauffer, "The Measurement of Corporate Rates of Return: A Generalized Formulation," *Bell Journal of Economics and Management Science*, vol. 2 (Autumn 1971), pp. 434–69.

25. See, for example, George J. Benston, "The Validity of Profits-Structure Studies with Particular Reference to the FTC's Line of Business Data," *American Economic Review*, vol. 75 (March 1985), pp. 37–67; and F. M. Scherer and seven others, "The Validity of Studies with Line of Business Data: Comment," *American Economic Review*, vol. 77 (March 1987), pp. 205–17.

mean, as some critics have urged, that they are useless for evaluating such questions as the profitability of mergers. If the errors are unsystematic or uncorrelated with the phenomenon (for example, merger or sell-off activity) under investigation, they merely add "noise" to any underlying profitability relationships, making them more difficult to detect. To extract such relationships from "noisy" data is what statistical technique is all about. More serious problems intrude when the errors present in accounting data are systematically associated with the phenomena analyzed, for example, if more merger-prone lines tend to be heavier advertisers, grow more rapidly, or use LIFO inventory accounting methods more frequently. Whether or not such potential biasing factors exist is an empirical question. Two things can be done about it. First, one can strive to identify whether associations exist that could bias the results, and test the sensitivity of measured returns to these biasing factors. Second, one can attempt to control explicitly for the biases, for example, by introducing into explanatory equations accounting choice variables and measures of R&D, advertising, and capital intensity and by differentiating among industries whose characteristics might bias profitability measures systematically in one direction or the other.

The Federal Trade Commission's "Line of Business" (LB) data analyzed in this book are ideally suited to such a research approach. They have already been the subject of systematic research on such questions as the impact of common cost allocations and transfer pricing methods.[26] The data base also includes explicit information on depreciation methods, plant asset age, inventory accounting methods, growth rates, R&D and advertising intensity, and (thanks to our augmentation) merger accounting methods. These and other data will be used to test for biases and the sensitivity of key results to bias control variables. Thus, care will be taken to ensure that the "signals" extracted from the "noise" accompanying the accounting profit data are not distorted.

In addition, we shall see that the data have considerable intrinsic plausibility. Concretely, they will be able to anticipate or predict important behavioral phenomena with a degree of power quite at odds with critics' claims that the data "are of doubtful value for the purposes of

---

26. See William F. Long, "Impact of Alternative Allocation Procedures on Econometric Studies of Structure and Performance" (FTC, July 1981); and David J. Ravenscraft, "Intracompany Transfer Pricing and Profitability" (FTC, December 1981).

economic analysis"[27] or that "there is no way in which one can look at accounting rates of return and infer anything about relative economic profitability."[28] We are confident our analysis will demonstrate that such objections are ill-founded.

Research Methodology

Our research objective, to repeat, was to penetrate beyond stock market manifestations of merger events and to determine what actually happened and why. Recognizing the limitations of any single methodology, we pursue an eclectic approach, combining case studies with the quantitative analysis of both accounting and (on a more limited scale) stock price data.

The most unique and ambitious facet of this multifaceted approach is our use of Line of Business data. For the years 1974 through 1977, the Federal Trade Commission required a panel of from 437 to 471 characteristically large U.S. manufacturing corporations to file domestic income statement and balance sheet data broken down according to 261 manufacturing and 14 (broader) nonmanufacturing industry categories. Companies reporting in 1977 disaggregated their operations into 8 manufacturing LBs on average (excluding a residual catch-all category), with a range of from 1 to 53 (averaging across the 5 leaders). For reports published by the FTC,[29] the individual company information was aggregated to present an overall view of profitability, advertising intensity, R&D spending, accounting method choice, and the like by industry category. In the research reported here, on the other hand, we analyze financial performance at the individual manufacturing Line of Business level.

The availability of Line of Business data only for 1974 through 1977 forces us to study economic history rather than analyzing current events—that is, the merger wave of the 1980s. But this necessity has a corresponding virtue, since a match of 1974–77 performance data to merger activity peaking in the late 1960s permits us to investigate fully the longer-run developments following merger.

27. Benston, "Validity of Profits-Structure Studies," p. 64.
28. Fisher and McGowan, "On the Misuse," p. 90.
29. See, for example, Federal Trade Commission, Bureau of Economics, *Statistical Report: Annual Line of Business Report, 1974* (Washington: FTC, 1981), which includes a detailed description of the reporting guidelines, methodology, and industry categories.

For the special purposes of this study, three sets of merger and sell-off data were linked to the individual manufacturing LBs. First, using the Federal Trade Commission's historical files on merger activity, augmented by numerous other sources, an attempt was made to identify each manufacturing company acquisition by Line of Business sample corporations over the period 1950–77 and surviving (that is, not divested) at least into 1975. Nearly 6,000 mergers were drawn into the sample, and relevant data on them were linked and coded to the individual LBs affected. Second, through a mail survey, research in company financial disclosures, and the use of a prediction model, the accounting method used on each known merger was identified. Third, tapping a variety of public and internal sources, we sought to identify all manufacturing unit sell-offs by sample companies over the 1974–81 time interval. Each such sell-off was traced to the individual LBs affected.

This linked Line of Business–merger–sell-off data base, whose compilation entailed several person-years of research effort, has been supplemented by various special data bases on pre-merger profitability, industry growth, and company stock price history. These will be described more fully as they are introduced and analyzed.

The other main research thrust encompassed 15 field case studies of conglomerate mergers (or clusters of mergers) that were made and subsequently sold off. Based upon library research and 70 interviews with parent and subsidiary unit executives and other participants, the case studies inquired why the acquisitions were made, what considerations led to sell-off, and how the acquired units' organization, motivation, and performance varied under diverse ownership structures.

In sum, our research approach attempts to combine the in-depth qualitative insights historical case studies can provide with more broadly representative quantitative insights stemming from the analysis of a large statistical data set.

Plan of the Book

We begin our presentation of results in chapter 2 with a statistical overview of U.S. merger activity, focusing especially on the preponderantly conglomerate merger wave that peaked in 1968 and continued at more reduced levels into the 1974–77 period covered by our Line of Business data. For the corporations in the 1975 Line of Business sample, we trace the changes in diversification occurring between 1950 and 1975 and the role mergers played in those changes. We then analyze industry characteristics associated with especially vigorous merger activity.

In chapters 3 and 4, Line of Business data supplemented by pre-merger profitability and asset size data are analyzed to derive broadly based generalizations about the performance consequences of various merger types—that is, horizontal, vertical, "related business," and pure conglomerate; those treated under pooling-of-interests accounting as compared to purchase accounting; equal versus unequal partner sizes; voluntarily negotiated versus "hostile," and so on. In addition, post-merger growth rates and the intensity of company-financed research and development support are investigated.

In chapter 5, the principal insights resulting from our 15 sell-off case studies are distilled. (Appendix B summarizes the individual case study findings in historical narrative form.) The quantitative evidence on sell-offs is analyzed in chapter 6. We begin by presenting our own evidence on how often, and how quickly, merger was followed by divestiture. Using Line of Business data, the antecedents of sell-off—environmental, organizational, and financial—are investigated. Chapter 7 integrates our findings both quantitatively and qualitatively. Chapter 8 explores their implications for managers, investors, and public policy.

CHAPTER TWO

The Contours of Merger
Activity Since 1950

WE BEGIN WITH AN overview of historical patterns in U.S. merger activity, examining its ups and downs, how it has affected the structure of large industrial corporations, and how it has been related to diverse industrial characteristics.

Merger Trends in Manufacturing and Mineral Industries

Figure 2-1 provides the broadest historical perspective. It adjusts and splices several data series to show as consistently as possible the fluctuations in real (constant-dollar) merger activity that have occurred between 1895 and 1985.[1] The focus is on acquisitions of manufacturing and mineral industry companies. Most of the detailed analyses that follow will be concerned even more narrowly with manufacturing company acquisitions. This is done largely because by far the richest data exist for manufacturing. In addition, however, manufacturing is of special interest because of the strategic position it occupies in a modern economy. Although originating only 21 percent of U.S. GNP during the early 1980s, manufacturers conducted more than 95 percent of the industrial research and development, generating new products and processes that enhanced productivity in every sector.[2]

1. See F. M. Scherer, *Industrial Market Structure and Economic Performance,* 2d ed. (Houghton Mifflin, 1980), p. 120, which provides details on the splicing methods used, for sources of data. For years following 1979, when the Federal Trade Commission's "large" merger series was discontinued, data published annually by W. T. Grimm & Co. had to be linked in. They cover consideration paid, not acquired firm asset values. To convert the consideration paid values to asset values, a specially constructed variant of Tobin's Q index was estimated. The asset values were in turn put on a constant 1972 dollar basis using a weighted average deflator index. Half of the merger activity classified by Grimm as "conglomerate" was assumed to be in the manufacturing and minerals sector.

2. See F. M. Scherer, *Innovation and Growth: Schumpeterian Perspectives* (M.I.T. Press, 1984), chap. 3.

Figure 2-1. *Constant-Dollar Volume of Manufacturing and Mineral Firm Acquisitions, 1895–1985*

Value of acquired firms
(billions of 1972 dollars)

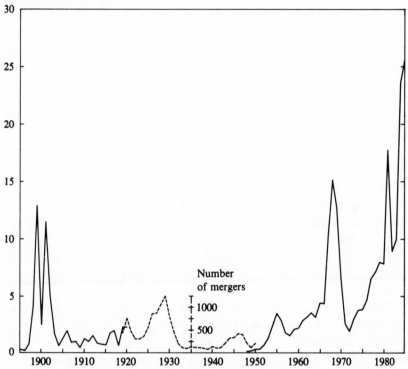

Sources: F. M. Scherer, *Industrial Market Structure and Economic Performance,* 2d ed. (Houghton-Mifflin, 1980), p. 120; extended using data from the U.S. Federal Trade Commission and W. T. Grimm & Co.

a. Data on the value of manufacturing and mineral company acquisitions are not available for the years 1921–47. The broken line reflects the number of acquisitions in those years.

Inspection of figure 2-1 reveals four great merger "waves" that have marked American industrial history—one peaking in 1901, a milder one during the late 1920s, a third with its peak in 1968, and a resurgence in the early 1980s. Each had quite distinctive characteristics. The turn-of-the-century merger wave was preponderantly horizontal, uniting large numbers of competitors into consolidations that often dominated the markets they served. The merger wave of the 1920s saw extensive activity in the public utility sector, outside the scope of figure 2-1.

Within manufacturing, there were many vertical and product line extension mergers, and the horizontal activity was better characterized as "mergers for oligopoly," in contrast to the "mergers for monopoly" at the turn of the century.[3] By the 1960s, antitrust constraints on horizontal mergers had become much more stringent, and perhaps in part as a result, the merger wave that peaked in 1968 was preponderantly "conglomerate" in character, that is, involving companies pursuing different, and often totally unrelated, lines of business. The mergers of the 1980s were different again. Antitrust enforcement ebbed, permitting more and larger horizontal mergers. In addition, financial intermediaries had become more free-wheeling in the kinds of mergers they would support, and as one consequence, hostile takeovers rose to unprecedented prominence.

Our main data sources for this volume cover the period from 1950 through 1977, whose most distinctive quantitative feature is the burst of activity peaking in 1968. Indeed, 44 percent of all the 1950–77 merger activity tracked by figure 2-1 fell within the five-year period 1966–70.[4] Thus, ours is in substantial degree a study of the 1960s conglomerate merger wave.

Just how "conglomerate" that wave was cannot be answered with certainty. Tables 2-1 and 2-2 present two alternative, somewhat divergent views.

Table 2-1 is drawn from classifications made by persons compiling the Federal Trade Commission's "large" merger series—that is, a series covering acquisitions of manufacturing and mining companies which have assets of $10 million or more. The merger types are defined as follows:[5]

> Horizontal: The merging companies produce one or more of the same, or closely related, products in the same geographic market.
> Vertical: The two companies had a potential buyer-seller relationship prior to the merger.

3. The terms are from George J. Stigler, "Monopoly and Oligopoly by Merger," *American Economic Review*, vol. 40 (May 1950, *Papers and Proceedings, 1949*), pp. 23–34.

4. A calculation using our chap. 4 data set for 1977 as the population puts 46.7 percent of the merger activity in 1966–70. The small discrepancy is attributable partly to sample coverage differences and partly to the greater relative weight accorded pre-1965 merger activity when a price level adjustment is made, as in figure 2-1.

5. U.S. Federal Trade Commission, Bureau of Economics, *Statistical Report on Mergers and Acquisitions: 1978* (FTC, 1980), pp. 108–09.

Table 2-1. *Distribution of Assets Acquired in Acquisitions of Large Manufacturing and Mining Companies by FTC Merger Type Classification, 1948–77*
Percent

Type of merger	1948–53	1956–63	1963–72	1973–77
Horizontal	36.8	19.2	12.4	15.1
Vertical	12.8	22.2	7.8	5.8
Conglomerate				
Product extension	44.8	36.0	39.3	24.2
Market extension	2.4	6.7	7.3	5.7
Other	3.2	15.9	33.2	49.2
Total	100.0	100.0	100.0	100.0

Sources: Adapted from U.S. Federal Trade Commission, *Economic Report on Corporate Mergers* (FTC, 1969), p. 673; FTC, Bureau of Economics, *Statistical Report on Mergers and Acquisitions: 1978* (FTC, 1980), table 17, and earlier issues.

Product extension: The acquiring and acquired companies are functionally related in production and/or distribution, but do not compete directly with another (for example, a soap manufacturer acquiring a bleach maker).

Market extension: The companies manufacture the same products, but sell them in different geographic markets.

Other, or pure conglomerate: The companies are essentially unrelated in the products they produce and distribute.

Mergers in the last three categories are all regarded as conglomerate of greater or lesser purity. The data show a significant decline in horizontal and vertical activity, at least through 1972, and an increase of conglomerate activity. The rise of "pure" conglomerate mergers in the 1960s and early 1970s is particularly pronounced.

Table 2-2 is drawn from our own tallies of acquired manufacturing business assets remaining with the acquiring company (that is, not sold off) by 1977. It embodies the following category definitions, which emphasize the presence or absence of acquiring company pre-merger experience in the acquired firm's line of business:

Horizontal: Acquiring company had at least five years experience in the same four-digit FTC industry category before acquisition.

Vertical: Acquired unit made at least 5 percent of its sales to, or purchases from, another unit operated by the parent company for at least five years before acquisition.

Related business: Acquiring company had at least five years experience in the same two-digit industry group before acquisition, but no horizontal or vertical connection.

Pure conglomerate: None of the above criteria satisfied.

Table 2-2. *Distribution of Manufacturing Industry Assets Acquired, by Experience-Oriented Merger Category, 1950–77*

Type of merger	1950–55	1956–63	1964–72	1973–77	1950–77
			Percent of total[a]		
Horizontal	70.1	49.1	38.2	39.4	41.4
Vertical	12.3	15.8	9.0	11.6	10.9
Related business	19.1	26.9	23.7	26.5	24.8
Pure conglomerate	5.3	18.4	36.2	32.4	31.3
			Billions of dollars		
Total assets	2.56	11.05	37.19	20.54	71.33

a. Percentages do not sum to 100 because some horizontal mergers are also classified as vertical.

The trends indicated by table 2-2 are similar to those shown in table 2-1: horizontal and vertical activity fell in relative importance, while pure conglomerate activity rose. However, the levels of activity are quite different. Table 2-2 shows relatively more horizontal and less conglomerate activity, especially in the related business category. There are several reasons for the differences between data sources. For one, the "horizontal" definition applied in table 2-2 is in most respects broader, including table 2-1's "market extension" mergers and using four-digit industry categories that are in some cases broader than the market boundaries favored in the antitrust enforcement context emphasized by the Federal Trade Commission. Second, the table 2-1 sample covers only large mergers, whereas ours includes mergers of all sizes, including horizontal mergers that may have been too small to pose antitrust difficulties. Third, table 2-1's sampling occurred at the time of merger, whereas our table 2-2 sample was for 1977, by which time disproportionately many conglomerate acquisitions had been sold off. Fourth, our classifications were made at the individual line of business level, which might include only part of an acquired company, whereas the FTC large merger series identified merger types at the whole acquired company level. Finally, our selection criteria were quantitative and rigid, whereas the FTC staff's were judgmental and flexible. Although the last two differences might work in either direction, it seems clear that our criteria are on balance more inclined to characterize mergers as horizontal.

The Sample Companies and Their Diversification

Even by our classification system, more merger activity entailed the movement into new lines of business than the expansion of existing lines. Over the entire period, 56.1 percent of the table 2-2 merger volume was "related business" and pure conglomerate, as compared to 41.4 percent horizontal. We now examine how that activity changed the structures of the corporations upon which our subsequent statistical analysis will focus.

What made our statistical analysis possible was the Federal Trade Commission's Line of Business reporting program, which collected disaggregated financial data from a panel of U.S. manufacturing enterprises for the years 1974 through 1977 before being discontinued. Counting jointly owned companies as one, the number of sample companies was 437 in 1974, 471 in 1975, 468 in 1976, and 459 in 1977.

Corporations were included in the FTC's survey if they specialized in manufacturing and had assets of $1 billion or more or were among the top 250 U.S. manufacturers measured in terms of sales. Beginning from this base, the sample was then expanded to ensure that each four-digit manufacturing industry category was represented by at least five participants and had at least 20 percent of its sales surveyed. Altogether, the 1975 survey covered approximately 70 percent of the gross plant and equipment assets in place in the U.S. manufacturing sector.[6] Line of Business sample companies made approximately 75 percent of the acquisitions, by value of assets acquired, recorded in the FTC's large merger series for the years 1950–76.

Our effort to develop a comprehensive historical record of merger activity begins with 1950 because for that year the Federal Trade Commission collected and later published its "Corporate Patterns" report—a detailed profile of product line sales of the 1,000 largest manufacturing enterprises.[7] Using that reference point, it is possible to trace the evolution of most Line of Business sample members' structures over time. In this chapter we make comparisons over a quarter century's span, between 1950 and 1975.

Of the 471 Line of Business sample companies for 1975, 311 were also present in the Corporate Patterns survey for 1950. Of the 160 newcomers, 17 were founded as start-up companies (that is, other than through the merger of existing firms) after 1950, 17 operated domestically in 1950 but had no manufacturing sales, and the rest had 1950 manufacturing

6. FTC, Bureau of Economics, *Statistical Report: Annual Line of Business Report, 1976* (FTC, 1982), p. 55.

7. FTC, *Statistical Report: Value of Shipments Data by Product Class for the 1,000 Largest Manufacturing Companies of 1950* (Government Printing Office, 1972).

activities too small (or in the case of some sizable private companies, too difficult to identify) to be included in the 1950 Corporate Patterns list of 1,000 leaders.

To pinpoint the industry structure of the Line of Business sample companies' activities, we use the FTC's four-digit industry category system. It has 14 broad domestic nonmanufacturing industry categories, 261 detailed four-digit manufacturing categories, and 1 catch-all category (99.99) in which reporting firms were allowed to combine manufacturing activities whose sales in a regular category were less than $10 million. The FTC manufacturing categories are somewhat broader on average than Standard Industrial Classification four-digit industries (of which there were 451 in 1972). They tend to be broadest when the products of a three-digit SIC sector were commonly produced within a single plant complex or were highly substitutable in consumption. In a few cases (pharmaceuticals, automobiles, and copying machines), the FTC classification is more narrowly segmented than the four-digit SIC industries.

To measure the degree to which Line of Business sample companies were diversified and how their diversification changed over time, we take as our unit of account the 261 FTC manufacturing Line of Business categories (excluding 99.99). For companies also covered by the 1950 Corporate Patterns survey, the 1950 sales information (broken down into some 1,000 product lines) was recoded to approximate as closely as possible the 1975 Line of Business reporting categories and rules. This reconciliation encountered numerous difficulties,[8] requiring in some

8. The 1950 Corporate Patterns survey (FTC, *Statistical Report: Value of Shipments*) sought value of shipments (roughly, sales) data only and was designed to track Census Bureau product line reporting conditions as closely as possible. The Line of Business surveys sought information on profitability and other aspects of financial performance and had to strike a balance between meaningfulness and consistency with company accounting structures. Because of these differing objectives, three main inconsistencies arose.

The 1975 Line of Business survey guidelines permitted respondents optionally to consolidate the activity of lines with sales of less than $10 million into a "miscellaneous" category (FTC code 99.99). A majority of the firms exercised this option. A corresponding procedure had to be implemented in recoding the data for 1950 retrospectively. Two alternatives were considered. One was to adjust the 1975 $10 million figure downward only for GNP deflator inflation; this would have put the 1950 miscellaneous threshold at $4.25 million. The other was to adjust for both nominal and real GNP growth, amounting to a factor of 5.4 between 1950 and 1975. An approximation to the latter rule was implemented: 1950 sales (aggregated to the LB level) totaling less than $2 million were consigned to the miscellaneous category.

A second option permitted 1975 Line of Business survey respondents to include in

cases that 1950 comparison figures be presented in terms of a minimum-maximum range. For sample companies not covered by the 1950 survey, information on product line structure was obtained from annual reports, trade publications, and in a few especially difficult cases, inspection of the invention patents received by the companies during the early 1950s.

Diversification in 1950 Compared to 1975

Table 2-3 arrays the 471 companies covered by the 1975 Line of Business survey according to 1975 domestic manufacturing sales and provides various measures of diversification for the years 1950 and 1975 for five size groupings. The LB count columns report the number of (non-catch-all) FTC four-digit manufacturing categories in which the companies operated. For 1950, "minimum" and "maximum" figures are presented, depending upon whether one counts the lines of both partners, or only the more diversified partner, in certain mergers to be described more fully in chapter 4 as "mergers of equals." The 1950 LB counts for companies incorporated after 1950 cover the number of lines served in the first year of operation (usually, but not always, only one line).

Two important insights emerge from the LB counts. First, the largest

---

their reports for an LB activities that did not truly belong there, as long as the sales of those "secondary product contamination" activities did not exceed 15 percent of individual LB sales and certain other criteria were met. The purpose of this convention was to avoid forcing companies to make breakdowns finer than what their books of account could adequately support. Companies exercised the option sparingly; secondary product contamination amounted to 3 percent of total 1975 manufacturing LB sales. To make the recoded 1950 data as comparable as possible, the lower-bound counts of tables 2-5 and 2-6 exclude 68 cases in which activities otherwise qualifying to be counted as separate 1950 LBs (that is, with sales over $2 million) were reported only as contamination with sales of less than $10 million in 1975. The upper-bound counts include all such 1950 LBs. The "high" and "low" estimates do not differ greatly.

A third significant option accorded Line of Business survey respondents was to report on an integrated basis vertically related activities. Indeed, in certain specified industries—notably, those in which most sales tended to be intra-company, or in which market-based transfer prices were otherwise difficult to establish—respondents were instructed that they *should* integrate vertically related activities. When companies made such integrations in their 1975 reports, the 1950 data were similarly integrated. In those cases, neither the integrated 1950 LBs nor their sales were included in computing 1950 LB counts and numbers-equivalent indexes. Eliminating vertically integrated sales in this way avoids the double-counting problem that occurs under product line reporting (for example, when shipments from a parts plant to an auto assembly plant are counted once, and then the sales of the assembly plant are counted again).

Table 2-3. *Manufacturing Sales and Line of Business Counts in 1950 and 1975 for the 471 Companies in the FTC's 1975 Line of Business Survey*

Company rank, by 1975 sales volume	Median 1975 sales (millions of dollars)	Average number of lines of business[a] 1950		1975	Average 1975 numbers-equivalent index[b]
		Minimum	Maximum		
Top 100	2,354	4.26	4.48	12.38	4.17
101–200	1,036	3.02	3.38	9.27	4.26
201–300	526	1.99	2.11	6.56	3.41
301–400	260	1.64	1.73	4.85	2.94
401–471	135	1.56	1.62	3.42	2.52
All 471	. . .	2.55	2.73	7.54	3.52

a. Average number of four-digit FTC manufacturing categories in which companies operated. For 1950, the count includes lines served in the first year of operation for companies incorporated after 1950. Minimum figures for 1950 count only the lines of the more diversified firm among mergers of equal partners; maximum figures count the lines of both.

b. See text.

companies as of 1975 were more diversified (that is, covered more lines) than their smaller compatriots both in 1950 and in 1975.[9] Second, companies of all sizes greatly increased their diversification over the quarter century analyzed. For all sample companies, the average number of lines increased by 2.85 times between 1950 (using median estimates) and 1975. The greatest proportional increase (3.20 times) was for companies 201–300. The smallest increase (2.15 times) was for companies 401–471, which may be distinctive for having been included in the Line of Business sample to increase coverage of some particular industry and may have continued in 1975 to specialize in that category.

The last column of table 2-3 offers an alternate means of measuring diversification: a "numbers-equivalent index," NE, obtained by inverting the Herfindahl-Hirschman index, as follows: $NE = 1/\Sigma \, S_i^2$, where S_i is the ith segment's share of total company domestic manufacturing sales.[10] NE has its minimum value of 1.0 when the company reports in only one manufacturing line of business. NE rises with increases in the number of equal-sized reporting segments. If each of a company's lines

9. By regressing the logarithm of the number of LBs in 1975 on the logarithm of median 1975 sales, one obtains a regression coefficient of 0.45, with $r = 0.998$, indicating that the number of lines rises at a rate slightly less than with the square root of sales.

10. An early use of the numbers equivalent to measure corporate diversification was Charles H. Berry, *Corporate Growth and Diversification* (Princeton University Press, 1975), pp. 62–66.

had the same sales, NE would rise in exact alignment with a simple LB count. But for a given number of lines, NE is lower, the more unequal the lines are in size. Thus, a company with many LBs, but with most of its sales concentrated in one or two lines, is likely to have a relatively low NE value.

Comparing the last two columns of table 2-3, we see that the Line of Business sample companies were not as diversified in terms of the numbers-equivalent index as with a straight LB count. Thus, there was considerable inequality of the typical company's LB sizes—about as much as when a seven-line firm had individual line shares of 45, 23, 14, 7, 5, 4, and 2 percent. Examined in terms of numbers equivalents, the companies in the several sales groupings differ from one another by much less than when a straight line count is employed. Indeed, companies 101–200 are found to be slightly more diversified than the very largest manufacturers. This suggests that the LBs of the top 100 are particularly unequal in size. That is, the top 100 appear to have added many lines of business that were quite small relative to their main lines.

Table 2-3 takes the 1975 Line of Business sample members (for the most part, the largest U.S. manufacturing enterprises) and asks what their structures looked like in 1950. A different perspective is obtained by identifying the leading manufacturers of 1950 and comparing their structures to those of the leading manufacturers in 1975. We do this for the top 200 of each period. The two cohorts are by no means necessarily the same. In fact, it is useful to begin with the top 200 of 1950 (reduced to 199 when the affiliated Kaiser-Frazer and Kaiser Steel Corporations are consolidated) and determine what their fate was in 1975. A summary follows:

	Number of companies
Survived to 1975 as a member of the leading 200 manufacturers in the Line of Business sample	121
Survived to 1975 as a lower-ranked member of the LB sample	27
Survived to 1975, but not in the LB sample	7
Acquired by a company among the top 200 in the 1975 LB sample	15
Acquired by another 1975 LB sample member	24
Acquired by a company not included in the 1975 LB sample	5
Total	199

Seventy-eight percent of the 1950 leaders survived as independent

Table 2-4. *Diversification of Top 200 Companies of 1950 and 1975, Ranked by Sales Quintile*

Company rank by current-year sales quintile[a]	Mean number of lines of business per company		Mean numbers-equivalent index	
	1950[b]	*1975*	*1950*[b]	*1975*
Largest companies	8.10	12.95	2.52	3.69
Second quintile	5.03	11.83	2.07	3.95
Third quintile	3.53	11.43	1.88	4.83
Fourth quintile	3.15	9.18	1.75	4.28
Smallest companies	4.00	9.08	2.02	4.32
All companies	4.76	10.89	2.05	4.22

a. The companies are grouped into quintiles in descending order of domestic manufacturing sales in each of the two years for which the analysis is presented.

b. These are computed on the same basis as the "low" counts of table 2-5.

entities. The remainder were acquired, mainly by members of the 1975 Line of Business sample.

In table 2-4, the two (only partly overlapping) cohorts of top 200 companies are compared, with a further breakdown into size quintiles, each year's quintile order reflecting that year's sales rankings. Again, a substantial increase in diversification between 1950 and 1975 is observed, although the proportionate rise of LB counts is not as great as for the top 200 of table 2-3. Table 2-3 shows more increase in diversification than table 2-4. This is so because in table 2-3 companies were assigned to the top 200 of both 1950 and 1975 according to their 1975 sales ranks, and where the two cohorts were not in fact synonymous, the 1950 leaders omitted from table 2-3 but included in table 2-4 were necessarily larger, and probably also more diversified, in 1950 than the companies replacing them. Table 2-4 also provides two new insights. For one, increases in diversification were much more pronounced for the smaller giants than for the very largest corporations. The largest 40 manufacturers (not necessarily identical between years) increased their diversification by some 60 percent when measured by a reporting LB count and 46 percent when measured by the numbers-equivalent average. For the smaller companies, the indicated degree of diversification doubled or even tripled. Second, with the more rapid increase in diversification among lower-ranked companies, the sharp differences evident in 1950 between the largest and smaller companies had faded by 1975. Indeed, corporations populating the highest sales volume quintile for 1975 had the *lowest* average numbers-equivalent index of the five groups.[11] What apparently

11. The standard error for comparing differences in mean numbers equivalents

happened between 1950 and 1975 is that the largest companies added new lines, but they were small relative to their principal lines, while companies that "made it" into the lower quintiles of the top 200 for 1975 added lines more evenly proportioned in size to their principal lines.

The mean values of table 2-4 conceal a considerable amount of diversity. Twenty-two of 1975's top 200 operated in 21 or more manufacturing LBs; in 1950, only two achieved that level of diversification. Ninety of 1975's top 200 occupied 10 or more lines, compared to only 19 for 1950's top 199. At the other extreme, 25 of 1950's leaders, but only 5 of 1975's, operated in a single line of business.[12]

As we have seen earlier, 148 top 200 companies of 1950 maintained sufficient manufacturing sales in 1975 to enter the Line of Business sample. For those survivors, there was a considerable degree of sales rank stability. The Spearman correlation between the 1950 sales ranks of those 148 and their 1975 ranks is $+0.58$ ($t = 8.66$). Since unusually complete and comparable data exist for those "constant-membership" companies, we embark upon a more extensive analysis of the changes in their internal structures.

Table 2-5 takes the first step. Each diversification index for 1950 now has two variants: a lower-bound estimate that excludes 1950 activities surviving into 1975 but subject to miscellaneous category or "contaminated" reporting in 1975, and an upper-bound estimate that includes those activities.[13] The 148 "constant-membership" companies are assigned to their 1950 top 200 sales quintiles. Thus, the cohorts compared in table 2-5 are identical between years.

Once again, we observe increases in diversification between 1950 and 1975, the more so for smaller enterprises than for the largest corporations. However, the changes are less pronounced than when nonconstant top 200 sets were compared. For all 148 companies, the mean increase in the number of LBs per company was in the range of 62 to 87 percent; the mean numbers-equivalent index increased by between 55 and 66 percent.

These differences between variable-membership top 200 lists and a tally for 148 constant-membership companies suggest that newcomers

---

between two samples of 40 is approximately 0.80. Thus, the quintile means are not significantly different from one another at conventional confidence levels.

12. For further details on the distribution of diversification indexes, see F. M. Scherer and David Ravenscraft, "Growth by Diversification: Entrepreneurial Behavior in Large-Scale United States Enterprises," *Zeitschrift für Nationalökonomie*, Supplement 4 (1984), p. 203, from which part of the material in this chapter is drawn.

13. See note 8.

Table 2-5. *Diversification of the 148 Top 200 Companies of 1950 Surviving in the 1975 Line of Business Survey, Ranked by 1950 Sales Quintile*

Company rank, by 1950 sales quintile[a]	Mean number of lines of business			Mean numbers-equivalent index		
	1950			1950		
	Low	High	1975	Low	High	1975
Largest companies	8.17	9.57	11.91	2.69	2.87	3.60
Second quintile	5.19	6.14	8.72	2.14	2.27	3.51
Third quintile	4.11	4.59	9.19	2.13	2.31	3.57
Fourth quintile	3.54	3.92	9.04	1.93	1.98	3.84
Smallest companies	4.00	4.46	9.62	2.05	2.31	4.00
All 148 companies	5.22	6.01	9.74	2.22	2.38	3.68

a. Companies are placed in the same 1950 sales rank quintiles as in table 2-4; the number of companies in each quintile ranges from 24 to 36.

to the 1975 list were more diversified than both the firms remaining on the list and the exiting companies they replaced. This is readily verified. The 78 newcomers to 1975's top 200 reported on average in 11.77 manufacturing LBs; the median value was nine lines. This exceeds the comparable figures for 148 constant-membership companies of 9.77 and eight lines respectively. Similarly, the newcomer companies had a mean 1975 numbers-equivalent index of 5.02 and a median of 3.77, compared to 3.68 and 2.79, respectively, for the constant-membership firms. Judged by their numbers equivalents, the 1975 newcomers were more diversified than even the most diversified quintile of the constant-membership group.[14]

The 44 companies that were on the 1950 top 200 list but exited by being acquired some time during the ensuing quarter century were less

14. The standard error for comparing differences in numbers-equivalent means between the constant-membership sample and the sample of newcomers is approximately 0.54. With a t-ratio of 2.47, the differences are significant at the 0.01 level in a one-tail test. This is not to say that all of the newcomers were highly diversified. In fact, the distribution of numbers equivalents was almost bimodal. Numerous new entrants into the top 200 list were fairly narrowly specialized in such rapidly growing fields as petroleum, chemicals, electronics, and aerospace. Of the 78 newcomers, only 6 were completely new firms in the sense that they began operations after 1950.

diversified in 1950 than their surviving counterparts. Their mean count of 1950 LBs (upper-bound estimate) was 3.64; their mean 1950 numbers-equivalent index was 1.59. In both instances, these values are below the lowest 1950 values for any constant-membership company quintile.

Although there were individual exceptions, a broad pattern is implied. Smaller enterprises that grew aggressively, among other things through diversification, tended to survive and move into the ranks of the leading manufacturers. Those that lacked diversification succumbed with greater than average frequency to acquisition by other corporations.

The Paths to Diversification

To determine how diversification was achieved, we extend our analysis of the 148 constant-membership companies. There are two main modes. Diversification can occur through entry into new lines by internal growth, for example, through the development of new products or services; or other firms already operating in different lines of business can be acquired. Table 2-6 traces the structural changes (and definitional ambiguities) accompanying the growth in the number of LBs attributed to the 148 companies between 1950 and 1975.

The first entries show that LBs may not only be added, but also subtracted. The difference between upper-bound and lower-bound counts for 1950 consists of lines that met 1950 reporting criteria but were small enough in 1975 to be buried among other LB reports. In addition, 181 full-fledged lines of 1950, or 20 percent of the upper-bound count, disappeared from their parents' operations by 1975. Thus, only 592 lines from 1950 survived as full-fledged 1975 LBs: 294 of them without any recorded acquisitions of other firms, and 298 with one or more acquisitions. They were joined in 1975 by 29 LBs with identifiable 1950 activity too small to qualify for the 1950 count.

By subtracting from the count of actual 1975 LBs (1,442) the LBs carried over from 1950 (592 + 29), one finds that 821 additional LBs appeared. These reflect the sample companies' success in diversifying. Through a detailed analysis of mergers consummated between 1950 and 1975, an attempt was made to determine the extent to which these additional LBs resulted from acquisition as distinguished from internal growth.

Some 191 lines of business appeared in 1975 reports without 1950 sales antecedents and without any indication of intervening mergers.

Table 2-6. *Accounting for Changes in the Number of Lines of Business for the 148 Top 200 Companies of 1950 Surviving in the 1975 Line of Business Survey*

Description		Number of lines
(1) Upper-bound count of 1950 LBs		889
(2) Less: LBs that disappeared into 1975 "contamination" or the 99.99 catch-all category		−116
(3) Lower-bound count of 1950 LBs		773
(4) Disappearances of lower-bound-count LBs from the 1975 reports		−181
(5) 1950 LBs continuing to report in 1975 (row 3 minus row 4)		592
Of which:		
LBs without any observed acquisitions	294	
LBs with one or more acquisitions	298	
(6) 1975 LBs with 1950 antecedents whose sales were less than $2 million and hence not counted as 1950 LBs		29
Of which:		
LBs that grew from a small start without acquisitions	13	
LBs with one or more acquisitions	16	
(7) Total LBs reporting in 1975		1,442
(8) Additions to LBs continuing from 1950 (row 7 minus rows 5 and 6)		821
Of which:		
New internal growth LBs	191	
New LBs from internal growth plus acquisition	11	
New LBs attributed to acquisitions	578	
Others (complicated by vertical integration or secondary product contamination)	41	
With acquisitions	35	
Without acquisitions	6	

Eleven other LBs were new to the 1975 report and had intervening mergers, but there was evidence that the companies had first entered the fields de novo and only later added to them through merger. Thus, the sum of 191 + 11 = 202, or one-fourth of the lines added, provides an approximation of the extent to which diversification occurred through internal growth. It is an overestimate in part because the merger data were incomplete, and some acquisitions that led to a new line for the constant-membership companies may have been overlooked, leading to the false conclusion that the line arose internally.

One means by which new lines are entered is through research and new product development. The 202 new "internal growth" LBs were on average considerably more strongly oriented toward the performance of R&D than LB sample members generally. With each of the 202 LBs counted separately, mean and median industry R&D/sales ratios (including both company-financed and contract R&D) were as follows:

	R&D as a Percentage of Industry Sales	
	Mean	Median
202 new internal growth LBs	4.20	2.00
All manufacturing industries	1.92	0.88

The differences are highly significant statistically. Only 51 of the 202 new internal growth LBs were in industries with R&D/sales ratios below the median for all manufacturing industries. A possible bias might intrude because three of the most R&D-intensive industry categories—semiconductors, guided missiles, and photocopying equipment—had no antecedents in the 1950 product field classification. LBs in those industries during 1975 were necessarily counted as "new," although (for those with a merger history) not necessarily as stemming from internal growth. When the 19 new internal growth LBs in those three categories are deleted from the sample of 202, the mean and median R&D/sales ratios of the remaining LBs continue to be significantly higher than the corresponding values for all manufacturing industries excepting semiconductors, missiles, and copiers.

Of the LBs unambiguously occupied in 1975 but not in 1950, 578 were associated with one or more acquisitions between 1950 and 1975. These we provisionally designate as cases of diversification through acquisition. This too can be only an approximation. It is possible that a company commenced operations de novo in some field after 1950 and only later added to its activity through acquisition. In the absence of supplementary evidence, such cases would be wrongly classified as cases of diversification through merger. That such classification errors have been made is certain. However, extensive cross-checking of alternative sources suggests that they occurred at most for only a small fraction of the LBs depicted as merger-originated.

The final rows of table 2-6 cover a residual category of 41 new LB appearances classified as "others." These entailed complex circumstances in which only "contaminating" or vertically integrated parts of the company's 1975 activity had 1950 antecedents.[15] Although the cases defy simple categorization, they resemble the more straightforward

15. See note 8.

Table 2-7. *Percentage of Added Lines of Business Attributed to Internal Growth versus Acquisition for the 148 Top 200 Companies of 1950 Surviving in the 1975 Line of Business Survey, Ranked by 1950 Sales Quintile*

Company rank, by 1950 sales quintile	Origin of 1975 lines of business	
	Internal growth	Acquisition
Largest companies	15.8	25.2
Second quintile	16.6	35.8
Third quintile	11.0	50.4
Fourth quintile	10.2	57.9
Smallest companies	14.0	50.4
All 148 companies	14.0	41.1

cases in the preponderance of intervening mergers and acquisitions observed.

Table 2-7 offers further perspective on the role of mergers and acquisitions as compared to internal growth in large enterprises' diversification history. It shows how the proportion of constant-membership companies' 1975 reporting LBs attributed to each diversification mode varied as a function of company size, with the firms grouped into their 1950 sales quintiles. There is no clear size-correlated pattern in the incidence of LBs added through internal growth. For diversification by acquisition, however, a pattern emerges: the smaller top 200 companies of 1950 were much more active than the largest companies in adding new lines by acquisition.[16] Indeed, fully half of their 1975 lines appear to have come through acquisitions.

The Conglomerates

The diversification efforts of smaller companies can be probed further. Some of the most active merger-makers of the period covered by our study were companies too small in 1950 to be part of the top 200 list for that year. These included many of the leading "conglomerates" of the

16. The standard error for comparing quintile acquired proportion means is approximately 12 percent. Thus, for a comparison between the first and third quintiles, the *t*-ratio is 2.10.

1960s and 1970s—companies that grew rapidly by acquiring large numbers of essentially unrelated businesses. Table 2-8 provides an introductory overview. It lists the 51 Line of Business sample members for which Federal Trade Commission historical records tallied 50 or more acquisitions, manufacturing and nonmanufacturing, between 1950 and 1978. The companies are ranked by the number of acquisitions made. The first dozen companies are particularly interesting. Only 1 of the 12, Beatrice Foods, was among the top 200 manufacturing enterprises in 1950, and 10 were not even listed among the top 1,000 for that year. Most of their many acquisitions were of a diversifying character, adding, or adding to, previously unoccupied lines of business and vaulting the acquirers to positions among the most diversified of U.S. corporations. They will play a prominent role in the case studies of chapter 5.

Table 2-8 underrepresents the population of conglomerate acquirers in two respects. For one, other Line of Business sample members made smaller but still significant numbers of diversifying mergers, and in some cases, the "conglomerate acquirer" appellation can be assigned to companies making only a few acquisitions of considerable size. Also, not all active conglomerate acquirers survived to be included in the Line of Business sample. Some stumbled and were acquired themselves or were forced to sell off such a large fraction of their previous conquests that they were too small to qualify for inclusion. Thus, although the exact bounds of the conglomerate acquirer group cannot be defined precisely, table 2-8 does not encompass it entirely. On the other hand, the table also includes some corporations that, despite an extensive merger history, were arguably not conglomerates. The most notable among them are the forest products companies such as Georgia Pacific, Boise Cascade, Champion International, and St. Regis Paper, which made many acquisitions to augment their timber reserves and wood or paper fabrication activities; petroleum companies such as Ashland Oil and Sun Oil, which acquired numerous crude oil reserve holders and gasoline retailers along with petrochemical operations; and publishing companies such as Gannett, Times Mirror, and Macmillan, which expanded by buying up other newspapers, magazines, publishing houses, and the like along with diversifying into less closely related media such as broadcasting. With at most a dozen exceptions, however, the companies in table 2-8 did achieve wide-ranging diversification through merger.

Table 2-8. *The Leading Merger-Making Companies in the Line of Business Survey, Ranked by Number of Acquisitions, 1950–78*

Company[a]	Number of acquisitions, 1950–78	1950 status[b]
Beatrice Foods Co.	290	200
U.S. Industries	190	M
W. R. Grace & Co.	186	Non
International Telephone & Telegraph Corp.	163	M
Consolidated Foods Corp.	158	M
Gulf & Western Industries	155	M
Chromalloy American Corp.	155	New
Whittaker Corp.	148	M
Teledyne	133	New
Textron	115	1,000
Republic Corp.	109	M
Walter Kidde & Co.	108	M
Genesco	101	1,000
Georgia-Pacific Corp.	101	1,000
Litton Industries	99	New
Ashland Oil	96	1,000
Boise Cascade Corp.	89	M
Control Data Corp.	75	New
Mead Corp.	74	200
Minnesota Mining & Manufacturing Co.	74	200
Borden	70	100
Evans Products Co.	67	1,000
Champion International Corp.	66	200
General Mills	64	100
Westinghouse Electric Corp.	63	100
Gannett Co.	63	M
Lear Siegler	63	M

The Stock Market's Reaction

It is worthwhile pausing to see how the stock market reacted to the most active merger-makers. Our principal vehicle for doing so is an analysis of two decades of common stock price history for 13 of the 15 most merger-prone companies listed in table 2-8. The Republic Corporation was excluded because it, unlike the other table 2-8 leaders, had fewer than 20 manufacturing acquisitions.[17] Georgia-Pacific is excluded

17. Harry H. Lynch also rejects Republic in his list of "acquisitive conglomerates," includes 9 of our 13, and fails to consider 5 of the 15 leaders in table 2-8. See Lynch,

Table 2-8 *(continued)*

Company[a]	Number of acquisitions, 1950–78	1950 status[b]
Royal Industries	63	M
Bendix Corp.	62	100
Foremost-McKesson	62	1,000
Koppers Co.	61	200
Combustion Engineering	60	1,000
Times Mirror Co.	60	1,000
Emerson Electric Co.	59	1,000
Dart Industries	58	1,000
LTV Corp.	58	New
Sun Oil Co.	55	100
St. Regis Paper Co.	55	200
McGraw-Edison Co.	55	1,000
Esmark	53	100
Allied Products Corp.	53	M
National Service Industries	53	M
Wickes Corp.	53	M
General Telephone & Electronics Corp.	52	200
Indian Head	51	1,000
Macmillan	51	1,000
Ogden Corp.	51	Non
Studebaker-Worthington	51	100
Sybron Corp.	51	M
American Standard	50	200
Bangor Punta Corp.	50	Non

Sources: Federal Trade Commission, historical files on mergers and acquisitions; *Moody's Industrial Manual;* annual reports of the companies.

a. Name used in 1977.

b. Categories are *100* for top 100 manufacturers by 1950 sales volume; *200* for next 100; *1,000* for next 800; *M* for manufacturing companies not in 1950's top 1,000; *New* for manufacturing companies founded after 1950; and *Non* for companies that had nonmanufacturing lines only in 1950.

because most of its acquisitions were horizontal or vertical rather than conglomerate.

The 13 remaining conglomerates made 2,001 of the 4,402 acquisitions tallied in table 2-8 and 16 percent of the maximum acquisition count for our full (471 corporation) Line of Business sample. For each of the 13, closing stock price quotations were compiled for June 30 of each year,

Financial Performance of Conglomerates (Harvard University, Graduate School of Business Administration, Division of Research, 1971), pp. 66–72.

Table 2-9. *Cumulated Stock Market Value of $1,000 Investments in Thirteen Leading Conglomerates, 1965–83 and 1968–83*[a]

	Thirteen conglomerates				Twelve conglomerates, excluding Teledyne			
	1965	1968	1974	1983	1965	1968	1974	1983
Investment initiated in June 1965								
Value of $1,000 invested in each conglomerate (dollars)	13,000	63,009	16,543	144,482	12,000	55,340	14,490	79,019
Value of equivalent amount invested in S&P 425 industrials portfolio (dollars)	13,000	17,382	19,177	53,377	12,000	16,046	17,701	49,271
Conglomerates as a percent of S&P portfolio value	100.0	362.5	86.3	270.7	100.0	344.9	81.9	160.4
Investment initiated in June 1968								
Value of $1,000 invested in each conglomerate (dollars)	…	13,000	5,686	31,115	…	12,000	5,418	22,578
Value of equivalent amount invested in S&P 425 industrials portfolio (dollars)	…	13,000	14,342	39,919	…	12,000	13,238	36,848
Conglomerates as a percent of S&P portfolio value	…	100.0	39.6	77.9	…	100.0	40.9	61.3

a. The thirteen companies are Beatrice Foods Co., Chromalloy American Corp., Consolidated Foods Corp., Genesco, W. R. Grace & Co., Gulf & Western Industries, International Telephone and Telegraph Corp., Litton Industries, U.S. Industries, Teledyne, Textron, Walter Kidde & Co., and Whittaker Corp.

Figure 2-2. *Stock Price Movements of a Portfolio of Thirteen Merger-Prone Conglomerates and the Standard & Poor's Industrials Portfolio, 1964–83*

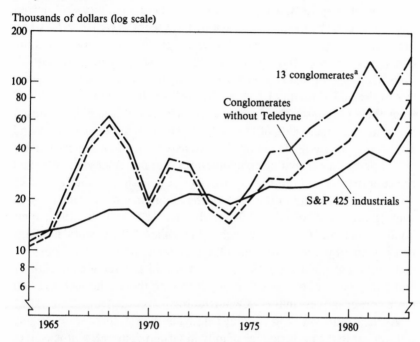

Thousands of dollars (log scale)

a. Beatrice Foods Co., Chromalloy American Corp., Consolidated Foods Corp., Genesco, W. R. Grace & Co., Gulf & Western Industries, International Telephone & Telegraph Corp., Litton Industries, U.S. Industries, Teledyne, Textron, Walter Kidde & Co., and Whittaker Corp.

or when June 30 was a holiday, for the previous trading day.[18] Stock splits and stock dividends were accounted for, and each year's cash dividends were assumed to have been reinvested at midyear. No transaction costs or tax leakages were assumed. A similar procedure was followed to track the market value of the Standard & Poor's 425 industrials portfolio. The results of the analysis are summarized in table 2-9 and figure 2-2. Table 2-9 assumes that a $1,000 investment was made in each company's common stock in 1965, before the conglomerate merger boom went into full swing, or in 1968, at the boom's peak.

Clearly, there were sharp fluctuations in the conglomerates' stock

18. For Whittaker and Teledyne, the first available quotations were for 1964, with which the figure 2-2 series begins. The 11 conglomerates, excluding those 2, outperformed the S&P 425 very slightly in the 1962–65 interval.

market fortunes, so that how well investors fared depended critically on when they bought in. If investors bought into the 13 budding conglomerates in 1965 (top half of table 2-9), they did 3.6 times better than the S&P portfolio by 1968, when conglomerate merger activity was viewed enthusiastically by the market, but only 86 percent as well in 1974, when the pace of merger activity had slowed and it had become clear that the conglomerates were having difficulty managing many of their acquisitions. By 1983, they had recouped nicely, with a portfolio value 2.7 times that of the S&P (but only 1.6 times the S&P's value if they had excluded from their purchases the spectacularly successful Teledyne, omitted from the right hand side of the table).[19] The period between 1974 and 1983 was characterized inter alia by extensive divisional sell-off activity on the part of most leading conglomerates (but not Teledyne). We shall see later that the sell-offs and the stock price gains are probably related.

Those who bought at the peak of the conglomerate merger wave in 1968 (bottom half of table 2-9) fared much less well. By 1974, their holdings had lost 56 percent of their value while S&P investors' holdings had gained 10 percent. Although the conglomerate investors' position had improved greatly by 1983, they had still not recouped, with or without Teledyne, to a position of parity with those who had invested more conservatively in the S&P portfolio.

As the results with and without Teledyne suggest, there were striking differences in the performance of individual conglomerates' stocks over the 1965–83 interval. This is shown more fully in table 2-10, which reports the June 30, 1983, values of individual $1,000 investments made

19. Generally similar results are obtained for a broader set of conglomerates, although it appears that the 13 companies on which our analysis focuses fared somewhat better on the stock market than conglomerates that made fewer mergers. In its annual "500" issues, *Fortune* magazine publishes ten-year stock price performance indexes computed similarly to ours. For the period 1965–75, the *Fortune* 500 industrials had a median annual return of +3.08 percent. Nine of our 13 conglomerates included as "acquisitive conglomerates" in Lynch, *Financial Performance*, had an average return of −0.30 percent, and 13 other conglomerates on Lynch's list averaged −1.32 percent. For 1974–84, discontinuation of *Fortune's* second 500 list permitted a comparison on only 7 of our 13, averaging +25.56 percent per year (or 21.44 percent without Teledyne). Nine of the remaining (less merger-intense) Lynch conglomerates averaged +20.24 percent. The 1974–84 median for *Fortune's* 500 industrials was 18.65 percent per year.

Seven companies on Lynch's list that were not included in the *Fortune* tabulations, in all cases but one because of intervening acquisition, had cumulative stock value gains 26 percent higher than the S&P industrials on average from 1965 to the time of their acquisition (or 1983), but fared only half as well from 1968 to the time of their acquisition (or 1983). Thus, they faded even more sharply after the 1968 peak.

Table 2-10. *Value in 1983 of a $1,000 1965 Investment in Each of Thirteen Leading Conglomerates and in the S&P Industrials Portfolio*

Rank	Company	1983 value of $1,000 investment (dollars)	Risk factor (β)	Market portfolio correlation (r_{im})
1	Teledyne	65,463	1.76	0.356
2	Whittaker Corp.	24,025	1.82	0.323
3	Gulf and Western Industries	16,287	2.33	0.373
4	U.S. Industries	7,152	1.40	0.580
5	Textron	4,947	1.38	0.668
6	Walter Kidde	4,813	1.32	0.546
7	Chromalloy American Corp.	4,672	1.06	0.366
...	S&P 425 industrials portfolio	4,106	...	...
8	Beatrice Foods Co.	3,992	0.95	0.807
9	Consolidated Foods Corp.	3,820	0.90	0.606
10	ITT Corp.	3,625	1.51	0.807
11	Litton Industries	2,691	1.72	0.629
12	W. R. Grace & Co.	2,587	1.12	0.775
13	Genesco	408	2.10	0.594

in 1965 and held, with reinvestment of dividends, to 1983. Six conglomerates fared worse than the S&P, three did slightly better, three considerably better, and one (Teledyne) 16 times as well. The distribution is extremely skewed. In fact, where S is the number of observations greater than or equal to some value V, if we plot in the logarithms the Pareto-Levy equation:

$$(2-1) \qquad S = \gamma V^{\alpha},$$

we find a close fit, with $r^2 = 0.85$ and an α value of 0.58. Such a low value of α implies that neither the mean nor the variance of the distribution is asymptotically finite.[20] This is the kind of distribution one might expect to encounter investing in individual high-technology company stocks, not from diversifying away risks by pooling the fortunes of numerous unrelated business entities.

That the most merger-prone conglomerates did not achieve risk-

---

20. See Benoit Mandelbrot, "New Methods in Statistical Economics," *Journal of Political Economy*, vol. 71 (October 1963), pp. 421–40. What matters most in determining whether the distribution is Paretian is the "fit" and α value in the large-value tail. For the five most successful conglomerates, $\alpha = 0.61$ and $r^2 = 0.976$.

reducing diversification is shown also by examining their stock market β values, computed according to the formula:

$$(2\text{-}2) \qquad\qquad R_{it} = a_i + \beta_i R_{mt} + \epsilon_{it},$$

where R_{it} is the year-to-year percentage gain or loss from holding company i's common stock and R_{mt} is the year-to-year performance of the "market" portfolio—in this case, the Standard & Poor's 425 industrials. The β values estimated in this way, along with the simple correlations r_{im} between the individual stock's performance with that of the market portfolio, are presented in the last two columns of table 2-10. Only 2 of the 13 stocks had β values (slightly) below 1.0, which is where common stocks of average risk tend to cluster. The average β for the 13 conglomerates was 1.49, indicating that the conglomerates carried much more market risk than the "normal" common stock. If the conglomerates' diversification merely canceled out individual line of business risks so as to make the portfolio of all their acquired activities like a mutual fund, one would expect their annual stock market returns to correlate closely with the S&P market portfolio's returns. In fact, however, the 13-company average r_{im} was 0.57, indicating much less than complete elimination of "unsystematic market risk" through diversification.

These findings track fairly closely those of Weston and others, who investigated the 1960–69 stock market records of 48 conglomerates, defined as companies operating in 10 or more three-digit SIC industries and with 20 percent or more of their asset growth attributable to merger.[21] Making explicit comparisons to a group of mutual funds, they found the conglomerates had achieved much less systematic risk reduction than could have been possible by simply buying share interests in a large collection of companies, as most mutual funds do. For their conglomerates, the average β was 1.93, compared to the average for our 13 of 1.49 and the average for their mutual funds of 0.88. Their average r_{im} was 0.54, which is quite close to our 0.57 and far below the mutual funds' 0.93. They conclude, as we must also with evidence on an additional 14 years, that "the major objective of conglomerate mergers was not

21. J. Fred Weston, Keith V. Smith, and Ronald E. Shrieves, "Conglomerate Performance Using the Capital Asset Pricing Model," *Review of Economics and Statistics*, vol. 54 (November 1972), pp. 357–63.

diversification in a risk-reducing sense alone."[22] Just what the conglomerates were seeking through their aggressive merger-making and what they actually achieved are questions that will recur in later chapters.

The Structural Correlates of Merger Activity

We ask now, what characteristics distinguished the companies that diversified actively through merger from other manufacturers? How did the lines they acquired differ from those with which they commenced their diversification programs? And more generally, did the industries marked by heavy acquisition activity differ in significant respects from those with only a sparse merger record? To secure some preliminary quantitative insights on these questions, we probe further into the Line of Business data.

Hypotheses

There is a large literature on the characteristics of industries from which, and toward which, U.S. corporations, conglomerate and otherwise, diversified.[23] Our link between Line of Business and merger data

22. Ibid., p. 362. We do not attempt here to evaluate the return/risk performance of our sample firms, as Weston and associates did, because the outcome depends critically upon the buy-in and sell-out dates chosen.

23. Pioneering analyses include Michael Gort, *Diversification and Integration in American Industry* (Princeton University Press, 1962); J. Fred Weston and Surenda K. Mansinghka, "Tests of the Efficiency Performance of Conglomerate Firms," *Journal of Finance*, vol. 26 (September 1971), pp. 919–36; Richard P. Rumelt, *Strategy, Structure, and Economic Performance* (Harvard University, Graduate School of Business Administration, Division of Research, 1974); and Berry, *Corporate Growth and Diversification*.

More recent contributions include Robert S. Harris, John F. Stewart, David K. Guilkey, and Willard T. Carleton, "Characteristics of Acquired Firms: Fixed and Random Coefficients Probit Analyses," *Southern Economic Journal*, vol. 49 (July 1982), pp. 164–84; James M. MacDonald, "Diversification, Market Growth, and Concentration in U.S. Manufacturing," *Southern Economic Journal*, vol. 50 (April 1984), pp. 1098–1111; William J. Marshall, Jess B. Yawitz, and Edward Greenberg, "Incentives for Diversification and the Structure of the Conglomerate Firm," *Southern Economic Journal*, vol. 51 (July 1984), pp. 1–23; James M. MacDonald, "R&D and the Directions of Diversification," *Review of Economics and Statistics*, vol. 67 (November 1985), pp. 583–90; Michael Gort, Henry Grabowski, and Robert McGuckin, "Organizational Capital and the Choice Between Specialization and Diversification," *Managerial and Decision Economics*, vol. 6 (March 1985), pp. 2–10; and (on Canada) André Lemelin, "Relatedness in the Patterns of Interindustry Diversification," *Review of Economics and Statistics*, vol. 64 (November 1982), pp. 646–57.

provides an opportunity to explore some of the received hypotheses in unusually fine detail. We proceed here with a two-pronged analysis, one at the company level and another at the industry level, using industry characteristic variables measured for the 261 FTC industry categories. The seven main variables and their theoretical rationale are as follows:

Growth. Most analyses of the 1960s merger wave indicate that acquirers moved from low-growth to high-growth industries. We retest that hypothesis using the variable *GROWTH*. It measures the average annual growth rate (in percent) of the current-dollar book value of industry plant and equipment plus inventories. It was estimated by fitting a time trend to the logarithms of appropriately aggregated Census and Survey of Manufactures data for the years 1957, 1962, 1967, 1972, and 1976.[24]

Profitability. Diversification efforts might be expected to flow toward higher-profit industries. However, the opposite trajectory might be observed if firms in high-profit industries sought investment opportunities elsewhere to avoid "spoiling" their home markets. Our ability to test this hypothesis is limited by the unavailability of Line of Business profitability data for a period preceding the conglomerate merger wave's peak. We make do with a crude surrogate—the average industry price-cost margin, *PCM*, over the two Census years 1963 and 1967. For a given year, *PCM* is computed as 100 x (industry value added − payroll costs) / industry value of shipments.

Seller Concentration. Firms in markets with high seller concentration ratios (whose price-cost margins tended to be higher)[25] may have been particularly conscious of the "spoiling" effect too much investment can have. This implies diversification away from concentrated markets. On the other hand, merger may have been viewed as an especially effective way of hurdling entry barriers and entering concentrated industries. Our measure of seller concentration, *CR4*, is the four-firm seller concentration ratio (in percent) for 1967, aggregated when necessary from the four-digit SIC industry level to the smaller number of FTC categories using value of shipments weights. For industries redefined more narrowly in the 1972 SIC revision, 1972 concentration ratios were substituted.

Capital Intensity. Census price-cost margin data do not by them-

24. The *GROWTH* variable is described further in chap. 4.
25. For our sample of 261 industry categories, the simple correlation between *PCM* and the four-firm 1967 seller concentration ratio was +0.237, which is significant at the 0.01 level.

selves reflect the necessity in equilibrium for higher returns on sales in more capital-intensive industries. Thus, in multivariate analyses, a capital-intensity variable should be controlled for in using *PCM* as an explanatory variable. We measure capital intensity, *CAP/S*, as the ratio of Line of Business category assets to sales in 1975. No attempt is made to use data for the 1960s, as with other variables, because differences in industry capital intensity are probably stable over time, and the 1975 data are superior to pre-LB surrogates.

Research and Development. Several earlier studies have suggested that U.S. corporations attempted to diversify toward industries of high technological opportunity, as reflected inter alia in high ratios of company-financed research and development to sales. However, managing an R&D-intensive activity may require special skills, so firms whose home-base industry does little R&D may have been less inclined to diversify in this way. We use the Line of Business company-financed R&D/sales ratios, *RD/S*, by industry category for 1975. There are no data of comparable quality for the 1960s, but for broader industry groups, R&D/sales ratios were highly correlated between the 1960s and 1970s.[26]

Advertising. Consumer goods industries with strong product differentiation, indicated in part by high advertising/sales ratios, may be attractive diversification targets. However, companies with little or no experience in selling such consumer goods may be at a disadvantage and may therefore have avoided moves into intensive-advertising fields. Our measure of industry advertising intensity, *ADV/S*, is the ratio of 1975 media advertising outlays to sales, drawn again from the Line of Business data base.

Other Selling Costs. "Other" selling costs—for example, for field sales representatives, point-of-sale displays, coupons, samples, customer service, and sales management—are on average 4.3 times as large as media advertising outlays.[27] For companies with extensive field sales organizations, diversification into industries in which such costs are important might yield scale economies. Our variable *OSELL/S*, industry selling costs (other than advertising) as a percentage of sales, is taken from the 1975 Line of Business survey. Again, similar data for the 1960s do not exist, but industry intensities are probably stable over time.

26. See F. M. Scherer, "Inter-Industry Technology Flows and Productivity Growth," *Review of Economics and Statistics*, vol. 64 (November 1982), p. 629.

27. See Leonard W. Weiss, George Pascoe, and Stephen Martin, "The Size of Selling Costs," *Review of Economics and Statistics*, vol. 65 (November 1983), p. 668.

The quantitative variables to be analyzed here, as in other chapters, are identified by mnemonic names. A more complete glossary of mnemonics used in the various chapters is provided in appendix C.

Company Diversification Trajectories

Our first analysis focuses on companies that diversified actively through merger. From the full Line of Business sample, we draw a subsample satisfying the following criteria:

(1) The company made at least 15 manufacturing company acquisitions between 1950 and 1977.

(2) The company operated at least one manufacturing line of business in 1975 that it also occupied in 1950. Whether or not they made intervening acquisitions, these are called *ORIG* lines.

(3) The company operated in 1975 at least as many manufacturing LBs stemming from post-1950 acquisitions as the number of lines qualifying under criterion (2). These are called *NEWMERG* lines.

(4) The company's merger history evidence was of acceptably high quality.[28]

Ninety of the 471 companies in the 1975 Line of Business sample satisfied these four criteria. The 90 subsample companies were mostly aggressive diversifiers; on average, the number of their *NEWMERG* lines was 4.7 times the number of original 1950 lines still operated in 1975.

We wish to know how the industries into which companies diversified by merger differed from the industries the firms occupied in 1950. For any given industry characteristic X_i, we compute the variables *X:ORIG*, which is the simple average of the characteristics in originally occupied LBs, and *X:NEWMERG*, which averages the characteristics of lines entered since 1950 by acquisition. The values of these variables are interesting in themselves. We also compute the relative change variable:

$$(2\text{-}3) \qquad X{:}DIFF = \frac{X{:}NEWMERG - X{:}ORIG}{X{:}ORIG + X{:}NEWMERG}.$$

If the new lines' characteristics are identical to those of the original lines, $X{:}DIFF = 0$. In the limiting case where the original lines' characteristic average has a zero value and the new lines' average has a finite value, $X{:}DIFF = +1$. The other extreme, $X{:}DIFF = -1$,

28. Merger histories were compiled from a variety of sources described in chap. 4.

occurs when the new lines' characteristic average is distinguished by a zero value.

Table 2-11 summarizes the results for all 90 companies together, and with the companies arrayed into quartiles in ascending order of their average original industry characteristics. The data are organized to shed light on three distinct questions: (1) Were the 90 diversification-prone companies "at home" originally in industries different in important respects from the population of all manufacturing industries? (2) Did the companies move into lines with significantly more or less of some characteristic than the lines they originally occupied? (3) Did the companies starting with relatively more of some characteristic select diversification lines with more of that characteristic than companies with a lower initial endowment, that is, did likes choose likes, or were target lines chosen essentially randomly with respect to original quartile position?

The first question is addressed using data presented in the first three numerical cells of the first row for each variable. The first-row entry in the t-ratio column gives the t-ratio in a test of equality between all-industry means (first numerical column) and 90-company means (second numerical column). The most striking result, which runs contrary to conventional wisdom, is that the active diversifiers' original industries were not marked by abnormally stagnant growth opportunities. To the contrary, the slowest-growing quartile of active diversifiers occupied industries of nearly average growth, and the rest started from faster-growing industries. The only other difference that passes statistical significance tests is for seller concentration. The active diversifiers began from relatively unconcentrated industries. The difference on other selling expenses is marginally significant ($t = 1.69$); the other differences are statistically insignificant by conventional standards.

Table 2-11 has two tests of the "original versus new line" characteristics question. The second t-ratio column entry for each characteristic tests the equality of means for *ORIG* as compared to *NEWMERG* industry characteristics. The third t-ratio column entry tests whether the relative change variable *X:DIFF* is significantly different from zero. Only for *GROWTH* and *CAP/S* do both tests indicate significant differences. That is, diversifying companies sought (slightly) more rapidly growing industries than those in which they were at home, and they moved into more capital-intensive industries.[29] There is equivocal evi-

---

29. This relationship might be spurious if merger per se led to asset write-ups (that

Table 2-11. Average Industry Characteristics of Newly Acquired and Original Lines of Business for Ninety Merger-Active Companies

Characteristic[a]	All-industry average (percent)	Ninety-company average (percent)	t-ratio	Quartile averages[b]				F-ratio (3, 86)[c]
				Lowest	Second	Third	Highest	
GROWTH:								
ORIG	4.61	7.08	8.26[d]	4.56	6.61	7.42	9.74	...
NEWMERG	...	7.76	2.52[e]	7.71	7.90	7.45	7.99	0.99
DIFF	...	0.062	3.68[f]	0.26	0.09	-0.01	-0.09	...
PCM:								
ORIG	27.3	26.0	1.26[d]	17.7	23.3	26.9	36.3	...
NEWMERG	...	27.2	1.27[e]	25.0	26.7	26.9	30.4	5.55
DIFF	...	0.034	2.45[f]	0.16	0.07	-0.003	-0.08	...
CR4:								
ORIG	41.0	35.8	2.27[d]	16.6	28.0	38.9	59.9	...
NEWMERG	...	32.4	1.66[e]	28.9	30.5	33.0	37.2	4.29
DIFF	...	-0.009	0.35[f]	0.27	0.02	-0.09	-0.23	...
CAP/S:								
ORIG	0.684	0.650	1.20[d]	0.37	0.56	0.70	0.98	...
NEWMERG	...	0.762	3.08[e]	0.68	0.72	0.88	0.77	2.84
DIFF	...	0.086	4.35[f]	0.25	0.11	0.09	-0.12	...
RD/S:								
ORIG	1.44	1.29	0.69[d]	0.015	0.31	1.09	3.80	...
NEWMERG	...	1.30	0.03[e]	0.35	1.25	1.11	2.48	4.32
DIFF	...	0.083	1.50[f]	0.60	0.10	-0.11	-0.25	...
ADV/S:								
ORIG	1.65	1.39	0.65[d]	0.07	0.30	0.83	4.46	...
NEWMERG	...	1.09	0.79[e]	0.46	0.49	1.15	2.30	10.52
DIFF	...	0.071	1.33[f]	0.45	0.05	0.03	-0.25	...
OSELL/S:								
ORIG	7.15	6.17	1.69[d]	1.15	4.34	6.95	12.42	...
NEWMERG	...	6.90	1.14[e]	4.89	6.28	6.43	10.13	9.69
DIFF	...	0.103	2.42[f]	0.48	0.13	-0.12	-0.09	...

a. Terms defined in text.
b. Companies are arrayed into quartiles according to their original characteristic values.
c. The relevant 5 percent point is 2.72; the 1 percent point is 4.04.
d. Tests the equality of all-industry and 90-company averages.
e. Tests the equality of ORIG and NEWMERG averages.
f. Tests whether the DIFF values are significantly different from zero.

dence that the companies gravitated toward industries with (at best, slightly) higher price-cost margins (perhaps in compensation for the greater capital intensity), and that they moved into lines in which "other" selling expenses were heavier than in their original lines.

The "like-for-like" hypothesis is subjected to an F-ratio test (last numerical column of table 2-11) of the equality of *NEWMERG* means across the four *ORIG* line quartiles. Rejection of the equal means hypothesis implies that diversification efforts were influenced by original line characteristic intensities.[30] Especially with respect to activities that demand special skills or permit economies of scale, there is strong evidence of like-for-like diversification. Companies originally in industries with a high intensity of R&D spending, advertising, or other selling activity moved into industries with significantly higher values of those characteristics than did companies diversifying from industries with low characteristic values. There is also evidence that firms in industries with unusually high price-cost margins targeted their diversification toward wider-margin industries than companies starting with relatively low margins. The similar result for *CR4* is difficult to interpret. Although the companies at home in the most concentrated industries chose relatively more concentrated targets than their peers, *all* of the quartiles moved into industries less concentrated on average than the 41 percent all-industry mean value. The weakest evidence of like-for-like movement is with respect to growth. Apparently, companies in unusually rapidly growing home industries had no superior ability to pick rapid-growth diversification targets, even though all of the active diversifiers moved toward relatively rapidly growing industries.

---

is, under purchase accounting), increasing indicated capital intensity in the *NEWMERG* lines, and if the *NEWMERG* lines chosen for diversification by our 90 sample companies were the subject of especially intensive merger activity.

30. No significance tests are performed on *ORIG* versus *NEWMERG* intra-quartile changes, since it is normal to expect some regression toward the mean from above-average or below-average starting positions. However, a corollary of the like-for-like hypothesis is that, for some characteristics, regression toward the mean may be greater than for others. A direct test is to compute the regression equation (where "regression" now has its more conventional statistical meaning):

$$X{:}NEWMERG_i = a + b \ X{:}ORIG_i + e_i.$$

More regression toward the mean is implied, the lower the value of the coefficient b. A b value of 0 implies total regression, while values approaching 1 support the like-for-like hypothesis. The b values, in descending order, were 0.40 for *OSELL/S*, 0.39 for *RD/S*, 0.27 for *PCM*, 0.22 for *CAP/S*, 0.17 for *CR4*, 0.10 for *ADV/S*, and 0.09 for *GROWTH*.

Industries Favored by Acquirers

An alternative means of investigating merger trajectories is to examine by industry the characteristics associated with high levels of acquisition activity.

One way of measuring merger activity is to count the number of LBs within an industry that entered their parents' folds through acquisition since 1950,[31] and divide it by the industry's total number of LBs in 1975. The distribution of this variable, *ICOUNT,* across the 251 industries with three or more reporting LBs (encompassing a total of 3,209 LBs) is interesting in its own right:

Acquired lines as a percent of total lines	Number of industries	Percent of all industries
0–19	20	8.0
20–39	64	25.5
40–59	87	34.7
60–79	67	26.7
80–100	13	5.2
Total	251	100.0

In the median (and mean) industry, nearly half of the LBs reporting in 1975 had come under their parents' control through acquisition, rather than being part of the parents' operations in 1950 or originating through new internal development.

Because it counts only cases in which companies entered a four-digit FTC industry category by acquisition, the *ICOUNT* variable captures only diversifying or vertical merger activity. To include the substantial number of horizontal cases too, we define the variable *IMERGSHR,* whose numerator is the estimated sum of all acquired assets at original acquisition values and whose denominator is total 1975 industry assets. Its individual line of business counterpart will play a prominent role in chapter 4.[32] The mean value of *IMERGSHR* across the 251 industries is 0.25. That is, on average, 25 percent of 1975 assets were merger-originated.

A difficulty with *IMERGSHR* is that it has a lower value, the more

31. These are the *NEWMERG* lines of our earlier analysis.
32. The prefix "*I*" distinguishes these industry aggregate variables from similarly named variables used in chap. 4 that are disaggregated to the individual line of business level.

rapidly an industry grew after the average acquisition occurred. Thus, a spurious negative correlation with our industry growth variable *GROWTH* may appear. An alternative approach (explained more fully in chapter 4) is to let each individual acquisition's assets be multiplied by a cumulative industry asset growth factor from the year of acquisition to 1975 before those assets are aggregated to the industry level. The "grown" summed assets are then divided by 1975 industry assets. This modified merger history variable, *IMERGROW,* has a mean value of 0.46 after the observations for 25 industries with values exceeding 1.0 are truncated at unity. Because the estimation of *IMERGROW* uses a variant of the 1957–76 industry growth rate variable *GROWTH,* we must again be wary of a spurious correlation—in this instance, positive—between the two.

In addition to the seven industry characteristics used in our 90-company analysis, three more are introduced into multiple regressions "explaining" industry merger activity. *EXPORT* is the ratio of industry exports to industry sales in 1972, *IMPORT* the ratio of 1972 imports to sales. Both are drawn from Input-Output tables for the United States. One might anticipate diversification away from import-impacted industries and toward export-intensive industries. *NATRES* is a dummy variable with a unit value for industries in which firms' operations may be constrained by available supplies of timber, crude oil, or other natural resources.[33] It was hypothesized that merger activity in such industries might be stimulated by the desire to secure sources of otherwise inexpansible input supplies.

Table 2-12 presents the regression equations with the three alternative measures of industry merger activity as dependent variable. Two-tailed hypothesis tests are applied, since many of the a priori predictions are ambiguous. Except with respect to the growth variable, the results are generally similar. Only the *ICOUNT* equation is free of spurious growth influences. Its significantly positive *GROWTH* coefficient reinforces our company-level finding that high-growth industries were favored diversification targets. Contrary to the findings of others using cruder measures, we observe that R&D-intensive industries experienced significantly less acquisition activity. The highly concentrated industries had a similar experience. Industries with relatively high selling expenses

---

33. The industries are beet sugar, logging, sawmills, pulp mills, paper, paperboard, sanitary paper products, fertilizers, petroleum refining, cement, gypsum products, primary copper, primary lead, and primary zinc.

Table 2-12. *Regression Equations Relating Measures*
of Industrywide Merger Activity to Industry Characteristics

	Dependent variable[a]		
	ICOUNT	IMERGSHR	IMERGROW
Intercept	0.52[b]	0.36[b]	0.40[b]
	(8.96)	(7.18)	(5.13)
GROWTH	0.0115[b]	−0.0074[c]	0.0264[b]
	(2.67)	(1.99)	(4.58)
PCM	−0.0020	−0.0008	−0.0010
	(1.08)	(0.51)	(0.39)
CR4	−0.0036[b]	−0.0033[b]	−0.0053[b]
	(6.03)	(6.46)	(6.65)
CAP/S	0.063	0.114[c]	0.111
	(0.98)	(2.06)	(1.29)
RD/S	−0.0143	−0.0204[b]	−0.0439[b]
	(1.61)	(2.64)	(3.66)
ADV/S	−0.0051	−0.0044	−0.0112
	(0.92)	(0.91)	(1.51)
OSELL/S	0.0113[b]	0.0085[b]	0.0097[c]
	(3.82)	(3.31)	(2.43)
EXPORT	0.0002	0.0004	0.0017
	(0.13)	(0.23)	(0.65)
IMPORT	−0.0002	0.0001	−0.0005
	(0.42)	(0.27)	(0.78)
NATRES	−0.099[d]	−0.065	−0.042
	(1.82)	(1.37)	(0.58)
R^2	0.2926	0.2907	0.3387

a. Based on 251 industries; numbers in parentheses are *t*-ratios.
b. Significant in a two-tailed test at the 0.01 level.
c. Significant in a two-tailed test at the 0.05 level.
d. Significant in a two-tailed test at the 0.10 level.

(other than media advertising), on the other hand, tended to attract above-average merger interest, all else equal. For the other explanatory variables, the estimated relationships are weak and sometimes (as for *NATRES*) in an unexpected direction.

Conclusion

American manufacturing industry experienced merger activity of impressive proportions between 1950 and 1976, with a sharp peak in the late 1960s. One-fourth of the average industry member's 1975 assets can be traced directly back to acquisitions. Although horizontal and vertical acquisitions were also in evidence, the mergers were preponderantly of a conglomerate, or diversifying, character. The typical large corporation nearly doubled the number of lines in which it operated through acquisitions. Correspondingly, half of the typical manufacturing industry's participants experienced a merger-related change in ownership. Line of Business sample members that were relatively small in 1950 tended to diversify more aggressively than the larger enterprises. Companies tended to diversify through acquisition toward high-growth industries and perhaps also toward industries in which they could realize selling and distributional scale economies. There are other signs of a pattern in diversification efforts—for example, as firms accustomed to spending heavily on research and development or advertising moved into lines requiring similar emphasis. The stock market reacted enthusiastically to the most aggressive diversifiers during the late 1960s, turned against them in the early 1970s, and then selectively returned them to favor in the late 1970s. A few conglomerates achieved spectacular stock market gains, although the market tended to evaluate their securities as extraordinarily risky.

CHAPTER THREE

The Profitability of
Acquired Companies

OUR NEXT and central task is to determine how mergers of the 1950s, 1960s, and early 1970s affected the operating efficiency and profitability of the companies involved. To begin, we investigate the profit potential of the acquired companies, as manifested in their pre-merger earnings records.

Prior Research

There is a substantial literature on the profitability of mergers generally and the pre-merger profitability of acquired entities.[1] Early qualitative analyses suggested that acquirees were in general a sickly lot. According to Donald Dewey in 1961, "Most mergers . . . are merely a civilized alternative to bankruptcy or the voluntary liquidation that transfers assets from falling to rising firms."[2] In his influential article on the theory of takeovers, Henry G. Manne saw voluntary mergers as a means of "lessening . . . wasteful bankruptcy proceedings" and "trying to establish more efficient management in poorly run companies."[3] These characterizations, although perhaps exaggerated, may have been reasonably accurate with respect to European conditions. Studies covering the United Kingdom, West Germany, and (less consistently) Belgium,

1. For surveys of the literature, see Peter O. Steiner, *Mergers: Motives, Effects, Policies* (Ann Arbor: University of Michigan Press, 1975), chap. 8; Dennis C. Mueller, "The Effects of Conglomerate Mergers," *Journal of Banking and Finance*, vol. 1 (December 1977), pp. 315–47; Dennis C. Mueller, ed., *The Determinants and Effects of Mergers* (Cambridge, Mass.: Oelgeschlager, Gunn & Hain, 1980); and F. M. Scherer, *Industrial Market Structure and Economic Performance*, 2d ed. (Houghton Mifflin, 1980), pp. 138–41.

2. Donald Dewey, "Mergers and Cartels: Some Reservations About Policy," *American Economic Review*, vol. 51 (May 1961, *Papers and Proceedings, 1960*), p. 257.

3. Henry G. Manne, "Mergers and the Market for Corporate Control," *Journal of Political Economy*, vol. 73 (April 1965), pp. 119–20.

Sweden, and the Netherlands have shown acquired companies to be appreciably less profitable on average than their acquirers or control groups.[4]

For the United States, the previously published evidence is more mixed, although it lends little support to a theory of mergers as a common alternative to bankruptcy. The most comprehensive analysis was by Boyle.[5] It covered 698 acquisitions of publicly traded manufacturing companies recorded on the Federal Trade Commission's "large" merger compendium (that is, with acquired firm assets of $10 million or more) for 1948–68, and for which five years of pre-merger data were available. Only 4.8 percent had negative profits in the year before merger. Acquired manufacturers with assets below $100 million had after-tax profit returns on assets 2 to 7 percent lower on average than those recorded for all manufacturing corporations of comparable size in the Federal Trade Commission's *Quarterly Financial Report*.[6] For acquired companies with assets above $100 million, on the other hand, the pre-merger record was significantly less favorable, averaging only 44 percent of the *QFR* benchmark in the above-$250 million category. Companies of all sizes acquired in horizontal mergers had final pre-merger year returns on stockholders' equity averaging 8.8 percent. The *QFR* benchmark was 10.0 percent. The returns of conglomerate acquisitions, averaging 10.2 percent, were slightly higher than those of the all-manufacturing universe.

Examining 287 U.S. companies acquired over the period 1962–72,

4. Dennis C. Mueller, "A Cross-National Comparison of the Results," in Mueller, *Determinants and Effects*, pp. 299–302; and Ajit Singh, *Takeovers: Their Relevance to the Stock Market and the Theory of the Firm* (Cambridge University Press, 1971), especially p. 76.

5. Stanley E. Boyle, "Pre-Merger Growth and Profit Characteristics of Large Conglomerate Mergers in the United States: 1948–1968," *St. John's Law Review*, vol. 44 (Spring 1970, *Special Edition*), pp. 152–70.

6. The *Quarterly Financial Report*, as the name suggests, records the quarterly returns on assets or stockholders' equity. The standard technique used by Boyle and most other analysts (including the Council of Economic Advisers) of averaging four quarters' ratios and multiplying by four to get an annual return is systematically biased as a benchmark for evaluating returns reported in companies' annual reports. If assets are growing, they will be larger when the company compiles its end-of-year annual report than in three of the four quarters for which quarterly returns are computed. Thus, returns compiled annually will have a larger denominator than returns averaged over four quarters. The overstatement of universe operating income/asset ratios using the four quarterly average method from 1965 through 1970 was on the order of one part in 27. For example, the four-quarter average rate for 1968 was 11.88 percent and the end-of-year rate 11.43 percent.

including only 28 horizontal acquisitions, Dennis Mueller found that the acquirees had pre-merger returns on assets slightly greater than those of a size- and industry-matched control group, and nearly a percentage point greater than the average return in their home industries.[7] In a still more recent study, Robert S. Harris and others examined the ratio of operating income to assets for 106 publicly traded U.S. manufacturing companies acquired in the period 1974–77.[8] Over the two years before acquisition, the acquired firms had average returns on assets slightly, but statistically insignificantly, above those of some 1,199 nonacquired corporations.

New York Stock Exchange Listing Application Evidence

The prior studies on pre-merger profitability support a conclusion that the acquired companies were not greatly different from the universe of U.S. corporations to which they belonged. There may have been some trend over time toward increased relative profitability of the acquisition targets, although the evidence on this point is not decisive.

All of the prior analyses, however, suffer from an important set of limitations. In order to obtain published profit information, the analyses were confined to acquisitions of "public" companies—those whose securities were listed on a stock exchange. Any sample so defined is necessarily skewed toward acquirees that were relatively large. It may also be biased in more subtle ways. Yet the conglomerate merger wave of the 1960s and surrounding years plainly encompassed a much larger set, including thousands of closely held and usually small corporations. For a balanced assessment, it is essential to find a sample that sweeps more widely.

Fortunately, an appropriate data source exists. When companies whose securities are traded on the New York Stock Exchange make acquisitions entailing the issue of new or additional shares, they are required under the NYSE rules to file a "listing application" describing

7. Dennis C. Mueller, "The United States, 1962–1972," in *Determinants and Effects*, p. 278.

8. Robert S. Harris, John F. Stewart, and Willard T. Carleton, "Financial Characteristics of Acquired Firms," in Michael Keenan and Lawrence J. White, eds., *Mergers and Acquisitions: Current Problems in Perspective* (Lexington Books, 1982), p. 236.

details of the transaction.[9] The information provided includes a recent income statement (occasionally covering less than a full fiscal year) and balance sheet for the acquired firm, the consideration to be paid, and the type of accounting (purchase or pooling-of-interests) to be used in bringing the acquired firm's assets onto the acquirer's books.

A virtually complete collection of hard-bound NYSE listing applications at the University of Pennsylvania was tapped to draw several pre-merger samples. The most comprehensive effort spanned three segments: one including all domestic manufacturing company acquisitions made during the first nine months of 1968, at the peak of the 1960s conglomerate merger wave; a second covering 1971 manufacturing company acquisitions whose financial results for 1970 (a year of recession) were disclosed;[10] and a third encompassing 1974 acquisitions. The three samples attempted to cover all domestic manufacturing company acquisitions, not only acquisitions made by Line of Business sample corporations. Thirty-eight percent of the sample acquisitions were *not* made directly by Line of Business respondents, although some of the non-LB acquirers were themselves later acquired by LB sample members. In any event, the listing application sample's scope is somewhat broader than most of the statistical analyses reported in this volume, although, as we shall see, the results are quite similar to those for Line of Business acquirer samples only.[11]

As expected, the listing application acquisitions were much smaller on average than those covered by samples including only public companies. Seventy-eight percent of the acquired companies had pre-merger assets of less than $10 million—the threshold for inclusion in the FTC's large merger file, on which Boyle's sample was based. The median acquired company's assets were $2.63 million. The comparable figure was $29 million for large public company acquisitions on the FTC's 1968 list. The distribution of acquired companies by asset size was highly skewed:[12]

9. See New York Stock Exchange, *Listed Company Manual* (New York: NYSE, 1983), especially paragraph 703.01.

10. To ensure that the reported profit figures were centered on 1970, the sample began with April 1, 1971, listing applications and terminated after September 1971, when the incidence of 1971 profit reports increased markedly.

11. See note 17 in this chapter and note 28 in chap. 4.

12. Among the values in this potentially unbounded range, the maximum was $749 million and the mean $319 million. A frequency distribution by *value* of assets, rather than by number of acquisitions, as in the table here, is presented in chap. 7.

Assets (millions of dollars)	Percent of all acquired companies
Less than 1	28.7
1–4.9	39.3
5–9.9	10.9
10–19.9	8.2
20–49.9	7.1
50–99.9	3.0
100 or more	2.8

Consistent with the analysis to follow in chapter 4, our profitability measure is the ratio of annual (or annualized) operating income to total end-of-period assets, expressed in percentage terms. Operating income is computed before income taxes, extraordinary charges or credits, and interest charges (or income). The simple average profit rates for pre-merger sample members, and the *QFR* manufacturing universe figures for the most closely comparable reporting period, are as follows:[13]

NYSE sample companies

Acquisition period	Number of companies	Average profit-ability (percent)	QFR profit benchmark (percent)
1968	392	20.8	11.3
1971	113	19.6	8.6
1974	129	18.9	11.6
All three years	634	20.2	10.9

For the three periods separately and together, the acquisition targets were substantially more profitable than the population of all manufacturing corporations. The differences are statistically significant, with *t*-ratios ranging from 11.48 (for all years combined) down to 4.08 (for 1974). Only 5.8 percent of the 634 acquired companies had negative operating income in the last accounting period before their acquisition.

To control more completely for industry and timing influences, each

---

13. To avoid the bias present in earlier studies, the *QFR* benchmark is defined as the sum of four quarters' operating income, divided by fourth-quarter assets. A more complex procedure was required to deal with a sizable discontinuity between 1973 and 1974.

Thirteen observations were excluded from the sample: seven because they used unconventional merger accounting methods (usually "dirty" pooling) and (consistent with the approach to be taken in chap. 4) six because operating income/assets percentages exceeded + 100 percent (in four cases) or − 100 percent (in two cases).

Table 3-1. *Average Supranormal Profitability of Acquired Companies before Merger, by Year of Acquisition and Merger Accounting Method*

Acquisition period	Pooling-of-interest acquisitions		Purchase acquisitions		All acquisitions	
	Number of companies	Supranormal return (percent)[a]	Number of companies	Supranormal return (percent)[a]	Number of companies	Supranormal return (percent)[a]
1968	337	9.09	55	4.01	392	8.37
1971	81	13.81	32	−1.58	113	9.45
1974	86	8.84	43	1.72	129	6.47
All three years	504	9.80	130	1.88	634	8.18

a. The supranormal returns are the averages of individual company operating income as a percentage of assets, less the comparable figure for the most closely corresponding *QFR* industry group.

company's operating income ratio was matched to its *QFR* counterpart in one of 17 possible two-digit manufacturing industry groups and to the four-quarter period most closely coinciding with the company's final pre-merger income report. In addition, mergers made under pooling-of-interests accounting were distinguished from purchase accounting acquisitions. As noted in chapter 1 and shown more fully in appendix A, acquirers have tended to adopt pooling accounting when they paid high acquisition premiums relative to the acquired firm's pre-merger book value, while purchase accounting has been adopted more frequently for low-premium acquisitions. The more profitable an acquired company was, the higher the above-book premium was likely to be. Thus, pre-merger profitability is expected to vary systematically with accounting method choice as well as home industry and business cycle stage.

Table 3-1 summarizes the results, with annualized pre-merger profitability now measured as supranormal returns, that is, the difference between the acquired firms' operating income/asset ratios (in percent) and the corresponding *QFR* industry benchmarks. Several findings stand out. Acquired companies are again found to be substantially more profitable than their manufacturing universe peers. However, their superiority is somewhat less when industry effects are controlled (8.18 percent for all acquisitions over all three years) than when not (from the earlier table, $20.2 - 10.9 = 9.3$ percent). As expected, pooling-of-interests acquisitions were significantly more profitable pre-merger than purchases. The relevant *F*-ratio (with 3 and 628 degrees of freedom) is 7.79, which exceeds the 1 percent point of 3.82. The supranormal profitability of purchase acquisitions is insignificantly different from zero; $F(3, 127) = 0.42$ in a test of the zero restriction. We cannot reject the hypothesis that the supranormal profitability averages for all acquisitions are insignificantly different from one another across the three years; $F(2, 631) = 0.80$.

How is it that our NYSE listing statement results can differ so strikingly from those of other studies, which found acquired companies to be either somewhat less, or insignificantly more, profitable than peer groups? Our sample covers more recent acquisitions than those analyzed in other studies except that by Harris, Stewart, and Carleton. If there has been a rising trend in the profitability of companies selected for acquisition, it should show up in our data. However, no clear trend is apparent over the seven years spanned by table 3-1. Much more important, our sample, unlike others, includes smaller and (often related to smallness) privately held companies.

The role of size is shown in part by a comparison of unweighted and asset-weighted means. The asset-weighted average operating income/ assets ratio, influenced strongly by a few very large acquisitions, was 12.98 percent. Since the simple average was 20.20 percent, our results were plainly influenced by the NYSE sample's extensive coverage of small acquisitions. Although both averages are meaningful, the un- weighted averages are of greater interest for the analyses in chapter 4, which will include numerous individual company lines of business formed through one or a few relatively small acquisitions.

Size can interact with private ownership to affect managerial salaries, and hence operating income after deduction of salaries. The bias could go either way: owners of small private companies might either overpay or underpay themselves from the salary account. Studies by George J. Stigler and Joseph L. McConnell covering the 1940s and early 1950s reveal a strong tendency toward overpayment, and hence an understate- ment of operating income for the smallest corporations.[14]

Further insight into the role of size, accounting choice, and two methodological problems encountered in compiling the NYSE listing application data is obtained by regressing *SUPRA*, the supranormal profitability variable analyzed in table 3-1, on four variables:

14. George J. Stigler, *Capital and Rates of Return in Manufacturing Industries* (Princeton University Press, 1963), pp. 59–61 and 125–27; and Joseph L. McConnell, "1942 Corporate Profits by Size of Firm," *Survey of Current Business*, vol. 26 (January 1946), pp. 10–16.

LOGSIZE   Logarithm (to base 10) of acquired company pre-merger assets, measured in thousands of dollars.

PURCH   Dummy variable with value of 1 if purchase accounting was adopted, and 0 otherwise.

PARTYR   Dummy variable with value of 1 if earnings were reported for less than a full year and had to be annualized, and 0 otherwise.

INTRST   Dummy variable with value of 1 if interest charges (or income) were subtracted from operating income.

Partial-year earnings had to be annualized in 10.3 percent of the 634 cases (with the possibility of biases like those analyzed in footnote 13 above). In 6.5 percent of the cases, interest items could not be purged from operating income, leading to an understatement of profitability if more interest was paid than earned. With *t*-ratios in subscripted parentheses, the regression equation estimated for all three years' supranormal profit data is as follows:

$$(3\text{-}1) \quad SUPRA = 17.62 - 2.20 \; LOGSIZE - 7.78 \; PURCH$$
$$\quad\quad\quad\quad (4.91) \quad (2.20) \quad\quad\quad\quad (4.24)$$
$$\quad\quad\quad\quad - 1.77 \; PARTYR - 1.22 \; INTRST.$$
$$\quad\quad\quad\quad (0.72) \quad\quad\quad (0.40)$$
$$R^2 = 0.037, N = 634.$$

Supranormal profitability falls by 2.2 percentage points with each tenfold increase in assets.[15] For the pooling-of-interests mergers, to which the intercept value of 17.62 applies, supranormal profitability is eliminated only beyond acquired company asset values of $100 billion (eight base-10 logarithmic cycles), a size attained by no acquisition in our sample. As in table 3-1, companies acquired under purchase accounting had returns nearly eight percentage points lower than pooling-of-interests acquisitions.[16] The need to annualize some partial-year operating income

15. The size coefficient was *positive* but insignificant ($t = 0.93$) for 1974. For 1968 and 1971, it was negative and significant, with a value of 3.28 for 1968 acquisitions and 3.45 for 1971. No implication is drawn from this regression that larger size (or purchase accounting) *causes* lower profitability. Rather, the regression is presented in the spirit of a covariance analysis to determine how the profitability of companies selected for acquisition varied across merger types. We thereby lay a foundation for the post-merger comparison to follow in chaps. 4, 6, and 7.

16. A similar analysis in chap. 7 provides statistically weak evidence that the purchase effect declined with acquired firm size.

items, and inability to exclude certain interest charges, apparently had no significant biasing effect.

The difference in profitability between purchase and pooling accounting acquisitions could affect the generality of our listing statement results in another more subtle way. Only 20.5 percent of the 634 acquisitions were treated as purchases. For a larger sample of companies analyzed in appendix A and not limited to NYSE listing application information, 44.6 percent of the acquisitions on which accounting choice disclosures were available were treated as purchases. Thus, the NYSE sample is biased toward more profitable pooling acquisitions, probably because the rules governing such choices, especially after 1970, called for the use of pooling mainly when new securities were issued, which in turn necessitated (at least for NYSE-listed acquirers) publication of a listing application. Taking the averages by accounting type in table 3-1 and reweighting them to reflect the 45-55 purchase-pooling division evident in our broader and more representative sample, we find the all-acquisition supranormal return for three years combined to have been approximately 6.3 percent.

Further Evidence

Several additional samples were drawn, from NYSE listing application sources and others, to examine certain pre-merger profitability questions in greater depth.

Sold-Off Lines

One question is whether acquired entities that were subsequently sold off were less profitable pre-merger than the entities that survived through 1980. To find out, a list of 615 known divisional sell-offs, augmented with original acquisition dates when known, was prepared. A comprehensive search of NYSE listing applications from 1962 through 1976 was then made to identify acquired companies subjected to later sell-off. A total of 215 matches (excluding 4 with unorthodox merger accounting choices) were found. Their median assets were $3.5 million, similar to the $2.6 million median found for the 1968–71–74 sample of 634 acqusitions. Their average operating income/assets ratio in the last pre-merger period was 20.7 percent, which differs insignificantly from the 20.2 percent average for the 634-acquisition group, selected without regard to subsequent outcome. The sell-off sample observations were pooled with the 634-company sample, with duplications eliminated. When an analogue of regression (3-1) was estimated to take into account the effect on profitability of acquired firm size and accounting choice, a dummy variable distinguishing the sold-off acquisitions was insignificantly different from zero, with a t-ratio of 0.02.[17] Thus, there is no reason to believe that units subsequently sold off were less profitable pre-merger than surviving units.

Adjustment for Macroeconomic Variations

In analyzing the pre-merger profitability of companies acquired at widely differing times, a comparability problem can arise. Manufacturing universe benchmark profit rates are lower in recession years than in boom years, and holding the business cycle phase constant, there was a tendency for profit rates to creep upward over time as inflation rates, and hence nominal capital costs, rose. Table 3-2 shows that operating income/assets ratios for all manufacturing corporations, compiled from periodic issues of the QFR series, varied from a low of 8.57 percent in recession year 1970 to 13.09 percent in 1977 (when our Line of Business data series ends). To adjust for changes in these macroeconomic conditions, a variable $MACRO$ was defined as:

$$(3\text{-}2) \qquad MACRO_t =$$
$$\frac{\text{(Operating income/assets) for } QFR \text{ manufacturing universe in year } t}{\text{Average } QFR \text{ (Operating income/assets) for 1974–77}}$$

---

17. Because individual industry profitability benchmarks were not compiled for the sell-off sample periods, the regression was estimated with the raw operating income/assets ratios $PROF{:}A$, not supranormal returns, as the dependent variable. Also included was an additional nonduplicating sample of Line of Business company acquisitions that were not sold off. Its members are designated by the dummy variable $MATCHED$. Their performance is analyzed further in chap. 4. The estimated regression is:

$$PROF{:}A = 32.8 \quad - \quad 8.91 \; PURCH - \; 3.10 \; LOGSIZE$$
$$\phantom{PROF{:}A = } (2.96) \quad (5.92) \qquad \qquad (3.68)$$

$$+ \; 0.02 \; SELLOFFS + \; 2.38 \; MATCHED.$$
$$(0.02) \qquad \qquad (1.28)$$

$$R^2 = 0.037, \; N = 893.$$

Table 3-2. *Operating Income as a Percentage of Assets for All Manufacturing Companies in the FTC's Quarterly Financial Report, 1962–77*

Year	QFR benchmark (percent)	MACRO valueª	Year	QFR benchmark (percent)	MACRO valueª
1962	10.75	0.860	1970	8.57	0.685
1963	11.16	0.893	1971	9.02	0.722
1964	11.88	0.951	1972	10.02	0.801
1965	12.71	1.017	1973	11.63	0.931
1966	12.74	1.020	1974	12.78	1.022
1967	10.91	0.873	1975	11.19	0.895
1968	11.43	0.914	1976	12.94	1.035
1969	10.75	0.860	1977	13.09	1.047

Source: U.S. Federal Trade Commission, *Quarterly Financial Report for Manufacturing Corporations* (Government Printing Office, various years).

a. Ratio of current year's value to average for 1974–77.

MACRO's denominator of 12.50 percent, the average of *QFR* values for 1974–77, establishes a consistent benchmark for evaluating the "normality" of earlier years' *MACRO*-adjusted profits. The years 1974–77 are chosen because the Line of Business data used in subsequent post-merger and pre-sell-off analyses are for that period. For the 634 NYSE sample companies, the figures are as follows when their annual averages are *MACRO*-adjusted:[18]

Acquisition period	Unadjusted return (percent)	MACRO-adjusted (percent)
1968	20.8	23.1
1971	19.6	28.6
1974	18.9	20.3
All three years	20.2	23.5

With adjustment, the pre-merger profitability averages strengthen even more our earlier conclusion that acquired companies were extraordinarily profitable. Also, after macroeconomic adjustment, as when adjusted with respect to individual industry returns, the acquisitions whose profits were reported for recession year 1970 turn out to be the most profitable among the three cohorts.

When individual company observations for the sample of 215 sold-off

18. Profit observations for 1968 are centered on a fiscal year ending in the third quarter of 1967, and so a *MACRO* value other than the one reported in table 3-2 is applied. For 1971 and 1974, the centering is on calendar years 1970 and 1973.

acquisitions are adjusted by *MACRO*,[19] the simple average operating income/assets percentage rises to 23.69 percent. This is quite close to the 23.51 percent value for the larger 1968–71–74 sample, indicating again that sold-off lines were not less profitable before their acquistion.

Time Trends

Because the sold-off acquisitions sample spans 14 years, it is worthwhile to inquire whether there are discernible time trends. The 215 *MACRO*-adjusted operating income/assets observations were regressed on a linear time trend variable, the logarithm of pre-merger assets, and a purchase accounting dummy variable. The time coefficient was positive and statistically significant ($t = 2.92$), suggesting a 1.38 percentage point average annual increase in pre-merger profitability. However, further analysis revealed that this result stemmed from a clustering of high-profit observations in the 1968–71 reporting years and low-profit observations in 1964–65. The pattern was not linear, and when the individual observations were aggregated to annual averages, no significant linear time correlation remained.

Analysis of other acquisition samples confirms the absence of a simple time trend. Boyle's 1951–66 time series, using public reports for acquired companies on the FTC's large merger lists, revealed different profitability time patterns among three groups—acquired companies with assets of less than $50 million, those with $50 million to $100 million, and all sizes together.[20] For the all-sizes group, the ratio of net profits after tax to assets, adjusted for variations in the corresponding all-manufacturing figures, was perceptibly lower in the 1961–65 period than in earlier or later years.[21]

We replicated and extended Boyle's series to 1977 using net profit

19. Positive profit ratios were deflated by *MACRO*; the nine negative values were multiplied by *MACRO*.

20. Boyle, "Pre-merger Growth and Profit Characteristics," p. 165.

21. That ratio, which is the only one available in the FTC merger files, is an inferior measure of profitability, since it deducts interest payments but does not take into account differences in companies' relative reliance upon interest-bearing debt as compared to equity. See Stigler, *Capital and Rates of Return*, pp. 123–25. An analysis of mid-1960s data showed no consistent correlation between manufacturing corporation size and debt/equity ratios, once industry effects were controlled. See F. M. Scherer and others, *The Economics of Multi-Plant Operation: An International Comparisons Study* (Harvard University Press, 1975), pp. 286–87. Smaller corporations did pay higher interest rates—a point analyzed further in chap. 7.

and asset data contained in the FTC's large merger series files. That series also exhibited a period of depressed acquired company returns relative to all-manufacturing benchmarks in the early 1960s.[22] Over the entire span of 28 years, the net profit/assets ratio for acquired companies was 90 percent of all-manufacturing values, both in simple annual averages and in averages weighted by the number of mergers per year. Pre-merger profits for the years 1961–65 had an unweighted average amounting to 72 percent of universe values. Over the 28-year interval, the ratio of annual average acquired company returns to manufacturing universe returns had an insignificant correlation of −0.04 with a linear time trend.

Tender Offer Targets

Most mergers are effected through negotiation between the managements of the acquiring and acquired corporations, leading eventually to a "deal" recommended by management to the acquired (and in relatively large mergers, also acquiring) company shareholders for approval. Some mergers, however, occur through the quite different tender offer mechanism. Then the acquirer deals directly with the target firm's shareholders, offering a price (or complex set of prices) at which it will buy out their interests and (usually) assume control over the target. Some such tender offers are openly opposed by the target's incumbent management, in which case they are called "hostile." On others, management may remain neutral (even if unenthusiastic) or actively approve.

Corporations included in the Line of Business sample, on which most of our research is based, were involved in at least 96 manufacturing company tender offer acquisitions, as reported on lists compiled by Douglas V. Austin and Arnand Desai.[23] In a few cases the Line of

22. Caution is advised in interpreting the results, since work reported in chap. 4 disclosed that the listed asset values were occasionally erroneous.

23. The Austin lists appear in Douglas V. Austin and Jay A. Fishman, "The Tender Takeover," *Mergers & Acquisitions*, vol. 4 (May-June 1969), pp. 4–23; Austin, "Tender Offers Revisited: 1968–1972; Comparison with the Past and Future Trends," *Mergers & Acquisitions*, vol. 8 (Fall 1973), pp. 16–29; "Tender Offer Statistics: New Strategies Are Paying Off," *Mergers & Acquisitions*, vol. 10 (Fall 1975), pp. 9–18; and "Tender Offer Update: 1978–1979," *Mergers & Acquisitions*, vol. 15 (Summer 1980), pp. 13–32. The Desai list, to which Michael Bradley, Peter Dodd, and Richard Ruback apparently contributed, was kindly provided by Ellen Magenheim. Twenty-two relevant tender offers were on the Desai list but not the Austin lists; 15 verified tender offers were on

Business companies themselves were taken over, usually by foreign acquirers who maintained the targets as separate entities. In most cases the LB companies acquired other firms by direct tender offer, in a negotiated deal precipitated by the LB sample member's earlier tender offer, and/or as "white knights" favored by target company management over some other (hostile) tenderer.

Since most tender offer targets have stock traded on public exchanges, it was possible to find pre-merger financial data for 95 of the 96. Their median pre-tender assets were $83.5 million—much larger than the NYSE listing application sample median. Profitability data were sought for the two years preceding, or at most only partly overlapping, the date of the first (of sometimes multiple) tender offer announcements. The measure used, as with the NYSE sample, is operating income as a percentage of assets. To take into account shifting macroeconomic and industry conditions, the comparable *QFR* ratio for the most closely comparable two-digit industry in the most closely corresponding fiscal year was subtracted out. As with the NYSE listing application sample, the difference between target company and peer industry returns will be called *SUPRA*.

The mean level of target company profits before deduction of industry benchmark ratios was 11.15 percent in the last year before (or partly overlapping) the first tender offer and 11.01 percent for the previous year. The comparable average *SUPRA* values were -0.86 percent and -1.08 percent for the later and earlier years.[24] Although there is a hint of rising profitability as the tender offer date approached, the differences between years are far from statistically significant, with *F*-ratios of less than 0.05. Thus, we pool the two years' data in the analysis that follows.

For all 95 tender offer targets together, the two-year average operating income/assets ratio was 11.08 percent. The average *SUPRA* value was -0.97 percent, with a *t*-ratio of 1.90 in a test of the zero null

---

the Austin lists but not on the Desai list.

The criterion for inclusion in our sample was that a manufacturing company acquisition was precipitated by a tender offer in which target company management played no visible shaping role. Some marginal cases were eliminated on the basis of *Wall Street Journal* chronicles—for example, when the tender offer merely "mopped up" outstanding shares after a negotiated merger transferred control over the target company, or when key management shareholders agreed in advance to a merger through tender offer.

24. Similarly, when the raw profit figures are *MACRO*-adjusted, the average values are 12.17 percent for the later year and 12.13 percent for the earlier year. The *MACRO* norm is 12.50 percent.

hypothesis. Thus, the tender offer targets were slightly less profitable than the industries to which they belonged—about 8 percent less profitable relative to the 12.055 percent average of their industries. The comparable average for all manufacturing industries together during the same time periods was 11.485 percent, revealing that the industries in which the tender offer targets operated were marginally more profitable than all manufacturing. Since the average 0.40 percent deviation of tender offer targets' profitability from that of all manufacturing has a t-ratio of only 0.78, it would appear that the targets were underperformers relative to their home-base industries, even if not (or less significantly so) relative to the entire manufacturing corporation population.

When the target companies are divided into three distinct tender offer history groups, the average *SUPRA* values are as follows:

Group	SUPRA value (percent)
25 companies acquired in "hostile" tender offers opposed by incumbent management	-2.28
20 companies acquired by "white knights"	-0.56
50 companies acquired in other tender offers uncontested overtly by management	-0.49

There is a suggestion that the companies acquired in "hostile" takeovers were the worst underperformers. However, the differences among category means are not statistically significant; $F(2, 187) = 1.61$, which falls short of the 0.05 point value of 3.05.[25]

The pre-tender profitability data span a time interval from 1957 through 1975, with a mean centered on early 1969. The correlation between *SUPRA* and the year for which profits were reported was -0.05, which falls well short of statistical significance. This result parallels the lack-of-trend finding for the extension of Boyle's profitability series.

Multiyear Dynamics

One might have supposed, contrary to the equivocal evidence yielded by our tender offer sample, that takeover attempts are triggered by

25. When the tender offer targets are divided into two classes, "hostile" and "other," the F-ratio is 2.33, which is below the 0.05 point of 3.90.

For the 25 hostile takeover targets, *SUPRA* was lower in the last year before tender offer than in the prior year: -2.45 percent as compared to -2.11 percent. This is the opposite of the weak rising profitability pattern observed for the full tender offer sample. However, the difference is not statistically significant; $F = 0.04$.

declining profitability. For mutually negotiated mergers, a different hypothesis seems appropriate. The companies acquired might choose a time of peak profitability, following a period of rising profits, to elicit the most favorable acquisition price. A corollary, holding that the peak pre-merger profitability is unsustainable over the longer run and must be followed by decline, is examined in chapter 4.

New York Stock Exchange listing applications typically provide acquired firm income statement data for only one pre-merger year plus or minus a fraction thereof. Therefore, they cannot be used for an analysis of longer-term pre-merger profitability patterns. We are forced to focus on companies whose securities are publicly traded, which in turn means a bias toward acquired entities larger than those in our listing application samples.

One such sample is the set of Line of Business company mergers we shall call "mergers of equals" in the next chapter. These were pooling-of-interests mergers in which the merging parties differed from one another in size by no more than a factor of two. Given the selection criterion, the companies involved were relatively large and hence more likely to publish financial reports. Among the 69 mergers of equals cases, pre-merger financial data were available for 45. Median assets of the smaller partners among those 45 cases were $73 million; median assets of the larger partners were $135 million.

For the 41 larger and 40 smaller mergers of equals partners with three years of pre-merger profitability data available, average operating income as a percentage of assets, adjusted by the *MACRO* variable, was as follows:[26]

	Profitability (percent), by year before merger		
Merger	*Final year*	*Two years*	*Three years*
Larger partners	12.27	12.33	11.57
Smaller partners	13.30	11.80	11.33

For the smaller partners and (less clearly) for the larger, profitability

26. Final year averages for all 45 mergers were 12.10 percent for the larger partners and 14.46 percent for the smaller.

When a quadratic time trend regression equation was fitted, the *MACRO*-adjusted pre-merger profitability of mergers of equal partners had a local minimum in the year 1962. This result parallels our earlier finding for the much more comprehensive FTC large merger series that acquired companies were least profitable relative to the manufacturing universe in the early 1960s.

apparently rises as the merger date approaches. However, the standard errors for comparing the two means are approximately 1.57 for the larger partners and 1.63 for the smaller. Thus, none of the differences between larger and smaller cohorts, or among years within the groups, is significant. Nor do any of the averages differ significantly from the 12.50 percent value for the manufacturing corporation universe.

That the mergers of equals companies, like the tender offer companies but unlike the NYSE listing application companies, realized no supranormal pre-merger returns suggests the need for a sample more like the NYSE group. Therefore, an additional sample was drawn to satisfy several criteria:

(1) The company was acquired by a Line of Business sample member between 1965 and 1976.

(2) The company's financial statements for at least five years before merger were included in the COMPUSTAT data files.

(3) The company had final pre-merger year assets of less than $50 million.

Sixty-one corporations met these criteria. Their median final year assets were $23.2 million. Their average final-year *MACRO*-adjusted operating income/assets ratio was 16.5 percent—above the all-manufacturing value of 12.5 percent, but below NYSE sample averages. To bring the sample into still closer conformity with the NYSE cohort, a fourth criterion was applied:

(4) Operating income was 15 percent or more of assets in the last year before the firm's acquisition.

This screen narrowed the sample to 33 companies with average final-year profitability of 25.2 percent, which comports reasonably closely to the mean (macroeconomically adjusted) of 23.5 percent for the 634 companies in the NYSE sample. We shall call the 61-member COMPUSTAT sample the "full sample" and the high-profit 33-company subset the "truncated sample."

Letting T-1 be the last financial reporting year before merger, the time pattern of pre-merger profits was as follows:[27]

---

27. The averages are sensitive to the influence of a few extremely high or low observations in certain years. When we exclude companies whose operating income/assets percentages exceeded plus or minus 50 percent in any year, the revised averages for the 57 full-sample members for the final through the fifth year before merger were 16.40, 16.34, 13.19, 14.84, and 15.90 percent, respectively, and for the 30 truncated-sample firms 24.59, 22.89, 17.10, 19.27, and 20.41 percent, respectively.

	Profitability (percent) by year before merger				
Sample	Final year	Two years	Three years	Four years	Five years
Full	16.53	15.00	13.00	14.34	15.30
Truncated	25.19	20.79	16.94	18.56	21.07

For both samples, the last year before merger was a peak year among the five. Averages for the earlier years suggest that the firms had experienced setbacks approximately three years before their acquisition and that, although they may have seized the opportunity to be acquired on an upswing and perhaps even at a peak, they also had the staying power to recover from their past adversities.[28] This must be considered speculative, however, since the differences in profitability across years are not statistically significant, with $F(4, 160) = 0.42$ for the full sample and 1.24 for the truncated sample.

Summary

What one finds concerning the pre-merger profitability of acquired enterprises depends upon the sample one draws and perhaps also upon timing and the choice of measures. Previous U.S. studies focusing on large publicly traded companies found acquired firms' profitability to be slightly below that of their peers (in the early analyses) and the same or slightly above (in the later studies). Our several investigations of operating income/assets ratios turned up only one cohort—the tender offer targets—in which the average acquired firm's final-year performance was inferior to that of a broader comparison group by an amount approaching statistical significance. And for the New York Stock Exchange samples that, unlike previous studies, include the large number of small, privately owned, acquired companies, the acquirees' average pre-merger profitability was well above industry peer values. Evidently,

28. This result differs from the finding in Boyle, "Pre-Merger Growth and Profit Characteristics," p. 165, that profitability was *higher* three years before merger than in the year before for companies with assets of less than $50 million. On the other hand, for larger acquisitions, Boyle's results are similar to ours.

The possibility that profitability was peaking following a period of growth is consistent with evidence that publicly traded acquisition targets' stock prices tended to decline in the year or so before acquisition. However, we have not been able to link these two strands of evidence.

a selection bias (detected also in our case studies)[29] was at work. When would-be acquirers "fished" among the population of relatively small manufacturing enterprises for noncoercive acquisitions, they tended to haul in mainly the specimens with superior profit records. The most profitable catches were taken in under pooling-of-interests accounting; those of only average profitability were treated as purchases.

No clear trend is apparent in the attractiveness of the average acquired company over time. There are hints that acquirees were least profitable relative to all-manufacturing benchmarks in the early 1960s, but the pattern is sufficiently inconsistent that no confident conclusion is warranted.

For the acquired company samples on which pre-merger profitability data spanning multiple years were available, the general pattern is one of rising profitability as the merger date approaches. Especially for voluntarily negotiated mergers, the implication may be that acquired company management picks a time of improving performance (and commensurately optimistic acquisition price offers) to surrender its independence. This interpretation must be tentative, however, since the pre-merger profitability timing patterns seldom achieve statistical significance by conventional standards.

29. See chap. 5.

CHAPTER FOUR

Post-Merger Financial Performance

CORPORATE ACQUIRERS of the 1960s and early 1970s took into their fold large numbers of extraordinarily profitable enterprises, especially when they targeted their search toward relatively small and/or nonpublic firms. How did they fare with their catches? How profitable were their acquisition programs? How much growth was achieved? And upon what did post-merger success or its absence depend?

The Line of Business Merger Data Link

Our main vehicle for addressing these questions is the set of Federal Trade Commission performance reports for the years 1974–77. As noted earlier, the Line of Business data solve some of the most serious problems encountered in assessing post-merger performance.[1] For each reporting company (numbering from 437 in 1974 to 471 in 1975), financial statistics for domestic manufacturing operations were broken down into appropriate industry categories chosen from a list of 261, mostly defined at the three- or four-digit level of the U.S. Standard Industrial Classification. In 1977, the average sample company reported on 8.0 manufacturing lines of business (not counting the catch-all category 99.99) plus 1.4 nonmanufacturing LBs (with which we will not be concerned). With this degree of disaggregation, individual acquisitions small relative to the acquiring company need not be lost within a sea of unrelated parent activities. Moreover, it is possible to form sharply focused control groups—notably, the collection of all units in the same narrowly defined industry category, using similar technology and subjected to similar demand and supply shocks.

A major data collection effort was required to link merger histories to the Line of Business files. The time frame was from 1950, for which the

1. See chap. 1.

Federal Trade Commission gathered five-digit product line sales data from the 1,000 largest manufacturers,[2] to 1977, for which the last Line of Business reports were submitted. The linking process began with the extensive list of acquisitions tabulated in the FTC's "all mergers" series, covering both the "large" acquisitions with assets of $10 million or more and (less comprehensively) acquisitions of smaller concerns. The FTC compilation was supplemented using company histories recorded in multiple volumes of *Moody's Industrial Manual,* company financial reports, the company Line of Business documents, and diverse other sources. Each of more than 7,000 acquisitions by Line of Business sample companies had to be traced to one or more individual company LBs or (when appropriate) coded as already sold off by 1974.[3] Invaluable in this linking process were Schedule I of the companies' Line of Business filings, which listed incorporated subsidiaries not yet dissolved into the parent corporation, and Schedule II, which listed the "basic components" of each LB by division name and/or plant location.

Table 4-1 arrays the 2,955 lines of business in what will be our main 1977 sample according to the number of nondivested acquisitions coded per line. Nearly a fourth of the lines had no recorded acquisitions. Of the lines with acquisitions, 45 percent had only one, while 2.3 percent had ten or more.

As the merger history research progressed, it became clear that sometimes it was difficult to ascertain who acquired whom. Small fish occasionally swallowed larger ones, and the name or corporate charter location that survives a merger is not always that of the acquirer. To handle such cases, a special "merger of equals" category was created. It included all pooling-of-interests mergers between firms that differed from one another in size by not more than a factor of two.[4] In a few

2. U.S. Federal Trade Commission, Bureau of Economics, *Statistical Report: Value of Shipments Data by Product Class for the 1,000 Largest Manufacturing Companies of 1950* (Government Printing Office, 1972).

3. The comprehensive file from which coding began covered 12,399 acquisitions. Of these, 5,966, including 69 "mergers of equals," were nonmiscellaneous manufacturing lines. The reasons and counts for not coding the remaining acquisitions were as follows: miscellaneous (99.99) manufacturing, 813; merger completion date 1978 or later, 728; positive evidence of nonmanufacturing locus, 2,023; divested before 1975, 678; less than 50 percent ownership interest acquired, 172; no confirmation of FTC file report that acquisition was consummated, 655; no Standard Industrial Classification information and no independent evidence of manufacturing locus, 858; other reasons (including noncoding because of deficient company data), 506.

4. Usually assets were taken as the measure of size, but in a few cases involving

Table 4-1. *Distribution of Lines of Business by the Number of Nonequals Acquisitions Surviving into 1977*

Number of acquisitions per line of business	Number of lines	Percent of lines with acquisitions
0	717	. . .
1	1,014	45.3
2	530	23.7
3	269	12.0
4	143	6.4
5	111	5.0
6–9	119	5.3
10–14	37	1.7
15 or more	15	0.7
Lines with acquisitions	2,238	100.0
All lines	2,955	. . .

instances, wholly new companies formed through multiway mergers of previously independent firms were also treated as mergers of equals. Altogether, 69 mergers of equals encompassing 267 nonmiscellaneous 1977 LBs were identified. They are not included in the table 4-1 tallies. For both mergers of equals partners, acquisitions made previously by either partner were counted as part of the combined company's acquisition history. No attempt was made to trace the second-order acquisition histories of other acquisitions. Thus, when LB sample company ABC acquired in a nonequals transaction company XYZ, which had previously acquired JKL, the acquisition of JKL was not coded.

In addition to determining *whether* lines of business experienced mergers between 1950 and 1977, we needed to know *when* and *how much* merger activity occurred. The size measure chosen was the value of acquired assets. Numerous problems had to be overcome in quantifying this variable. The FTC's large merger series includes data on pre-merger assets of the acquired entity and the "consideration paid" (that is, the cash, stock value, and/or bond value) in obtaining control of the acquiree. These were found to be not only incomplete but also inaccurate; occasional decimal point transpositions imparted order-of-magnitude errors. All such estimates were triple-checked against alternate sources,

---

activities of widely differing capital intensity, or where assets data were unavailable, employment was substituted. On the median asset sizes of the larger and smaller mergers of equal partners, see chap. 3.

when available, and for general plausibility. Asset values for small acquisitions were commonly lacking in the FTC records. When they could not be estimated from alternative sources such as *Moody's* or New York Stock Exchange listing applications, they were "plugged" at the average 1968 asset size of corporations with assets of from $100,000 to $10 million in the same two-digit industry group.[5]

Asset Values and the Choice of Accounting Method

How much acquired firm asset value is taken onto the acquiring corporation's books depends upon the method of accounting used— usually, purchase or pooling of interests.[6] Under pooling-of-interests accounting, it will be recalled, acquired firm assets are recorded by the acquirer at their pre-merger book values, while under purchase accounting, they are recorded at the effective purchase price paid. To illustrate more fully, suppose the XYZ Corporation has the following pre-merger balance sheet:

Current assets	$70	Current liabilities	$50
Plant and equipment	130	Stockholders' equity	150
	$200		$200

Assume now that ABC Enterprises acquires all of XYZ's common stock, paying XYZ stockholders $250 in cash, securities, or some combination, and agreeing also to assume XYZ's current liabilities (payrolls, accounts payable, and accrued taxes). ABC has in effect given up $250 plus an

5. The data are from U.S. Department of the Treasury, Internal Revenue Service, *Statistics of Income: Corporation Income Tax Returns, 1968* (IRS, 1972), table 5. The $10 million ceiling was imposed because virtually all free-standing manufacturing corporations with assets of $10 million or more were included in the FTC's *Quarterly Financial Report* sample, so the data were available for coders using the FTC's internal (confidential) "large" merger files. Probable exceptions were researched further. The $100,000 floor was imposed because few acquisitions of smaller size were found among the many small mergers on which data were available. Thus, there were only 10 firms below that threshold in our NYSE listing application pre-merger profitability sample of 634. The plug values ranged from $0.5 million to $1.1 million.

6. Other methods are used infrequently. "Dirty pooling," not permitted in the United States after 1970, entailed a mixture of purchase and pooling accounting. Dirty poolings are coded in our sample with fractions denoting the amount of each major form. "Equity" accounting is used when acquirers buy a stock interest in some company without taking control. A change is normally made to purchase or pooling when control is assumed, as has been the case for the acquisitions qualifying for inclusion in our Line of Business sample.

obligation to pay $50, or $300 in total, for XYZ assets whose book value was $200 pre-merger. Under pooling accounting, ABC would debit $70 to its own current asset account, debit $130 (the book value of XYZ's plant) to its plant account, credit $50 to its current liabilities account, and credit its cash, stockholders' equity, or debt account by the acquisition consideration of $250. After debits of $200 and credits of $300, ABC then makes its books balance by debiting (reducing) its stockholders' equity account $100, the premium of the acquisition price over XYZ's pre-merger book value. In contrast, under purchase accounting, ABC would not enter the last stockholders' equity debit, but instead would debit its plant and equipment account by $130, the pre-merger book value, *plus* $100, the acquisition premium over book. Or if an appraiser finds XYZ's plant and equipment to be worth only $130, ABC would create a "goodwill" asset account debited with the acquisition premium of $100.

Our main profitability index in the following analysis will be the ratio of operating income to assets. In the average merger, where the acquisition price exceeds book value, post-merger asset values will be higher under purchase accounting than under pooling, all else equal. Therefore, it was important to identify the accounting method adopted for each acquisition by sample companies. Through extensive effort, we were able to obtain accounting method codings for 67 percent of the manufacturing industry acquisitions traced to Line of Business companies.[7] Because disclosure of accounting method choices was more complete for larger acquisitions, the codings covered approximately 87 percent of total acquired entity assets. Using the coded acquisitions, a logit model was developed to predict the accounting method used, given other variables. A fuller discussion is presented in appendix A. The model successfully "predicted" 84 percent of all known accounting method choices. It was then applied to predict the method used in the acquisitions for which no direct evidence was available.

7. The effort began in June 1982 when co-author Scherer sent a personalized letter and list of acquisitions to the chief financial officer of most Line of Business sample companies. The letter asked that accounting methods be coded and that sold-off (or not actually acquired) entries be crossed off. Usable (but not always complete) replies were obtained from 50 percent of the companies with recorded mergers. A team of researchers then invaded the Securities and Exchange Commission's Washington public records library to search company annual reports, 10-K reports, and other filings. Gaps and conflicts identified after this two-pronged attack were followed up using NYSE listing applications and corporate annual report collections at three major university libraries.

The question of accounting method choice interacts with the estimation of acquired asset values, since for pooling mergers previous book values will be carried forward, whereas asset restatements will occur for purchases. When data on the acquired company's pre-merger assets were available, they were used to approximate the value of pooled merger activity, subject to correction for subsequent sell-offs and nonmanufacturing components. When data on consideration paid were available, they were used to estimate purchase method acquisition value. This understates the value of purchased assets to the extent that assumed payables are not counted, and so pre-merger asset values were substituted when they exceeded consideration paid. For purchase acquisitions on which no consideration paid data were available, post-merger asset values were estimated by multiplying pre-merger assets by an appropriately modified value of Tobin's Q index for the year of acquisition.[8] For pooling acquisitions on which only consideration paid data were available, assets were estimated by dividing the appropriate year's Q index into consideration paid.

The acquired asset measures are necessarily imprecise as a consequence of these complex estimation procedures, the need to apportion acquired assets across more than one line of business in many cases,[9] and the need to plug asset values for many small acquisitions (with appropriate Tobin's Q corrections for purchase accounting acquisitions). Biases could also intrude.[10] To ensure that our results are not systemat-

---

8. Tobin's Q is normally defined as the market value of corporate stocks and bonds divided by the replacement value of corporate assets. The Q values used in our analysis were derived by taking the annual average ratio of consideration paid to *book* (not replacement) value of assets for the acquired corporations in our data base with information on both variables. See appendix A.

9. Thirteen percent of all nonequals acquisitions affected more than one surviving LB. For them, the average number of LBs per acquisition was 2.42. The apportionment across LBs was based upon detailed product line sales data from the FTC's Corporate Patterns surveys for 1950 (*Statistical Report: 1,000 Largest Companies*) and 1972, NYSE listing application information, listings ranking the relative importance of four-digit product line sales in *Standard & Poor's Register of Corporations, Directors, and Executives,* company annual reports, the Line of Business reports, and diverse other data sources. A fair amount of informed guesswork could not be avoided.

10. The bias possibilities here are extremely complex. One problem is that consideration paid will tend to rise in relation to book value, the higher a company's expected profitability is. For purchase acquisitions on which both consideration paid and asset data are used, the "consideration paid or assets, whichever is higher" rule underestimates post-merger asset values for acquisitions of high expected profitability, but the understatement is nonlinear, being greater for mergers of very high or middling profitability

ically biased as a consequence, a simpler alternate merger activity measurement approach was also pursued. Under it, the relevant measures are categorical, not continuous. Either a line experienced non-divested acquisitions between 1950 and the year analyzed, or it did not. However, in making such distinctions, it is also important to differentiate between lines of long standing that simply expanded through merger and new lines, most of which (we saw in chapter 2) entered the parent company through diversifying acquisitions. Therefore, the following mutually exclusive categories were established:

	Category	Number of lines in 1977 sample
ORIG	Line operated by the parent company in 1950 (or at the company's founding, if later), with no post-1950 acquisitions (other than mergers of equals)	442
ORIGMERG	Line operated by the parent company in 1950 with subsequent nonequals acquisitions	723
NEW	Line not operated by the parent in 1950 (or at its founding, if later), with no subsequent acquisitions	275
NEWMERG	Line not operated by the parent in 1950, with at least one nonequals acquisition	1,515

Under the categorical measurement approach, a line of business has a dummy variable with value of unity for either *ORIGMERG* or *NEW-*

---

than for those in between. As acquisitions move from middling to very low profitability, the bias goes to zero and then turns toward overestimation of post-merger values. These nonlinear effects will yield profits-merger activity regression coefficient biases only with certain special distributions of acquired firm profitability expectations.

When pre-merger asset values are available for pooling mergers, there is no bias. When Q-deflated consideration paid values must be substituted for missing asset values on poolings, high-profit companies' assets will be overestimated and low-profit companies' assets underestimated, leading to a possible positive bias on regression coefficients. When Q-adjusted asset values are substituted for missing consideration paid values, high-profit companies' post-merger assets will be underestimated and a negative bias on regression coefficients can intrude. Working against these last two biases is the tendency for regression coefficients to be biased toward zero when there are unsystematic errors in measuring post-merger asset values.

A further potential bias associated with differing rates of post-merger asset growth is discussed later when the *MERGSHR:G* variable is introduced.

MERG if it had an affirmative acquisition history; otherwise those variables have zero values.

Sample Composition

The sample we analyze most fully, and to which the categorical breakdown count above applies, is for 1977—macroeconomically the most normal year for which Line of Business data are available. It contains a total of 2,955 individual company LB observations. It was winnowed down from a larger set of 3,674 manufacturing lines (excluding the 99.99 catch-alls) operated by 456 sample companies on the basis of several criteria, in part overlapping. First, because of a partial-year bias problem, 171 lines with substantial acquisition or divestiture activity in 1977 were excluded.[11] Second, 303 manufacturing lines that had been assigned by the company in 1975 to the 99.99 miscellaneous category (usable only for lines with sales below $10 million) were excluded because their merger histories were incomplete. Third, 243 lines of 12 companies for which the merger histories were of poor quality were dropped. Finally, 19 lines were eliminated because their profitability ratios (in percentage terms) exceeded plus-or-minus 100 percent, since such "outlier" values could overwhelm the statistical patterns among more normal lines. The sensitivity of results to the last two exclusion rules will be tested.

The same criteria were applied de novo in developing samples for 1975, 1976, and the three years 1975–77 combined. The samples differ somewhat in size and composition as a result. No substantial analysis is done for the 1974 Line of Business reporting year, in part because the company sample was appreciably smaller and partly because govern-

---

11. Suppose a merger occurs in the middle of the acquiring corporation's fiscal year and there is no change in acquired entity baseline profitability. Under pooling, the acquirer normally "reaches back" and reports the acquired entity's profits for the acquirer's entire fiscal year. Under purchase accounting, profits are recorded only for the post-acquisition period (for example, one-half year). When profits are related to assets under the standard end-of-year convention, the profit/assets ratio under purchase accounting will be biased toward zero relative to the ratio under pooling and probably also relative to a competitive rate of return. If a sell-off occurs in midyear, the opposite bias results with either purchase or pooling accounting. See Geoffrey Meeks and J. G. Meeks, "Profitability Measures as Indicators of Post-Merger Efficiency," *Journal of Industrial Economics*, vol. 29 (June 1981), pp. 335–44.

ment price controls were in force until April 30, possibly distorting observed profitability relationships.

Variables and Model Specification

Our principal index of individual LB profitability $PROF_t{:}A$ is the ratio of operating income in year t (after depreciation, but before deduction of interest charges, extraordinary items, and income taxes) to end-of-year assets.[12] It is expressed uniformly in percentage terms. We also analyze more briefly the ratio of operating income to sales $PROF_t{:}S$ and the ratio of cash flow (before depreciation) to sales $FLOW_t{:}S$. Comparison of these ratios is informative because the choice of a merger accounting method can affect both the numerator and the denominator of $PROF_t{:}A$, but only the numerator of $PROF_t{:}S$. It does not affect $FLOW_t{:}S$.

The extent of merger activity is measured in two main ways: through the continuous variable $MERGSHR_t$, dividing the original value of assets acquired (in other than mergers of equals) to end-of-period t assets, and through the zero-one categorical variables $ORIGMERG$ and NEW-$MERG$. In addition to the measurement problems already identified, a potential problem with MERGSHR is that when, because of losses, write-offs, or sell-offs, an LB's assets have shrunk over time, $MERGSHR$ can exceed 1.0, possibly greatly. Twelve percent of the non-zero 1977 $MERGSHR$ values exceeded 1.0, and 1 percent exceeded 2.5. To avoid letting such outlier values dominate the analysis and to reflect the fact that an LB cannot have been more than 100 percent merger-originated, the outlying values were truncated at 1.0. The sensitivity of results to this and other key data assumptions will be tested.

The $MERGSHR$, $ORIGMERG$, and $NEWMERG$ variables are in most analyses multiplied by the fraction of acquired assets (in other than mergers of equals) subjected to a given accounting treatment. Thus, the variable $POOL$ is $MERGSHR$ times the fraction of acquired assets treated as poolings; $PURCH$ is $MERGSHR$ times the fraction of assets recorded under purchase accounting; $NEWMERG(POOL)$ is the dummy variable 1 for post-1950 lines times the fraction of pooling assets; and so

---

12. A sensitivity test showed little change in key coefficients when profits were related to average rather than end-of-year assets. More complete coverage is possible with end-of-year assets.

on. The accounting treatment multipliers are bimodally distributed, since nearly half of all LBs with acquisitions had only one acquisition and because, for multiple acquisition lines, accounting choices were often consistent. Thus, of all LBs with acquisitions, 31.5 percent had 97.5 percent or more of their acquired assets recorded under pooling, while 40 percent had an equivalent disproportion treated as purchases.

Our objective is to assess the impact on profitability of mergers and their accounting treatment, other relevant variables being held equal. The "other variables" that must be controlled are those that lead to differences in profitability owing to demand, supply, and structural influences affecting particular industries.

A traditional way to do so is to introduce a battery of industry-specific (not LB-specific) variables believed to affect profitability. For the analysis of 1977 profitability, we shall employ the following control variables, each with a history of use in industrial organization studies sufficiently extensive that the underlying rationale need not be spelled out.[13] Each is measured in percentage terms:

Variable		Mean value (percent)
CAPINT	1977 industry assets/industry sales	66
RD/S	1977 industry company-funded research and development outlays/sales	1.56
ADV/S	1977 industry advertising/sales	1.63
IMPT	1975 imports of industry products/production for domestic use	6.5
EXPT	1977 industry exports/sales	9.4
CR4	1977 four-firm seller concentration ratio at four-digit industry level	39
MES	1977 estimate of minimum efficient plant scale (average top 50 percent plant employment/ total industrywide employment)	3.1
ΔOUTPUT	Industry real output growth over 1972–77	15.9

Under this approach, the effects of merger activity are assessed relative to no-merger lines or low-merger lines with similar values of the industry characteristics variables.

A simpler and more comprehensive approach is a "fixed industry

13. See David J. Ravenscraft, "Structure-Profit Relationships at the Line of Business and Industry Level," *Review of Economics and Statistics*, vol. 65 (February 1983), pp. 22–31.

effects" model under which each of 257 four-digit industry categories with reporting LBs has its own intercept dummy variable.[14] Variations in LB profitability associated with more or less intense merger activity are then measured relative to an adjusted average of the home industry's profitability. The control group in this instance is the set of lines in a given industry with zero acquisition activity, or with arbitrarily small acquisition activity. Of 1977 sample LBs, nearly one-fourth had zero values of *MERGSHR* and 38 percent had *MERGSHR* values of 0.05 or less.

Three additional independent variables, defined at the individual line of business level, will be carried through most of our analyses. *EQUALS* is a dummy variable with a value of unity if the LB experienced a merger of equals, as defined previously, and zero otherwise. No attempt is made to quantify the value of merger of equals assets. *NEW* is a dummy variable with a value of unity for LBs in which the parent corporation did not operate in 1950 and for which no acquisitions were recorded. Such lines usually resulted from internal diversification efforts. SHR_t measures (in ratio, not percentage, form) the market share in year t of an LB in its four-digit FTC industry category, nationally defined. In prior studies using line of business data, profitability has been found to increase significantly, the larger a line's market share was, presumably because of scale economies, first-mover advantages, and the lagged reaction of sales to cost advantages and the pricing strategies they influence.[15] Other variables to be introduced later will be motivated as they appear.

The Cross-Sectional Results

We have two quite different ways of measuring merger activity and two alternative ways of controlling for industry effects. With multiple years and a variety of other influences to be analyzed, the results can proliferate to unmanageable proportions. We therefore begin by esti-

14. See, for example, Richard Schmalensee, "Do Markets Differ Much?" *American Economic Review*, vol. 75 (June 1985), pp. 341–51.

15. See Ibid.; Ravenscraft, "Structure-Profit Relationships"; and F. M. Scherer, "On the Current State of Knowledge in Industrial Organization," in H. W. de Jong and W. G. Shepherd, eds., *Mainstreams in Industrial Organization* (Boston: Kluwer Academic, 1986), pp. 5–22.

Table 4-2. Basic Merger Effect Regressions[a]

	Regression number and dependent variable									
	1:PROF77:A	2:PROF77:A [257 values][b]	3:PROF77:A [257 values][b]	4:PROF77:A [257 values][b]	5:PROF75:A [257 values][b]	6:PROF76:A [257 values][b]	7:PROF75–77:A [257 values][b]	8:PROF77:S [257 values][b]	9:FLOW77:S [257 values][b]	10:FLOW75–77:S [257 values][b]
Intercept	14.4[b] (35.2)	...	...	...	...	−1.60 (1.31)	...	...	...	...
MERGSHR	−1.60[c] (1.77)	−2.35[d] (2.50)	...	...	...		...	...	...	...
POOL	...	...	1.99 (1.56)	3.36[b] (2.63)	1.29 (1.04)		0.36 (0.32)	1.09 (1.50)	0.96 (1.30)	0.38 (0.57)
PURCH	...	...	−5.27[b] (4.35)	−3.74[b] (3.05)	−3.31[b] (2.64)	−3.48[b] (2.88)	−3.84[b] (3.26)	−1.46[d] (2.10)	−1.64[d] (2.33)	−1.23[c] (1.75)
NEW	...	...	1.82 (1.59)	3.11[b] (2.70)	0.76 (0.67)	−0.39 (0.35)	0.77 (0.77)	1.19[c] (1.82)	1.24[c] (1.89)	0.14 (0.24)
EQUALS	...	...	1.61 (1.46)	2.00[c] (1.82)	1.55 (1.43)	2.29[d] (2.13)	1.37 (1.43)	0.97 (1.56)	0.75 (1.20)	0.71 (1.23)
SHR	...	...	...	39.25[e] (6.34)	30.11[e] (4.73)	28.07[e] (4.91)	30.16[e] (5.67)	25.37[e] (7.20)	24.81[e] (6.99)	23.11[e] (7.29)
Summary statistics										
R^2	0.0011	0.1338	0.1421	0.1547	0.1862	0.1474	0.1804	0.1791	0.1930	0.2387
Number of lines	2,955	2,955	2,955	2,955	3,223	3,101	2,732	2,955	2,955	2,732
Mean dependent variable value (percent)	13.9	13.9	13.9	13.9	11.7	13.4	13.3	7.8	10.3	10.1

a. Numbers in parentheses are *t*-ratios.
b. Significant in a two-tailed test at 0.01 level of confidence.
c. Significant in a two-tailed test at 0.10 level of confidence.
d. Significant in a two-tailed test at 0.05 level of confidence.
e. Significant in a one-tailed test at 0.01 level of confidence.

mating the fixed-industry-effects model with a continuous merger activity index, since it was preferred on a priori grounds for its simplicity and power. Ordinary least squares regression models[16] using the alternative industry characteristics variables and categorical merger history variables will then be compared to ensure that the results are not sensitive to the basic model structure choice.

The "Core" Model Results

Table 4-2 presents the results of increasingly comprehensive models, beginning with no control at all for industry effects, accounting method, or market share and then adding those variables sequentially before turning to other years and other profitability measures. The numbers in parentheses under the regression coefficients are t-ratios. In all cases, two-tailed statistical significance tests are applied for the merger effect variables, since it was unclear a priori whether mergers would increase or decrease profits relative to control group values.

Regressions 4-2(1) and 4-2(2) make no distinction between merger accounting methods and therefore correspond most closely to the methodology of earlier studies.[17] Both before and after controlling for industry effects, they reveal that intensive merger activity had a significantly negative effect on 1977 sample profitability.

Regressions 4-2(3) and 4-2(4) distinguish between pooling and purchase acquisitions and add other variables to identify the effects associated with internal growth, mergers of equals, and market share. Important differences materialize. Pooling-of-interests acquisitions and mergers of equals (also treated on a uniform pooling basis) show higher, though not always significantly higher, profitability with more intensive merger activity. Purchase acquisitions, on the other hand, are not only less profitable than poolings, as expected, but also significantly less profitable than no-merger lines of otherwise similar industry and market

16. Ordinary least squares yields biased standard error coefficients if the error structure is heteroscedastic. However, a regression of the absolute values of prediction errors from regression 4-2(4) on *POOL* and *PURCH* revealed no significant association. *NEW* lines did have greater residual profit variability, while increases in *SHR* significantly dampened variability.

17. The only known exception is Geoffrey Meeks, *Disappointing Marriage: A Study of the Gains from Merger* (Cambridge University Press, 1977), who adjusts British acquired company asset values to take out acquisition premiums and finds, with or without the adjustment, a deterioration of post-merger profit returns.

share characteristics. Moreover, there are sizable differences in the *POOL* and *PURCH* coefficients, depending upon whether or not the market share variable is included. With *SHR77* included, merger activity is found to be more profitable, or (for *PURCH*) less unprofitable, than when it is not. The reason for this (and the similar behavior of the *NEW* coefficients) is discovered by comparing the average market shares of LBs across relevant merger activity categories:

Category	Mean value of SHR77
Parent active in line in 1950, no acquisitions or mergers of equals	0.076
Parent active in line in 1950, with acquisitions	0.056
No 1950 parent presence, no acquisitions or mergers of equals	0.020
No 1950 parent presence, with acquisitions	0.021
Mergers of equals	0.035

The lines with acquisitions, and especially the lines not served in 1950, had much smaller market shares on average than the lines without mergers, which serve as the base against which merger effects are measured when *NEW* has its own dummy variable.[18] And since profitability rises by 2.16 percentage points with an increase in market share from 0.021 to 0.076, taking into account separately the merger-prone lines' smaller market shares removes a profit-depressing influence otherwise embodied in the merger effect estimates. This correction would be inappropriate if the chain of causation ran from merger to lower market share and hence (at least in part) to lower profitability. Dennis Mueller has shown that there is reason to believe such a linkage exists.[19] However, it is also possible that antitrust fears diverted even conglomerate merger activity toward acquisition targets of relatively low market share. We choose to err conservatively on the side of controlling separately for market share, thereby enhancing the indicated profitability of merger activity.

Alternative Controls

We leave table 4-2 temporarily to examine the sensitivity of our results

18. The association exists within groups as well as between groups. For the subset of LBs appearing after 1950 and with acquisitions (the *NEWMERG* group), the correlation between *SHR77* and *MERGSHR* is -0.06, which is significant at the 0.01 level.

19. Dennis C. Mueller, "Mergers and Market Share," *Review of Economics and Statistics*, vol. 67 (May 1985), pp. 259–67.

to alternative ways of controlling for industry effects and measuring merger activity. The requisite regression equations, all but one using 1977 operating income as a percentage of assets as the dependent variable, appear in table 4-3. Regressions without and with *SHR77* are alternated. All pairs affirm that controlling for market share differences raises the indicated profitability of merger activity. Comparing regressions 4-3(2) and 4-2(4), we see that the coefficients on *POOL* and *PURCH* are of similar magnitude, whether LB profits are analyzed relative to the averages of 257 different industry categories, as in table 4-2, or relative to a set of continuous industry characteristics variables. The main differences occur in R^2 values, with the 257 fixed-effect variables explaining much more of the industry-specific variance in profitability. Because of its greater control but otherwise similar results, we retain only the fixed-industry-effect approach in subsequent analyses.

The most clearly focused test between continuous and categorical merger activity measures is achieved by comparing regressions 4-3(4) with 4-2(4). Since "newness" per se is controlled by the *NEW* coefficient, the *NEWMERG(POOL)* coefficient indicates that post-1950 lines with acquisitions were 1.87 percentage points more profitable on average than 1950 no-merger lines of comparable market share, all else equal. To compare it with the *POOL* coefficient of regression 4-2(4), we must recognize that the latter estimates the effect of moving from zero merger activity to having 1977 assets 100 percent originated in pooling mergers. In fact, however, the average *NEWMERG* line had acquired assets amounting to 48 percent of total 1977 assets. To make the two coefficients directly comparable, *NEWMERG(POOL)* must be inflated by 1/0.48. With this transformation, the average 100 percent pooling profitability effect is estimated at 3.90 percentage points by categorical regression 4-3(4) and 3.36 percentage points by continuous merger measure regression 4-2(4). The average 100 percent purchase acquisition effect is estimated at −6.29 by the categorical regression and −3.74 by regression 4-2(4). Here the differences are much larger. In both cases, the categorical estimates are larger in absolute value—the opposite of what one might fear if there were systematic biases in the asset estimates underlying *MERGSHR*.[20] For the 723 *ORIGMERG* lines, in which the parent already had a presence by 1950, acquired assets amounted to only 20 percent of 1977 assets on average. *ORIGMERG(PURCH)*/0.20 = −4.50 is of the

20. See note 10.

Table 4-3. Merger Effect Regressions for 1977 with Continuous Industry Controls and Categorical Merger Activity Variables[a]

	Regression number and dependent variable					
	1:PROF77:A	2:PROF77:A	3:PROF77:A [257 values][b]	4:PROF77:A [257 values][b]	5:PROF77:A	6:PROF77:S [257 values][b]
Intercept	16.25[b] (11.25)	16.25[b] (11.30)			16.86[b] (10.55)	
POOL	1.83 (1.49)	2.93[c] (2.36)	...	...	...	...
PURCH	-4.46[b] (3.76)	-3.25[b] (2.70)	...	...	...	...
NEWMERG (POOL)			0.58 (0.54)	1.87[d] (1.73)	1.51 (1.45)	1.54[c] (2.50)
NEWMERG (PURCH)			-4.46[b] (4.15)	-3.02[b] (2.76)	-3.04[c] (2.88)	-0.55 (0.88)
ORIGMERG (POOL)			-0.67 (0.47)	-0.61 (0.43)	0.059 (0.04)	0.37 (0.45)
ORIGMERG (PURCH)			-0.93 (0.78)	-0.90 (0.76)	-1.18 (1.03)	-0.17 (0.25)
NEW	1.53 (1.38)	2.52[c] (2.25)	1.00 (0.75)	2.68[c] (1.98)	1.97 (1.50)	1.61[c] (2.09)
EQUALS	1.99[d] (1.84)	2.28[c] (2.11)	1.46 (1.31)	2.02[d] (1.82)	2.23[c] (2.05)	1.13[d] (1.80)
SHR77	...	28.84[e]	...	39.45[e]	28.39[e]	26.89[e]

		(5.25)		(6.25)	(5.10)	(7.50)
CAPINT	-0.040[c]	-0.046[b]	...	...	-0.045[b]	...
	(2.31)	(2.64)			(2.59)	
RD/S	-0.56[c]	-0.49[c]	...	...	-0.49[c]	...
	(2.34)	(2.06)			(2.04)	
ADV/S	0.33[b]	0.31[b]	...	...	0.31[b]	...
	(2.79)	(2.62)			(2.67)	
CR4	0.004	-0.020	...	...	-0.023	...
	(0.18)	(0.89)			(1.01)	
MES	0.038	-0.103	...	...	-0.105	...
	(0.36)	(0.96)			(0.97)	
ΔOUTPUT	0.008	0.011	...	...	0.011	...
	(0.53)	(0.74)			(0.72)	
IMPT	-0.18[b]	-0.19[b]	...	...	-0.20[b]	...
	(4.22)	(4.64)			(4.76)	
EXPT	0.15[b]	0.18[b]	...	...	0.18[b]	...
	(3.98)	(4.53)			(4.62)	
Summary statistic						
R^2	0.0224	0.0315	0.1440	0.1562	0.0340	0.1814

a. Based on 2,955 lines of business; numbers in parentheses are t-ratios.
b. Significant in a two-tailed test at 0.01 level of confidence.
c. Significant in a two-tailed test at 0.05 level of confidence.
d. Significant in a two-tailed test at 0.10 level of confidence.
e. Significant in a one-tailed test at 0.01 level of confidence.

same general magnitude as the *PURCH* coefficient in regression 4-2(4), but *ORIGMERG(POOL)* has the wrong sign, and matters only become worse when it is inflated by 1/0.20. It seems probable that the merger effects in these original 1950 lines were submerged in the "noise" associated with the preponderantly nonacquired assets. Taken as a whole, the experiment with categorical variables suggests that the attempt to measure merger activity with *MERGSHR* and its *POOL* and *PURCH* derivatives does not lead to patently inferior or biased results, and indeed, its implications are more conservative than those obtained using cruder categorical methods. We therefore employ the continuous *POOL* and *PURCH* variables exclusively in what follows.

Differences among Years

We return now to table 4-2. Regressions 4-2(5) and (6) extend the analysis to 1975, a year of sharp recession, and 1976, a recovery year. The negative impact of purchase acquisition activity remains fairly steady. However, there are marked changes in the pooling coefficient, which is insignificantly above zero in 1975 and turns (insignificantly) negative for 1976. For some reason, the pooling acquisitions were particularly hard hit by the recession and its aftermath, and they recovered more slowly than purchase accounting lines and manufacturers generally. Their lagged recovery is shown by an analysis of year-to-year changes in sales and operating income for LBs with consistent data on all three years.[21] Pooling LB sales grew at an unusually rapid pace from 1976 to 1977, but not from 1975 to 1976. Profits of the pooling LBs grew more slowly than those of no-merger LBs from 1975 to 1976 and more rapidly in the following year. One reason, although not the only one, for the pooling LBs' 1977 recovery was the sell-off of unprofitable lines. Fifty-seven lines included in the 1976 regression of table 4-2 were sold off totally in, or beginning in, 1977. If those lines are excluded from the 1976 regression, the coefficient on *POOL* rises from −1.60 (the value reported in regression 4-2(6)) to −0.47. There is no clear evidence that pooling lines in general were intrinsically more susceptible to recession shocks. We recall from table 3-1 that companies acquired in 1971 pooling mergers had recession-year 1970 pre-merger profit performance superior to that of acquirees for whom boom-year 1967 and 1973 profits were reported. Thus, we can only conclude that the pooling lines had unusual

---

21. Deleting the LBs with fewer than three years of consistent data did not alter the coefficient time pattern.

difficulty coping with the 1975 recession, perhaps because of some peculiar constellation of chance elements.

Regression 4-2(7) averages the profitability, merger activity, and market share variables across all three years 1975–77 for lines of business that satisfied each year's inclusion criteria. This means among other things that lines sold off at any time during the interval are excluded, and so an important source of profit depression is removed.[22] The purchase accounting lines continue to exhibit significantly negative returns relative to no-merger lines. For the pooling lines, profitability is insignificantly superior to that of no-merger lines, holding industry effects and market share constant.

Preliminary Interpretation

The *POOL* coefficients are sufficiently variable over the business cycle that the conclusion drawn depends in part upon whether one emphasizes the three-year result or the more favorable 1977 coefficient. The latter implies that moving from having no acquisitions to 100 percent pooling acquisition origin of 1977 asset values brought above-control profitability of 3.36 percentage points. Even if the more optimistic view is taken, we recall from table 3-1 that pooling acquisitions had pre-merger operating income/assets ratios exceeding those of their home industries by 9.8 percentage points on average. Thus, by any criterion, profitability *fell* on average following pooling mergers. This implication will be analyzed further in later sections.

For all years and regression specifications, the *PURCH* coefficients are consistently negative and significant. Given the table 3-1 evidence that the pre-merger profits of companies acquired under purchase accounting were insignificantly different from those of their manufacturing peers, this too implies a post-merger decline. One possible reason is the payment of premiums over the acquired entity's book value, raising post-merger asset values and depreciation charges. Both numerator and denominator of 1977 assets-deflated regression 4-2(4) are affected by this phenomenon, but only the numerator of operating income/sales regression 4-2(8) is affected. With the latter, the *PURCH* effect remains significantly negative, though smaller because operating income is a much smaller fraction of sales than assets. If higher depreciation charges

---

22. On the depressed profitability of sold-off lines, see chap. 6.

were an important reason for the reduced profitability of purchase accounting acquisitions, that effect should vanish when the dependent variable is measured in terms of cash flow (operating income plus depreciation). In fact, as cash-flow regressions 4-2(9) and 4-2(10) reveal, the negative *PURCH* effect is slightly greater in relation to sales, not smaller, with a cash-flow definition.[23] A systematic depreciation effect might not be observable if asset revaluations went preponderantly into goodwill, which did not have to be amortized before 1970 and was subjected to long (for example, 40 years) amortization periods thereafter.

That asset "step-ups" occurred is suggested by the relative differences between the *PURCH* and *POOL* coefficients in assets-deflated 1977 regression 4-2(4) as compared to sales-deflated regression 4-2(8). That is, we compute the absolute difference between the *POOL* and *PURCH* coefficients and relate it to average all-sample profitability, augmented by the 1977 merger-related premium implied by *POOL*. For assets-deflated regression 4-2(4), the relative *POOL-PURCH* differential is 100 [7.10 / (13.9 + 3.36)] = 41 percent, compared to 100 [2.55 / (7.8 + 1.09)] = 29 percent for sales-deflated regression 4-2(8). The implication is that asset denominators rose (in regression 4-2(4) only) while operating income fell (in both regressions).

The consistently positive, although not always significant, coefficients for the *EQUALS* variable suggest that mergers of equals may have been more successful in avoiding profitability declines. This inference is augmented by an analysis of 43 cases (out of 69) on which pre-merger profitability data for both partners were available, and for which the acquired LBs remained in the sample in all three years 1975–77. After adjustment for business cycle and trend (*MACRO*) influences, final pre-merger-year operating income averaged 12.36 percent of assets for the larger of the partners, 13.97 percent for the smaller, and 12.55 percent for the asset-weighted average of the two.[24] By this average of the weighted averages, the mergers of equals partners started out slightly but insignificantly below the 1975–77 LB sample average return of 13.31 percent. If a simple average is taken of the returns of the 43 *EQUALS* partners' LBs included in the 1975–77 sample, the result (uncorrected

23. The three-year operating income/sales regression analogous to regression 4-2(10) is not explicitly reported. Its *PURCH* coefficient is −1.18 (t = 1.67) and its *POOL* coefficient +0.38 (t = 0.57).

24. This sample differs slightly from that of chap. 3 because 2 of the 45 companies did not qualify for inclusion in all three of the 1975–77 sample years.

for industry or market share effects) is 14.98 percent—1.67 points better than the all-sample average. This is quite close to the +1.37 point *EQUALS* coefficient in 1975–77 regression 4-2(7)—for all *EQUALS* LBs, not just those belonging to companies on which pre-merger information was available. However, to match the pre-merger situation as closely as possible, the individual LB returns must be reaggregated up to their constituent company level with weights equal to individual LB assets. The simple average of those weighted company 1975–77 returns is 12.36 percent—slightly (and insignificantly) less than the partners' *MACRO*-adjusted 12.55 percent pre-merger average. Evidently, the mergers of equals companies outperformed the 1975–77 control group in their more numerous smaller lines, but underperformed it in their largest lines. The implication concerning their post-merger performance is therefore equivocal, depending upon the weighting scheme used in computing the averages.

Except in 1976, positive coefficients also appear for the categorical variable *NEW,* although statistical significance is achieved only for 1977 after controlling for market share (which for *NEW* lines was well below the all-sample average). The *NEW* lines were those not operated by the parent in 1950 and without evidence of merger activity. Although a few may have originated in mergers too small to be detected, most undoubtedly came from internal growth, based at least in part on research and the development of new products.[25] Like acquired lines, *NEW* lines typically had to obtain their physical assets at post-1950 market prices. Yet the *PURCH* coefficients are consistently more negative than the *NEW* coefficients, suggesting that on average growth by purchase acquisition was less profitable than growth by internal development.

Other Explanatory Variables

We now investigate the role of other variables that might expand our understanding of how mergers affected profitability. Our focus will again be 1977, the strongest year macroeconomically, presenting the most favorable picture of mergers' financial results. Our point of departure is "core" regression 4-2(4), which is repeated for purposes of comparison as regression (1) in table 4-4. To avoid confounding the influences of

25. See chap. 2, p. 35.

Table 4-4. *Merger Effect Regressions Testing Additional Variables, with Fixed Industry Effects, 1977 Operating Income/Assets as Dependent Variable*[a]

	Regression number						
	1	*2*	*3*	*4*	*5*	*6*	*7*
	[257 values][b]	[257 values][b]	[257 values][b]	[257 values][b]	[257 values][b]	[257 values][b]	[257 values][b]
Intercept	3.36[b] (2.63)	…	…	2.77[c] (2.13)	3.50[b] (2.73)	3.55[b] (2.76)	3.59[b] (2.79)
POOL	…	…	…	…	-3.13[c] (2.44)	-2.74[c] (2.09)	-2.81[c] (2.14)
PURCH	-3.74[b] (3.05)	-3.74[b] (3.06)	…	-2.11 (1.52)	…	…	…
NEW	3.11[b] (2.70)	3.10[b] (2.69)	2.72[c] (2.40)	2.18[d] (1.80)	3.11[b] (2.70)	3.15[b] (2.74)	3.15[b] (2.73)
EQUALS	2.00[d] (1.82)	1.96[d] (1.78)	2.18[c] (1.99)	2.04[d] (1.85)	2.03[d] (1.85)	1.97[d] (1.79)	2.03[d] (1.84)
SHR77	39.25[e] (6.34)	39.12[e] (6.31)	41.13[e] (6.81)	39.39[e] (6.36)	39.20[e] (6.33)	39.52[e] (6.38)	39.45[e] (6.37)
HORIZ × POOL	…	4.18[d] (1.73)	…	…	…	…	…
VERT × POOL	…	1.77 (0.42)	…	…	…	…	…
RELAT × POOL	…	5.61[b] (2.74)	…	…	…	…	…

CONG × POOL	...	1.18 (0.66)	...	...	...	...	...
POOL × NUMM	...	...	0.195 (0.93)	...	...	...	...
PURCH × NUMM	...	...	−0.724[b] (3.54)	...	...	...	...
Q	...	...	...	−1.33[c] (2.53)	...	...	...
PART	...	...	...	...	−4.84 (1.63)	...	...
WHITE	...	...	...	...	...	+0.00 (0.02)	...
HOSTILE	...	...	...	...	...	−3.65 (1.49)	...
OTHER	...	...	...	...	...	−3.81[d] (1.95)	...
TENDER	...	...	...	...	...	...	−2.66[d] (1.94)
Summary statistic							
R^2	0.1547	0.1557	0.1521	0.1567	0.1555	0.1564	0.1559

a. Based on 2,955 lines of business; numbers in parentheses are *t*-ratios.
b. Significant in a two-tailed test at 0.01 level of confidence.
c. Significant in a two-tailed test at 0.05 level of confidence.
d. Significant in a two-tailed test at 0.10 level of confidence.
e. Significant in a one-tailed test at 0.01 level of confidence.

diverse variables, new variables are added singly or in small clusters to that core regression.

One set of variables characterizes the type of merger according to the degree to which acquired companies complemented existing lines. The following variables are used, each estimating the fraction of an LB's acquired assets (in other than mergers of equals) belonging to the specified category:[26]

	Variable	Percent of total 1950–77 acquired assets
HORIZ	Acquiring company had at least five years experience in the same FTC four-digit category before the acquisition	41.4
VERT	Acquired unit made at least 5 percent of its sales to, or purchases from, another unit operated by the parent for at least five years before the acquisition	10.9
RELAT	Acquiring company had at least five years experience in the same two-digit industry group, but no horizontal or vertical connection	24.8
CONGLOM	None of the above criteria satisfied	31.3

The definitions emphasize the accumulation of experience facilitating effective management, and hence the avoidance of control loss problems. Since the antitrust laws were fairly strictly enforced with respect to mergers during most of the period covered, HORIZ effects larger than those for the other categories, if observed at all, are more likely to reflect managerial competence rather than the augmentation of monopoly power.[27]

Each merger category share variable is multiplied by the pooling

26. Since HORIZ and VERT are not mutually exclusive and overlap, the shares sum to more than 100 percent. A more complete breakdown is provided in table 2-2.

27. Among other things, the companies acquired in horizontal mergers were smaller on average than those acquired in vertical or conglomerate mergers. The mean and median acquired company asset sizes (in millions of dollars, adjusted for merger accounting revaluations) by category were as follows:

	Mean	Median
HORIZ	7.94	1.3
VERT	9.55	1.5
RELAT	12.25	2.9
CONGLOM	13.90	2.5

merger fraction variable *POOL* (and also, in an unreported regression that failed to exhibit significant purchase merger differences, by *PURCH*). Regression 4-4(2) shows the result. There is a slight but statistically significant increase in explanatory power, as evidenced by the increase in R^2 relative to core regression 4-4(1) and an incremental F-ratio of 3.18 (exceeding the 2.99 five percent point). Only the "related business" and horizontal acquisitions have statistically significant positive coefficients. Conglomerate acquisitions, comprising 36 percent of all acquisition activity by asset value in 1964–72 and 26 percent in other years, were the *least* profitable. These differences imply that acquirers managed more successfully the lines on which they had relevant experience.[28] The vertical acquisitions were too few in number, and too collinear with horizontal mergers, to yield significant coefficient values.

Regression 4-4(3) multiplies the *POOL* and *PURCH* variables by a variable *NUMM,* counting the number of separate nonequals acquisitions recorded in each individual line of business. (The distribution of *NUMM* by LB was tallied in table 4-1.) The merger impact coefficients

28. An alternate hypothesis is that the acquired companies differed systematically by type of acquisition in their pre-merger endowments, carrying those differences into post-merger performance. It is also important to rule out the possibility that horizontal acquisitions had subnormal profitability before merger but rose to supranormal performance through the exercise of monopoly power.

The 634-company New York Stock Exchange listing application sample of chap. 3 was tapped to explore these questions. Line of Business sample companies made 392, or 62 percent, of the 634 acquisitions. Of these 392, 251 survived long enough to be linked to manufacturing LBs in one or more of the years 1975–77. Nonlinked companies, with median pre-merger assets of $0.99 million, were significantly smaller [$F(1, 390)$ = 75.95] than linked companies, with median assets of $4.81 million. The nonlinked acquisitions were not significantly different from the linked acquisitions in pre-merger profitability; $F(1, 390) = 0.53$.

The 93 linked acquisitions that were strictly horizontal (that is, without elements of verticality or conglomerateness) had mean supranormal profitability (that is, with two-digit industry averages subtracted out) of 11.75 percent. For the other lines, the mean was 7.84 percent. The difference is significant at the 0.10 level ($F = 3.88$). The variable *SUPRA* (in percentage terms) for the 251 linked acquisitions was regressed on the logarithm of acquired company assets and a purchase accounting dummy, as in regression 3-1 of chap. 3. An additional dummy variable identifying strictly horizontal acquisitions had a coefficient of +3.33, with $t = 1.66$. In a separate regression, a dummy variable distinguishing all acquisitions with some element of horizontality from the others had a coefficient of +3.14, with $t = 1.63$. Thus, it seems clear that the horizontal acquisitions were not *less* profitable on average pre-merger.

The second most populous group of linked acquisitions comprises the pure conglomerates, with 82 cases and mean supranormal profits of 9.93 percent. There were only 6 strictly vertical cases, with mean *SUPRA* of −6.97 percent. There were 16 mixed horizontal and vertical cases, with mean *SUPRA* of 13.67 percent.

retain the signs previously attained. However, R^2 and the coefficient t-ratios fall in the *NUMM* version, showing that profitability is better explained by an index of merger activity in relation to assets than by a mere count of acquisitions, regardless of relative size. Adding quadratic values of *NUMM* to take into account possibly diminishing or increasing marginal returns with increased numbers of mergers improved the regression "fit" insignificantly (not explicitly reported in table 4-4). The implication was one of slight diminishing returns in both the *POOL* and the *PURCH* relationships.

In regression 4-4(4), we add a modified Tobin's Q index. It measures the average ratio of consideration paid to acquired firm book asset value for mergers consummated during years in which an LB made acquisitions, weighted by the value of assets the LB acquired in that year. It was anticipated that the higher Q was on average in a year when acquisitions were made, the higher would be the premium paid over acquired company book values, and hence the more the post-merger operating income/assets ratio of purchase acquisitions would be depressed. The Q variable does have the expected negative coefficient. The increase in R^2 it permits relative to regression 4-4(1) leads to a statistically significant F-ratio of 6.38. Equally important, its inclusion substantially reduces the coefficient on *PURCH* relative to that of core regression 4-4(1), revealing that at least part of the *PURCH* coefficient's negative value stemmed from bidding up the acquired asset denominator in years of relatively high common stock prices. The -2.11 and -1.33 point *PURCH* and Q coefficients of regression 4-4(4) are a decomposition, with 9 percent error, of the -3.77 point *PURCH* value in regression 4-4(1).

The variable *PART* appearing in regression 4-4(5) measures the fraction of assets acquired by an LB from other companies selling only part of their own assets. In other words, *PART* captures the buyer's side of the divisional sell-off market to be analyzed in chapters 5 and 6. Since virtually all partial acquisitions were subjected to purchase accounting, the takeover prices buyers paid should be reflected in the denominator of their operating income/assets ratios. If sold-off lines had inferior profits, as we shall find to be true on average, buyers should have bid sufficiently low that after the transfer of ownership, "normal" returns would be realized. In fact, the coefficient on *PART*, although slightly below the 10 percent level of statistical significance,[29] implies that, on

---

29. Two hundred eighty-two LBs had non-zero values of *PART* in 1977.

average, the acquirers of sell-offs erred on the side of optimism. Having a line whose assets originated fully from some other company's divisional sell-off was associated with a 4.84 percentage point depression of returns on assets *in addition to* the 3.13 point depression associated with using purchase accounting to value acquired assets.

Regressions 4-4(6) and (7) address the question of whether the post-merger performance of units acquired following tender offers differs from that of units acquired through mutually negotiated mergers. As indicated above,[30] Line of Business sample members were involved in 96 tender offer acquisitions, 73 of which had surviving LBs included in the table 4-4 sample. A dummy variable *TENDER* identifies lines so acquired. The set of *TENDER* offer lines was also broken down into three subsets, each categorized by a dummy variable: *HOSTILE,* for the 52 LBs in which incumbent management opposed a tender offer that nevertheless succeeded; *WHITE,* for the 52 LBs in which a management-approved "white knight" came to the rescue and made an acquisition that otherwise might have been accomplished by a hostile tenderer; and *OTHER* for the 84 tender offer cases in which incumbent management maintained, at least publicly, a neutral posture.

In regression 4-4(6), the influence on 1977 profitability of these three tender offer history variables is estimated separately, and in regression 4-4(7) the three categories are combined. Post-merger profits are found to be below control group levels in the wake of hostile and "other" tender offers and for all tender offers combined, while a zero effect is found for the white knight acquisitions. However, the white knight effect was negative when tested for the years 1975 and 1976.

Because of this instability, and given the relatively small number of tender offer observations generally, the data for all three years were averaged, as in regression (7) of table 4-2. The resulting 1975–77 regressions were as follows:

$$PROF75\text{--}77: A = [257 \text{ values}] + \underset{(0.60)}{0.68} \; POOL - \underset{(2.24)}{2.82} \; PURCH$$

(4-1)
$$+ \underset{(0.83)}{0.84} \; NEW + \underset{(1.51)}{1.46} \; EQUALS + \underset{(5.67)}{30.15} \; SHR$$

$$- \underset{(1.65)}{3.65} \; HOSTILE - \underset{(1.69)}{3.77} \; WHITE - \underset{(1.18)}{2.23} \; OTHER.$$

$$R^2 = 0.1824, N = 2{,}732.$$

30. See chap. 3.

$$PROF75-77: A = [257 \text{ values}] + \underset{(0.58)}{0.66 \ POOL} - \underset{(2.24)}{2.81 \ PURCH}$$

(4-2)
$$+ \underset{(0.82)}{0.83 \ NEW} + \underset{(1.48)}{1.43 \ EQUALS} + \underset{(5.68)}{30.18 \ SHR}$$

$$- \underset{(2.41)}{3.10 \ TENDER.}$$

$$R^2 = 0.1823, N = 2,732.$$

The tender offer coefficients in equation (4-1) are of similar magnitude, and as the near identity of R^2 values between equations (4-1) and (4-2) shows, distinctions among the three tender offer categories provide no explanatory power. The combined, statistically significant *TENDER* coefficient of regression (4-2) implies that having a tender offer history, which on average predated the 1975–77 profitability period by nine years, was associated with operating income/assets ratios 3.1 percentage points lower than in lines of comparable industry membership, market share, acquired assets share, and accounting method.

To probe this result further, the cash flow/sales analogue of asset-deflated regression (4-2) was estimated, as follows:

$$FLOW75-77: S = [257 \text{ values}] + \underset{(0.72)}{0.49 \ POOL} - \underset{(1.16)}{0.87 \ PURCH}$$

(4-3)
$$+ \underset{(0.27)}{0.16 \ NEW} + \underset{(1.26)}{0.73 \ EQUALS} + \underset{(7.29)}{23.12 \ SHR}$$

$$- \underset{(1.43)}{1.09 \ TENDER.}$$

$$R^2 = 0.2393, N = 2,732.$$

The tender offer coefficient remains negative, but is smaller and statistically insignificant. This indicates that the main reason for the relatively poor operating income/assets performance of tender offer acquisitions was the substantial write-up of asset values (normally handled under purchase accounting) that follows seller-initiated tender offers. That the cash-flow *TENDER* coefficient did not turn positive reveals that acquiring corporation managements were unable to bring the average performance of the units they acquired above control group norms. And since our chapter 3 analysis found that, on average, tender offer targets were only slightly less profitable pre-merger than their all-manufacturing peers, no significant *increase* in operating income or cash flow was achieved through changes in control induced by tender offers.[31] For the debate occurring during the 1980s concerning the consequences of tender offer acquisitions, these are important findings. Unfortunately, our sample of tender offer acquisitions is small, and since collection of the vital Line of Business profitability data was discontinued after 1977, it will be difficult to achieve similar insights into the effects of the burgeoning number of tender offers since then.

Sensitivity Analyses

Numerous assumptions and estimates had to be made in measuring the merger intensity variables and culling the LB sample to a set of acceptably reliable observations. The sensitivity of our results to the use of alternative control approaches and the substitution of categorical merger activity measures has been examined already. We now carry the sensitivity tests further in several directions.

Some critics argue that, because of the widely varying accounting conventions used by companies and the difficulty of matching accounting values to "real" economic magnitudes, little or no economic meaning can be attributed to inferences drawn from accounting data.[32] However,

31. An extension to the chap. 3 results provides essential perspective. Only 62 companies with a tender offer history had LBs qualifying for this three-year analysis. Eleven companies dropped out because the tender offer mergers occurred in 1975 or 1976, and the remaining members of the original 96-company cohort were excluded because of prior sell-offs or failure to meet the sample composition criteria enumerated above. For the 62 included companies, pre-tender operating income as a percentage of assets averaged 1.57 percentage points below peer two-digit industry values—a deviation greater than the -0.97 percentage point figure for the full 95-company group on which pre-tender profitability data were available. Pre-tender, the 62 companies were 12.9 percent less profitable on average than their peers. In regression 4-3, the *TENDER* coefficient (purged of revaluation effects) is 10.8 percent lower than full LB sample cash flow/sales averages. Thus, a slight and insignificant operating performance improvement (ignoring the effect of asset step-ups on *PURCH*) is observed. For further analysis of the pre- and post-tender results, see David J. Ravenscraft and F. M. Scherer, "Life After Takeover," *Journal of Industrial Economics*, vol. 36 (September 1987).

32. See George J. Benston, "The Validity of Profits-Structure Studies with Particular Reference to the FTC's Line of Business Data," *American Economic Review*, vol. 75 (March 1985), pp. 37–67; and Franklin M. Fisher and John J. McGowan, "On the Misuse of Accounting Rates of Return to Infer Monopoly Profits," *American Economic Review*, vol. 73 (March 1983), pp. 82–97. Compare William F. Long and David J. Ravenscraft, "The Misuse of Accounting Rates of Return: Comment," *American Economic Review*, vol. 74 (June 1984), pp. 494–500; and F. M. Scherer and others, "The Validity of Studies with Line of Business Data: Comment," *American Economic Review*, vol. 77 (March 1987), pp. 205–17.

Table 4-5. *Sensitivity Analyses Testing Additional Accounting Variables, MERGSHR Growth Variants, and Adjusted Sample Coverage, with 1977 Operating Income/Assets as Dependent Variable*[a]

	Regression number and explanation						
	1: Core regression	*2: Accounting variables added*	*3: Predicted accounting method lines deleted*	*4: MERGSHR truncated at 3.0*	*5: Growth-adjusted MERGSHR truncated at 3.0*	*6: Outlying profit values included*	*7: Poor merger history companies included*
	[257 values][b]	[257 values][b]	[257 values][b]	[257 values][b]	[257 values][b]	[257 values][b]	[257 values][b]
Intercept	3.36[b] (2.63)	3.57[b] (2.78)	2.96[c] (2.03)	3.06[b] (2.87)	1.25[c] (2.04)	3.85 (1.48)	3.32[b] (2.65)
POOL	−3.74[b] (3.05)	−3.29[b] (2.67)	−4.42[b] (3.09)	−3.39[b] (3.48)	−1.84[b] (2.71)	−9.04[b] (3.62)	−3.45[b] (2.93)
PURCH	3.11[b] (2.70)	2.92[c] (2.54)	3.15[c] (2.51)	3.10[b] (2.72)	3.04[b] (2.63)	1.85 (0.79)	3.71[b] (3.57)
NEW	2.00[d] (1.82)	2.08[d] (1.89)	2.90[d] (1.93)	2.00[d] (1.82)	1.97[d] (1.79)	3.44 (1.53)	1.82[d] (1.67)
EQUALS							
SHR77	39.25[e] (6.34)	36.91[e] (5.91)	41.03[e] (5.72)	39.15[e] (6.35)	39.12[e] (6.34)	35.21[e] (2.78)	38.37[e] (6.23)
LIFO	⋯	−0.22 (0.29)	⋯	⋯	⋯	⋯	⋯
STLINE	⋯	−3.38[b] (3.62)	⋯	⋯	⋯	⋯	⋯
Summary statistics							
R^2	0.1547	0.1588	0.1770	0.1558	0.1526	0.0669	0.1483
Number of lines	2,955	2,955	2,235	2,955	2,955	2,974	3,179

a. Numbers in parentheses are *t*-ratios.
b. Significant in a two-tailed test at 0.01 level of confidence.
c. Significant in a two-tailed test at 0.05 level of confidence.
d. Significant in a two-tailed test at 0.10 level of confidence.
e. Significant in a one-tailed test at 0.01 level of confidence.

as we have seen in table 4-2, there is little difference between the merger effect estimates obtained using operating income/sales as the dependent variable and those produced with cash flow/sales as the focus. Thus, the results are robust, whether depreciation charges are deducted or left in.

In table 4-5, regression (2) explores another facet of the accounting choice sensitivity question. The new variable *LIFO* measures the fraction of an LB's inventory assets (usually, because of tax law constraints, either 1 or 0) covered by last-in, first-out accounting. The variable *STLINE* measures the fraction of depreciable assets covered by straight-line depreciation (as contrasted to accelerated schedules). The *LIFO* coefficient is statistically insignificant, but *STLINE* is negative and significant. On average, the assets in the sample lines were five to ten years old, by which time the main burden of accelerated, but not straight-line, depreciation had already been absorbed. Thus, lines using straight-line depreciation reported lower profitability because sizable depreciation charges continued and because undepreciated assets (in the denominator of the profitability ratio) were larger. What is more important for our present purposes is that the merger effect coefficients are little affected by this additional control for accounting method differences. Relative to core regression 4-5(1), the most altered coefficient is that for *PURCH,* but the new value is reduced by only 12 percent relative to that of the core regression, and it remains highly significant.

One of the thorniest conceptual problems associated with Line of Business reporting is how costs and assets common to multiple lines are to be allocated among individual lines. Under the FTC Line of Business program, companies were instructed to allocate "nontraceable" costs and assets, averaging 2.2 percent and 9.5 percent of LB sales, respectively, according to the criteria they considered most reasonable. Studies by William Long of alternative allocation methods, including a "market-based" criterion, showed standard industrial organization structural coefficient estimates to be fairly insensitive to plausible alternatives.[33] For our purposes, the key question is whether the recorded profitability of merger-intense lines might have been artificially depressed by excessive allocations from parents to acquired LBs. This problem would arise if allocated cost/sales or asset/sales ratios were positively correlated with *MERGSHR,* our principal index of merger intensity. In fact, for the

33. William F. Long, "Impact of Alternative Allocation Procedures on Econometric Studies of Structure and Performance" (Federal Trade Commission, July 1981); and Scherer and others, "The Validity of Studies," pp. 208–11.

ratio of allocated nontraceable costs to sales, the correlation with *MERGSHR* is negative ($r = -0.038$) and significant at the 0.05 level. For allocated nontraceable assets/sales, the correlation is negative (-0.032) and significant at the 0.10 level. Similarly negative but statistically insignificant correlations of -0.021 and -0.019 emerged when the allocated cost and assets ratios were normalized to the averages of their four-digit industry categories. Thus, there is no support for the hypothesis that excessive cost or asset allocations systematically depressed acquired lines' returns. To the contrary, the negative correlations might be interpreted as weak evidence of overhead-sharing economies gained through merger.[34] Alternatively, some acquired lines may have been kept sufficiently separate from their parents' main operations that they drew proportionately less benefit from common corporate functions, and hence were assessed lower overhead charges.[35]

As indicated earlier, for some acquisitions, and particularly the smaller ones, it was impossible to determine what merger accounting method was adopted. In such cases, the choice was predicted using the logit model presented in appendix A. Regression 4-5(3) tests sensitivity to this approach by deleting 720 LB observations in which the logit predictions were used for more than 25 percent of a line's acquired assets. The *POOL* and *PURCH* coefficients change somewhat, as might be expected with such a large reduction in sample size, but the basic implications remain unaffected.

To avoid having coefficient estimates dominated by a few extreme values, and because a line's assets cannot have been more than 100 percent merger-originated, values of *MERGSHR* were truncated at a maximum of 1.0. Regression 4-5(4) allows *MERGSHR* values to be as high as 3.0. Although the *POOL* and *PURCH* coefficients (derived from *MERGSHR*) fall, as one expects when the mean value of the variable whose effect they measure rises, there is again no fundamental change in the model's implications.

MERGSHR is likely to be lower, the more rapidly a line has grown since it made acquisitions and the longer a post-merger period there was for growth to accumulate. The time dynamics of profitability changes

34. The cost allocation relationship is such that moving from a *MERGSHR* value of 0 to 1.0 reduces average costs by 0.51 percent of sales.

35. On functions retained by acquired units, see Jesse W. Markham, *Conglomerate Enterprise and Public Policy* (Harvard University, Graduate School of Business Administration, Division of Research, 1973), pp. 64–76.

will be scrutinized in subsequent sections. For the moment, we present an alternative version of *MERGSHR* obtained by multiplying acquired assets by a growth factor $G = e^{g(T) \times T}$. Here T is the number of years between 1977 and the asset-weighted year of acquisition, and $g(T)$ is the rate at which current-dollar assets grew over the (1977 - T) interval in the four-digit industry category to which an LB belonged.[36] For *NEW-MERG* lines, the average value of *MERGSHR:G* estimated using these growth-adjusted acquired asset values was 1.18, compared to 0.56 with the unadjusted (and untruncated) *MERGSHR*. When *MERGSHR:G* is truncated at 3.0 and used in computing *POOL* and *PURCH*, the resulting *POOL* and *PURCH* coefficients (regression 4-5(5)) decline, as expected when independent variables are rescaled upward, but the basic structural pattern persists. When *MERGSHR:G* is truncated at 1.0, the *POOL* and *PURCH* coefficients (not explicitly reported in table 4-5) are 2.55 and -2.27, respectively.

In all of the analyses presented thus far, 19 lines of business whose operating income/assets percentages exceeded plus-or-minus 100 percent were excluded. Although this treatment of "outliers" is prudent, its impact must be tested. Regression 4-5(6) brings back the extreme value lines. R^2 drops sharply and standard errors rise, but most of the regression coefficient values change by moderate amounts. The exception is *PURCH*, which jumps to -9.04, indicating that some of the excluded lines had extensive, highly unprofitable operations stemming from purchase acquisitions. Since the results are not altered qualitatively, conservative statistical practice supports continuing exclusion of the extreme-valued observations to maintain insight into more normal cases.

Finally, regression 4-5(7) adds lines of business for 12 companies whose merger histories were of poor quality. Again, relative to core regression 4-5(1), the changes are not dramatic.

Altogether, the results appear robust across a wide array of sensitivity tests. No test changes the basic qualitative implications, and in most

36. The raw data were Census and Survey of Manufactures estimates of gross plant and equipment values plus inventories for survey years from 1957 (the first year plant value data were collected) through 1976. To those values, growth equations of the form $A(T) = A_0 \exp gT$ and $A(T) = A_0 \exp (gT + hT^2)$ were fitted. G values were interpolated from the estimated parameters of those equations, with the quadratic form being used only when it increased R^2 by more than 0.05 and the resulting R^2 was greater than or equal to 0.80. A fuller analysis of *MERGSHR:G* values follows in a later section.

cases, quantitative magnitudes are affected only modestly, or by the amount consistent with independent variable rescalings.

The Time Structure of Profit Effects

The *POOL* and *PURCH* coefficient values estimated thus far assume an impact of merger activity on profitability that is constant, no matter when acquisitions were consummated. In other words, a rectangular time structure is implied. That assumption is now tested. To do so, we define a variable *YEAR*, which is the asset-weighted year of acquisition, or for lines with only one acquisition, the year in which the acquisition was made. The median value of *YEAR* occurs at 1967.

Since a complete profit time series was not available, alternate time lag structures were pre-specified and imposed upon the merger effect coefficients. The best-fitting specification was then sought. The simplest formulation is a triangular lag structure under which *POOL* (or *PURCH*) is weighted by:

$$(4\text{-}4) \qquad YLAG = YEAR - 1950,$$

where *YEAR* is the average acquisition year. This specification assumes profit effects that diminish linearly to zero in 1950. Alternatively, *POOL* (or *PURCH*) is weighted by $(27 - YLAG)$ for a structure with increasing effects.

For both the pooling and the purchase effects, the best-fitting triangular lag structure of this type was the diminishing effect version, reported as regression (1) in table 4-6. Adding the triangular *POOL* lag coefficient to a regression with rectangular effects alone (regression (4) in table 4-2) leads to a reduction of unexplained variance significant at the 15 percent level: $F(1, 2692) = 2.53$. The declining triangular *PURCH* lag was not significantly different from its rectangular counterpart: $F(1, 2692) = 0.43$. The decreasing triangular structure was significantly superior to lags that *increased* triangularly over time for both *POOL* and *PURCH*: $F(1, 2692) = 7.33$ and 6.55, respectively.

The pooling acquisition above-control profitability profile implied by regression 4-6(1) is illustrated by the dot-dash line in figure 4-1. For comparison, the rectangular lag structure of regression 4-2(4) is shown by a long-dashed line. With the regression 4-6(1) structure, pooling acquisitions consummated in 1976 brought 1977 profitability averaging 5.15 percentage points above no-merger levels. The "older" an acqui-

Table 4-6. *Best-Fitting Time Lag Structure Regressions*[a]

	Regression number and lag structure		
	1:Constrained triangular	*2:Unconstrained triangular*	*3:Pooling quadratic, purchase triangular*
Intercept	[257 values][b]	[257 values][b]	[257 values][b]
POOL × *YLAG*	0.198[b]	0.357[b]	0.059
	(3.00)	(3.05)	(0.18)
POOL × *(YLAG)*^{2}			0.007
			(0.43)
PURCH × *YLAG*	−0.178[b]	−0.130[b]	−0.181[b]
	(3.11)	(3.23)	(3.14)
NEW	3.17[b]	3.06[b]	3.13[b]
	(2.78)	(2.69)	(2.73)
EQUALS	1.97[c]	1.97[c]	1.97[c]
	(1.80)	(1.79)	(1.79)
SHR77	39.66[d]	39.30[d]	39.53[d]
	(6.43)	(6.38)	(6.40)
Summary statistic			
R^2	0.1553	0.1555	0.1554

a. Numbers in parentheses are *t*-ratios.
b. Significant in a two-tailed test at 0.01 level of confidence.
c. Significant in a two-tailed test at 0.10 level of confidence.
d. Significant in a one-tailed test at 0.01 level of confidence.

sition was, the more its above-control profitability deteriorated. A similar interpretation of the *PURCH* effect (not graphed) implies returns 4.63 percentage points *below* the control group (or 4.63 + 5.15 = 9.8 points below the pooling acquisition returns) for the most recent (1976) acquisitions. They depreciate linearly to zero for 1950 acquisitions.

Regression 4-6(1) constrains the lag effects to equal zero in 1950. When this restriction is removed by adding a variable intercept year constant, the best-fitting specification was regression 4-6(2). The fit is slightly, but not significantly, superior to that when both merger effects are constrained to have a 1950 intercept. For the unconstrained *POOL* effect, graphed by the solid line in figure 4-1, profitability for 1977 (the first year whose mergers are excluded, and implicitly the last pre-merger year) is estimated at 9.64 percent. This is strikingly close to the 9.8 percent pre-merger supra-normal profitability of pooling mergers in table 3-1. For *POOL* lines acquired before 1959, returns are negative relative to the control group. For *PURCH* acquisitions (not graphed), recent-year effects are negative, and a crossover occurs at 1941. This slow rate

Figure 4-1. *Pooling Merger Effect Lag Structures from Regressions in Tables 4-2 and 4-6*

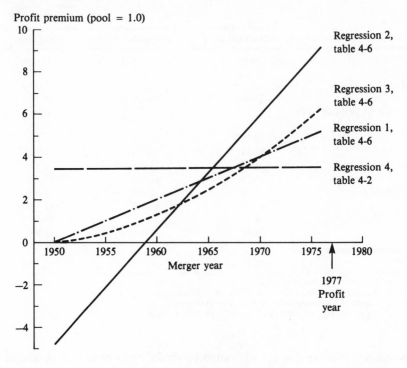

Profit premium (pool = 1.0)

of depreciation explains why one cannot distinguish statistically between triangular and rectangular lag structures for the purchase acquisitions.

It seems clear that pooling acquisition profitability effects were decreasing over time, not increasing or constant. However, it is possible that acquisitions need a few "shakedown" years before reaching maximum profitability, and only then does decline commence. To test this hypothesis, three nonlinear models were estimated. First, *YLAG* was introduced quadratically in the 1950 intercept-constrained version. If the shakedown hypothesis were correct, an inverted U shape, with a negative squared-term coefficient, should appear. Actually, as regression 4-6(3) shows for a model with quadratic *POOL* effects only, both the linear and the squared terms are positive but (because of extreme collinearity) insignificant. The *F*-ratio for the additional squared term is only 0.18. The resulting *POOL* lag structure, shown by a short-dashed line in figure 4-1, differs little from the triangular structure of regression

4-6(1). Results for a quadratic *PURCH* effect were similarly weak. Second, the years 1974, 1975, and 1976 were allowed to have their own intercept shift dummy variables interacting with the merger effect variables. The shakedown hypothesis received no support. All dummy coefficient values were insignificantly different from zero, with *t*-ratios of less than 0.32 for the three *POOL* shift dummies. Third, an inverted U shape was forced upon the data by estimating nonlinearly a binomial *POOL* lag structure. The best-fitting variant, with a peak profit effect in 1973, was significantly inferior in fit to all of the simpler declining lags graphed in figure 4-1. Thus, the nonlinear tests compel no revision of our conclusion that profitability declines monotonically following the time of pooling mergers.

Matched Pre- Versus Post-Merger Analysis

Let us pause to take our bearings. From chapter 3, we know that acquirers of the 1960s and early 1970s absorbed numerous small companies whose profitability averaged well above all-manufacturing norms, especially for acquisitions treated as poolings of interests. The cross-sectional Line of Business analysis in this chapter demonstrates that over the eight or nine years following the median acquisition, profitability declined, perhaps gradually for the pooling acquisitions and sharply (owing to an instant revaluation of assets) for the purchases. The profitability drop for pooling acquisitions, which had no visible asset revaluations, shows up whether one analyzes 1977, the most favorable year, or the average of three years, which has pooling returns insignificantly above no-merger returns. The decline materializes even though many lines realizing negative returns were sold off, as we shall see in chapter 6, leaving only the more profitable survivors for the analysis in this chapter. The question that remains is, why did profits decline following merger?

The case studies to be presented in chapter 5 will yield two hypotheses: profits fell because of managerial control loss problems, or they fell because units were treated as "cash cows" and allowed to decline in product appeal and plant modernity. The control loss hypothesis is consistent with evidence that post-pooling acquisition profitability was lowest for conglomerate acquisitions, on which acquiring company managers had the least pertinent experience. The cash cow hypothesis

Figure 4-2. *Capital Allocation Decisions under Capital Rationing and Elastic Capital Market Conditions*

Internal rate return, cost of capital

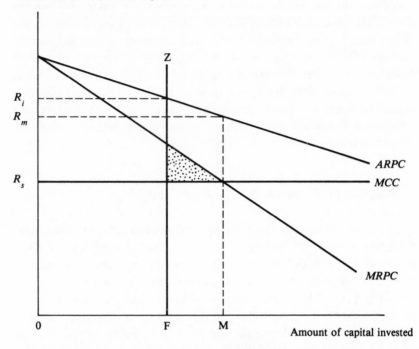

has more dubious support, in part because not *all* businesses, and especially the survivors, are likely to have been milked, and in part because our nonlinear time structure analyses show no early post-merger profitability bulge, as would be expected if generalized cash cow behavior prevailed. Still it should not be ruled out without further testing.

A corollary of the cash cow hypothesis provides an alternative explanation which, unlike the control loss hypothesis, is consistent with a view of mergers as efficiency-enhancing. The high observed pre-merger profitability of the NYSE listing application companies in chapter 3 could have stemmed from capital rationing. Most of those companies were privately or closely held, without ready access to stock markets. Their capital investment may have been limited to what could be raised through internal cash flow and limited bank credit. Then the situation may be schematized as in figure 4-2. *MRPC* is the firm's marginal revenue product of capital function, or in Keynesian terms, the marginal efficiency of capital schedule. *ARPC* is the corresponding average revenue product function. *MCC* is the marginal cost of capital *if* the firm could tap an elastic external capital market. But for privately held companies, this schedule may not be available. Instead, the firm is confined to the inelastic internal funds flow constraint *FZ*. If so, capital investment will be limited to *OF*, and the firm's average return on capital (estimated by our empirical operating income/asset ratios) will be OR_i. If a merger makes available an elastic supply of investible funds along the schedule R_sMCC, either from external sources or cash cow divisions, expansion to *OM* will occur (where the marginal return on capital equals marginal cost) and average returns will drop to OR_m. In the process, an efficiency gain measured by the shaded triangle with base *FM* will occur.

A fourth possibility is that the high pre-merger profitability observed in chapter 3 may not have been sustainable. The analysis there indicates that the typical bilaterally negotiated merger was made when the acquired firm's profitability was on an upswing, and the acquiree's owner-managers may have believed that they were catching a peak. If so, and if there was a tendency for acquirers to select targets whose pre-merger profitability was high at least partly by chance, Galtonian "regression" toward some more normal level will occur.[37]

The Matched Merger Analysis

To help discriminate among these alternatives, a more ambitious pre- versus post-merger analysis was undertaken. It was limited to lines of business satisfying several criteria:

(1) The line was new to the parent company, originating from a single acquisition not augmented by further acquisitions.

(2) Pre-merger financial data were available on the acquired company (usually from NYSE listing applications).

(3) Post-merger data were available for all the years 1974–77.

(4) The acquisition was accounted for as a pooling, so that no asset revaluation ensued.

37. The tendency was first identified by the eminent biologist Francis Galton. On the application of the Galton effect to business enterprise profitability, see Dennis C. Mueller, *Profits in the Long Run* (Cambridge University Press, 1986), and Geoffrey Whittington, *The Prediction of Profitability and Other Studies of Company Behaviour* (Cambridge University Press, 1971), pp. 101–06.

These stringent criteria were satisfied in 67 cases.[38] The "matched merger" sample is probably biased on the side of more successful acquisitions, since the resulting lines survived several years of high sell-off activity, and since parent corporations were not required to disaggregate their Line of Business reports for lines with sales of less than $10 million. The reporting threshold together with the single acquisition criterion imply not only survival fitness, but also a bias toward larger pre-merger size. Median pre-merger assets were $12.0 million, compared to $2.6 million for the less constrained NYSE listing application sample of table 3-1.

Like the much larger table 3-1 sample, the matched merger sample firms enjoyed returns well above all-manufacturing averages in the year before their acquisition. Their simple average operating income/assets ratio was 21.0 percent unadjusted, or 25.2 percent when the profitability ratios were adjusted to reflect cyclical and trend changes in the concurrent *Quarterly Financial Report* manufacturing figures relative to a 1974–77 benchmark value of 12.50 percent. The matched lines' simple average 1974–77 operating income/assets ratio was 12.24 percent—a decline of more than half over the average of seven years from the time of their pre-merger earnings report to the midpoint of the 1974–77 period. Despite the passage of time and substantial inflation, only 57 percent of the matched lines experienced an absolute (that is, not asset-denominated) increase in current-dollar operating income between the pre- and post-merger periods.

Although there was little increase in operating income and a sharp decline in profit rates, considerable asset growth occurred. Fifty-two percent of the lines experienced nominal asset growth rates exceeding those of the four-digit industry category to which they belonged. The mean asset growth rate was 8.93 percent per year, compared to a mean of 7.68 percent over matched time periods for the counterpart four-digit industries. Thus, there is no evidence that the acquired and surviving

---

38. The attrition rate should not cause surprise. The population from which the selection began was the 1,515 *NEWMERG* lines of 1977, winnowed to 1,164 by the four-year data requirement. Roughly 55 percent of all acquisitions were poolings, and 45 percent of the lines with acquisitions had only one acquisition. This leaves a group of approximately 288 on which the pre-merger profit data availability screen operated.

When a single acquired company gave rise to more than one LB, which occurred in a few cases, the post-merger profits for that company were computed as the asset-weighted average of the individual LB profits.

lines were on average treated as cash cows or otherwise deprived of investible funds. Some lines grew extraordinarily rapidly. Nine of the 67 had asset growth rates of 20 percent or more per year. Their average pre-merger operating income/assets ratio was an unusually high 27.6 percent; their average post-merger ratio was 14.4 percent. However, among the 9 there was no visible relationship between growth and 1974–77 profitability. Some remained supranormally (though less) profitable while some overshot and had subnormal 1974–77 returns.

To probe further, the 1974–77 operating income/assets percentage *POSTPI* was regressed on two variables: the comparable ratio *PREPI* for the last pre-merger year, and the average annual percentage growth rate of acquired entity assets *OWNGROW*. Pre-merger profits were adjusted to macroeconomic comparability with the 1974–77 experience.[39] To capture the spirit of the Galtonian regression-toward-normal hypothesis, we subtracted from each profit figure 12.5 percent, the average operating income/assets value for all manufacturing corporations over 1974–77. The resulting regression equation was:

$$(4\text{-}5) \quad POSTPI = \begin{array}{cccc} -2.84 & + & 0.10 \ PREPI & + & 0.15 \ OWNGROW. \\ (1.31) & & (0.81) & & (0.81) \end{array}$$

$$R^2 = 0.034.$$

The coefficient on *PREPI* would have a value of 1.0 if there were no regression toward "normal" and zero if there were complete regression.[40] It is not significantly different from zero—the standard test shown by the subscripted t-ratio. But it differs from 1.0 with high significance ($t = 7.18$).

There remains the counterfactual question of whether profits would have declined as much had merger not occurred. Like all counterfactuals, it can have no certain answer. However, to test it as fully as possible, a special control sample was drawn. It consisted of all corporations in Standard and Poor's COMPUSTAT file from 1965 through 1980 primarily engaged in manufacturing, whose 1965 assets were $50 million or less, and whose 1965 operating income was 15 percent or more

39. See table 3-2.
40. If 12.50 is not the correct norm toward which Galtonian regression occurs, the intercept will be biased away from what should otherwise be a zero value—negatively if the norm is set too high, as appears to be the case in our regressions. Thus, from regression 4-5, it would appear that the norm should have been approximately 9.5 percent.

of assets. The median 1965 assets of the 261 "independent survivors" meeting these criteria were \$13.8 million, close to the 67 matched merger company pre-merger value of \$12.0 million. The survivors' 1965 operating income/assets ratios, adjusted for macroeconomic changes, averaged 24.1 percent, again approximating the matched merger company value of 25.2 percent. Thus, the two samples were as alike as possible in key respects, except that one group remained independent and the other did not.

When the matched merger and independent survivors groups were pooled, and letting DM be a dummy variable identifying the 67 matched merger lines,[41] the regression analogous to equation 4-5 was:

$$POSTPI = -4.55 + 0.32 \ PREPI - 0.19 \ DM \times PREPI$$
$$(4.68) \quad (5.76) \quad\quad (2.78)$$
(4-6)
$$+ \ 0.24 \ OWNGROW.$$
$$(3.48)$$

$$R^2 = 0.157, N = 328.$$

The 0.32 coefficient on $PREPI$ again suggests considerable regression toward the norm. However, the negative and significant coefficient on $DM \times PREPI$ reveals that the profits of matched merger lines regressed (mostly fell) more rapidly than those of the control, even though, with an average pre-merger profit reporting date of 1968, they had less time to do so than the control group (with data uniformly for 1965).[42]

By selecting our control group with a 15 percent floor on 1965 operating income/assets, a variable subject to more or less random fluctuation over time, we have virtually guaranteed a Galtonian regression effect on the coefficient of $PREPI$ in equation 4-6. However, case study interviews suggested that acquiring companies at least tried to find candidates with sustainable profitability, not one-year flashes in the pan.[43] The five-year pre-merger profit analysis in chapter 3 also suggests sustainability. Therefore, the independent survivor group was culled to eliminate companies whose 1966 or 1967 operating income/assets ratio was less than 70 percent of the 1965 value. For the 179 companies that survived this screen, the counterpart regression is:

41. This methodology follows Mueller, "Mergers and Market Share," pp. 260–66.

42. An alternate formulation of regressions 4-5 and 4-6, with $PREPI$ multiplied by a variable measuring the interval between the last pre-merger (or 1965) profit report and 1975.5, had slightly, but insignificantly, more explanatory power. It revealed an even larger difference between the independent survivor and matched merger companies.

43. See chap. 5 and appendix B.

$$POSTPI = -3.59 + 0.40 \; PREPI - 0.29 \; DM \times PREPI$$

(4-7)   (3.13)   (5.06)   (3.54)

$$+ \; 0.19 \; OWNGROW.$$
(2.36)

$$R^2 = 0.160, N = 246.$$

Here the control group regression effect is smaller, as expected, while the matched merger offset coefficient increases commensurately. In each of equations 4-5 through 4-7, the matched merger lines retained only 10 percent to 13 percent of their pre-merger supranormal profits, while the control group retained 32 percent to 40 percent. Thus, it would appear that something more than Galtonian regression underlay the acquired units' declining profitability.

The positive and significant coefficients on *OWNGROW* in regressions 4-6 and 4-7 suggest that rapid growth is associated with higher end-of-period profitability. Although the matched merger firms' average growth rate of 8.9 percent per year was higher than that of the firms' home industries, the independent survivors ($N = 261$) grew even more rapidly, at 13.1 percent per year. The difference is highly significant ($t = 3.85$). Evidently, the small, profitable companies that chose to remain independent were not deprived of growth capital relative to lines that were acquired and tapped an internal corporate funds market. Had the mostly private, highly profitable acquired firms in our matched merger sample chosen to remain independent but list their securities on public markets, their growth in the counterfactual situation might not have been stunted.

Merged Unit Growth

The question of post-merger growth is sufficiently important that it is worthwhile pushing our data further for a broader sample. We focus on the 1,515 *NEWMERG* lines surviving in 1977 that were not part of their parents' 1950 operations. For the vast majority of those lines, an acquisition was the means by which the parent entered the industry category. After the initial acquisition, growth could have occurred by additional acquisitions, internal investment, or some combination of the two.

We know what the end-of-1977 assets were for lines that survived sample quality controls. Let us call those assets for the ith line $A77_i$. We also have estimates of the value of assets A_{ij} gained by line i in its jth acquisition, adjusted when appropriate to reflect purchase accounting revaluations. We define the variable T_{ij} to be 1977 minus the date of acquisition j by line i. Using Census and Survey of Manufactures data on plant and inventory values, compounded growth curves were fitted for each four-digit Line of Business category.[44] Thus, if over interval T_{ij} line i's acquired assets grew at the average rate $g_k(T_{ij})$ experienced in its home industry k, we predict the line's assets at the end of 1977 to be:

$$(4\text{-}8) \qquad A_i^* = \sum_{j=1}^{N} A_{ij} \exp\left[g_k(T_{ij}) \times T_{ij}\right].$$

This prediction is subject to appreciable error, in part because the acquired "seed" assets A_{ij} were, as observed earlier, subject to estimation uncertainties. Especially for acquisitions below \$10 million in asset value, the "plugging" approach that was often used could introduce errors as large as a factor of two or even three, which in turn become multiplied by the exponential growth factor of equation 4-8. Most such errors are expected to be random, although biases might also intrude. Because assumed liabilities were not counted, our purchase accounting asset estimators are probably biased on the low side for the more profitable acquisitions. On the other hand, ignoring initial investment seeds planted before any acquisitions were made imparts an opposite bias in the procedure that follows.

For each of the 1,515 lines that made post-1950 acquisitions, equation 4-8 was used to predict 1977 asset values. Those predictions were then related to actually reported 1977 assets by the formula:

$$(4\text{-}9) \qquad MERGSHR{:}G = \frac{A_i^*}{A77_i},$$

where $MERGSHR{:}G$ is the same as the growth-adjusted variant of $MERGSHR$ used in an earlier sensitivity analysis. Values exceeding 1.0 reflect actual growth at *less* than the industry rate. That is, the predicted numerator exceeds the actually realized denominator value. $MERGSHR{:}G$ values below 1.0 indicate that the line grew faster than its industry (unless pre-merger internal investment seeds were overlooked).

44. See note 36.

Table 4-7. *Distribution of Asset Growth MERGSHR:G Values for Post-1950 Lines of Business with Acquisitions*

MERGSHR:G value	Number of lines	Percent of all lines	Cumulative percent
0.00–0.25	267	17.6	17.6
0.26–0.50	193	12.7	30.3
0.51–0.75	189	12.5	42.8
0.76–1.00	201	13.3	56.1
1.01–1.25	177	11.7	67.8
1.26–1.50	116	7.7	75.5
1.51–2.00	153	10.1	85.6
2.01–2.50	82	5.4	91.0
2.51–3.00	42	2.8	93.8
3.01–4.00	52	3.4	97.2
4.01 and above	43	2.8	100.0

Table 4-7 presents a frequency distribution of the computed *MERGSHR:G* values. The mean value of 1.182 implies actual growth slower than industry norms on average, but it is heavily affected by the *MERGSHR:G* distribution's long tail, which arises because some lines (often those with a sell-off history) have 1977 assets that can approach zero. A more reliable indicator of central tendencies is the median, whose value of 0.89 implies actual growth greater than that of the industries to which the LBs belonged in a majority of cases. With a standard error of approximately 0.047, the median is significantly below the 1.0 value expected if the typical line grew no more rapidly than its home industry.

This finding provides additional support for rejecting the hypothesis that acquired lines surviving through 1977 were on average treated as cash cows and deprived of investible funds. Because of the large potential error component in the original merged asset values, however, the support must be considered fragile.

Expenditures on Research and Development

A further facet of firms' growth strategy is investment in research and development to create new and improved products and devise superior production processes. Have acquired lines been more or less ambitious than their no-merger peers in supporting such technology investments?

The Line of Business data base contains among other things the most richly disaggregated information on company-financed R&D expenditures available. Previous research using LB, as well as more aggregated, data has shown that R&D intensity, measured by the ratio of R&D expenditures to sales, varies widely across four-digit industry categories.[45] It is doubly important here to control for such interindustry differences, since, as we learned in chapter 2, diversification by merger during the 1950–75 period was targeted toward industries of lower-than-average R&D intensity. Thus, in analyzing the ratios of individual lines' R&D to sales, *RD:S* (scaled in percentage terms), we employ a "fixed-effects" model that in essence allows each LB to be evaluated relative to the average ratio for the industry category (out of 256) to which it belongs.

Earlier research has found a weak tendency for company-financed R&D outlays to rise more than proportionately with LB sales. We take this phenomenon into account by including the market share variable *SHR*. In the most detailed analysis, parent firm diversification proved to have no significant impact on R&D outlays, once industry category and relative LB size were controlled.[46] However, there has been no equivalently detailed analysis of how merger history and intensity affected R&D. We investigate that relationship using our *MERGSHR* variable in one case and the categorical *NEWMERG* and *ORIGMERG* variables in another. Also included will be the mergers of equals dummy variable *EQUALS*, the post-1950 no-merger line variable *NEW*, and (in two versions) the tender offer dummy variable *TENDER*. We focus on 1977, macroeconomically the most normal year for which we have data. The sample is the same as the one used for our core profitability analysis in tables 4-2, 4-3, and 4-4, which covers 2,955 LBs.

The results are presented in table 4-8. All of the merger activity variables but *TENDER* reveal a negative influence, although only the *MERGSHR* coefficient is statistically significant. The *TENDER* variable adds little to R^2 relative to the two regressions from which it is omitted; the incremental F-ratios are 1.66 and 0.55, with the 5 percent point being 3.84. From regression 4-8(1), moving from having had no acquisition history to 100 percent of 1977 assets originated through merger reduces an LB's R&D/sales ratio by 0.28 percentage points, or by 18 percent of

45. F. M. Scherer, *Innovation and Growth: Schumpeterian Perspectives* (M.I.T. Press, 1984), chap. 11. On the literature more generally, see William L. Baldwin and John T. Scott, *Market Structure and Technological Change* (New York: Harwood, 1987).

46. See Scherer, *Innovation and Growth*, pp. 235–36.

Table 4-8. *Regressions with Ratios of 1977 Company-Financed R&D Outlays to Sales as Dependent Variable*[a]

	Regression number			
	1	2	3	4
Intercept	[256 values][b]	[256 values][b]	[256 values][b]	[256 values][b]
MERGSHR	−0.28[c]	−0.33[b]	. . .	. . .
	(2.41)	(2.67)		
NEWMERG	. . .	. . .	−0.133	−0.146
			(1.16)	(1.25)
ORIGMERG	. . .	. . .	−0.074	−0.079
			(0.59)	(0.63)
NEW	0.26[d]	0.26[d]	0.26	0.26
	(1.94)	(1.92)	(1.62)	(1.61)
EQUALS	−0.12	−0.13	−0.11	−0.11
	(0.96)	(0.99)	(0.86)	(0.87)
TENDER	. . .	0.20	. . .	0.11
		(1.27)		(0.71)
SHR77	2.59[b]	2.58[b]	2.77[b]	2.77[b]
	(3.54)	(3.53)	(3.71)	(3.72)
Summary statistic				
R^2	0.3873	0.3877	0.3863	0.3864

a. Based on 2,955 lines of business; numbers in parentheses are *t*-ratios.
b. Significant in a two-tailed test at 0.01 level of confidence.
c. Significant in a two-tailed test at 0.05 level of confidence.
d. Significant in a two-tailed test at 0.10 level of confidence.

the all-industry average R&D/sales ratio of 1.555 percent. From the categorical measures, the average R&D-reducing effect lies in the range of 5 percent to 8.5 percent. The *MERGSHR* coefficient is larger because it assumes the maximum change (from 0 to 1) in merger intensity, not the average experience (48 percent asset origination through merger for *NEWMERG* lines, 20 percent for *ORIGMERG*) assimilated by the categorical variables. *MERGSHR*'s higher *t*-ratios may also reflect its tendency to approach its maximum unit value in LBs that have experienced little asset growth beyond what was achieved directly through acquisition (perhaps because of deficient R&D) and in financially distressed LBs, as evidenced by post-merger sell-offs and/or asset write-offs. Even when such influences are absent, however, as in the categorical variables, we find no support for the hypothesis that R&D was *stimulated* by the parent-subsidiary relationships following merger. If acquired lines achieved more rapid growth, it did not happen because of extraordinary technological effort.

As expected, R&D/sales ratios rise with higher market shares. The size of the effect is more surprising: having a pure monopoly position more than doubles R&D intensity compared to what an atomistic rival would achieve in the average industry. *NEW* lines have above-average R&D/sales ratios, all else equal, most likely reflecting the product R&D that let them enter new industries without the aid of merger.

Conclusion

We conclude by repeating the question with which we began this chapter: how well did corporate acquirers fare with their catches? The preliminary answer must be, in most respects, not very well. On pooling-of-interests acquisitions without systematic asset revaluations, profitability was barely above control group levels over the three years 1975–77, and even in the best year, 1977, it was much lower than the average acquired unit's pre-merger return. Purchase acquisitions had sub-control returns, at least in part, but not entirely, because of the asset revaluations that accompanied merger. To this preponderantly negative picture, there are two positive offsets: mergers of equals out-performed the control group and (less clearly) their pre-merger records; and lines joining their parent through acquisition had strong asset growth experiences, even though they were below-par R&D performers. A fully balanced assessment of these and other findings must await the completion of our analysis and, in particular, our investigation of the sell-off phenomenon.

CHAPTER FIVE

The Economics of Sell-Off:
Case Study Evidence

IF THE 1960s were the decade of conglomerate mergers, the 1970s and early 1980s can be called the era of divestiture and "back to basics" restructuring.[1] Evidence on quantitative dimensions of the sell-off phenomenon will be presented in the next chapter. Here we address qualitative questions: What happened? Why were so many mergers undone? And what does the experience of divested acquisitions teach us about the motivations and success of mergers generally?

Methodology

Insight into these questions is provided by a set of case studies. Sixteen acquisitions (or clusters of acquisitions) were selected for case study research, and 15 of the case studies were successfully executed. An attempt was made to choose a sample spanning a broad and representative array of experiences, subject to certain feasibility constraints. The selection process began with the identification of 70 potentially

An earlier version of this chapter appeared in Lacy Glenn Thomas, ed., *The Economics of Strategic Planning: Essays in Honor of Joel Dean* (Lexington Books, 1986), pp. 143–70.

1. The move toward sell-off following acquisition was recognized early by the journal *Mergers & Acquisitions*, which established a regular column on sell-offs in 1968. In 1971 it predicted "that the sell-off trend has only begun. Many more companies will undoubtedly discover that it's easier to dump an unprofitable operation than to turn it around—particularly if its operation is in an area outside the parent company's primary expertise." "Corporate Sell-Off," *Mergers & Acquisitions*, vol. 6 (Spring 1971), p. 58. Likewise, in 1968, merger consultant Frederick Lovejoy criticized conglomerates for retaining poorly performing divisions, urging that "what is needed is for management to devote valuable corporate resources to opportunity areas and stop trying to do repair jobs in those areas with little or no potential for meeting corporate objectives." *New York Times*, October 9, 1968.

feasible sell-off cases through a systematic screening of the journal *Mergers & Acquisitions*. Both in preparing this preliminary list and winnowing it down, several criteria were stressed. First, to ensure that participants were still accessible and that memories were reasonably fresh, a 1977–83 sell-off time frame was imposed. Second, all of the original sampled entity acquisitions were conglomerate or diversifying in character, and with only 4 ultimate exceptions, the parent (that is, divesting) corporations had been active conglomerate acquirers, with 30 or more acquisitions recorded on the Federal Trade Commission's merger history file. All but 5 of the parent corporations are included in the table 2-8 (50 or more acquisitions) list, and 8 of the case studies involve parents included in the table 2-9 (99 or more acquisitions) list. Third, an effort was made to cover a wide spectrum of industrial conditions, with an even division between consumer and producer goods, some large acquired-and-divested units and some small, a sprinkling of both dynamic and mature technologies, and diverse degrees of capital intensity. Fourth, a rough balance was sought between large companies and small companies (or internal management groups) as the ultimate acquirers of the sold-off subsidiaries. Fifth, because of budget constraints, only companies located within 350 miles of Philadelphia or Chicago (the interview team members' home bases) or on a convenient travel route between those two points were chosen. Few exceptions to this constraint could be allowed. Finally, as the list of potential case studies was narrowed using these criteria, literature searches were carried out to ensure that a reasonable amount of published information was available, so that a preliminary history could be compiled before the interviewing began, and so that current and former executives could be identified and targeted for interviews. This criterion biased the case studies toward relatively sizable acquired-and-divested business units. Median assets of the principal acquired case study sample companies were approximately $26 million in the year before their acquisition—ten times the median size of acquisitions comprising our New York Stock Exchange listing application samples.

It is important to recognize a criterion that was *not* systematically applied in the selection process. There was no attempt deliberately to load the sample with cases on which there was prior evidence of managerial failure by the original acquiring company. Indeed, at the time the final sample selection decisions were made, the reasons for divestiture were typically known only in vague terms from public statements: for example, that growth prospects or returns on investment had been found unsatisfactory, or that a continuation of operations was deemed inconsistent with the divesting company's strategic plan.[2] Thus, if there is a bias in the sample toward problem-ridden acquisitions, it is there by chance, not by design.

One case study, on Borden's 1963 acquisition and 1980 sell-off of transparent and adhesive tape maker Mystik, had to be abandoned when Mystik's new parent, Chemical Investors Inc., filed for bankruptcy.[3] The Chapter XI petition coincided with our requests for interviews, leading to negative responses and making it clear that a balanced perspective would not be achieved.

Once the case study sample was chosen, the literature search was intensified, and as complete a history as could be drawn from public sources was assembled. From this, preliminary research questions were formulated. Lists were also compiled of current executives and "alumni" of the acquired-and-divested unit, the original acquirer, and the ultimate buyer (except in management buyout cases). In some instances, labor union officials were also identified. Potential interviewees were sent letters explaining the research, spelling out disclosure guidelines, and setting out several questions to focus the proposed interview. In all, 70 interviews were conducted, 12 by telephone (counting only substantive discussions) and 58 face-to-face. Excluding the abandoned Mystik Tape case, there were 13 clear refusals to be interviewed, along with an unknown number of referrals that led eventually to interviews with others in the same organization. In all but a few cases, it was possible to find adequate substitutes for refused interviews. In no completed case study were there fewer than three independent interviews. A rough

2. Only two exceptions need noting. Co-author Scherer, who was solely responsible for the case study research, had participated as an advisor to the U.S. Attorney General in antitrust deliberations precipitated by a 1978 merger involving the Youngstown Sheet & Tube Co. From this role he had reason to believe that Youngstown's earlier acquisition led to financial and managerial problems. The case was included because of substantial uncertainty about the nature of those problems and whether a new (horizontal) merger could correct them. The Talon case study was included in part because the *New York Times*, December 7, 1981, reported substantial market share losses and suggested inconclusively that those losses came from a short-sighted financial strategy pursued by parent corporation Textron.

3. See "Fast-Growing Company's Fall Attributed to Flawed Accounting and Risky Buyouts," *Wall Street Journal*, August 2, 1983.

categorization of interviewees by organizational position, listing only the senior official of multi-person interviews, is as follows:

Interviewee	Number
Parent corporations	
Chairman or president	7
Vice president or equivalent	11
Other staff	1
Divested entities	
Chairman or president	20
Vice president or division head	6
Plant manager	3
Other staff	9
Other	
Union representatives	8
Journalists or consultants	3
Competitors or customers	2
Total	70

Thirty-four interviews were conducted solely by research assistants, 15 were made jointly by co-author Scherer and research assistants, and the remainder were done by Scherer alone. Co-author Ravenscraft did not participate in the case study effort.

Nondirective interviewing methods were used to the maximum possible extent. That is, after a brief introduction, the interviewee was asked to tell his or her story of the relevant events, interrupted mainly for clarifying questions or follow-up questions on significant facts or interpretations that had not been volunteered directly. To enhance rapport, notes were taken during the interviews only on names, addresses, and an occasional figure. Immediately following the interview, detailed notes were written or dictated. These were subsequently expanded into full interview protocols totaling approximately 225 single-spaced pages. The telephone interviews followed this approach less consistently, being used in some cases primarily to verify or clarify disputed or questionable points emerging from face-to-face interviews. Follow-up calls to a previous interviewee are not included in the interview tally.

Various assurances of anonymity and confidentiality were provided. All material that identifies particular companies, or that could conceivably be traced to a particular source, has been cleared with appropriate interviewees. When key persons refused to grant an interview, they were asked to review the pre-publication version for accuracy.

The Sample

Table 5-1 provides an overview of the 15 business units on which the case studies focused. The sales figures for the last year before divestiture began are sometimes extrapolations from earlier years, and in some cases they exclude modest amounts of previously divested unit sales. The sample's diversity in terms of product offerings and divested unit size—spanning a sales range from $3.5 million to $1.5 billion, with a median of $55 million—is evident. For two parent corporations, Bendix and Chromalloy American, two subsidiary sell-off histories were examined, largely to isolate the role of unit-specific variables within a common corporate environment. Both of the Bendix acquisitions were unique in having been sold off by earlier large-corporation parents. The emphasis of our field research was on the period beginning with Bendix ownership. With one minor exception, other sample members were independent entities, or clusters of independent entities, before their acquisition.

Table 5-2 provides insight into the pre-merger profitability of the 11 acquired companies for which the requisite information was available.[4] As in chapters 3 and 4, the focus is on operating income as a percentage of assets in the last reporting year before acquisition. For the 11 acquired companies, the unweighted average profit return was 15.3 percent; after adjustments to a constant macroeconomic base, the average was 16.6 percent. Although above all-manufacturing norms, the averages are lower than those reported for the 634-company sample studied in chapter 3, largely because our case study companies were much larger than the typical NYSE acquisition sample member. Seven case study members had returns lower than those predicted on the basis of size and accounting method variables from the regression equation in footnote 17 of chapter 3; only four had higher-than-predicted returns. On average, the case study members' returns were 1.1 percentage points lower than what the NYSE sample-based regression predicted. The difference is not statistically significant; $t = 0.59$.

A more detailed factual summary of the case histories is provided in

---

4. Data on the two Bendix acquisitions were unavailable because only parts of the parents were acquired. Chromalloy Glass came together through multiple small acquisitions in a two-stage process, so that no useful NYSE listing application existed. Sintercast was too small to publish financial statements.

Table 5-1. *Merger and Divestiture Highlights for Fifteen Case Study Units Sold Off between 1977 and 1984*

Acquired and divested unit	Principal product	Acquired by	Year	Sold to	Year	Annual sales at divestiture (millions of dollars)
A.S.R. Products Corp.	Razors and blades	Philip Morris	1960	Management	1977	42
Bendix Home Systems	Mobile homes and recreational vehicles	Boise Cascade Corp.	1968	Bendix Corp.	1972	210
		Bendix Corp.	1972	Commodore Corp.	1978	175
Robert Bruce	Sportswear	Consolidated Foods Corp.	1973	Savoy Industries	1980	50
Caradco Corp.	Wooden windows	Scovill Manufacturing Co.	1968	Bendix Corp.	1979	18
		Bendix Corp.	1979	Kusan Division of Bethlehem Steel Corp.	1981	n.a.
Chromalloy Glass Products	Architectural glass and mirrors	Chromalloy American Corp.	1968–71	Diverse interests	1982–83	25
ESB	Batteries	International Nickel of Canada	1974	Diverse interests	1982–83	880
Great Lakes Screw	Specialty fasteners	U.S. Industries	1967	Allied Products Corp.	1979	15
Harley Davidson Motor Co.	Motorcycles	AMF	1968	Management	1981	290
Harman International Industries	High fidelity equipment	Beatrice Foods Co.	1977	Former management and Shin Shirasuna Co.	1979–80	137
Letisse	Leather handbags	W. R. Grace & Co.	1969	Lane Wood	1977	8
Marquette Cement	Portland cement	Gulf & Western Industries	1976	Lone Star Cement	1982	139
Sintercast	Sintered titanium carbide	Chromalloy American Corp.	1959	Middle management	1981	3.5
Talon	Zippers	Textron	1968	Nucon Holdings	1981	180
S. S. White Co.	Dental supplies	Pennwalt Chemicals Corp.	1966	Outside manager[a]	1984–86	55
Youngstown Sheet & Tube Co.	Steel products	Lykes Corp.	1969	LTV Corp.	1978	1,500

a. Later sold to diverse interests.

Table 5-2. *Profitability of Eleven Case Study Companies in the Year before Their Acquisition*

Company	Operating income as a percent of assets	MACRO-adjusted profit (percent)[a]	Assets (millions of dollars)
A.S.R. Products Corp.	15.0	15.9	21.9
Robert Bruce	16.8	23.3	20.3
ESB	8.9	9.4	315.1
Great Lakes Screw	30.7	30.1	5.7
Harley Davidson Motor Co.	11.2	12.4	29.7
Harman International Industries	14.8	14.3	86.4
Letisse	26.1	28.6	2.0
Marquette Cement	2.9	3.2	155.4
Talon	26.3	30.1	74.6
S. S. White Co.	9.5	9.4	33.5
Youngstown Sheet & Tube Co.	5.6	6.1	1,026.7
Average of 11 companies	15.25	16.62	. . .

a. See table 3-2 for the values used to adjust profitability to a 1974–77 basis.

appendix B. The emphasis here is analytic and synthetic. Because sensitive questions of strategy, motivation, and managerial competence are explored, the names of companies and executives are sometimes suppressed.

The Reasons for Merger

As is true more generally, the mergers covered by our case studies had complex motivations. In all but the two overtly contested takeover cases, merger appeared mutually desirable to the managements of both partners.

A common contention concerning unilateral takeover attempts is that management of the target company has been derelict in its duty to maximize profits and that, by reorganizing and reorienting operations, the acquiring entity will improve matters.

The hostile takeover of ESB by International Nickel (INCO) did not fit this model. Inco sought ESB because it wanted to diversify, had the resources to do so, concluded from careful study that the battery business was where it could best achieve its goals, and (after an unsuccessful approach to a British company) viewed ESB as its best feasible prospect.

The Youngstown Sheet & Tube case is more complex. Ocean shipper-become-conglomerate Lykes sought Youngstown despite opposition from Youngstown's management because, with depressed stock prices following low earnings that were expected to increase, Youngstown seemed a good diversification investment. Stock analysts had been critical of Youngstown management for being relatively tardy in modernizing their plants and then for investing heavily in modernization in an industry with uncertain prospects. But the largely completed Indiana Harbor modernization was creating one of America's most modern and promising integrated steel works. Whether Lykes planned from the outset not to invest further in the older Youngstown, Ohio, works is unclear. The subsequent failure to invest, including cancellation of a plan to install basic oxygen furnaces, appears in hindsight attributable more to disappointing earnings and stringent capital servicing needs than to a preconceived resource allocation plan.

The Harley Davidson case occupies a halfway position, since merger with AMF was triggered by another firm's hostile takeover attempt. A thin market for the company's stock, and the desire of family member-owners to diversify their portfolios, were the main reasons why takeover would have been possible. For AMF as "white knight," the acquisition was a natural and attractive complement to its other recreational equipment businesses. If there was any failure on Harley's part, it was a failure to move out of its niche and take advantage of the rapidly growing, Japanese-dominated small-cycle market. For such an expansion, AMF's greater access to capital could be of help. It is significant that after buying Harley, AMF did not make wholesale managerial reorganizations, but left Davidson family members in key positions.

At least 9 of the remaining 12 cases were in large measure seller-initiated. Most entailed some mixture of three motives: the desire of owners to diversify stock portfolios and make them more liquid; the perceived need for more elastic sources of finance; and problems of managerial succession owing to age or sickness or (with Harman International Industries) accession of the chief executive to a high government position. In all of these cases, the buying company perceived the target firm as highly promising, not as a business in trouble. The two exceptions to the pattern among seller-initiated acquisitions were Bendix Home Systems and Caradco, both sell-offs from large corporations. Boise

Cascade sold Home Systems because it desperately needed cash owing to losses on other operations. Home Systems was said (not altogether accurately) to have been one of its "crown jewels." Scovill sold Caradco because of disappointment with its performance; Bendix bought Caradco because it thought it could do better, taking advantage inter alia of complementarities with other components of its Forest Products Division. Caradco's acquisition by Bendix is the only clear case of an original sample acquisition driven by the belief that prior management had performed poorly and that a change would improve matters.

The ASR, Chromalloy Glass, and S. S. White mergers are best described as jointly initiated. In each, the parties anticipated substantial "synergies" (as well as greater portfolio liquidity for seller stockholders) from their union. It was thought that ASR's advertising effectiveness could be enhanced through a piggyback relationship with Philip Morris. The owners of the numerous fragments that came to make up Chromalloy Glass saw advantages in joining a much larger family of glass specialists. And for Philadelphia firms S. S. White and Pennwalt, merger seemed to offer diversification, financing, and technical research complementarities. It is of interest that in two of the three cases, ASR and S. S. White, the acquiring and acquired firms had interlocking directorates before merger was proposed.

That the acquisitions in our sample were motivated only negligibly by pre-merger managerial failures is also revealed by the rarity of planned management shake-ups at the time of acquisition. In six cases, including both contested takeovers and most of the larger friendly acquisitions, the acquiring company moved fairly quickly to install a chief executive from its own organization, but the next tier of management was changed little except in response to newly emerging needs. In most of the other cases, the acquiring corporation saw compelling advantages in retaining existing top managers, who had knowledge, experience, and a record of accomplishment for which no ready substitutes were at hand. Eleven of the 15 sample acquisitions were announced by New York Stock Exchange listing applications. In ten cases, the listing statements declared either explicitly or in describing employment incentive contracts that the incumbent management team was invited to stay on. In the other case, the previous president had announced his intention to retire. To be sure, many of the acquisitions led sooner or later to major managerial changes, sometimes voluntarily (for example, when four Youngstown executives took advantage of the golden parachutes Lykes offered them) and sometimes not. But these were a reaction to unanticipated developments, not an initially planned corrective to problems perceived at the time of merger.[5]

What Went Wrong?

Our case study sample is biased by design toward corporate marriages that ended in divorce. One's natural inclination is to suppose that if the marriage ended in divorce, something went wrong. This is not necessarily true. If the purchase of corporations were like buying blocks of common stock or soybean futures contracts, one would not be surprised when purchases were followed by sales. But the analogy is false. Organizations are not inanimate objects or market abstractions; their behavior is affected by the act and consequences of sale or purchase. Moreover, it is clear from our case study interviews that none of the 15 sample acquisitions was made as a purely speculative play, nor was there evidence that sell-off was considered at the outset as a likely sequitur to the purchase decision. Rather, mergers were made because the marriage itself was expected to bring substantial rewards. Divestiture followed most commonly because, in one way or another, the acquirer's expectations were not fulfilled. This occurred in most cases because unanticipated problems emerged, but in a smaller subset, disappointment came because the acquiring company's objectives and expectations were revised.

It is useful at the outset to distinguish between problems that were latent in the situation—already germinating when the acquisition was made, or about to spring up with a new roll of the market environmental dice—and those that were directly caused by the merger and change of control. In practice the distinction is difficult to implement, partly

5. Seven of the 15 acquired firms (or clusters of firms) experienced substantial top management turnover—in only two cases, anticipated beforehand—during the three years following merger. Two others had significant turnover in the fourth year. This tendency for turnover to be unplanned but appreciable is also noted in other studies. See, for example, Harry H. Lynch, *Financial Performance of Conglomerates* (Harvard University, Graduate School of Business Administration, Division of Research, 1971), pp. 84–85; Jesse W. Markham, *Conglomerate Enterprise and Public Policy* (Harvard University, Graduate School of Business Administration, Division of Research, 1973), pp. 85–86; "After the Merger: Keeping Key Managers on the Team," *Business Week*, October 30, 1978, pp. 136–45; and "Takeovers: Who Stays On?" *Dun's Business Month*, January 1982, p. 107.

because there is an important domain of interaction between the two categories. But we begin by doing the best we can to use and illuminate the distinction.

The Inspection Problem

Making a corporate acquisition is risky. After the fact, some acquisitions turn out well, some badly. There are things one can do to identify problems before a commitment is made, but often the pressures of time, competition, or acquired entity reticence prevent a thorough examination. Even when a careful pre-merger inspection is undertaken, some problems are so subtle that they elude detection. In many cases, they are not visible even to the incumbent management, and when they are perceived, there may be disagreement within the organization over their significance. Those who take a relatively pessimistic view of latent or newly emerging problems are not likely to be paraded before the visitors from a prospective acquirer. Would-be sellers naturally present their best face.

How far one goes, or is required to go, in the pre-merger show-and-tell game depends upon both ethical and legal constraints as well as upon the relative sophistication and eagerness of the negotiating parties. Our case studies provided examples spanning a wide spectrum. At one extreme, the negotiator for an acquisition candidate did what was called a "snow job" on the acquirer's representatives, among other things deflecting attention from accounting practices that had been selected to enhance the company's reported value. Apparently much less common was a case at the opposite extreme, in which an experienced acquirer induced the target firm's management to accept provisions that, the acquired entity discovered only later, made the acquisition virtually self-financing in a very short period.

Hostile takeovers pose especially high risks of failing to identify detectable latent problems, since by definition, the target firm's management declines to cooperate in supplying operational details. Thus, in buying ESB, International Nickel was unaware of new product developments that would eventually lead to grief; it failed to perceive significant weaknesses at certain key operating management positions; and it was surprised by vast differences in "corporate culture" that eventually made it difficult for the two organizations to reconcile their approaches to problems.

The Nature of the Emerging Problems

The latent problems that escape detection in merger negotiations are enormously varied. If this were not so, a cookbook could be prepared to save the unwary from most mistakes. Detection often requires a good understanding of the relevant business—something conglomerate acquirers normally lack. A few examples must suffice to illustrate the range of problems. In acquiring ASR, Philip Morris tacitly assumed that making good razor blades was not very difficult for a firm skilled in the art, and so it was totally surprised by ASR's deficient know-how for entering the new era of stainless steel blades. In acquiring Caradco, Bendix underestimated the problems of achieving high productivity with a relatively inexperienced plant work force, and it was overcome by paint-peeling problems that came to light only after Caradco's windows had been in use for some time. It took many years for Textron's top management to comprehend that the Japanese could produce top-quality zippers, that they were serious about making a concerted attack on the U.S. market, that their machinery was better than Talon's, that the Talon name alone was not sufficient to maintain buyer loyalty at price premiums, and that the lucrative home sewing market was on the wane. And Pennwalt failed to realize that S. S. White's organization had grown resistant to technological and marketing method changes. Once the problems *were* perceived, Pennwalt lacked the know-how to transform White's organization and maintain the right balance between sensitivity to the specialized requirements of the dental equipment market and willingness to try new things.

Some of the problems that led to disappointment with our sample acquisitions could not have been foreseen even with the most diligent and intelligently conducted pre-merger inspection. Rather, the acquirer's luck was simply bad. Thus, before Beatrice's acquisition of Harman International, the high fidelity equipment business had experienced almost uninterrupted growth. The recession that followed, like the quadrupling of the price of cobalt used in Harman's loudspeakers, was scarcely predictable. In acquiring Marquette Cement, Gulf & Western consciously gambled on rising prosperity and a construction industry boom. Through 1979, the gamble turned out to be mildly disappointing. Thereafter, a new Federal Reserve Board tight money policy wreaked havoc on cement demand. The 1973–74 energy price shock dealt a severe blow to the recreational vehicle sales of Bendix's newly acquired Home

Systems Division. Mobile home sales and (for Caradco, selling mainly to home builders) window sales were hit hard by the housing recessions of 1975 and 1980. The parallel developments that reduced automobile demand and shifted it toward smaller imported units hurt Great Lakes Screw, whose fasteners were designed for large traditional cars, and ESB, which lost automobile battery sales to importers and industrial battery sales to recession. A part of Talon's manifest difficulties came from the whims of fashion as women switched in large numbers to garments with more buttons and fewer zippers.

In at least ten of the acquisitions selected for our case study research, detectable latent problems unnoticed or unheeded by the buyer grew eventually to be a source of considerable distress. In eight of the acquisitions, including seven of the latent problem cases, subsequent bad luck, most commonly associated with macroeconomic events of the turbulent 1970s, contributed to disappointment and the ultimate decision to divest. Thus, if one sought the simplest and most sweeping explanation of why our sample mergers ended in divorce, the answer would be: reality often falls short of anticipations.

Interaction Effects

This is too simple. The truth of Murphy's Law (if anything can go wrong, it will) is well known. Why should the emergence of unexpected problems set in motion a chain of events leading to divestiture, and not to adaptations that correct the problems or, when that is impossible, minimize their adverse impact? In most cases, corrections were tried, and in some, they succeeded. But what came to light with great frequency in our case studies was evidence that the problem-solving mechanism failed to work, or worked poorly. This failure stemmed in many instances from organizational and motivational deficiencies resulting from the merger. In other words, there was an interaction between merger-induced behavioral changes and the effectiveness of problem-solving efforts that led eventually to divestiture.

When merger occurs, it is necessary for the new parent to establish control over the subsidiary. Although there were many detailed variations, this was done in two main ways. As noted earlier, in six cases, the parent soon installed as chief executive of the subsidiary a person from its own organization. In one case, this occurred because the original owner-manager wanted to retire and there was no internal successor. In the other five, control considerations outweighed chain of succession issues even when retirements were the precipitating factor. In the other nine cases, there was at least initially no external intrusion into the acquired unit's top management. Instead, control was exercised by close financial monitoring (most commonly, at monthly intervals) and by having the unit manager report to one or more members of corporate management—usually to a group or executive vice president.

These approaches were quite different behaviorally from the control system existing when the acquired unit was independent, and its top managers were responsible either to themselves as owners, or to a board of directors supposedly representing stockholders. Both post-merger control approaches can lead to difficulties, especially when problems arise and cause disappointing earnings performance. The possibilities here are very complex, because what happens depends at least as much on individual personalities as on formal organizational structures. For perspective, it must be emphasized that sometimes the control mechanisms worked well, even under stress. Here we accentuate the negative with illustrations from our case studies.

When an "outsider" is installed as chief executive to represent parent interests, two main (often interrelated) problems can occur. One is that there is resentment on the part of incumbents in the acquired unit. Morale suffers, and turnover of experienced operating executives and staff may accelerate. These problems need not happen, especially when the outsider has strong interpersonal relations skills, as three of the early outside appointees covered by our case studies did. But in other cases, the outsiders proved inept in this important respect and were seen by inside staff as authoritarian, threatening, and unsympathetic. Morale and motivation consequently suffered. Second and perhaps more important, at least in our sample, it appeared rare for an outsider to be able to take charge of a new and complex business and quickly master the nuances of its operation.[6] As long as things were going well, this lacuna

6. According to management consultant and philosopher Peter Drucker, "three out of four managers from outside do not prove out, partly because there is such a thing as a corporate culture. . . . The fellow who believes he is transferable is guaranteed to come a cropper." "Why Some Mergers Work and Many More Don't," *Forbes*, January 18, 1982, p. 36. In an interview, business school professor H. Edward Wrapp noted that the conglomerates "assumed that the staff at headquarters would know if something was wrong in one of the businesses. But many times the staff did not recognize the early symptoms of problems . . . until they were in deep trouble. The managers made another very important assumption—that if you were a successful manager in one company, you could be a successful manager in another. So they kept moving general

was not a serious problem. But when latent or new problems became acute, there was a risk of dangerously delayed or flawed reactions. Thus, in one company that experienced mounting difficulties, much of the blame was attributable to an externally imposed unit head who "had no idea how to run an [industry suppressed] company" and whose autocratic behavior drove many experienced executives out and alienated others to the point where rational problem-solving broke down. In another troubled company, a series of outsider managers were skilled in general managerial knowledge and interpersonal relations, but they met "considerable resistance from the old guard" and failed to acquire a finely honed instinct for their business' intricacies, making (and in interviews admitting having made) a number of serious errors as a consequence. As an "insider" executive of the same firm observed bitterly, "What is wrong with our company is MBAs who think they can manage anything without knowing anything about the company, who insist upon profits immediately, and who are dissatisfied if the profits don't continue growing from year to year."

When control is exercised over acquired subsidiaries primarily through a reporting link to corporate management, other problems can arise. To exercise just the right amount of managerial control over a subsidiary is extremely difficult. It is easy to err on either side of the optimum. In one case, the key controlling role was performed by a corporate official who so awed his subordinates that "no one could stand up to him." That individual had strong opinions inconsistent with the analyses and recommendations coming from acquired division executives confronted with escalating business problems. Interviews with the various parties made it clear that divisional management never really "got through" to corporate management, despite many meetings, and as a result, timely corrective measures were not undertaken. In another case, a strong but more open corporate head showed unusual sensitivity to divisional problems. Among other things, he settled a transfer pricing conflict between a division covered by our case studies and another division. When he was replaced by a much weaker person, however, the two divisions fell to quarreling again, no rapprochement could be worked out, and the profitability of the originating division was seriously impaired by the loss of business with its sister division.

Particularly delicate is the relationship of group or similar vice

managers around like players on a chess board, and then all of a sudden the businesses started to fall apart." "Don't Blame the System, Blame the Managers," *Dun's Review*, vol. 116 (September 1980), p. 82.

presidents to the operating units under their span of control. If things are going well at the operating level, the best thing for the group executive to do is nothing—except administer occasional doses of praise. To be nominally in control of a business unit and to refrain from active intervention, however, requires a strong sense of self. Weaker personalities are inclined to meddle simply to demonstrate their authority. In one of our sample cases, such intervention without good cause had catastrophic effects, driving out well-motivated operating-level managers and creating a climate of hostility that explained many of the unit's subsequent difficulties. When genuine operating problems do arise, the group executive should presumably intervene, but intervening effectively is not easy. There are two basic pitfalls. The group executive almost always knows much less about the details of the division's problems than operating-level managers, and there is little point in belaboring the obvious when operators realize they are in trouble. Group executive intervention is consequently perceived by operators as nagging over profit figures, nit-picking about operational details peripheral to the real problem, and harassing in general. When this happens, as it did in at least four and (to a less marked degree) two others of our case studies, a hostility dynamic unfolds, morale and motivation decline, problems go unresolved, and when operating managers have alternatives, they resign.[7]

The difficulties of maintaining control and motivation simultaneously when serious operating problems emerge are so great that direct supervisory intervention may be a strategy advisable only when interpersonal relations are abnormally favorable. Under more normal circumstances, it may be preferable for corporate management to refrain from intervening except by asking what it can do to help, to observe with cultivated patience whether the problems are being solved, and if in due course they are not, to replace the operating-level managers. Yet this is a gamble, since it may be hard to find replacements with the necessary ability and knowledge, and outsiders with a poor understanding of a complex business can do more harm than good when they are brought

7. A survey of executive retention patterns revealed that 68 percent of the top executives who left their acquired units after major acquisitions said the new parent exercised substantial control over their operations, whereas only 10 percent of those who remained viewed the parent's control as substantial. Robert H. Hayes, "What Happens to My People After I Sell?" in Steven James Lee and Robert Douglas Colman, eds., *Handbook of Mergers, Acquisitions, and Buyouts* (Prentice-Hall, 1981), p. 133.

in at a time of crisis. Recognizing this, one is forced into grudging admiration for the conglomerate subsidiary management strategy pursued during the 1970s by Beatrice Foods: if the problems of an acquired unit persist for several quarters, don't intervene operationally, sell the unit off.

The Influence of Corporate Financial Objectives

Assiduously watching "the numbers," either to guide cajoling and active intervention or to trigger sell-off, carries its own set of dangers. Many parents of acquired operating units placed considerable emphasis on the attainment of short-run profit and/or cash-flow objectives. Beatrice Foods had perhaps the clearest, although not necessarily the most stringent, policy. It communicated in no uncertain terms to operating-level managers its pride in an almost unbroken record of corporate profits rising each quarter, and it indicated that operating unit failure to conform to this pattern would not be taken lightly. Such an emphasis on short-run performance can create problems and aggravate difficulties that have emerged for other reasons.

Lykes's demand for a sizable continuing cash flow from its Youngstown Sheet & Tube subsidiary was a major contributor to the capital investment stringencies that left critical bottlenecks unbroken, impairing Youngstown's profitability, and prevented Youngstown from bringing its older plants up to a level of modernization that might have permitted them to survive a competitive struggle. Textron's insistence upon an ambitious rate of return on the investment it had already made in Talon, and on new physical investment proposals, interacted with internal Talon problems to leave the zipper maker incapable of stemming increasingly strenuous competition from Japanese rival YKK. In other acquired units covered by our case studies, the parent's stress on short-run results, or its decision to treat the subsidiary as a cash cow, led to scrimping on equipment maintenance (which eventually impaired operating efficiency), a failure to discontinue losing product lines because the immediate write-off to earnings was weighed more heavily than eventual profit gains, a failure to take advantage of one-shot profit-making opportunities because they would raise targets for subsequent accounting periods, and a failure to make strategic investments that could have reversed a deteriorating situation. In other instances, a combination of tight financial constraints and active corporate intervention in unit decisionmaking led to "penny-wise, pound-foolish" choices. For example, in one company, selling the product to industrial users required regional sales personnel with considerable technical sophistication. The market for individuals with such skills was tight, calling for compensation (salary plus bonus) higher than what corporate finance staff members earned. Corporate staff refused to permit offering the needed salary packages, in effect mandating that the job be done by less-skilled individuals incapable of building or even maintaining the division's sales.

Several parent firms followed more or less consciously a "portfolio" strategy, attempting to channel funds from cash-rich, slowly growing lines toward more rapidly growing lines with high prospective returns on investment.[8] The trouble with this strategy is that it assumes status as a cash cow to be both exogenous and event-invariant. Neither assumption held up well for our sample. A business unit's profitability and growth depend at least as much on how well it is managed as upon exogenous circumstances. Treating a unit as a cash cow can so demoralize the unit's management that profitable growth opportunities are not sought actively, and such treatment may, as in the Chromalloy Glass, Great Lakes Screw, and (in its late stages only) Sintercast cases, convert what would be a profitable if slow-growing venture into a lagging "dog." Also, today's stars may become tomorrow's dogs, as Lykes, Chromalloy, and AMF discovered when the transportation and oil field equipment businesses to which they consciously diverted their cash flow suddenly, because of unanticipated events, turned unprofitable.

Certain other detailed financial controls were merely burdensome or silly rather than counter-productive. Examples include the insistence on three- to ten-year plans in intrinsically volatile businesses, and the maintenance of tight controls on capital expenditures in operations of low capital intensity, but in which millions could easily be squandered through unwise materials procurement (subjected to no ex ante higher-level control).

Needless to say, financial crisis at the corporate level can have repercussions that make it more difficult for operating units to solve their problems. INCO in particular, experiencing a depression of the

8. On the relevant theory, see Bruce D. Henderson, *Henderson on Corporate Strategy* (Cambridge, Mass.: Abt Books, 1979), especially pp. 82–85 and 163–66; and George A. Steiner, *Strategic Planning: What Every Manager Must Know* (Free Press, 1979), chap. 9.

world nickel market and the consequences of huge overseas nickel mine investments that had to be mothballed, was in no position to help its ESB subsidiary retool and produce the new kinds of batteries toward which the market had turned. Lykes's ability to support modernization by Youngstown Sheet & Tube was constrained by heavy debt and preferred stock servicing obligations and (in 1976 and 1977) sharply declining ocean shipping income.

What Went Right

Our task has been to explain what went wrong and led to the divestiture of previously acquired businesses. Many things did go wrong, and they had much to do with subsequent sell-off decisions. Yet it would be misleading to suggest that all of our sample divestitures were the result of correctable self-inflicted wounds.

In two cases (Robert Bruce and Letisse), parent corporation management was satisfied with the unit's performance. In several others, the parent-subsidiary interaction had significant positive consequences, even though in the end it was concluded that unsolved problems warranted divestiture. Gulf & Western made an important contribution to the financing of Marquette's new Cape Girardeau, Missouri, cement plant while maintaining what all interviewees considered an enlightened management oversight relationship. The business cycle setbacks that led to sell-off were beyond either party's control. AMF financed and guided a substantial expansion of Harley Davidson's output and left its sold-off unit with a legacy of a nearly completed new motorcycle line development program. Philip Morris revamped ASR's management, brought in new technical talent, retooled its plant for successful stainless steel razor blade production, and left ASR strongly positioned in the private label and women's razor markets, even if not in the larger branded blade market toward which original business plans were targeted. And when the initial negotiations to sell S. S. White were concluded, White had a modern plant and a dominant position in dental burs, even though it was bruised and weakened in several other lines.

Our case study sample was selected without a deliberate slant regarding subsidiary or parent success. Partly because of this "performance blind" approach, but also because it had few recorded sell-offs, the most successful leading conglomerate parent by stock market standards—Teledyne—was not included. As we saw in chapter 2, an investor who bought Teledyne stock at $1,000 in mid-1965 and held on would have had a cumulated value of $65,463 in 1983. Even an investment made at the conglomerate merger wave's peak in 1968 would have increased 8.5 times in value by 1983.

To remedy an evident gap on "what went right," published sources on the history and management of Teledyne were analyzed.[9] Several insights stand out:

1. Many of the early acquisitions made after Teledyne's founding in 1960 were in high-technology fields, with strong growth potential. Only later did diversification into such areas as insurance, banking, and oil field services follow.

2. Teledyne's organization was similar to that of many other acquisitive conglomerates: a small corporate staff monitored the performance of approximately 130 operating units. But Teledyne was unique in loading its top management and board of directors with scientists and engineers possessing advanced degrees.

3. Teledyne headquarters imposed upon its operating units stringent cash-flow planning and monitoring—as strict as in any of the conglomerates covered by our case studies.

4. Teledyne operating-level managers were given considerable freedom "as long as they perform."[10] However, the company was said to be quick and ruthless in dismissing managers who failed to meet performance goals. And units in trouble were subjected to intense scrutiny by top management, including approval of payrolls by the president and detailed involvement by the chairman in decisions as to which branch offices of an insurance subsidiary would be closed and how the insurer's cash portfolio would be invested.[11]

5. Few divisions are known to have plunged into problems warranting

9. Useful analyses include: "Making Big Waves with Small Fish," *Business Week*, December 30, 1967, pp. 36–39; "Is Teledyne's Cash an Embarrassment?" *Business Week*, March 1, 1976, p. 20; "Two PhDs Turn Teledyne into a Cash Machine," *Business Week*, November 22, 1976, pp. 133–39; A. F. Ehrbar, "Henry Singleton's Mystifying $400–Million Flyer," *Fortune*, January 16, 1978, pp. 66–76; Robert J. Flaherty, "The Sphinx Speaks," *Forbes*, February 20, 1978, pp. 33–35; Flaherty, "The Singular Henry Singleton," *Forbes*, July 9, 1979, pp. 45–50; Steve Kichen, "Teledyne's Winning Roster," *Forbes*, August 17, 1981, pp. 35–36; "A Strategy Hooked to Cash Is Faltering," *Business Week*, May 31, 1982, pp. 58–62; and Nicholas D. Kristof, "Teledyne's Singleton To Yield One Top Post," *New York Times*, April 24, 1986.

10. "Two PhDs Turn Teledyne," p. 136.

11. Ibid., p. 133; and "A Strategy Hooked to Cash," p. 64.

such detailed intervention, and operating-level management turnover was reported to be low.[12]

6. Partly because of this, sell-off of Teledyne units was rare. When parts of operating divisions were in serious trouble, closure of the impacted operations, rather than sell-off, was the preferred solution.

7. Teledyne's philosophy during the 1970s was to treat most or all of its operating units as cash cows, expected to return net cash to corporate headquarters. Because of this, it was claimed, company spending on research and development was lower than all-manufacturing norms, despite the firm's high-technology orientation, and other investments were said to have been slighted, leading to market share erosion in several key businesses by the early 1980s.[13]

8. When its stock price plunged in 1969, Teledyne virtually ceased making acquisitions for the next 13 years. Instead, it focused on improving its effectiveness as an operating company and, more confident than the stock market of its eventual success, it repurchased 75 percent of its outstanding common stock and reduced its debt to conservative levels during the 1970s.

9. Beginning in the mid-1970s, Teledyne invested insurance subsidiary revenues and then the excess cash flow of its other operating units in the common stocks of other corporations, often conglomerates, whose shares Teledyne management considered undervalued by the stock market. Although Teledyne's ownership interest exceeded 35 percent of the equity of some targets, it avoided seeking control because of the substantial premiums required for full takeover. At the end of 1984, more than half its assets consisted of such investments.

10. In the 25 years of its existence through 1985, Teledyne paid no cash dividends, insisting that it could reinvest its cash flow (without the double taxation on dividends) more profitably than shareholders could.

Clearly, Teledyne was similar to the conglomerates covered by our case studies in some important respects and quite different in other respects. How one sorts out the similarities and differences to explain its success is problematic. Perhaps the most extraordinary feature of the Teledyne history is the infrequency of reported operating unit performance failures. It is unclear whether this was the result of unusually good luck; the impressive ability of its chairman, who reigned through

12. Compare Flaherty, "The Sphinx Speaks," p. 35, and "The Singular Henry Singleton," p. 48.
13. "A Strategy Hooked to Cash," pp. 58–64.

the first 26 years of the company's existence, and the aides he picked and motivated; the company's penchant for secrecy concerning detailed internal operations; or some other combination of circumstances. It is also uncertain whether the reported cash-cow treatment of operating units will eventually undermine their strength. The most that can be said is that what we observed in our case studies—festering problems resolved only through sell-off—is not an inevitable concomitant of aggressive conglomerate diversification. On this cautionary note, we proceed to our analysis of the case study sample members' sell-off experiences.

The Sell-Off Decision

Some combination of unresolved problems—latent, exogenous, and/or self-inflicted—with a failure of the acquired unit to satisfy the parent corporation's financial goals was a crucial element in the decision to divest most of our case study members.[14] In 11 cases—ASR, Bendix Home Products, Caradco, Sintercast, Chromalloy Glass, ESB, Great Lakes Screw, Harman, Talon, S. S. White, and Youngstown—it was probably the most important specific underlying cause. In two others, Harley Davidson and Marquette, the impetus came not so much from what had happened in the past as from the expectation of problems and depressed returns in the future. In the two remaining cases, corporate management was satisfied with the performance of Robert Bruce and Letisse, but suffered from problems like those analyzed here in several related units. Once they decided to divest those businesses, a fear of new problems in the future and a desire for organizational tidiness led them also to exit the broad field (in both cases, fashion-sensitive consumer goods) altogether, shedding the winners along with the losers.

Many of our sample member divestitures were part of wider-sweeping parent efforts to prune their corporate trees. Consolidated Foods, Bendix, Chromalloy American, U.S. Industries, Beatrice, W. R. Grace, Gulf & Western, and Textron each made dozens of divestitures during the late 1970s and early 1980s. Underlying the sell-off decisions of sample

14. Similarly, Irene M. Duhaime and John H. Grant found in interviews with 40 corporations concerning 59 divestitures, that at the time of sell-off 40 percent of the divested units were sustaining losses and 44 percent had unacceptably low profits. "Factors Influencing Divestment Decision-Making: Evidence from a Field Study," *Strategic Management Journal*, vol. 5 (October-December 1984), pp. 301–18.

parents were certain broader rationales as well as the unit-specific problems analyzed previously.

For one, most of the companies that had pursued conglomerate growth with abandon in the 1960s came to realize during the 1970s that they could not manage anything and everything well. There was virtue in specialization, they learned—if not in narrow product lines, then at least in broad areas that demanded similar technical and marketing skills. This realization came in part from the kinds of corporate headquarters–subsidiary control problems analyzed here and the aggravated performance failures that followed in their wake. It was reinforced by the verdict of the stock market, which had been entranced by conglomerates during the 1960s, but fell out of love in the early to mid-1970s.[15]

A second consideration leading to sell-off was that large corporations, conglomerate and otherwise, learned that the costs of managing small subsidiaries might be too high to justify the realizable gains. As one group vice president put it, management talent is scarce, and a three-day trip to work on an operation with sales of $10 million offered less potential gain than three days spent at a $100 million unit. In another company, corporate managers came to view small units as a "bother." A third company's small division characterized itself as "a flea on an elephant's tail."

In more cases than not, these alterations in corporate views as to how diversified they should be and what businesses they should maintain followed changes in top management—notably, when the executive responsible for a conglomerate acquisition spurt, or for particular acquisitions, departed. Certain divestitures were also motivated by event-driven changes in a chief executive's view of the macroeconomic environment—for example, as Gulf & Western chairman Charles Bluhdorn shifted from optimism to pessimism on the prospects for resource-based industries like portland cement.

Finally, chance events sometimes play a key triggering role in the sell-off decision. Philip Morris was more or less resigned to retaining ASR indefinitely, despite the unit's relatively insignificant size and

15. See the analysis accompanying fig. 2–2. AMF, Bendix, Lykes, and Pennwalt were clearly conglomerates, but had too few acquisitions to be included among the 13 leading conglomerates analyzed in chap. 2. The combined value of $1,000 investments in each of the four during 1965 would have risen to $7,070 in 1968—a smaller percentage gain than for the 13 leading conglomerates. In 1974, the value of an original $4,000 investment would have been $4,777.

disappointing profits, had Bic Pen not come forward and proposed a purchase. When the transaction was blocked by antitrust action, Philip Morris, having made the hard decision to divest, carried it through to an unanticipated buyout by management. And although Bendix was ready to sell its Home Systems Division almost from the moment it was acquired, it waited for six years in a thin, often depressed market until an interested potential buyer took the initiative and proposed a deal.

The "Lemons" Problem

Clearly, many sell-offs are products of a troubled environment. This suggests a puzzle. If our sample is representative, potential buyers must know there is a substantial probability of taking on problems that have defied previous solution and that pose appreciable risks. Although the buyer of a sell-off is put on warning, even the most careful inspection may not disclose all the pitfalls, for as we have seen, latent problems are hard to discover, and some may have remained latent. A variant of the classic "lemons" problem arises.[16] If a unit's profits are depressed and if there is reason to believe no turnaround is in sight, the prudent would-be buyer should bid at most the discounted present value of a continuing stream of depressed profits, discounted further to reflect the possibility that the situation may deteriorate even more. But if the would-be seller sees that it can obtain no more for an ailing subsidiary than the discounted present value of the profits with which it is already disappointed, and perhaps less, why should it sell? Why not hang on and make the best of a bad situation—unless the situation is even worse than outside inspection is likely to disclose? If prospective buyers perceive this, they will bid so cautiously that sellers will find it worthwhile to retain all but the most (secretly) hopeless of their ailing subsidiaries. The market for sell-offs may implode.

This sell-off market problem is quite different from the inspection and bidding problem on "new" or first-time acquisitions. There are many "normal" reasons why the managers of an independent firm may want to secure more diversified or liquid ownership, and there are many good new firms on the merger market. Despite the risk, and in part because of it, the acquirer may consider itself to enjoy a reasonable likelihood of

16. See George A. Akerlof, "The Market for 'Lemons': Quality Uncertainty and the Market Mechanism," *Quarterly Journal of Economics*, vol. 84 (August 1970), pp. 488–500.

making an advantageous buy. But when one buys a sell-off, one must be especially wary of the seller's motives, for only the overvalued cases may be let go.

Although there is in principle a dilemma here, it is easily resolved. The market for problem-ridden subsidiaries will thrive if there is a substantial class of potential buyers who can do a better job solving the sell-off candidates' problems, and hence expect to receive from their operation higher after-tax profits, than the incumbent parents. We shall see momentarily that this has almost surely been true.[17]

Accounting and Market Valuation Consequences

Whether the existence of such potential buyers is the entire explanation for the lively sell-off market is less certain. Even when buyers are expected to have no advantages in operating a poorly performing unit, parents may wish to sell the unit off because of their desire to "clean up the balance sheet."

Suppose a unit's current and anticipated performance implies a stream of after-tax cash flows, for either the incumbent parent or a prospective buyer, with a net discounted present value of $10 million, which is only one-fourth the unit's net accounting book value (that is, assets less assumable liabilities) of $40 million. Assuming other parts of the parent's operations to be healthy, the unit's depressed profits will pull down overall corporate returns on stockholders' equity. If the unit is sold off, the buyer will pay at most $10 million for it. When the sale is recorded in the parent's books, relevant assets and liabilities will be written off, and there will be a one-time charge against stockholders' equity of approximately $30 million. With healthy profits in the future and $30 million less stockholders' equity, the parent's return on stockholders' equity (or on assets) will rise to "normal" levels. The sell-off is analogous to having an impacted wisdom tooth extracted: there is an interval of pain, and then one lives happily ever after.

How painful the nonrecurring charge interval is depends in part upon

17. It is important to recall from table 4-4 that, on average, the profitability of *PART* lines—those acquired through another firm's divisional sell-off—was 4.8 percentage points lower than on other purchase accounting acquisitions. Evidently, second-order acquirers overestimated their ability to improve matters and/or paid too high an acquisition price, even though that price may have been lower than the seller's book value.

how the stock market reacts. If share prices fall permanently to reflect the reduction of stockholders' equity, the pain may be both severe and nontransitory. But there is no reason to believe this will happen.[18] If "the market" sees through what is going on, the parent's stock price will fall when the sell-off candidate gets into trouble and experiences an anticipated depression of the net present value of its cash flows to $10 million, and this should happen well in advance of the sell-off per se, with its accompanying accounting adjustments. If subsidiary problems are recognized and anticipated by the market, there should be *no* fall in share prices when a sell-off at discounted present value occurs. To be sure, if the sell-off is made at "fire sale" prices below the discounted present value of cash flows from hanging on to the unit, stock prices should fall at the time of sale (or at the announcement that a fire sale will follow). But this effect may be of second-order magnitude, too small for analysts and investors to discern and act upon in the confusion that accompanies trouble in a subsidiary and the unit's eventual sell-off on terms often left vague in public announcements.

Whether sell-off announcements are in fact painful in the sense that they precipitate stock price declines is an empirical question. The weight of evidence suggests a fairly uniform tendency for stock prices to rise, not fall, at the time a voluntary sell-off (as we have used the term) is announced.[19] Not surprisingly, significant effects are more likely to be detected when the sell-off is large in relation to the divesting firm's total market value. April Klein found in addition that positive stock price increases were associated mainly with cases in which the parent announced the amount being paid by the new acquirer.[20] She hypothesized (with negative empirical results) that the transaction price announcement

18. An exception might occur if the write-off breaches equity coverage restrictions in loan contracts, inhibiting future financing.

19. See Kenneth J. Boudreaux, "Divestiture and Share Price," *Journal of Financial and Quantitative Analysis*, vol. 10 (November 1975, *Papers and Proceedings, 1975*), pp. 619–26; Gordon J. Alexander, P. George Benson, and Joan M. Kampmeyer, "Investigating the Valuation Effects of Announcements of Voluntary Corporate Sell-offs," *Journal of Finance*, vol. 39 (June 1984), pp. 503–17; James D. Rosenfeld, "Additional Evidence on the Relation Between Divestiture Announcements and Shareholder Wealth," *Journal of Finance*, vol. 39 (December 1984), pp. 1437–48; and Prem C. Jain, "The Effect of Voluntary Sell-off Announcements on Shareholder Wealth," *Journal of Finance*, vol. 40 (March 1985), pp. 209–24.

20. April Klein, "The Timing and Substance of Divestiture Announcements: Individual, Simultaneous, and Cumulative Effects," *Journal of Finance*, vol. 41 (July 1986, *Papers and Proceedings, 1985*), pp. 685–96.

signaled a higher likelihood that the sell-off would actually occur. An alternative hypothesis consistent with our case study research is that management is reluctant to disclose "fire sale" prices unless forced to do so because the divested unit and its problems attracted special investor interest, in which case news of an impending fire sale is likely to have leaked out in advance. Further stock price research using the large sample of sell-offs studied in the next chapter is contemplated as a follow-on project to the work reported in this book.

That sell-offs cause some pain to management is suggested by evidence from our case studies. Managers do not like the admission of failure a special sell-off charge implies. If incentive compensation formulas are linked to a "bottom line" below the "nonrecurring losses" line, managers' pay is also adversely affected. When an ailing unit's troubles have not reached the crisis stage, companies often appear to follow a crude stopping rule: hold on until a buyer comes along who is willing to pay book value (and hence requires no nonrecurring charge). Or they use the book value as a focal point in price negotiations. In at least four of our case studies, sell-off prices were quite close to book values. On the other hand, in eight cases, conditions had deteriorated so seriously, and/ or the sales were made in such haste, that special nonrecurring charges resulted.

Developments after Sell-Off

We move on now to ask what happened after the businesses in our sample were sold off. We shall be especially concerned with ascertaining whether the buyers were somehow better able to solve the units' problems and operate them more profitably than the original parents.

Table 5-3 provides a summary of salient buyer characteristics. The change in organizational patterns is striking. At the outset, by sample design, all 15 case study members stood in a conglomerate relationship to their parent; that is, the parent was either an acknowledged conglomerate, or the parent's original lines of business were quite different from that of our case study subject. After sell-off, only three conglomerate relationships remained for the main survivors (in what were sometimes multiple divestitures). Robert Bruce was the first acquisition of a new leveraged buyout venture group that later acquired a toy maker and a real estate developer; Bethlehem Steel acquired Caradco through a

Table 5-3. *Characteristics of New Buyers in Fifteen Sell-Off Cases*

Divested unit	Buyer characteristics
A.S.R. Products Corp.	Leveraged buyout by management
Bendix Home Systems	Leveraged market-extension acquisition
Robert Bruce	Leveraged buyout by conglomerate venture holding company
Caradco Corp.	Product-line extension by conglomerate subsidiary
Chromalloy Glass Products	Numerous management buyouts and one market-extension acquisition
ESB	Numerous leveraged buyouts by venture groups and management
Great Lakes Screw	Horizontal acquisition
Harley Davidson Motor Co.	Leveraged buyout by management
Harman International Industries	Buyout by former manager, one vertical acquisition
Letisse	Acquisition by miniconglomerate
Marquette Cement	Market-extension acquisition
Sintercast	Leveraged buyout by management
Talon	Leveraged buyout by interim management, one vertical acquisition
S. S. White Co.	Buyout by former head of another dental equipment manufacturer (subsequently undone)
Youngstown Sheet & Tube Co.	Horizontal acquisition (ignoring Lykes component, subsequently spun off)

conglomerate subsidiary that used marketing channels similar to Caradco's; and Letisse was acquired by a three-field miniconglomerate, which proceeded then to buy two additional leather goods companies complementary to Letisse. In eight cases, the principal divested entities moved from conglomerate ownership to being single-line specialists, usually with their managers (and in a large subset, the same managers as in their conglomerate subsidiary days) holding a substantial equity interest. All eight cases as well as Robert Bruce were typical of the leveraged buyouts that soared to prominence in the United States during the early 1980s. In the remaining four cases, the sample member's acquisition was for the acquirer a horizontal merger or an only slightly different "market extension" merger, that is, one in which the acquirer and the acquired company offer the same products in different geographic markets.

Horizontal Merger Efficiencies

At least three of the four essentially horizontal acquisitions yielded efficiencies apparently unattainable in the original conglomerate organizational framework. A full description is provided in appendix B; here a brief synopsis must suffice.

Perhaps the most important contribution made by LTV's Jones & Laughlin Steel Company to Youngstown Sheet & Tube was the infusion of competent, highly motivated management that cracked production bottlenecks, instituted better production scheduling, and began a drive to improve badly eroded labor relations. In addition, complementarities among adjacent J&L and Youngstown plants were exploited, most notably to implement greater rolling mill specialization and the use of lower-cost hot-metal capacity in making seamless steel tubes. Costs were also reduced by closing Youngstown's headquarters and paring field sales forces. Iron and coke procurement savings claimed as a consequence of the merger stemmed from apparent market failures reflecting the unwillingness or inability of steel makers to buy raw materials at arm's length from more conveniently located competitors with excess capacity.[21]

With the merger of Lone Star Cement and Marquette Cement, headquarters staff costs were cut. Savings were also realized by coordinating the production of geographically linked plants to utilize low-cost kilns more fully and achieve greater product specialization.

The Commodore Corporation closed Bendix Home Systems' headquarters, consolidating the central office's functions at a new, lower-cost site. To tap a larger market, it offered product design changes Bendix had been unwilling to make. Plant rationalization was inhibited by the typically large distances between Commodore and Bendix plants and the high costs of shipping manufactured homes.

Allied Products' efficiency gain from acquiring Great Lakes Screw was least impressive of the four horizontal cases. Great Lakes' plant was closed following the acquisition. It is unclear why Allied could not have purchased only the machinery it moved to another plant, along with the patent Great Lakes held on an exclusive product. The acquisition of what was left of Great Lakes' customer goodwill was undoubtedly viewed as a benefit by Allied, although gains of this sort are zero-sum in a broader sense, offset by equal sales losses of either a continuing Great Lakes operation or, assuming shutdown to be unavoidable, Allied's remaining competitors.

It is probably coincidental that despite their cost-reducing efforts, all

21. See F. M. Scherer and others, *The Economics of Multi-Plant Operation: An International Comparisons Study* (Harvard University Press, 1975), pp. 264–66 and 386–88.

four preponderantly horizontal sell-offs covered by our case studies experienced severe financial stress following the transfer of control. All four, supplying products in the capital goods sector that are interest rate sensitive, were hit hard by the monetary policies and recessions of the early 1980s. LTV-J&L-Youngstown was driven into bankruptcy by the post-merger collapse of demand for seamless oil well tubing—the most important product the two companies manufactured in common. Low capacity utilization and financial pressures led Lone Star subsequently to sell off Marquette's principal plants in the Northeast. Commodore was forced into filing for bankruptcy in 1985, and, as we have seen, Great Lakes Screw's plant was closed.

The nonhorizontal acquisition of Caradco by Bethlehem Steel's Kusan Division was expected also to increase Caradco's sales and capacity utilization by tapping complementary distribution channels, although this had not been accomplished four years later. Whether Kusan would succeed better than Scovill and Bendix in solving quality control and labor productivity problems remained uncertain at the time our main interviews were concluded.

The Motivational Consequences of Leveraged Buyouts

Our sample includes numerous leveraged buyout cases. Because the phenomenon was relatively new and quantitatively important, considerable research effort was devoted to ascertaining how behavior changed as sample units were reorganized from conglomerate subsidiary status into a leveraged buyout form.[22]

As its name suggests, a leveraged buyout is a reorganization in the ownership of a business unit to a corporate financial structure with a high degree of leverage. Characteristically, borrowing provides 75 to 90 percent of the capital structure (other than current accounts payable) and common stock equity the balance, in contrast to the 30/70 debt/ equity average prevailing for all U.S. manufacturing corporations in

22. See Nicholas Wallner, "Leveraged Buyouts: A Review of the State of the Art, Part I," *Mergers & Acquisitions*, vol. 14 (Fall 1979), pp. 4–13, and vol. 15 (Winter 1980), pp. 16–26; "Who's Who in Buyout Financing," *Venture*, August 1983, pp. 102–04; "A Leveraged Buyout: What It Takes," *Business Week*, July 18, 1983, pp. 194–98; Irwin Ross, "How the Champs Do Leveraged Buyouts," *Fortune*, January 23, 1984, pp. 70–78; and "Leveraged-Buyout Empires," *New York Times*, August 5, 1985. On the parallel British experience, see Mike Wright and John Coyne, *Management Buy-Outs* (London: Croom Helm, 1985).

1980. Thus, the capital structure of leveraged buyouts is more like that of the typical Japanese industrial enterprise than of U.S. corporations. In most but not all cases, the unit's managers are among the principal equity holders. Indeed, one reason for the high reliance on outside borrowing is to permit managers with limited capital to have an important ownership stake in the enterprise they control. The number of common stockholders is usually small, and in most cases the stocks are not publicly traded, so leveraged buyout managers are spared the burdens of security registration, publicity, and large-scale investor relations borne by more conventionally financed industrial corporations.

The most obvious attractions of the leveraged buyout, then, are a close coupling of ownership and control, with its presumed incentive-altering effects, and some ability to escape the goldfish bowl of day-to-day stock market price fluctuations. In addition, four important tax advantages may be realized. First, most of the financing is provided by debt, whose interest payments are tax-deductible, rather than stock, whose dividends provide no shield from corporate income taxation. Given the differences in tax treatment, debt is normally (at least infra-marginally) a lower-cost mode of financing than equity. Second, if the enterprise does well, its anticipated future earnings can be capitalized and sold (through stock issues or mergers), and the owner-managers could (until 1987) capture the fruits of their effort largely in the form of lightly taxed capital gains rather than more heavily taxed dividend payout. Third, under a leveraged buyout (but also under more conventional company purchases), if a premium above original book value is paid, the buyer can "step up" the value of assets and then depreciate that higher value, gaining a depreciation shield against income taxes larger than that enjoyed by the original owner. Since our case study businesses were not sold at substantial premiums over book value, this feature was not significant in the acquisitions studied. Fourth, and also with or without leveraging, a purchase of assets after the enactment of major U.S. tax law changes in 1981 allowed buyers in many instances to adopt shorter depreciation lives than were applicable for the original owner, and hence to enjoy larger early depreciation shields. This leads, all else equal, to higher after-tax cash flows, at least in the early years following the buyout.

There is a well-known scarcity of free lunches, and leveraged buyouts are no exception. For a given amount of capital raised, heavy debt financing imposes larger mandatory capital service payments than under equity-intensive financing, since dividends on common stock can be waived without default in a pinch, whereas debt interest cannot. If sales decline or costs rise so that net cash flows turn out to be much lower than anticipated, the risk of default and possible bankruptcy is greater with high leverage. This is in itself a cost, even if only psychic, to the leveraged buyout equity holders. Also, recognizing the smaller equity cushion and greater risk of default, unsecured lenders demand a risk premium in the interest rates they charge leveraged buyouts. For the short-term component of our sample members' debt structures, premiums above prime rate of one-half to three percentage points were common. Also, because of unusually turbulent capital market conditions during the early 1980s, the leveraged buyouts we studied bore appreciable risks that, say, the 14 percent interest rate initially negotiated on short-term loans could suddenly be rolled over into a 20 percent or higher rate.

The behavioral effects of moving from conglomerate ownership to this high-risk, high-potential-gain environment were striking. Cost-cutting opportunities that had previously gone unexploited were seized. Austere offices were substituted for lavish ones. Staffs were cut back sharply. New and more cost-effective field sales organizations were adopted. Inexpensive computer services were found to substitute for expensive in-house operations. Make versus buy decisions were re-evaluated, and lower-cost alternatives were embraced. Efforts were made to improve labor-management relations by removing bureaucratic constraints that had been imposed by the previous conglomerate's headquarters. Tight inventory controls were implemented, cutting holding costs by as much as one-half. Low-volume items were pruned from product lines to trim inventories and reduce production set-up costs. Tighter control was exercised over accounts receivable. There were also a few staff increases—notably, to monitor all-important cash flows more tightly. And in one case, key managers were paid more than before the buyout in the expectation that they would perform better. Still our case studies left no doubt that the change in incentives under a leveraged buyout led to tighter cost control than had been prevalent before.[23]

23. Likewise, Wright and Coyne, in *Management Buy-Outs*, reported substantial improvements in British units' operations following buyouts, 61 percent of which came from parent firm divestitures. Of 34 cases in which the reorganized firm had survived for two years or more (p. 144), only 23.6 percent experienced a decline in profits while 38 percent achieved substantial stable growth of profits. The managing director of the first buyout to be listed on the London Stock Exchange claimed (p. 2), "Without the

Not all cost reductions are unambiguous blessings. There is a danger that the strong incentives to maximize current cash flow will lead to scrimping on "costs" that are really investments in future strength: for example, on equipment maintenance, research and development, and advertising.[24] Although the evidence was not completely consistent, such a tendency was revealed by our case studies. Several leveraged buyouts cut equipment investment appreciably, more because of compelling cash constraints than out of a deliberate trade-off sacrificing future for current benefits. In only one case, where the buyer acquired a particularly well-equipped and well-maintained plant, were the investment reductions considered innocuous. A consumer goods company cut its advertising budget by two-thirds and decided to "harvest" its best-accepted product, that is, to let the product's market share be eroded by lower-quality rival brands. In five engineering-oriented companies, R&D budgets were cut back—in two cases totally, in one case sharply, and in another through the stretch-out of ongoing projects. However, in one medium-technology company, the R&D budget was increased substantially in the belief that important sales opportunities had been sacrificed under the conglomerate's mantle. In a second situation, the engineering budget was increased to rescind some of the sharp cuts made before the sell-off took place. In another case, managerial staff reductions were so severe that doubts were expressed as to whether the company could continue to control its operations adequately over the longer run. Most of the interviewees who had made such cuts expressed unease and hope that, once their debt burdens became lighter through repayments, they would be able to invest more in future-building activities.

Most of the leveraged buyouts in our case study sample had a past history of trouble and low or negative profits. All came into being during, or just before, a period of unprecedented interest rate levels and volatility. By the time of our interviews, some had already survived

---

buy-out we would not have achieved what we did because the motivation would not have been the same." Another chief executive officer whose unit had a 50 percent sales increase and whose previous large loss was turned into a sizable profit said (p. 3), "We would not have done as well without the buy-out. . . . What we have now is the freedom to take decisions and take risks."

24. In 111 cases studied by Wright and Coyne, 18 percent of the newly formed enterprises experienced cash-flow problems both before and after buyout, and 13.5 percent experienced them after buyout but not before. Forty-seven percent reported no cash-flow problems and 22 percent had problems only before buyout. See *Management Buy-Outs*, p. 146.

difficult tests. Others were still being severely tested. One sample member, Great Lakes Screw, was liquidated, but it was not the subject of a leveraged buyout. The heavy debt load incurred by Commodore to purchase Bendix Home Systems was a material factor in Commodore's subsequent bankruptcy. S. S. White failed to obtain financial backing to replace Pennwalt's temporary support, and what was left of its operations was sold piecemeal. Letisse was forced to close its doors in 1986. An intended sample member, Mystik, was also acquired in a highly leveraged deal and plunged into bankruptcy before we could commence interviews.[25] Other sample member fragments were only marginally viable at the time of our interviews, although later follow-up research revealed some progress in "turning the corner" to profitability. Overall, there was a high mortality and debility rate following our once-healthy sample companies' decline and the attempt to revive them through sell-off. Out of 16 acquisitions selected for study, there were 7 clear failures (Mystik, Bendix Home Systems, Great Lakes Screw, Letisse, S. S. White, Youngstown, and substantial parts of Chromalloy Glass) and at least 2 other borderline cases. Unfortunately, no detailed statistical assessment of post-buyout profitability is possible, either for our sample members or more generally, because financial reports are seldom published once a company "goes private."

Transitional Behavior

For some of the business units in our sample, there was a lag of as much as three years between the time when a decision to sell was taken and a buyer was found to conclude the transaction. Such delays appear to have a number of effects. For one, morale often suffers, especially among workers and at the intermediate-staff level. Most of the unit heads we interviewed expressed less concern (in all but one case, retroactively), usually because they anticipated (sometimes wrongly) a continuing key role in the organization and a potentially more satisfying relationship with new owners. In some cases an attempt was made to maintain staff morale and minimize turnover by keeping the sell-off decision secret except among unit heads. Second, there was evidence in two cases that capital investment and nonroutine maintenance were cut back as sell-

25. On the risks of leveraged buyouts more generally, see Fred R. Bleakley, "S.E.C. Chief Cautions on Leveraged Buyouts," *New York Times*, June 8, 1984; and "Leveraged Buyouts: There's Trouble in Paradise," *Business Week*, July 22, 1985, pp. 112–13.

off became imminent. Third, research and development cutbacks occurred. In one case, one whole segment of a unit's R&D staff, including
a senior engineer with more than a dozen patents, was dismissed shortly
after the decision to sell was taken, even though the actual sell-off came
much later. Finally, in two clear-cut instances and several less tidy ones,
parts of the organization's production operation were shut down in an
attempt to make the remaining package more attractive to potential
buyers.

Conclusion

Why do corporate marriages end in divorce? For our sample, the
preponderant answer is clear: because problems arose that could not be
solved to the acquiring firm's satisfaction, making the marriage fall short
of original expectations. To expect that industrial life will be problem-
free is unrealistic. The important question, therefore, is whether the
merger contributed to, or inhibited, the emergence of problems, and
how it affected problem-solving reactions.

For 7 of our 15 cases—Caradco, Chromalloy Glass, ESB, Great Lakes
Screw, Talon, S. S. White, and Youngstown—it seems reasonably clear
that conglomerate control made matters worse by delaying or distorting
reactions to emerging problems, draining from the business resources
needed for problem-solving, and (in a subset) sapping managerial morale.
In 4 cases—ASR, Harley Davidson, Marquette, and (until late in its
history) Sintercast—conglomerate control lacked significant negative
consequences and probably helped the businesses react to their problems
and opportunities, usually by making available financial resources that
would otherwise have been harder (but not impossible) to secure. In the
4 remaining cases, either there were few traceable consequences, or
positive and negative effects were fairly evenly balanced. In 2 of those 4
(Letisse and Robert Bruce), sell-off occurred because the control mechanism had failed in other businesses sufficiently closely related that the
successful cases were considered atypical and unsustainable.

No counterfactual judgment is required for another conclusion: that
efficiencies not realized under conglomerate control were achieved when
our sample businesses became self-standing entities or were integrated
within a larger organization operating complementary activities. For the
self-standing businesses, there was sometimes a cost that is the mirror

image of the conglomerate success stories: financial constraints bit harder, and intrinsic riskiness increased. In some cases, the problems handed over through sell-off were so grave that the divested unit was unable to survive.

Our case study sample was deliberately biased, so we must refrain from generalizing to the larger population of divested and nondivested acquisitions. Chapter 6 expands the coverage statistically to the quantitatively substantial collection of units divested by corporations in the Line of Business sample.

CHAPTER SIX

The Economics of Sell-Off: Statistical Evidence

WE STRIVE now to understand the economics of sell-off on a broader plane than the case studies permit. Our principal focus will be the companies covered by the Federal Trade Commission's Line of Business surveys for the years 1974 through 1977. Those companies accounted for roughly three-fourths of all manufacturing and minerals company acquisitions by dollar value over the period 1950–76. Thus, to the extent that acquisition and sell-off are associated, the sample provides solid representation of an important universe.

The Frequency of Sell-Off

First, we must sharpen an impression left imprecise in chapter 1. There we observed that, according to data published by W. T. Grimm & Co., there were 40 divestitures during the 1970s for every 100 recorded acquisition transactions.[1] Nevertheless, the Grimm series is an inexact measure of how often sell-off followed merger for two main reasons.

For one, with an exception noted later, there is no necessarily close linkage between the units in which the Grimm divestiture counts are measured and those subsumed in the acquisition counts. A sold-off line may have originated through internal development and growth, not acquisition. And diverse bundlings of acquired and sold-off lines can occur: a single acquired unit may be split into several parts for multiple sell-offs, or several acquisitions may be grouped for a single divestiture. Also, there is some ambiguity in the Grimm definition of divestitures, which includes "divisional sales," where "a product line, a subsidiary, or a division" is sold, and also "partial sales where 10% or more of a

1. The most complete series appears in W. T. Grimm & Co., *Mergerstat Review, 1985* (Chicago: Grimm, 1986), p. 92.

company's equity is purchased."[2] The latter category, which among other things includes partial tender offers, is quite different from what we mean by sell-offs. The emphasis in Grimm narratives is on sell-offs in our sense of the term, and in some years "partial sales" are not mentioned at all. Still the Grimm series evidently contains at least a small amount of activity we would not view as sell-offs.

The 40 percent sell-off figure also provides an inaccurate link to acquisition counts because there is usually an appreciable lag from a line's acquisition to its sell-off. Merger activity peaked in 1968 and then declined. Many and perhaps most of the divestitures occurring during the 1970s came from the larger flow of acquisitions that took place during the 1960s. Thus, the unlagged Grimm data might overstate the true sell-off ratio.[3]

Figure 6-1 suggests that more can be inferred about the timing relationship between acquisition and sell-off. It combines the Grimm all-industry divestiture series with the acquisition value series (for manufacturing and mining industry only) first presented in chapter 2. Acquisition activity peaked in 1968, dropped to a trough in 1972, and then rose gradually until a new merger boom took hold in the early 1980s. Sell-off activity accelerated in the late 1960s and peaked three years after the merger wave peak, declining thereafter, but less precipitously than the prior fall in acquisition volume.[4] That the two peaks are related is

2. W. T. Grimm & Co., *1974 Merger Summary* (Chicago: Grimm, 1975), p. 15.

3. In another sense, the sell-off ratio is understated, since most units counted by Grimm as divested were also counted as an acquisition for the company to whom the unit was sold. If one relates 1970s decade divestitures to nonduplicating 1970s acquisitions, one must subtract the divested-and-acquired units from the denominator. The sell-off ratio relative to "fresh" acquisitions is then $100 [0.40 / (1 - 0.40)] = 67$ percent.

4. Where $S(t)$ is the number of sell-offs counted by Grimm & Co. between 1965 and 1985 and $M(t-3)$ is the three-year lagged value of acquisition activity (in billions of 1972 dollars) from fig. 2-1, a simple explanatory regression can be estimated:

$$S(t) = 622 + 54.0 \quad M(t-3).$$
$$(2.54)$$

$$r^2 = 0.253; \text{ Durbin-Watson} = 0.37.$$

With a Koyck transformation, the regression is:

$$S(t) = 329 (1 - 0.761) + 29.1 \quad M(t-3) + 0.761 \, S(t-1).$$
$$(2.91) \qquad\qquad (8.67)$$

$$R^2 = 0.856; \text{ Durbin-Watson} = 1.37.$$

The 0.761 lag coefficient suggests that the prior impact of mergers extends for a

Figure 6-1. *Trends in Sell-off and Merger Activity, 1965–85*

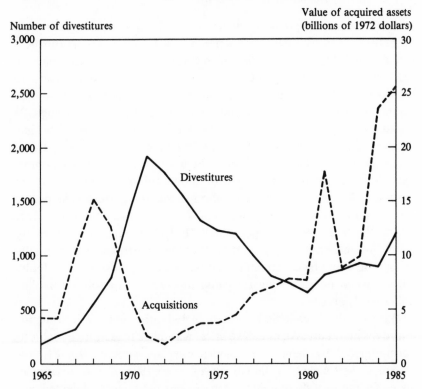

Sources: Figure 2-1; W. T. Grimm & Co., *Mergerstat Review, 1985* (Chicago: Grimm, 1986), p. 92.

suggested by predictions as early as 1968 that many ill-digested conglomerate acquisitions would sooner or later have to be sold off.[5] The resumption of an upward sell-off trend in 1981 can be attributed to the late 1970s rise in merger activity and/or to the emergence in the early 1980s of a new acquisition form—the "bust-up" takeover, in which companies were acquired and quickly dismembered because whole-company takeover prices were lower than the sums that could be realized by reselling the pieces separately.

---

considerable period, for example, with mergers in year $t-7$ having one-third as much effect as mergers in year $t-3$. The full effect over time of $1 billion in merger activity is $29.1 / (1 - 0.761) = 122$ sell-offs.

5. See "Corporate Sell-Off," *Mergers & Acquisitions*, vol. 6 (Spring 1971), p. 58; and *New York Times*, October 9, 1968, p. 62.

The Line of Business Sell-Off Data

To estimate more precisely what fraction of acquisitions ended in sell-off before the early 1980s sea change, we turn to the Line of Business sample data. Along with tracing the mergers made by each company to individual LBs, we also compiled detailed sell-off records. The two efforts were closely related, since one reason why recorded manufacturing company acquisitions could not be traced to manufacturing LBs is that the lines were sold off before 1974, the first year for which we had detailed LB data. Of the 12,399 manufacturing and nonmanufacturing acquisitions recorded on our comprehensive list for all sample companies, 809 were eliminated because of known sell-offs before 1974.[6] For the pre-1974 cases with known sell-off dates, the pattern is similar to that of the Grimm series: the number of divestitures per year rose sharply during the late 1960s to a peak in 1971. However, the documentary materials were sparse. For nearly half of the pre-1974 sell-off cases, no exact date could be ascertained, and many other divestitures undoubtedly escaped notice, being relegated to diverse "reason for nonlink unknown" cohorts.

With LB data available beginning in 1974, the relevant information improves markedly. An intensive effort was made to identify all sell-offs consummated by sample companies over the period 1974–81. The evidence is strongest for the LB survey years 1974–77. The disappearance of a line, or a sharp reduction in its sales, was readily detected, and reporting companies were instructed to annotate the elimination of "basic components" making up each LB. Several outside information sources were also tapped. They included the chronologies and product listings in *Moody's Industrial Manual,* the "Corporate Sell-Off" column published regularly in the journal *Mergers & Acquisitions,* the Federal Trade Commission merger files sorted by Line of Business company members (or more accurately, parts thereof) as *acquired* entity, and an exhaustive search of relevant *Wall Street Journal* items under the sample company heading. No source is comprehensive. Indeed, the *Wall Street Journal* search was undertaken last in an attempt to resolve puzzles posed when lines disappeared from LB reports without any outside evidence of sell-off. It led to a substantial increase in the verified sell-off

---

6. This number is greater than the sell-off tally reported in chap. 4, note 3, because the count here includes 99.99 and nonmanufacturing acquisitions.

Table 6-1. *Number of Manufacturing Lines of Business Sold Off per Year, 1974–81*

Initial year	Lines fully sold off by 1981	Lines partially sold off by 1981
1974	31	35
1975	57	51
1976	58	58
1977	62	66
1978	56	60
1979	50	55
1980	61	53
1981	51	39
Exact date unknown	10	38
Eight-year total	436	455

count. Despite this multifaceted tracing effort, some sell-offs were undoubtedly overlooked, especially for the years 1978–81, when LB reports were unavailable. Business firms are more reticent about publicizing their sell-offs (often, as we have seen, implying failure) than their acquisitions. Still from the high concordance of external and internal LB information for the years 1974–77, we believe an acceptably comprehensive statistical profile has been achieved.

Sell-offs were categorized as "full," when an entire line of business by FTC definitions was eliminated, or "partial," when the line continued to exist in 1981 even though a part had been divested. This distinction was implemented for post-1977 sell-offs by consulting 1982 product line descriptions in *Moody's Industrial Manual, Standard & Poor's Register of Corporations, Directors, and Executives*, company annual reports, and other sources. Full sell-offs often took place in stages. They are dated here by the year in which the process began, usually with a significant divestiture, but sometimes with an announcement that the entire line was for sale.

Table 6-1 summarizes the sell-off tallies for all nonmiscellaneous (non-99.99) manufacturing LBs. The maximum number of reporting LBs in any single year was 3,684, for 1977, although with year-to-year turnover, 4,409 LBs existed in one or more of the years 1974–77. Altogether, 891 lines, or 20 percent of the lines existing in any reporting year, experienced full or partial sell-off. In contrast to the pattern found with Grimm data, the year of maximum sell-off activity was 1977 in both the full and the partial categories. Our series shows no sign of a declining trend over the 1974–81 span, during which the number of divestitures reported annually by Grimm fell by 38 percent. Our figures for 1974, however, are probably underestimates, since lines totally sold early in the year would not have filed LB reports and may have escaped our notice. Also, the lack of data on 1973 line structure may have obscured the existence of some partial divestitures.

Our objective is to estimate the fraction of acquisitions sold off. To do so, we must go beyond table 6-1, which counts lines, not acquisitions. Sell-off and acquisition are clearly related. Whereas 24 percent of the LBs in our main 1977 sample of chapter 4 had no acquisitions, only 14 percent of the LBs with sell-offs had no prior acquisition history. On average, LBs fully sold off between 1974 and 1981 had 1.58 nonequals acquisitions recorded for the years 1950 through 1976. LBs with partial divestitures were more merger-prone; they averaged 2.62 acquisitions each. The information on sell-offs cannot be linked closely to individually named mergers, so it is impossible to know what fraction of the acquisitions in partial sell-off lines was divested. Making the conservative assumption that only one acquisition was divested per partial sell-off line, we estimate the total number of divested acquisitions between 1974 and 1981 as (436 × 1.58) + (455 × 1.00) = 1,143. This amounts to 19.4 percent of the 5,896 acquisitions (other than mergers of equals) made between 1950 and 1976 and coded to reporting manufacturing LBs. It is almost surely an underestimate of the sell-off ratio for several reasons.

First, our count of sell-offs is undoubtedly incomplete, especially for 1974 and the late 1970s. And if sell-off activity was higher in the early 1970s, as indicated by the Grimm series, large numbers of divestitures occurred before our 1974–81 count begins.

Equally important, there is usually a substantial lag between acquisition and sell-off. Since the flow of new acquisitions per year exceeded the number of sell-offs, the acquisition *stock* with respect to which 1970s sell-offs must be compared was smaller in the 1960s than in the 1970s. For the 288 fully divested *NEWMERG* lines (that is, those that were not part of their parents' operations in 1950, having entered the parent company by acquisition), the mean lag between acquisition and sell-off was 9.75 years, with a median of 10 years and a standard deviation of 4.56 years.[7] Letting T be the date of sell-off and L the acquisition-to-

---

7. Patterns for the "bust-up" takeover movement of the 1980s may have been different.

divestiture lag, we characterize that frequency distribution as $f(T-L)$. Then given the number of mergers $M(T-L)$ coded for year $T-L$, the number of acquired unit sell-offs $S(T)$ can be estimated as a function of past merger flows:

$$(6\text{-}1) \qquad S(T) = k \int_{1950}^{T} f(T-L)\, dt \left\{ \frac{M(T-L)}{1 - k \int_{50}^{74} f(T-L)\, dt} \right\},$$

where k is the fraction of acquired units eventually sold off. $S(T)$ would be a simple function of past acquisition dates, the sell-off rate k, and the sell-off lag structure $f(T-L)$ were it not for the fact that not all acquisitions were coded. The denominator of the bracketed term in equation 6-1 "blows up" observed acquisitions $M(T-L)$ to correct for acquisitions divested before the 1975 date with which our merger coding began. Assuming a stable sell-off lag distribution with mean of 9.75 years and standard deviation of 4.56 years, the only unknown in equation 6-1 is the sell-off rate k. Entering sell-off values for the years 1975 through 1978 and solving equation 6-1 by iterative methods, we find the average sell-off rate k to have been 46.6 percent. This is surprisingly high, probably because both the number of acquisitions $M(T-L)$ and the lag distribution $f(T-L)$ clustered around the merger boom period 1966–70, when acquisitions may have been made hastily, leading to unusually high sell-off probabilities. By projecting that experience to acquisitions made earlier, we may have given those acquisitions too little weight, and hence overestimated the probability of sell-off from the total accumulated acquisition stock. In this sense, 46.6 percent must be viewed as a high-side estimate of the sell-off rate.[8]

Finally, our analysis covers only conventionally defined manufacturing lines and excludes the FTC's 99.99 category, in which reporting companies could collect businesses with sales of less than $10 million each. No systematic attempt was made to identify and code 99.99 category acquisitions and sell-offs. Our impression was that many small acquisitions were included in 99.99 and that, because of their insubstantiality and ill fit, they had an especially high sell-off rate.

8. In a study of 33 large, diversification-prone U.S. corporations, Michael E. Porter found that 56.5 percent of the diversifying acquisitions made by those companies before 1976 had been divested by January 1987. "From Competitive Advantage to Corporate Strategy," *Harvard Business Review*, vol. 65 (May–June 1987), p. 50.

Thus, we estimate the sell-off rate for acquisitions made in the 1960s and early 1970s to have been somewhere in the range of 19 to 47 percent. Our best compromise of these estimates, one biased on the low side and the other on the high, is 33 percent.

This conclusion appears roughly consistent with Leonard W. Weiss's estimate.[9] He analyzed Line of Business sample members' 1950–70 acquisitions of manufacturing and minerals companies with pre-merger assets of $100 million or more. He identified 154 FTC-definition LBs operated by the 68 acquired companies in 1950 and found that 54, or 35 percent, had disappeared from the acquirers' LB reports for 1975. This estimate errs on the high side to the extent that lines were divested before the target companies were acquired, but understates the sell-off rate for lines added by the target companies after 1950 and divested after the targets were acquired. Given the low rates of sell-off until the late 1960s, post-1950 acquisition activity of the target companies was probably more intensive than pre-1970 sell-off activity, and so the Weiss tallies most likely underestimate the sell-off rate.

The Determinants of Sell-Off

We advance now to the question, what circumstances lead an enterprise to sell off one or more of its lines? To answer it, we use our information on the 436 full and 455 partial manufacturing line divestitures by LB sample companies over the years 1974–81.

The Role of Profitability

An important finding from our case study research is that sell-off occurs in response to profit performance deemed unsatisfactory by corporate management. The LB data permit a more general test. Table 6-2 provides preliminary insight.[10] It reports operating income/assets percentages for fully and partially divested lines, arrayed according to the time interval between the date of first sell-off and the year for which

9. Leonard W. Weiss, "The Extent and Effects of Aggregate Concentration," *Journal of Law & Economics*, vol. 26 (June 1983), pp. 440–41.

10. Part of the table appeared originally in David Ravenscraft and F. M. Scherer, "Mergers and Managerial Performance," in John C. Coffee, Jr., Louis Lowenstein, and Susan Rose-Ackerman, eds., *Knights, Raiders, and Targets: The Impact of the Hostile Takeover* (Oxford University Press, 1987).

Table 6-2. *Average Operating Income as a Percentage of Assets for Lines of Business with Sell-Offs, by Interval between the Date of Profit Report and Initiation of Sell-Off, 1974–81*

Years between profit report and first sell-off	Lines with full sell-off		Lines with partial sell-off	
	Number	Profit (percent)[a]	Number	Profit (percent)[a]
7	58	8.77 (2.94)	57	10.66 (1.80)
6	110	9.32 (1.99)	104	11.00 (1.44)
5	155	8.29 (1.38)	155	12.35 (1.40)
4	191	7.07 (1.24)	189	12.38 (1.23)
3	204	3.46 (1.14)	218	10.04 (0.93)
2	201	2.93 (1.15)	226	9.26 (1.08)
1	210	−1.09 (1.60)	219	9.72 (0.97)
0	121	−0.29 (2.27)	198	11.43 (1.06)
< 0[b]	39	7.49 (3.74)	238	13.02 (0.91)
Unknown[c]	19	−4.35 (5.13)	147	12.97 (1.55)

a. Values in parentheses are the standard error of the mean.
b. Profits reported after first sell-off.
c. Sell-off date not known (mostly after 1977).

profits are recorded. Thus, the row entries for two years before sell-off include 1974 profits for LBs whose divestiture commenced in 1976, 1975 profits for 1977 sell-offs, 1976 profits for 1978 sell-offs, and 1977 profits for 1979 divestitures.

For the 10,912 cases with no coded full or partial sell-offs, operating income averaged 13.93 percent of assets, with a standard error of 0.17 percent.[11] Over the seven years of pre–sell-off history, LBs subjected to full divestiture had returns averaging 4.76 percent—significantly less than those of nondivested lines.[12] In the third year before full sell-off,

11. A line that was not divested, but for which four years of profit data were available, is counted four times here.
12. The *t*-ratio in a test of equality of means is $(13.93 − 4.76) / 0.58 = 15.80$.

Table 6-3. *Deviations of Divested Lines' Profitability from the Average Operating Income/Assets Percentages of Nondivested Lines in the Same Industry, by Interval between the Date of Profit Report and Initiation of Sell-Off, 1974–81*

Years between profit report and first sell-off	Lines with full sell-off		Lines with partial sell-off	
	Number	Deviation (percent)[a]	Number	Deviation (percent)[a]
7	58	−1.54	57	−0.34
		(3.01)		(1.78)
6	110	−3.48	104	−0.56
		(2.07)		(1.59)
5	155	−3.72	155	−1.01
		(1.44)		(1.36)
4	191	−6.40	189	−2.33
		(1.36)		(1.18)
3	204	−9.92	218	−3.30
		(1.21)		(0.95)
2	201	−10.60	226	−4.10
		(1.22)		(1.11)
1	210	−13.54	219	−3.76
		(1.61)		(0.99)
0	121	−12.73	198	−1.96
		(2.15)		(1.12)
< 0[b]	39	−4.91	238	−1.34
		(3.80)		(0.94)

a. Values in parentheses are the standard error of the mean.
b. Profits reported after first sell-off.

profitability falls visibly, turning *negative* in the year before sell-off.[13] For partially divested lines the pattern is similar, but less dramatic. The impacted lines' returns are not materially different from those of non-divested lines until three years before sell-off. Once the surgery is completed, essentially normal profitability is observed for the retained components.

The fall in profitability preceding sell-off is not primarily a result of industry-wide shocks, as distinguished from matters more directly under the control of operating-level management. This is shown by table 6-3, in which the average profitability of *nondivested lines* in the industry

13. The 7.49 percent profitability figure for fully divested lines in < 0 years covers LBs for which sell-off proceeded in stages. It supports our case study insight that the most seriously distressed components are sold off first, leaving more profitable units for later "tidying-up" divestitures.

category to which divested lines belonged is subtracted from the operating income/assets percentages of the divested lines. Thus, the nondivested line norm is 0.00 percent. The pattern is quite similar to that of table 6-2, showing that sold-off lines' profitability diverged by increasingly wide margins from industry averages as the divestiture date approached.

These results provide striking confirmation of our case study evidence. And since the majority of sell-offs involved acquired units, it is important to recall the evidence presented in chapter 3 on the pre-merger profitability of divested units. We observed there that 215 companies acquired by Line of Business sample members and subsequently sold off had a simple average operating income/assets percentage of 20.7 percent—far above the comparably defined 8–12 percent returns realized by all U.S. manufacturing corporations. When the pre-acquisition profit data for the acquired-and-divested units were pooled with similar data for a much larger sample of 634 acquisitions, most of which were *not* sold off, no significant difference between the two groups could be detected.[14] Thus, the units acquired and later divested were on average in robust good health at the time of their acquisition, but became gravely ill thereafter.

Variables "Explaining" Sell-Off

To elucidate more fully the conditions that precede sell-off, we formulate a regression model in which the dependent variable distinguishes divested lines from retained lines and is in turn related to an array of explanatory variables.

We expect profitability of the lines to be an important variable. It will be designated *LBPROF* and measured as the ratio (not percentage) of LB operating income to LB assets. The lag structure will be clarified later.

Our case studies suggested that some lines are divested not because they themselves are in trouble, but because the parent company is experiencing financial distress and chooses to raise funds by selling "good" businesses. We test this hypothesis with a variable *COPROF*, which is the ratio of company-wide operating income to assets, averaged over the two years prior to sell-off for divested LBs.[15] We expect it to

14. See chap. 3, note 17.
15. The source of this variable, and most other company-level variables, was the Standard & Poor's COMPUSTAT computer tape.

have a negative sign; for given LB profitability, divestiture is more likely the lower company profits are.

An alternative or complementary approach is to view companies forced to raise cash by selling off lines as potential bankruptcy candidates. There is a substantial literature on the quantitative precursors to bankruptcy.[16] From those studies, we draw (in addition to the company profitability variable) two additional regressors. *WORKAP* is the average ratio of working capital (current assets less current liabilities) to total company assets one and two years prior to sell-off. The higher its value, the less likely bankruptcy and hence divisional sell-off should be. *EQUITY* is the average ratio of company equity to debt (both in book values) one and two years prior to sell-off. We anticipate a negative relationship between it and the probability of sell-off. Because the *COPROF, WORKAP,* and *EQUITY* variables all attempt to capture the same phenomenon, we introduce them separately rather than together.[17]

There were hints from our case studies that new top managers were more likely to sweep house through sell-offs, presumably because they had less emotional commitment to prior acquisition decisions. We therefore define a variable Δ *CEO*, which has a value of 2 if there was a change in the identity of the company's chief executive officer in the previous two years, or if both the chairman and the president changed; 1 if the company designated no CEO but had both a chairman and a president, one of whom changed; and 0 when the company's apparent head was unchanged. The annual movements of this variable are interesting in their own right, and hence are summarized in table 6-4.[18] The statistics imply leadership turnover on average every 11.3 years. Turnover may have accelerated somewhat during the recession of 1975. However, the year-to-year turnover ratio differences are not statistically significant; the Chi-square value is 8.35, which lies only at the 70 percent confidence threshold.

16. See Edward I. Altman and Arnold W. Sametz, eds., *Financial Crises: Institutions and Markets in a Fragile Environment* (Wiley, 1977). Our *COPROF, WORKAP,* and *EQUITY* variables approximate three of the five variables used in Altman, "Z Score Bankruptcy Model," in ibid., pp. 89–108.

17. The variables are moderately intercorrelated. The Pearsonian correlation for the 2,362 LB sample in our main analysis for *COPROF* and *WORKAP* is +0.367, for *COPROF* and *EQUITY* +0.433, and for *WORKAP* and *EQUITY* +0.155. All three correlations are statistically significant at the 0.01 level.

18. The number of companies covered varies from year to year mainly because information on the identity of the chief executive officer became unavailable for some companies that were acquired.

Table 6-4. *Annual Turnover Rates for Chief Executive Officers of Companies in the Line of Business Sample, 1973–80*

Year	Change in chief executive ($\Delta CEO=2$)	Change in chairman or president ($\Delta CEO=1$)	Total changes	Number of companies covered	Turnover rate
1973	32	9	41	446	0.092
1974	25	8	33	446	0.074
1975	41	5	46	447	0.103
1976	32	10	42	445	0.094
1977	23	3	26	443	0.059
1978	36	7	43	438	0.098
1979	37	5	42	436	0.096
1980	34	6	40	433	0.092

During the 1980s, companies sometimes viewed the consummation of a large merger as an occasion to reorganize, selling off selected units because of their poor "fit" with the new structure or to replenish depleted cash coffers. It is less clear whether such behavior was common during the 1974–81 period covered by our divestiture sample. To test the hypothesis, a dummy variable *ACQUI* was defined to have a value of 1 if the company acquired in the previous two years another firm with assets greater than or equal to $50 million, and 0 otherwise. Nineteen percent of the lines used in our main subsample belonged to companies with *ACQUI* values of 1.

At the individual line of business level, having a relatively high market share is likely to be viewed as strategically advantageous, inhibiting sell-off. We therefore introduce the variable *SHR*, measuring the line's share of its relevant national industry category two years before sell-off for divested lines or, for retained lines, in 1977. *SHR* is correlated positively with LB profitability; $r = 0.092$. Strategic advantages, and the accompanying expectation of future quasi-rents, may also accrue from having substantial reputational capital stocks built up through advertising and technological capital generated by research and development programs. These capital stocks should be larger the higher the ratios of advertising and R&D to sales are. However, the rent-yielding effects of advertising have been shown to depreciate much more rapidly (at about 85 percent in the first year) than the effects of company-financed R&D.[19] We

19. See Darral G. Clarke, "Econometric Measurement of the Duration of Advertising Effect on Sales," *Journal of Marketing Research*, vol. 13 (November 1976), pp. 345–57;

therefore expect the divestiture-inhibiting effects of R&D to be greater than those of advertising. Each variable is measured for two years before sell-off on divested lines and for 1977 on retained lines.

Although, as noted earlier, most of the LBs identified as divested between 1974 and 1981 had a prior history of acquisitions, 14 percent did not. We hypothesize that lines with an acquisition history, and especially lines that joined the company through merger, are more likely to be sold off. This is so in part because the parent's managerial know-how is less well adapted to operating conglomerate subsidiaries and partly because managers may have shallower emotional commitments to newly acquired units than to lines of long standing.

We have several measures of merger history, some substitutes and some complements. Because all were used in chapter 4, they can be described more succinctly here. Two dummy variables making an important distinction are *ORIGMERG,* with unit value if the LB was operated in 1950 and made subsequent acquisitions, and *NEWMERG,* with unit value for lines that were not operated in 1950 and had subsequent acquisitions. *NEWMERG* lines typically entered the company through acquisition, and hence might be expected to be especially vulnerable to sell-off. Finer discrimination is achieved by estimating the fraction of an LB's acquired assets (measured by chapter 4's *MERGSHR*) resulting from four distinct types of acquisitions:

HORIZ	Acquiring company had at least five years experience in the same four-digit industry category before acquisition.
VERT	Acquired unit made at least 5 percent of its sales to, or purchases from, other units operated by the company for at least five years before the acquisition.
RELAT	Acquiring company had at least five years experience in the same two-digit industry group before acquisition, but no horizontal or vertical connection.
CONGLOM	None of the above criteria satisfied.

Lines with high *CONGLOM* values are expected to be especially sell-off prone, all else equal. *HORIZ* lines and *VERT* lines (with strategic ties to other company LBs,[20] and with possibly distorted profitability figures if transfers were made at nonmarket prices) should have lower sell-off probabilities.

---

and David J. Ravenscraft and F. M. Scherer, "The Lag Structure of Returns to Research and Development," *Applied Economics,* vol.14 (December 1982), pp. 603–20.

20. Compare Kathryn Rudie Harrigan, "Exit Barriers and Vertical Integration," *Academy of Management Journal,* vol. 28 (September 1985), pp. 686–97.

The merger intensity variable *MERGSHR* can also be divided, as in chapter 4, into *POOL* and *PURCH* derivatives measuring the fraction of LB assets originating under each main form of merger accounting. Divestiture of pooling acquisition lines may be more likely because, not having experienced the asset value step-ups common under purchase accounting, their sale is less apt to entail nonrecurring disposition losses. The disclosure of such losses embarrasses management and, if managerial bonus plans are linked to profitability after nonrecurring charges, it may have an adverse impact on executive compensation.

In all of the analyses, we identify with 1-0 dummy variables lines that experienced mergers of equals (*EQUALS*), lines with a tender offer takeover or a "white knight" alternative (*TENDER*), and lines without any recorded acquisitions that were not part of the parent's 1950 structure (*NEW*). All are defined more fully in chapter 4. Especially for later years, when "bust-up" takeovers became popular, one might expect high sell-off rates for *TENDER* lines. Since *EQUALS* acquisitions were found in chapter 4 to have unusually successful profit records, lower sell-off rates might be anticipated. The effects of *NEW* are not clear a priori.

Finally, we introduce a variable *IGROWTH,* embodying the hypothesis that LBs were less likely to be divested if the industry in which they specialized was experiencing rapid growth. Growth might among other things make managers expect a profit setback to be only temporary. The *IGROWTH* variable is measured as the annual average percentage rate of industry output growth over the years 1974–81.[21]

Table 6-5 recapitulates the explanatory variables and provides information on their means and predicted coefficient signs. For the 1-0 dummy variables, the mean value indicates the fraction of sample LBs having the specified characteristic.

Model Specification

Some difficult conceptual and timing choices had to be made in structuring the model explaining sell-off behavior. One problem is the lack of a natural starting date. Our company history information goes

21. Four-digit industry sales and price deflators used in calculating this variable were kindly supplied by Vesta Jones of the National Income and Product Accounts Office, U.S. Department of Commerce.

Table 6-5. *Recapitulation of Explanatory Variables Used in the Analysis of Full Sell-Offs*

Variable		Mean value[a]	Predicted sign
LBPROF.L	Triangularly lagged line of business operating income/assets	0.133	−
COPROF	Two-year average company operating income/assets	0.128	−
WORKAP	(Current assets − current liabilities)/assets	0.275	−
EQUITY	Book equity/debt	6.16	−
ΔCEO	Change in chief executive	0.305	+
ACQUI	Large acquisition in previous two years	0.191	+
SHR	Line of business market share	0.037	−
RD/S	R&D/sales	0.0136	−
ADV/S	Advertising/sales	0.0144	−
ORIGMERG	1950 lines with acquisitions	0.218	[b]
NEWMERG	Post-1950 lines with acquisitions	0.525	+
HORIZ	Horizontal merger share	0.080	−[c]
VERT	Vertical merger share	0.024	−
RELAT	Related merger share	0.085	+
CONGLOM	Conglomerate share	0.141	+
POOL	Pooling merger share	0.172	+
PURCH	Purchase merger share	0.145	[d]
EQUALS	Mergers of equals	0.086	−
TENDER	Tender offer merger	0.053	+
NEW	Post-1950, no mergers	0.101	[b]
IGROWTH	1974–81 industry output growth rate	1.25	−

a. 2,362 lines of business covered.
b. No prediction.
c. Negative or zero.
d. Less than value of *POOL*.

back at best to 1950, focus of the first FTC Corporate Patterns survey,[22] but some LBs are much older, while the *NEWMERG* lines are younger. And reliable sell-off data are available beginning only in 1974 or 1975. Equally important, individual line profitability was expected to play a key role in explaining sell-offs. Yet the data are limited to the years 1974–77 for which Line of Business surveys were conducted. If one assumes that four years of lagged profits data are needed for a thoroughgoing sell-off analysis, the pattern of data availability (X) and gaps (O)

22. U.S. Federal Trade Commission, *Statistical Report: Value of Shipments Data by Product Class for the 1,000 Largest Manufacturing Companies of 1950* (Government Printing Office, 1972).

Table 6-6. *Availability (X) and Gaps (O) in Data for Estimating a Four-Year Lagged Relationship between Profitability and Line of Business Sell-Offs, 1970–80*

Profit Data Needed for	Year of first sell-off							
	1974	1975	1976	1977	1978	1979	1980	1981
1970	O	...	...	...	...	...	...	...
1971	O	O	...	...	...	...	...	...
1972	O	O	O	...	...	...	...	...
1973	O	O	O	O	...	...	...	...
1974	...	X	X	X	X	...	...	...
1975	...	...	X	X	X	X	...	...
1976	...	...	...	X	X	X	X	...
1977	...	...	...	...	X	X	X	X
1978	...	...	...	...	...	O	O	O
1979	...	...	...	...	...	...	O	O
1980	...	...	...	...	...	...	...	O

shown in table 6-6 appears. For 1974 sell-offs, none of the desired lagged profits data are at hand. Only for 1978 sell-offs do all four years of profit data exist.

There is no completely satisfactory solution to the data gap problem. Here we make the best of a difficult situation by using the full set of lagged profitability data when they are available, substituting the next-best data when the best are not available, and testing the sensitivity of our results by comparing subsamples with relatively satisfactory and unsatisfactory coverage.

Because the relevant LB profit data are completely lacking, 1974 sell-offs are excluded from the sample. Also excluded are 1975 sell-offs, in part because at best only 1974 profitability data were available. The FTC's expansion of Line of Business sample coverage from 437 corporations in 1974 to 471 in 1975 left substantial 1974 data gaps. Also, merger data links were not attempted for lines that existed in 1974 but filed no LB report in 1975—for example, because they were sold off in that year.

The phenomenon to be explained is sell-off, and so we take as our dependent variable a dummy variable with a value of 1 if sell-off occurred and 0 otherwise. With a dichotomous dependent variable of this sort, the error structure of the explanatory regression equation is likely to be bimodal, and so ordinary least squares (OLS) methods (which assume normally distributed errors) are inefficient. We therefore use logit analysis to determine how the sold-off lines differ.[23] A logit regression estimates the probability that the dependent variable will have unit value, that is, that the line will be sold off, as the function:

$$(6\text{-}2) \qquad Pr\,(Sell\text{-}off) = \frac{e_i^{\Sigma b_i x_{ij}}}{1 + e_i^{\Sigma b_i x_{ij}}}\,,$$

where X_{ij} is the ith explanatory variable for LB_j. The regression coefficient b_i is estimated nonlinearly. Although $\Sigma\,b_i X_{ij}$ can have positive or negative values without bound, the logistic transformation ensures that $Pr(Sell\text{-}off)$ lies in the range of 0 to 1. A disadvantage of the logit method is the difficulty of interpreting its estimated b_i coefficients' practical meaning. Therefore, we also present ordinary least squares regressions, whose coefficients have a more directly intuitive meaning. We shall see that the results with either technique are quite similar.

A final specification choice involves the dating of explanatory variables for the control group, or the set of lines without observed divestitures. Because of profit data limitations, lines that were sold off, say, in 1979, are treated as a single observation with dependent variable value of 1, and not as lines with a value of 0 in earlier years before sell-off. We in effect pose the question as, "Did the line survive from 1975 through 1981, or was it divested?"[24] If divestiture occurred, explanatory variables predate the time of sell-off by as appropriate a lag as was possible, given data limitations.

For the company-level variables *COPROF, WORKAP, EQUITY,* Δ *CEO,* and *ACQUI,* this choice means that for divested lines, the two-year intervals range from 1974–75 (for 1976 sell-offs) to 1979–80 (for 1981 sell-offs), while for nondivested lines, data for 1977 and 1978 are used uniformly. The interval for the nondivested lines approaches as closely as possible the midpoint of the divested line intervals.

For the LB-specific profit variable *LBPROF,* the matching situation is more complex, since three alternative forms using up to four years of

23. See Takeshi Amemiya, "Qualitative Response Models: A Survey," *Journal of Economic Literature,* vol. 19 (December 1981), pp. 1483–1536.

24. An alternative approach is taken in David J. Ravenscraft and F. M. Scherer, "Divisional Sell-off: A Hazard Function Analysis," forthcoming. With hazard function analysis, the focus is the time duration from some initial year (for example, 1975) before sell-off occurs. Annual sell-off "hazard rates" and cumulative sell-off probability distributions (for example, logistic, Weibull, exponential, and normal) are also estimated. The hazard function results are quite similar to the logit results reported in this chapter.

data were specified. The theoretically preferred version, *LBPROF.L,* attaches more weight to the most recent years by imposing a triangular lag structure. When four years of LB profit data could be employed— that is, for most nondivested lines and for lines divested between 1978 and 1981—the lag weights were 0.4 for 1977 profitability, 0.3 for 1976 profits, 0.2 for 1975 profits, and 0.1 for 1974 profits. The match is exact for 1978 sell-offs, off by one year for 1979 sell-offs, and has a maximum three-year mismatch for 1981 sell-offs. For 1976 and 1977 sell-offs, the profit data for fewer years were triangularly lagged—for example, for 1976 sell-offs, with weight of 0.6 on 1975 profitability and 0.4 on 1974 profitability.[25] Although imperfect, this matching was the best attainable compromise in view of the unavoidable data gaps.

A second profit specification *LBPROF.A* takes a simple average of LB profits for all four years when appropriate or for two or three years on 1976 and 1977 sell-offs. The matching implications are identical to those of the previous paragraph; the only difference is that the lag structure is rectangular rather than triangular. A third specification LBPROF.1 uses a single year's profitability data only—1977 for all retained lines and 1978–81 sell-offs, 1976 for the 1977 sell-offs, and 1975 for the 1976 sell-offs.

The LB-specific R&D, advertising, and market share variables are lagged two years, permitting perfect matches for retained lines and lines sold off between 1976 and 1979. One- to two-year mismatches are accepted for 1980 and 1981 sell-offs.

Sample Selection

From the total set of manufacturing LBs, various deletions were made in forming the principal sample. Some occurred because of data quality and bias problems discussed earlier.[26] In particular, lines were excluded if their operating income/assets ratios exceeded (in percentage terms) ± 100 percent in any year,[27] if their merger history was of unacceptable quality,[28] if for some reason other than sell-off 1976 and 1977 LB data

25. Similar reweightings were required to deal with missing observations.

26. See the discussion of "Sample Composition" in chap. 4.

27. This condition was waived for divested LBs violating it in period $T-1$; instead the $T-1$ profit data were excluded from the lag structure.

28. Biases discussed more fully in chap. 4, note 11, can intrude when lines had a substantial merger in a year for which LB profit data are included. This problem was solved by excluding the impacted years and reweighting the lag structure appropriately.

were unavailable, or if the LB was discontinued without sell-off between 1975 and 1981. Company-level financial data were taken from the COMPUSTAT files, which exclude companies whose securities are not listed on organized exchanges. Thus, all LBs of privately owned companies and most foreign parents fell from the sample. Also dropped were the LBs of companies for which 1977 and 1978 COMPUSTAT records were unavailable, usually because the parent was acquired by some other corporation, and companies that filed bankruptcy petitions between 1975 and 1981.

Although a combined analysis is reported later, lines with partial sell-offs were excluded from the full sell-off analysis.

After these deletions, the number of fully divested lines in the full sell-off analysis is 278, and the control group, or the set of nondivested lines, contains 2,084 LBs. Of the 436 full sell-off lines counted in table 6-1, 88 LBs were excluded because divestiture began in 1974 or 1975 and 70 because of data availability or quality problems. Also, 455 LBs were ineligible for inclusion in the full sell-off analysis because they had partial sell-offs. In view of this, the sample size of 2,362 is not greatly different from that of profitability regression 4-2(7) in chapter 4, which focused on the 2,732 LBs for which data of acceptable quality over the three years 1975 through 1977 were continuously available.

The Full Sell-Off Results

Table 6-7 presents the principal regression results for the analysis of full sell-offs. Regressions estimated by logit techniques (the "a" equations) and by ordinary least squares (the "b" equations) appear in most cases side-by-side. The pattern of coefficient signs and t-ratios (in subscripted parentheses) is similar regardless of the technique used.

Regression (1) is the core model, differentiating acquisition histories solely through dummy variables. The highest t-ratio (on the null hypothesis of a zero impact) is for individual LB profitability $LBPROF.L$. As noted already, the intuitive meaning of its logit regression coefficient— in regression (1a)—is difficult to grasp. To evaluate the effect of the $LBPROF$ variable, other variables held constant, one must solve nonlinear equation 6-2 over the desired range of $LBPROF$, holding the other variables constant. If, for example, one is interested in what happens when LB profitability moves from 0.1393 (13.93 percent) to -0.0109— the average $(T-1)$ difference between retained and divested LBs in table

6-2—one evaluates equation 6-2 for those two values, given all the relevant coefficient estimates of regression 6-7(1a) and holding all other variables at their means. One finds that such a change in *LBPROF.L* increases the probability of sell-off from 0.073 to 0.147, or by 0.074. With the analogous OLS regression 6-7(1b), the same intuition can be gained more readily. We simply multiply the *LBPROF.L* change of 0.1502 by the value of the partial regression coefficient -0.479, determining that the probability of sell-off is altered by 0.072, ceteris paribus. In this case the results are quite close, and in most instances they are similar. Still to maximize insight, table 6-8 shows the sell-off probability changes resulting when all logit variables but one are held at their means, and the subject variable is moved from two standard deviations below its mean to two standard deviations above (for the continuously scaled variables) or from 0 to 1 (for the dummy variables). From that perspective also, the *LBPROF.L* variable is found to have the largest single impact on sell-off probabilities, in part because of its sizable coefficient and partly because of the wide range over which LB profit rates vary.

Higher company profitability also has a significant negative effect on sell-off. From table 6-8, a four-standard-deviation increase in *COPROF* (which is less variable than *LBPROF.L*) reduces the probability of sell-off by 0.123, which is quite close to the value of 0.122 computed using the OLS regression (1b).

Higher market shares retard divestiture, as expected, although the OLS coefficient is statistically significant only at the 0.10 level.[29] R&D-intensive lines are significantly less likely to be sold off, presumably because past R&D investments support the expectation of future quasi-rents. The analogous advertising intensity variable has the wrong sign but is statistically insignificant. The insignificance of *ADV/S* is consistent with our hypothesis that advertising capital stocks depreciate rapidly. Contrary to our strongly held hypothesis, more rapid home industry growth in the 1974–81 period did not discourage sell-off.

Having had a change in management in the two years preceding significantly increases the likelihood of sell-off, apparently because new brooms attempt to sweep clean and/or emotional commitments to past

29. As we have seen in chap. 4, *SHR* is mildly collinear with both the profit and merger history variables. Thus, for the sample here, the correlation with *LBPROF.L* is $+0.092$ and with *NEWMERG* it is -0.251. Reestimating regressions (1a) and (1b) without the *SHR* variable strengthened the *LBPROF.L* and *NEWMERG* effects slightly, but otherwise made little difference.

Table 6-7. Logit and Ordinary Least Squares (OLS) Regressions Explaining Full Sell-Offs[a]

	(1a) Logit	(1b) OLS	(2a) Logit	(2b) OLS	(3a) Logit	(3b) OLS	(4a) Logit NEWMERG	(5a) Logit OTHER	(6a) Logit	(7a) Logit	(8b) OLS 1976–79	(9b) OLS 1980–81
							Regression number and method					
Intercept	−0.88[b] (3.18)	0.231[b] (9.74)	−0.621[b] (2.88)	0.238[b] (12.12)	−0.633[b] (2.94)	0.241[b] (12.19)	−0.126 (0.53)	−0.743[c] (2.20)	−1.87[b] (6.65)	−1.51[b] (6.16)	0.188[b] (9.12)	0.062[b] (3.93)
LBPROF.L	−5.24[d] (9.67)	−0.479[d] (10.63)	−5.22[d] (9.61)	−0.470[d] (10.47)	−5.33[d] (9.82)	−0.482[d] (10.69)	−5.20[d] (8.09)	−5.37[d] (5.46)	−5.78[d] (10.75)	−5.60[d] (10.41)	−0.425[d] (10.84)	−0.114[d] (3.56)
COPROF	−7.72[d] (5.15)	−0.566[d] (4.57)	−7.75[d] (5.16)	−0.567[d] (4.60)	−7.91[d] (5.26)	−0.604[d] (4.88)	−8.25[d] (4.43)	−7.48[d] (2.80)	⋯	⋯	−0.451[d] (4.20)	−0.166[e] (2.01)
WORKAP	⋯	⋯	⋯	⋯	⋯	⋯	⋯	⋯	0.803 (1.40)	⋯	⋯	⋯
EQUITY	⋯	⋯	⋯	⋯	⋯	⋯	⋯	⋯	⋯	−0.041[c] (2.09)	⋯	⋯
ΔCEO	0.174[e] (1.97)	0.021[d] (2.34)	0.171[e] (1.93)	0.021[d] (2.34)	0.163[f] (1.84)	0.020[e] (2.23)	0.312[d] (3.14)	−0.324 (1.57)	0.210[d] (2.39)	0.202[d] (2.31)	0.012[f] (1.51)	0.014[d] (2.21)
SHR	−7.47[d] (3.10)	−0.184[e] (1.81)	−8.53[d] (3.58)	−0.238[d] (2.39)	−8.57[d] (3.57)	−0.228[e] (2.28)	−3.94 (1.30)	−13.57[d] (3.19)	−6.96[d] (2.92)	−7.04[d] (2.95)	−0.166[e] (1.89)	−0.022 (0.34)
RD/S	−8.16[e] (2.27)	−0.669[d] (2.30)	−6.54[e] (1.84)	−0.569[e] (1.96)	−7.31[e] (2.05)	−0.633[e] (2.17)	−10.28[e] (2.21)	−3.11 (0.58)	−9.47[d] (2.55)	−8.87[d] (2.42)	−0.539[d] (2.10)	−0.182 (0.94)
ADV/S	1.19 (0.59)	0.174 (0.90)	0.360 (0.17)	0.095 (0.49)	0.533 (0.26)	0.122 (0.63)	−0.437 (0.16)	3.27 (0.99)	−0.767 (0.36)	0.369 (0.18)	0.216 (1.30)	−0.031 (0.25)
IGROWTH	−0.002 (0.14)	0.0008 (0.53)	0.0007 (0.04)	0.0011 (0.76)	0.0038 (0.24)	0.0013 (0.86)	0.0080 (0.43)	−0.023 (0.76)	−0.0008 (0.05)	0.0009 (0.06)	0.0012 (0.96)	−0.0005 (0.53)
ORIGMERG	−0.159 (0.54)	−0.020 (0.95)	⋯	⋯	⋯	⋯	⋯	⋯	−0.248 (0.85)	−0.216 (0.74)	−0.0094 (0.51)	−0.012 (0.88)
NEWMERG	0.903[d] (3.82)	0.079[d] (4.11)	⋯	⋯	⋯	⋯	⋯	⋯	0.802[d] (3.44)	0.772[d] (3.30)	0.057[d] (3.40)	0.034[d] (2.65)

HORIZ	⋮	⋮	⋮	⋮	⋮	⋮	⋮	⋮	0.053 (1.56)	0.595 (1.60)	⋮	0.295 (1.11)
VERT	⋮	⋮	⋮	⋮	⋮	⋮	⋮	⋮	−0.110[e] (1.99)	−2.12[e] (1.99)	⋮	−0.498 (1.62)
RELAT	⋮	⋮	⋮	⋮	⋮	⋮	⋮	⋮	0.092[d] (3.18)	0.801[d] (2.75)	⋮	0.048 (0.14)
CONGLOM	⋮	⋮	⋮	⋮	⋮	⋮	⋮	⋮	0.173[d] (7.08)	1.34[d] (5.92)	⋮	−0.377[c] (2.06)
POOL	⋮	⋮	⋮	⋮	⋮	⋮	0.145[d] (6.06)	1.31[d] (5.59)	⋮	⋮	⋮	⋮
PURCH	⋮	⋮	⋮	⋮	⋮	⋮	0.075[d] (2.88)	0.648[d] (2.53)	⋮	⋮	⋮	⋮
EQUALS	−0.005 (0.29)	0.025 (1.22)	0.152 (0.58)	0.164 (0.62)	h	h	0.007 (0.30)	0.127 (0.49)	0.014 (0.60)	0.165 (0.63)	0.018 (0.79)	0.295 (1.11)
TENDER	0.008 (0.43)	−0.075[c] (2.98)	−0.436 (1.43)	−0.378 (1.24)	h	h	−0.062[c] (2.06)	−0.503 (1.57)	−0.088[b] (3.01)	−0.738[c] (2.32)	−0.058[c] (2.03)	−0.498 (1.62)
NEW	0.003 (0.16)	0.005 (0.23)	−0.028 (0.09)	−0.013 (0.04)	h	h	0.004 (0.16)	−0.171 (0.62)	−0.0005 (0.02)	−0.213 (0.78)	0.008 (0.29)	0.048 (0.14)
ACQUI	0.013 (1.17)	−0.059[b] (4.06)	−0.372[c] (2.03)	−0.303[g] (1.65)	h	h	−0.042[c] (2.57)	−0.413[c] (2.23)	−0.042[c] (2.55)	−0.391[c] (2.12)	−0.040[c] (2.46)	−0.377[c] (2.06)
Summary statistics												
R^2	0.0277	0.0972	⋮	⋮	⋮	⋮	0.0983	⋮	0.1064	⋮	0.0989	⋮
Chi-square	⋮	⋮	243.9	237.5	75.6	136.6	⋮	259.4	⋮	274.1	⋮	263.6
Number of lines	2,174	2,272	2,362	2,362	1,121	1,241	2,362	2,362	2,362	2,362	2,362	2,362

a. Numbers in parentheses are *t*-ratios.
b. Significant in a two-tailed test at 0.01 level of confidence.
c. Significant in a two-tailed test at 0.05 level of confidence.
d. Significant in a one-tailed test at 0.01 level of confidence.
e. Significant in a one-tailed test at 0.05 level of confidence.
f. Significant in a one-tailed test at 0.10 level of confidence.
g. Significant in a two-tailed test at 0.10 level of confidence.
h. Excluded from regression.

Table 6-8. *Changes in the Probability of Sell-Off Indicated by Logit Regression (1a) in Table 6-7 with a Four-Standard-Deviation Increase in Individual Variables, Other Variables Held at Their Mean Values*

| Variable | Standard deviation | Probability of sell-off, two standard deviations[a] | | Change |
		Below mean	Above mean	
LBPROF.L	0.146	0.272	0.017	−0.255
COPROF	0.054	0.157	0.034	−0.123
SHR	0.067	0.180	0.029	−0.151
RD/S	0.023	0.105	0.053	−0.052
ADV/S	0.033	0.070	0.081	0.011
IGROWTH	4.39	0.076	0.074	−0.003
ΔCEO	0.708	0.060	0.094	0.034
NEWMERG[b]	0.499	0.048	0.111	0.063
ORIGMERG[b]	0.413	0.077	0.067	−0.011
NEW[b]	0.301	0.075	0.078	0.003
EQUALS[b]	0.281	0.073	0.096	0.023
TENDER[b]	0.225	0.077	0.048	−0.029
ACQUI[b]	0.393	0.080	0.056	−0.024

a. The mean sell-off probability is 0.075 when all variables are held at their means.
b. The dummy variable values are changed from 0 to 1.

decisions are broken. With a CEO change scaled at 2 and no change at 0, a CEO change increases the sell-off probability by 0.027 (from logit regression (1a)) or by $2 \times 0.0213 = 0.043$ (from OLS regression (1b)).

The merger coefficients reveal a significant difference between lines that were already operated by the parent in 1950 and those joining the parent thereafter through merger. The *ORIGMERG* variable is statistically insignificant, whereas with *NEWMERG* lines, the probability of sell-off is six to eight points higher than for control group lines, that is, those existing in 1950 and without a subsequent acquisition history. No significant effects are detected for no-merger *NEW* lines or lines with mergers of equals. Lines subjected to a prior tender offer were less likely to be sold off, perhaps because having "gone public" with a tender offer was a highly visible act that, if reversed, caused embarrassment to top management before bust-up takeovers came into vogue. Contrary to expectations, companies that made a large ($50 million or more) acquisition in the previous two years were significantly less likely to sell off existing lines, all else equal.[30]

30. One reader of a draft of this chapter suggested that companies go through

Although the differences are small, the best-fitting LB profitability lag structure is the triangular form reported in table 6-7. Compared to logit regression (1a), with a *t*-ratio on the triangularly lagged *LBPROF.L* of 9.67, the *t*-ratio for the average rectangular lag *LBPROF.A* was 9.61, and for *LBPROF.1*, including only the most recent year's profitability, it was 9.03. The corresponding Chi-square ratios for the full logit regressions with these alternative profit measures show the same goodness-of-fit ranking. The weaker performance of the single-year variable suggests that sell-off is induced by a series of low returns, and not simply by poor LB profitability in one year.

Regressions (2a) and (2b) in table 6-7 substitute the merger-type variables *HORIZ, VERT, RELAT,* and *CONGLOM* for *ORIGMERG* and *NEWMERG*. New insights are gained. Lines with a preponderantly conglomerate acquisition history are most likely to be sold off. From regression (2b), 100 percent origination of a line's assets in "pure" conglomerate acquisitions raises the probability of sell-off by 0.173. "Related business" acquisitions are also significantly more likely to be divested, although with a marginal probability only half as great as for purely conglomerate acquisitions. Vertical acquisitions are significantly *less* likely to be divested.

In regressions (3a) and (3b), LBs' merger histories are represented by the *POOL* and *PURCH* derivatives of *MERGSHR*. Both variables exhibit a positive and statistically significant impact on the probability of sell-off.[31] However, the *POOL* coefficients are roughly twice as large as the *PURCH* coefficients,[32] supporting the hypothesis that managers divest lines more readily when acquired assets were not subjected to purchase accounting step-ups that increase the probability and size of reported nonrecurring disposition losses.

In regressions (4a) and (5a), the role of mergers is explored in still another way. The main sample is divided into two parts: 1,241 LBs with *NEWMERG* values of 1—that is, those that entered their parent's fold after 1950 through acquisition (other than mergers of equals); and the

---

extended acquisition and consolidation phases, and that the immediate sequitur to large acquisitions was likely to be more acquisitions rather than a shift to sell-offs.

31. Note, however, that the Chi-square and R^2 values with these continuously scaled merger history measures are lower than in their regression (1a) and (1b) counterparts with *NEWMERG* and *ORIGMERG*. Evidently, experience matters more than the intensity of prior merger activity.

32. *PURCH* is significantly different from *POOL*, with *t*-ratios on the difference of 2.36 for regression (3a) and 2.31 for regression (3b).

remaining 1,121 *ORIG, ORIGMERG,* and *NEW* lines that were either operated by the parent in 1950 or (for the *NEW* cases) arose de novo without detectable mergers. Our purpose is to learn whether the determinants of sell-off differ between lines in which acquisition was seminal and those in which it was not. As one would have expected from regression (1a), the two groups differ sharply in the extent to which they experienced sell-offs. The 1,241 *NEWMERG* lines had 204 full sell-offs, while the 1,121 (mostly pre-1950) lines of regression (5a) had only 74. With sell-off rates of 16.4 and 6.6 percent, respectively, it is clear that full divestiture was disproportionately a phenomenon associated with lines joining their parents through post-1950 conglomerate acquisitions.

Comparison of regressions (4a) and (5a) reveals both similarities and differences. The coefficient values for the line of business and company-level profit variables are quite close across cohorts. However, application of logit equation 6-2 yields important differences in the sell-off probabilities triggered by profitability changes. With a four-standard-deviation decline in *LBPROF.L,* the probability of sell-off rises by 0.366 for *NEWMERG* lines but only by 0.146 for other lines.[33] *NEWMERG* line divestitures were also more responsive to changes in company-level profitability. Evidently, there is more inertia in deciding to divest lines that have been part of the company for a quarter century or more. A large market share significantly inhibited the sale of long-standing and internally developed lines, but for the *NEWMERG* cohort, the effect is statistically insignificant.[34] A change in top management significantly increased the probability that *NEWMERG* lines would be sold off, whereas for LBs of longer standing (whose origins almost always predated the reign of the displaced managers) the effect is negative but insignificant. Higher R&D/sales ratios significantly retarded divestiture only for *NEWMERG* lines. As in other regressions, the advertising and industry growth effects remain insignificant, with erratic coefficient signs.

Regressions (6a) and (7a), which are presented only in logit form,

33. The differences between cohorts came mainly from differences in the logit regression intercept terms and not from differing degrees of profit variability across subsets. For the *NEWMERG* lines, the standard deviation of *LBPROF.L* was 0.144; for the other LBs, it was 0.147.

34. Here the disparate predictive power may be attributable in part to differences in the range of market share values. The standard deviation of *SHR* was 0.086 for the regression (5a) LBs but only 0.034 for the *NEWMERG* LBs. Mean market share was 0.021 for the *NEWMERG* LBs and 0.055 for the others.

substitute the bankruptcy model variables *WORKAP* and *EQUITY* one-by-one for lagged company profitability. Relative to regression (1a) with *COPROF,* the fit is appreciably poorer, and the working capital variable has the wrong sign. Evidently, sell-off was more apt to be induced by poor company profitability than by a weak working capital position or high leverage.

The last two regressions in table 6-7 show what happens when the sample is divided between 1976–79 sell-offs, for which a reasonably good matching of lagged LB profitability measures is achieved, and 1980–81, for which the LB profit data predate sell-off by three or more years. The 1980–81 subsample may measure sell-offs less accurately as well, since only public sources could be tapped.

The results, reported only for the more easily interpreted OLS version, are consistent with our expectations. Regression (8b) for 1976–79, with 188 sold-off lines, is quite similar in most respects to its full-sample counterpart (1b). Regression (9a) for 1980–81 is qualitatively similar on the profitability, *NEWMERG,* and management change variables, but much weaker in terms of *t*-ratios and R^2. The loss of power is attributable both to poorer data quality and to the relatively small number, 90, of dependent variable observations with a value of 1 in a sea of 2,084 with 0 values. The R&D variable fades to insignificance. The large merger and tender offer variables change signs, perhaps revealing wider managerial acceptance of bust-up acquisitions, although neither coefficient approaches statistical significance.

Partial Sell-Offs

Thus far, lines that experienced only partial sell-off have been excluded from the sample. We now bring them under scrutiny. The method is multinomial logit analysis, which estimates separate coefficients for each sell-off category. The results are seen in table 6-9. For the LBs with full sell-offs (second numerical column), there is little change in coefficient estimates compared to regression 6-7(1a). However, important differences materialize for the lines with partial sell-offs (first numerical column). Higher LB and company profitability continue to discourage sell-off, although both effects are much weaker for partial divestitures. *NEWMERG* remains positive and significant, but it is overshadowed by *ORIGMERG,* whose sign has changed to positive for the partial sell-offs. Evidently, when divestiture was contemplated with

Table 6-9. *Multinomial Logit Results from Analysis of Partial and Full Sell-Offs for 2,683 Lines of Business*[a]

	Partial sell-offs	Full sell-offs
Intercept	−1.66[b]	−0.813[b]
	(6.71)	(2.95)
LBPROF.L	−1.64[c]	−5.20[c]
	(3.36)	(9.83)
COPROF	−4.21[c]	−7.95[c]
	(3.27)	(5.29)
ΔCEO	0.063	0.171[d]
	(0.74)	(1.97)
SHR	−1.35	−7.85[c]
	(1.21)	(3.25)
RD/S	4.02[e]	−8.30[d]
	(1.77)	(2.27)
ADV/S	2.62	1.22
	(1.64)	(0.61)
IGROWTH	0.015	−0.004
	(1.11)	(0.24)
ORIGMERG	0.849[b]	−0.151
	(4.03)	(0.52)
NEWMERG	0.479[d]	0.841[c]
	(2.31)	(3.58)
EQUALS	0.553[b]	0.243
	(3.06)	(0.94)
TENDER	−0.042	−0.418
	(0.17)	(1.38)
NEW	−1.31[b]	0.017
	(2.86)	(0.05)
ACQUI	−0.407[f]	−0.343[e]
	(2.36)	(1.89)

a. Numbers in parentheses are *t*-ratios.
b. Significant in a two-tailed test at 0.01 level of confidence.
c. Significant in a one-tailed test at 0.01 level of confidence.
d. Significant in a one-tailed test at 0.05 level of confidence.
e. Significant in a two-tailed test at 0.10 level of confidence.
f. Significant in a two-tailed test at 0.05 level of confidence.

respect to a line operated by the company for at least a quarter century, it was apt to be only a pruning job, not full sell-off. The same appears true of lines that experienced mergers of equals. For *NEW* lines, on the other hand, partial sell-off was even less likely than full sell-off, perhaps because *NEW* lines by definition had no reported acquisitions and may therefore have had especially simple organizational structures. Both the R&D/sales and (insignificant) advertising/sales coefficients have unexpected signs for reasons that are not obvious. Changes in top management appear less influential in partial sell-off decisions.

An Afterword

The profitability results are so consistent and strong that a final comment is warranted. A fundamental proposition of microeconomic theory is that "exit" occurs in response to low profitability (in the long run) or operating losses (in the short run). For large corporations like those in the Line of Business sample, exit from an industry takes place mainly through sell-off; companies rarely shut down a whole division or line of business.[35] Both the regression analyses and our findings in tables 6-2 and 6-3 are in accord with these propositions. Relying solely on conjecture as to what accounting bias problems *might* intrude, without any empirical analysis, a critic of the Line of Business program has asserted that the "data do not reflect economic market values well" and concluded that they are "of doubtful value for purposes of economic analysis."[36] Others have argued (again, with nothing more than anecdotal or conjectural evidence) that accounting data quite generally depart so widely from "economic rates of return" that economists "who believe that analysis of accounting rates of return will tell them much . . . are deluding themselves."[37] We believe our results show that their pessimism is unwarranted. The data have been put to the test of predicting an important aspect of business behavior. They pass with flying colors.

Pre-Divestiture Investment Behavior

Some of the business units covered by our sell-off case studies were treated as cash cows—that is, deprived of internal cash flow for investment in modernization, research and development, and (less clearly) advertising. In other instances, deteriorating profitability left so little

35. See Ravenscraft and Scherer, "Divisional Sell-off," where the sell-off rate is found to be at least 13 times the plant closure rate.
36. George J. Benston, "The Validity of Profits-Structure Studies with Particular Reference to the FTC's Line of Business Data," *American Economic Review*, vol. 75 (March 1985), p. 64.
37. Franklin M. Fisher and John J. McGowan, "On the Misuse of Accounting Rates of Return To Infer Monopoly Profits," *American Economic Review*, vol. 73 (March 1983), p. 91.

cash flow that investment cutbacks were necessitated. In one case, a long time interval passed between the decision to divest and its implementation, during which expenditures for R&D and facilities shrank.

Our question here is, is such investment-scrimping behavior before sell-off more general? Can it be detected statistically in the Line of Business sample?

The LB data base contains no explicit information on new capital outlays for plant and equipment. Our analysis must be limited, therefore, to two aspects of the cash cow hypothesis—spending on company-financed R&D and advertising.

Preliminary insight is provided by comparing the unweighted average R&D/sales and advertising/sales ratios (converted to percentages) of fully divested lines to those of their partially and nondivested counterparts. All years for which pre-divestiture data existed are included:[38]

	Nondivested lines		Fully divested lines		Partly divested lines	
	Mean ratio (percent)	Number of lines	Mean ratio (percent)	Number of lines	Mean ratio (percent)	Number of lines
R&D/sales	1.40	10,980	0.97	1,147	1.82	1,193
Advertising/sales	1.59	9,483	1.76	975	1.72	1,114

The differences in mean R&D/sales ratios for sold-off lines, as compared to nondivested lines, are statistically significant[39] and consistent with our regression analysis finding that full sell-off was less likely, but partial sell-off more likely, with high R&D/sales ratios. The divested lines' advertising/sales ratios are not significantly different from those of retained lines.[40]

Further analysis shows that the observed differences stem partly from characteristics of the industries to which the sold-off lines belonged. When average industry R&D/sales and advertising/sales ratios are subtracted from the individual LB values, the following pattern of

38. For the number of lines, each year's observation on a given LB is counted separately. The advertising/sales counts are smaller because LBs with no advertising were excluded. All relevant lines, with or without R&D, are included in the R&D tally.

39. With standard errors of 0.065 and 0.100 for the differences between the nondivested LB versus the full and partial sell-off means, respectively, the t-ratios are 6.62 and 4.21.

40. The standard errors are approximately 0.12 percentage points.

Table 6-10. *Average Deviations of the Ratios of R&D to Sales and Advertising to Sales from Industry Norms for Fully Divested Lines of Business, by Years before Sell-Off*

Number of years before sell-off	R&D/sales		Advertising/sales	
	Deviation (percent)	Number of lines	Deviation (percent)	Number of lines
6	−0.45	110	−0.07	98
5	−0.27	155	0.17	129
4	−0.09	191	−0.24	164
3	−0.29	204	−0.19	177
2	−0.22	202	−0.14	169
1	−0.41	214	−0.07	176
All years	−0.27	1,147	−0.09	975

average "deviations from industry norms" emerges:

	Non-divested lines (percent)	Fully divested lines (percent)	Partly divested lines (percent)
R&D/sales	0.00	−0.27	+0.08
Advertising/sales	0.00	−0.09	−0.05

Only the R&D/sales deviation for the fully divested lines is statistically significant ($t = 5.28$), and it is more than a third lower than the 0.43 point difference between fully divested and retained line ratios unadjusted for industry effects. Divested lines are now found to be (insignificantly) *less* advertising-intensive relative to their industries, not more so. Thus, the only firmly supported conclusions are that fully sold-off lines belonged to industries performing below-average amounts of company-financed R&D, that fully sold-off LBs tended to have sub-par R&D/sales ratios in their own industries, and that partly divested lines were roughly typical of their above-average R&D-intensity home base industries.

We ask now, did R&D and advertising intensities change for the divested lines as sell-off drew near? Since industry characteristics matter, we analyze only individual LBs' deviations from home industry averages. We focus on the full sell-offs, for which pre-divestiture changes are apt to be more clearly evident.[41] Table 6-10 summarizes the evidence. For research and development, there is a hint of less intense

41. The average deviations for the partial divestitures in the six years before sell-off were +0.07 percent for R&D and −0.05 percent for advertising, with no clear trend.

investment in the last year before sell-off, but that change is not significantly different from the previous year's value ($t = 1.12$). In advertising, the pattern, if any, is even weaker. Thus, the evidence does not support a conclusion that firms cut back their investment in R&D and advertising disproportionately as the conditions precipitating sell-off gathered momentum.

This does not mean that *absolute* levels of R&D and advertising outlays were maintained. Current-dollar LB sales grew more slowly in sold-off lines than in retained lines as sell-off neared.[42] The most that can be said is that the to-be-divested lines cut back on their R&D and advertising no more rapidly than their sales base shrank.

Conclusion

To sum up, a sizable fraction of the acquisitions made during the 1960s and early 1970s were subsequently resold. Our best estimate within a wide range of uncertainty is one-third. Acquired units were much more likely to be subjected to divestiture, and especially full divestiture, than lines already operated by the parent companies in 1950. Poor and declining profitability, at the LB or company level or both, characteristically preceded sell-off. Pooling acquisitions, which were unusually profitable pre-merger, were more likely to be sold than the purchase accounting acquisitions on which asset value step-ups had been recorded. A change in top management encouraged the divestiture of acquired LBs, while a strong market position, reflected by high market shares and/or large prior investments in research and development, diminished the probability of sell-off. There appears to be no general evidence that R&D and advertising spending were cut back disproportionately in anticipation of sell-off.

For both acquired and original lines, sell-off was on average a manifestation of financial distress. This does not mean that the sell-off per se was in some sense bad; rather, bad conditions precipitated the

42. The clearest comparison of sales changes can be made for the sample of LBs that qualified for inclusion in the combined 1975–77 regression 4-2(7) in chap. 4. The 82 LBs in that sample that were fully sold off in 1978 or 1979 had mean and median current-dollar sales growth rates between 1975 and 1977 only about a half as large as those of the remaining LBs. The differences are statistically significant. Even for the divested lines, however, the average nominal sales growth rates were positive, although standard deviations were three to four times the mean values.

decision to sell. Our case studies reveal that substantial efficiency increases often occurred under the new organizational structures established following divestiture. Restructuring through sell-off was not a complete solution, as evidenced by the bankruptcies afflicting particularly distressed, highly leveraged divestitures reported in the case studies of chapter 5 and the average 1977 return of roughly 5.9 percent achieved by sold-off units acquired by Line of Business sample corporations.[43] But the restructuring appears at least to have been a significant step in the right direction.

43. See regression 4-4(5) in chap. 4 and the discussion in chap. 5.

CHAPTER SEVEN

Pulling the Threads Together

WE ATTEMPT now to answer the questions posed at the beginning of our study. How successful have manufacturing mergers of the 1960s and early 1970s been? Did they serve the economy well by increasing the efficiency of resource allocation and utilization? To the extent that benefits were achieved, how were they distributed? It is generally acknowledged that acquired firm shareholders secured attractive acquisition premiums, but how well did acquiring companies' stockholders fare? What behavioral inferences can be drawn from the tally of gains and losses?

The Efficiency Consequences

One important insight is that corporate acquirers of the 1960s and 1970s began by selecting good material. They sought promising, well-managed acquisition targets, and on average, they succeeded in finding them. The typical acquired company reported operating returns on assets well above the norms for all manufacturing industry in the last year before surrendering its independence. The typical acquiree was also small, and the target selection process had a size bias: the smaller the target, the more its profitability tended to surpass peer industry norms. Yet even the larger acquired firms had good records. For one cohort of acquired companies near the upper extreme of the size distribution—mergers of equals partners—pre-merger profitability was statistically indistinguishable from that of all manufacturing enterprises. For tender offer targets, it averaged only 8 percent below peer industry norms.

The Sell-Offs

After merger, the acquired entities sooner or later divided into two groups—the sell-offs and the survivors. Our estimate of the sell-off

192

fraction remains uncertain; a compromise between the solidly based extreme values suggests that roughly a third of all acquisitions were eventually divested, with an average lag of nearly ten years.

For the divested entities, the story from an efficiency perspective is overwhelmingly one of failure. Operating income fell, turning negative on average in the year preceding divestiture. The reasons for this decline are not rooted simply in industry-specific problems. The fall was nearly as severe in relation to four-digit industry averages as in absolute terms. Our case studies illuminate the reasons. The targets were often acquired at or near a profit peak, and some subsequent disappointment was virtually inevitable. Bad luck struck frequently. But the fault was not only in the stars. The acquired entities often coped poorly with adversity because the new and more complex organizational structures imposed upon them slowed corrective responses and sapped motivation. Crises aggravated the organizational mismatch between parent and subsidiary and impaired constructive problem-solving. Although it is impossible to prove the counterfactual, the evidence points strongly toward a conclusion that the loss of control was worse under merger than it would have been in the simpler organizational structure of an independent entity. And in a smaller set of cases, organizational complexity and incentive breakdowns actively precipitated new problems, rather than merely impeding the solution of exogenously generated problems.

Surviving Lines

For the more numerous acquisitions that were survivors, the evidence on efficiency effects is most clear-cut for those treated under pooling-of-interests accounting, and hence without the asset revaluations accompanying purchase acquisitions. Our cross-sectional analysis finds operating income/assets ratios to be erratically, and for the years 1975–77 together insignificantly, above the returns achieved by no-merger lines of comparable industry base and market share. However, that nearly normal performance represented a sharp drop from the high pre-merger returns achieved by pooling acquisition companies. The full cross-sectional analysis suggests a post-merger profitability decline of roughly one-half percentage point per year; the smaller pre- versus post-merger analysis (limited to LB-originating conglomerate acquisitions) shows more rapid decline. Although some of the decline is attributable to the unsustainably high level of pre-merger profits, an appreciable fraction appears to be a scaled-down manifestation of the control loss problems that led to sell-off in more extreme cases. Not surprisingly, the problems were most serious following pure conglomerate acquisitions, in which the parent's managerial experience was least well-suited to crisis problem-solving. Even for the "related business" and horizontal acquisitions, however, post-acquisition profitability was depressed relative to the levels identified in our pre-merger analysis.

Declining average post-merger profitability is not the only symptom of deteriorating efficiency. Examining a smaller but richly disaggregated sample, Dennis Mueller found systematic market share losses following horizontal and (especially) conglomerate mergers.[1] Had we not controlled in our cross-sectional regressions for the relatively small 1975–77 market shares of acquired lines, we would have estimated even larger declines from pre-merger profitability levels.

As always, exceptions exist. Concealed in the disappointing averages for pooling acquisition survivors must be some strong success stories. The mergers of equals are a more systematic exception. The cross-sectional analyses point to a modest but consistent operating income/assets gain relative to no-merger lines and pre-merger averages. The mergers of equals experience is probably explained in managerial control terms. By definition, a merger of equals avoids the size asymmetries that leave previously independent company heads laboring under an unaccustomed control hierarchy. The stakes involved also compel the investment of more managerial energy into making the merger "work" than does the typical nonequals acquisition.

Acquisitions consummated using purchase accounting, and the tender offer acquisitions that fall mostly within the purchase accounting cohort, are more difficult to evaluate. On average, the nontender purchases entered the world of mergers with profit returns insignificantly above peer industry levels. After merger, returns on assets were significantly below no-merger peer levels. Merger-related asset revaluations precipitated some of the decline, but the purchase mergers also fared poorly relative to *NEW* lines. And even when the analysis focuses on the ratio of cash flow to sales—magnitudes unaffected by merger accounting choices—the purchase acquisitions exhibit below-par performance. Evidently, they too suffered from managerial control loss problems. The

1. Dennis C. Mueller, "Mergers and Market Share," *Review of Economics and Statistics*, vol. 67 (May 1985), pp. 261–66.

tender offer targets are an apparent exception. Starting from a profit position slightly below that of industry peers, they fell appreciably after merger. However, most of the change came from asset revaluations. Although the tenderers apparently failed to improve their targets' operating efficiency, they at least managed to avoid having it fall to significantly lower levels.

The Combined Efficiency Consequences

To bring our findings into better-integrated perspective, we make a number of assumptions, some heroic. The payoff in heightened insight, we believe, warrants the risk of pressing our data to their limits and perhaps beyond.

One important assumption is that, at least for the pooling-of-interests mergers, profitability movements reflect changes in operating efficiency relative to industry norms, and not waxing or waning monopoly power or income redistributions between the acquired entity and its managers, employees, or input suppliers.

Our opening wedge is figure 7-1. It plots the estimated regression equation relating pre-merger profitability to acquired company size for the 634 acquisitions analyzed at length in chapter 3.[2] That analysis was for profit returns in the years 1967, 1970, and 1973. The short-dashed line in figure 7-1 shows the raw operating income/assets regression equation for poolings as a function of company size; the solid line adjusts the relationship to be comparable with 1974–77 macroeconomic conditions. The long-dashed line is the analogous *MACRO*-adjusted pre-

---

2. The fitted regression equation is:

$$PROF:A = 32.32 - 3.02 \log_{10} ASSETS - 18.39 \ PURCH$$
$$ (8.13) \quad (2.66) \phantom{\log_{10} ASSETS -} (2.26)$$

$$+ \ 2.855 \ PURCH \times \log_{10} ASSETS,$$
$$ (1.25)$$

$$R^2 = 0.0450, n = 634.$$

where *PROF:A* is pre-merger operating income/assets (in percent), *ASSETS* is pre-merger assets (in thousands of dollars), and *PURCH* is a purchase accounting dummy variable. Although the size–purchase-accounting interaction term is not statistically significant, it seems important to account for the nonlinearity it introduces. For the pooling acquisitions, whose values are plotted by leaving out the terms with *PURCH*, the results are not much affected by using this interactive regression as compared to one lacking the interaction.

Figure 7-1. *Pre-Merger Profitability as a Function of Acquired Company Size*

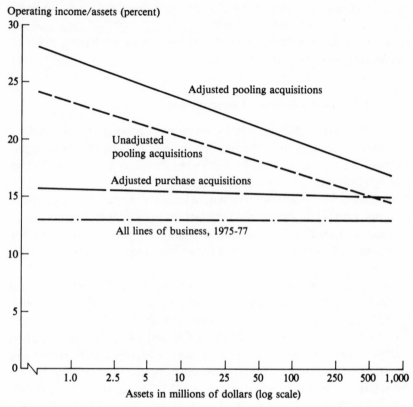

Operating income/assets (percent)

Adjusted pooling acquisitions

Unadjusted pooling acquisitions

Adjusted purchase acquisitions

All lines of business, 1975-77

Assets in millions of dollars (log scale)

merger profit equation for purchase acquisitions. The dot-dash line shows the average 13.31 percent return of Line of Business sample units for the years 1975–77. If acquired entities' post-merger profits fell uniformly into parity with the LB sample mean, we might estimate the resulting efficiency loss as the difference between macroeconomically adjusted pre-merger profits (declining with size) and 13.31 percent, weighted by the fraction of assets included in each acquired company size class. However, certain adjustments are required before the desired computations can be carried out.

For one, pooling acquisitions actually fared somewhat better than all-sample averages, as shown by the +0.36 *POOL* coefficient in chapter 4's 1975–77 regression 4-2(7), while purchases, with a coefficient of

−3.84, fared worse.[3] The coefficients' values tell the amount by which profitability is elevated or degraded with a change from no acquisition history to 100 percent merger origin of LB assets, other things such as industry membership and market share held equal. But on average, only 39 percent of the assets of LBs with acquisitions stemmed directly from acquisition.[4] Thus, the average *POOL* surplus above "normal" levels is $0.36 \times 0.39 = 0.14$; the average *PURCH* deficit is $-3.84 \times 0.39 = -1.50$.

Second, the profitability average for all LBs is not necessarily the correct no-merger norm. Pooling acquisitions raised the all-LB average, purchase acquisitions lowered it. From appendix A, we estimate that 55 percent of all acquisitions were poolings and 45 percent purchases, with no discernible size bias.[5] Thus, for 100 percent asset origination by merger, the weighted average impact is $(+0.36 \times 0.55) - (3.84 \times 0.45) = -1.53$ percentage points. On average, then, mergers pulled down the all-sample average. The no-merger norm must be higher than 13.31 percent. Recalling that 25 percent of total sample assets (from LBs with and without acquisitions) originated directly from acquisitions,[6] we solve for the "norm" P^* as $13.31 = 0.75\, P^* + 0.25\,(P^* - 1.53)$; thus, $P^* = 13.69$.[7]

To solve for the average post-merger profitability of pooled acquisition LBs, we add to P^* the $+0.14$ value derived two paragraphs earlier, obtaining a return of 13.83 percent. Likewise, for purchase acquisitions, the relevant post-merger benchmark is $13.69 - 1.50 = 12.19$ percent. The gap between these 1975–77 values and the pre-merger values traced in figure 7-1 is our first approximation to the efficiency loss associated with mergers. However, because pre-merger profits vary with acquired company size, those deviations must be weighted by the relative fre-

3. Results for 1975–77 are used not only because of their broader coverage, but because 1975–77 as a whole had macroeconomic conditions more like the ensuing 1978– 85 period than 1977. Average civilian unemployment rates were 7.8 percent in 1975–77, 7.1 percent in 1977, and 7.6 percent in 1978–85.

4. This figure is an LB count-weighted average of the *NEWMERG* and *ORIGMERG* fractions given in the section on "Alternative Controls" in chap. 4.

5. For the 634-acquisition sample, the correlation between the logarithm of acquired company assets and the purchase dummy variable was +0.031, which is not statistically significant.

6. See the analysis of "Industries Favored by Acquirers" in chap. 2.

7. We do not calculate P^* by the more straightforward method of averaging no-merger LBs' profit ratios because those lines had above-average market shares. The method used here controls for industry and market share effects.

Table 7-1. *Derivation of Asset-Weighted Deviations of Post-Merger from Pre-Merger Profitability in 634-Company Sample*

Pre-merger asset range (millions of dollars)	Asset weight (1)	Pooling acquisitions		Purchase acquisitions	
		Predicted pre-merger return (percent)[a] (2)	MACRO-adjusted return (percent) (3)	Predicted pre-merger return (percent)[a] (4)	MACRO-adjusted return (percent) (5)
Less than 1.0	0.0083	24.31	28.28	13.50	15.71
1.00–2.49	0.0212	22.67	26.37	13.41	15.61
2.50–4.99	0.0385	21.61	25.14	13.36	15.54
5.00–9.99	0.0456	20.71	24.09	13.31	15.48
10.00–14.99	0.0389	19.99	23.25	13.27	15.44
15.00–19.99	0.0295	19.53	22.72	13.25	15.41
20.00–29.99	0.0625	19.08	22.19	13.22	15.38
30.00–49.99	0.0865	18.48	21.50	13.19	15.34
50.00–99.99	0.1120	17.69	20.58	13.15	15.30
100.00–249.99	0.1260	16.69	19.41	13.09	15.23
250.00–500.00	0.1950	15.58	18.12	13.04	15.16
More than 500.00	0.2360	14.80	17.21	12.99	15.12
Resulting deviation	1.000[b]	. . .	6.20[c]	. . .	3.076[d]

a. Computed from the regression equation in text note 2.
b. Σ col. (1) = 1.000.
c. Σ col. (1) × [col. (3) − 13.83] = 6.20.
d. Σ col. (1) × [col. (5) − 12.19] = 3.076.

quency of acquisitions in diverse asset size classes. Table 7-1 does the job, using as size weights the distribution of acquired company assets found in the 634-company sample of chapter 3.[8] For pooling acquisitions, the asset-weighted average deviation between pre-merger and post-merger returns is 6.20 percent of assets. This value is lower than it would be if the estimates were based upon an unweighted count of acquisitions, since the largest acquisitions had relatively small deviations, but account for a disproportionate share of acquired assets. For the purchase acquisitions, the asset-weighted deviation is 3.08 percent of assets.

Additional adjustments must be made. Not all of the average 6.20 percent fall in pooling mergers' profitability can be attributed to merger-related inefficiencies. Some would have occurred in any event. Splitting the difference between the *DM* × *PREPI* coefficients of chapter 4's text

8. For each size interval, pre-merger profitability is predicted at the interval's geometric mean (for the closed intervals) or at the median acquired company value (for open-ended intervals).

equations 4-6 and 4-7, we take 0.24 as our best estimate of the merger-induced fraction—that is, the average of 0.19 and 0.29. Thus, the efficiency loss for pooling merger lines is estimated to be 0.24 × 6.20 = 1.488 percent of 1975–77 assets. Likewise, not all of the drop in purchase accounting acquisitions' profitability can be attributed to reduced efficiency. Given the much lower pre-merger level from which purchase acquisitions began, the main alternative factor must be merger-induced asset revaluations. The − 3.84 *PURCH* coefficient in operating income/assets regression 4-2(7) was 28.9 percent of mean 1975–77 operating income/assets for all LBs. Purging all revaluation effects, the − 1.23 *PURCH* coefficient in cash-flow regression 4-2(10) was 12.2 percent of 1975–77 cash flow/sales. Thus, the effect without revaluations is about 42 percent (that is, 100 [12.2 / 28.9]) of the effect with revaluations. Choosing to err on the conservative side, we assume that one-third of the − 3.84 percentage point asset-deflated effect was efficiency-related. Thus, the efficiency loss on purchase acquisitions is estimated at 3.076 percent (from table 7-1) × 0.33 = 1.015 percent of relevant 1975–77 assets.

These efficiency loss percentages must be applied to appropriate asset universes. Our tally of the FTC's "large" merger data for the years 1950–76 showed total acquired manufacturing and mining company assets of $88.9 billion. This must be adjusted upward by 1 / (1 − 0.1136) to correct (from the table 7-1 asset weight data) for omitted acquisitions of companies with assets below $10 million. The result must be adjusted downward to reflect the fact that our analysis covers manufacturing only, which in 1975–77 originated 90.5 percent of manufacturing plus mining gross national product.[9] The adjusted acquired asset population is found to be $90.8 billion.

A more difficult conceptual question must also be addressed. Our estimates of the profit rate decline in table 7-1 compare pre-merger returns with post-merger returns on 1975–77 assets. The merger-impacted LBs had much larger assets in 1977 than they acquired at the time of merger. From the average growth experience of post-1950 merger-originated (*NEWMERG*) lines, 1977 merger-related assets exceeded time-of-acquisition assets by an average factor of 1 / 0.56 = 1.786.[10] The

9. This percentage is based upon current-dollar GNP data before the general revision of GNP accounts. See the *Economic Report of the President, February 1985,* p. 244.

10. This is the factor obtained using untruncated *MERGSHR* values for the *NEWMERG* group. See the "Sensitivity Analyses" in chap. 4.

counterfactual question is, would the assets resulting from post-merger investment have yielded only normal returns, or would they have been as profitable (after allowing for regression and revaluation effects) as the acquired companies were before merger? Truth probably lies somewhere between the extremes, but without a clear answer, we proceed to make upper- and lower-bound estimates of the relevant asset universes (in billions of dollars):

	Total manufac- turing universe	Poolings (total × 0.55)	Purchases (total × 0.45)
Lower bound	90.81	49.95	40.86
Upper bound (lower × 1.786)	162.19	89.20	72.99

To arrive at our basic estimate of the 1975–77 efficiency loss in the wake of nondivested acquisitions, we multiply the asset universe values by the average efficiency loss percentages, arriving at the following values (in billions of dollars per year):

	Poolings	Purchases
Lower bound	0.743	0.415
Upper bound	1.327	0.741

Mergers of equals were an exception to the tendency for profits to fall. For our impact estimate, we use the +1.37 percentage point *EQUALS* coefficient of 1975–77 regression 4-2(7).[11] Because mergers of equals partners had an unusually high fraction of nonmanufacturing and foreign assets and because it is unreasonable to expect sold-off mergers of equals lines to have fared as well as retained lines, we estimate the mergers of equals asset base directly from our 1977 sample at $35.0 billion. Although the Line of Business sample covered 75 percent of all 1950–76 manufacturing and mining sector acquired assets, it probably includes nearly all relevant companies large enough to have entered mergers of equals as we have defined them. We therefore inflate the asset base by a more conservative 0.90 sampling ratio. Multiplying the $38.9 billion asset base by the 0.0137 impact coefficient, our estimate of the annual efficiency *gains* from mergers of equals is $0.53 billion per year.[12]

11. See chap. 4.

12. An implicit assumption is made that, but for merger, the post-merger assets of *EQUALS* lines would have realized only normal returns. Although mergers of equals

Sell-offs pose special estimation challenges. In contrast to the pattern assumed here for retained lines, their profitability may have deteriorated rapidly, at least for the divestitures occurring in the early 1970s. Once profits fell, recovery was at best slow. Substantial capital value write-offs accompanied many sell-offs, and as regression 4-4(5) shows, operating income/assets ratios for divested lines acquired by Line of Business sample companies rose by 1977 to an average of only 5.9 percent after purchase accounting asset revaluations. Since lines sold off in 1975, 1976, and 1977 are all excluded under the sampling assumptions governing regression 4-2(7), the losses attending pre-1978 sell-offs are not captured by our surviving line efficiency loss estimates. However, the 1975–77 continuing line loss estimate does anticipate the deteriorating profitability of post-1977 divestitures. Ignoring the resurgence of late 1970s mergers that probably induced a reversal of sell-off trends in 1981, we extrapolate linearly the downward 1971–80 trend and estimate that between 1965 and 1984, there were 17,050 sell-offs attributable to pre-1978 mergers, of which 13,562, or 79.5 percent, occurred prior to 1978. Thus, the cumulated sell-off fraction relevant to a 1977 loss estimate is 0.795.

Some lines would have encountered difficulties and been sold off even if they had not been merged. However, lines with no merger history were only half as likely to be divested as lines with a merger history.[13] We therefore assume that 50 percent of the 1965–77 sell-offs were attributable to merger. Splitting the difference between the extreme (19 and 47 percent) estimates of chapter 6, we assume that 33 percent of acquired entities were divested. Leonard W. Weiss's study yields as high a sell-off rate for large acquisitions, so we make no asset weighting distinctions.[14] Thus, our merger-caused sell-off ratio is 0.33 × 0.795 × 0.50 = 0.13 relative to the total merger count. It is doubtful whether

---

are found to be efficiency-increasing and other pooling mergers efficiency-reducing, it is not appropriate to subtract the mergers of equals assets from the ordinary pooling merger asset base. The mergers of equals had pre-merger profit ratios insignificantly different from those of all manufacturing corporations. If the assets on which they realized only normal returns were subtracted from the general pooling merger asset base covered by figure 7-1, the pre-merger profitability ratios of nonequals acquisitions would have to be raised commensurately. We accomplish the same effect more simply by leaving the asset base unadjusted.

13. Using regression 6-7(1a) from chap. 6, the probability of sell-off with both *NEWMERG* and *ORIGMERG* set at zero, other variables held at their means, is 0.0496. With both set at unity, it is 0.0989, or 1.99 times as great. Similar relationships hold for partial sell-offs, as shown in table 6-9.

14. Leonard W. Weiss, "The Extent and Effects of Aggregate Concentration," *Journal of Law & Economics*, vol. 26 (June 1983), pp. 440–41.

sold-off lines experienced as much post-merger growth as lines surviving through 1975–77, partly because they were less successful and partly because some were divested prior to 1975. We conservatively split at the one-third point the difference between the lower-bound merged asset figure of $90.81 billion and the upper-bound figure of $162.2 billion, obtaining an asset base of $114.6 billion. Applying the 0.13 merger-caused sell-off fraction, we estimate the relevant asset impact base at $14.9 billion.

For the average full sell-off, operating income was 1.73 percent of assets in the three years before divestiture, which is 11.96 points below the no-merger norm. Using this to estimate immediate pre-divestiture conditions and those persisting after asset write-downs and partial profitability recovery, we estimate the annualized sell-off efficiency loss in 1975–77 as $14.9 billion × 0.1196 = $1.78 billion.

Summing up, we estimate the following lower- and upper-bound annual 1975–77 merger impacts (in billions of dollars):

	Lower bound	Upper bound
Loss on retained pooling mergers	−0.74	−1.33
Loss on retained purchase mergers	−0.42	−0.74
Gain on mergers of equals	+0.53	+0.53
Loss on sold-off acquisitions	−1.78	−1.78
Total	−2.41	−3.32

The estimated annual efficiency losses are in the range of 0.59 to 0.81 percent of current-dollar gross national product ($410.4 billion) originating in the manufacturing sector during 1976. It seems reasonable to assume that these efficiency losses began accumulating in significant amounts at the peak of the conglomerate merger wave in 1968. If they grew by roughly equal increments in each subsequent year up to 1976, the midpoint of our post-merger evaluation period, they in effect reduced the annual *growth* of total factor productivity by the amount of the increment divided by GNP. Over the assumed eight-year period, the annual percentage reduction in productivity growth must have been between 0.074 percentage points (that is, 0.59/8) and 0.101 points. Between 1968 and 1976, the annual growth rate of total factor productivity in the U.S. manufacturing sector averaged 1.84 percent, a decline of 0.96 percentage points per year relative to the 1960–68 rate.[15] Thus,

15. U.S. Bureau of Labor Statistics, "Multifactor Productivity Measures," USDL 85–40 *News,* October 3, 1985, p. 8.

merger effects help explain roughly a tenth of the productivity decline—a modest contribution, but not so small that it can be ignored.[16] Whether our findings for manufacturing can be extrapolated to other sectors of the economy, which experienced even more alarming slumps in productivity growth, cannot be determined on the basis of our research.

Still to be considered is the merger-related reduction in research and development outlays discovered in table 4-8. From the negative (but statistically insignificant) ORIGMERG and NEWMERG coefficients of 0.074 and 0.133, respectively, our best estimate of the average effect for all manufacturing LBs (with and without mergers) is [(0.074 × 723) + (0.133 × 1,515)] / 2,955 = 0.086, where the nondecimal values are LB counts in the two merger categories and the full 1977 sample.[17] The estimated 0.086 percentage point reduction is a decline of 5.5 percent relative to the 1.555 percent average R&D/sales ratio for all manufacturing industries. Applying R&D–productivity growth relationships estimated elsewhere,[18] we find that a 5.5 percent reduction in R&D lowers the ratio of R&D used by industries relative to their sales by 0.055 × 0.73 = 0.0402. Taking into account both the benefits of R&D to industries doing process R&D and to those buying the products emanating from other industries' product R&D, the estimated productivity growth rate multiplier applicable to this last figure is 0.74.[19] Thus, the productivity growth shortfall attributable to mergers is approximately 0.0402 × 0.74 = 0.030, or roughly one thirty-third the overall annual productivity decline of the mid-1970s. Because approximately 96 percent of all privately financed industrial R&D is performed in the manufacturing sector, and because roughly half of the new technology originated through manufacturing R&D "flows" out for use in other sectors,[20] this shortfall affected the entire economy and was not confined to manufacturing. Again, the impact is small numerically, but not so small that it can be shrugged off.

16. For a more wide-ranging investigation, see Edward F. Denison, *Trends in American Economic Growth, 1929–1982* (Brookings, 1985), especially chap. 3.

17. Alternatively, the statistically significant *MERGSHR* coefficient in regression 4-8(1) is −0.28. Multiplied by 0.39, the average ratio of acquired to 1977 LB assets for lines with acquisitions, the estimated impact is −0.109. Thus, the estimate in the text errs on the conservative side.

18. See F. M. Scherer, *Innovation and Growth: Schumpeterian Perspectives* (M.I.T. Press, 1984), pp. 288–89.

19. This is the *USERD1* coefficient of productivity regression 3.1 in ibid., p. 279.

20. Ibid., pp. 50–51.

Were Mergers Profitable for the Acquirers?

That operating efficiency fell on average following merger does not necessarily mean that acquisition activity was unprofitable for the acquirers. The companies acquired, we have seen, were highly profitable before acquisition, and it took time for their profitability to deteriorate. Meanwhile, the acquisitions may have yielded handsome cash flows. To determine how well the acquiring corporations fared, we must consider how much they invested in securing those cash flows.

Purchase Acquisitions

The purchase accounting effect coefficients provide preliminary insight. For a line of business whose assets originated 100 percent from purchase acquisitions, according to regression 4-2(7), the ratio of operating income to assets was 3.84 percentage points below no-merger levels averaged over 1975–77, or, according to regression 4-2(4), 3.74 percentage points for the single year 1977. The 1975–77 no-merger norm, we recall, was approximately 13.69 percent. Thus, the implied average return (before taxes and financing costs) on retained purchase acquisitions was approximately $13.69 - 3.84 = 9.85$ percent. For divested acquisitions, needless to say, it had to be much lower. Because the *PURCH* coefficients are significantly negative in all operating income/ assets regressions while the *NEW* coefficients are preponderantly positive, purchase acquisitions were less profitable on average than new (internal growth) lines, whose assets also had to be acquired at current market prices, as well as no-merger lines already operated in 1950.

This does not necessarily mean that purchase acquisitions were unprofitable. Since the marginal efficiency of investment schedule undoubtedly slopes downward, *marginal* returns in established and new lines could have been lower than the returns on purchase acquisitions. And the returns on acquisitions may have exceeded the cost of new capital. On this, more will be said later.

The depression of operating income/assets ratios measured by the *PURCH* coefficients reflects, as we have seen, a combination of efficiency losses, merger-induced asset revaluations, and higher depreciation charges. Our comparison of cash flow/sales with operating income/

assets results suggests that the efficiency loss component was nearly as large as the revaluation component.

Pooling Acquisitions

For pooling-of-interests acquisitions, the revaluations attending merger were buried in adjustments to stockholders' equity accounts, and hence are not detectable in operating income/assets ratios. However, insight into the relevant magnitudes can be drawn from our analysis of accounting method choices in appendix A. We found that in exchange-of-securities acquisitions, pooling accounting was much more likely to be chosen over purchase accounting if the acquisition price substantially exceeded the book value of the acquired company's assets. Now we add a further datum. For the 1,409 acquisitions on which statistics measuring both "consideration paid" and pre-merger asset value were available, the consideration paid/asset ratio averaged 1.75 for acquisitions treated as poolings, but only 1.05 for purchase acquisitions. Both ratios are underestimates, since they do not count as part of the consideration paid the net value of accounts payable, bank debt, and other liabilities assumed. Still it is clear that if the profitability of purchase acquisitions was pulled down by the payment of acquisition prices exceeding book value, the profitability of pooling acquisitions would be affected even more sharply under comparable accounting.[21]

A step toward comparability can be taken by applying the information derived from our accounting choice analysis. Using the all-industry norm constructed earlier, the average 1975–77 operating income/assets ratio for 100 percent pooling acquisitions was $13.69 + 0.36 = 14.05$ percent.[22] That return is calculated on the book value of assets, unadjusted for the acquisition price paid. Since the average price paid was at least 1.75

21. To permit comparison with no-merger lines that had no similar asset revaluations, our stress here is on the premium of the acquisition price over the acquired company's book value. That premium can be decomposed into two parts: the acquisition price premium per share over pre-merger stock prices, and the premium (if any) of the pre-merger stock price over book value per share. W. T. Grimm & Co. data on public company acquisitions indicate that the first of these premiums averaged 25 percent in 1968–69, 33 percent in 1970–72, and 44 percent in 1973–76. *Mergerstat Review, 1982* (Chicago: Grimm, 1983), pp. 70–71. The second premium fluctuates with values of Tobin's Q ratio.

22. We focus here on lines whose assets originated entirely from pooling acquisitions. Little can be said about the incremental returns on new investments made after acquisition.

times pre-merger book value, the denominator of the operating income/ assets ratio for 100 percent pooling-originated lines must be multiplied by 1.75 to arrive at a value comparable to the average return observed for purchase accounting acquisitions. We thus take 14.05 / 1.75 = 8.03 percent as our best estimate of the average 1975–77 pre-tax, pre-interest return on surviving 100 percent pooling acquisition assets. This is lower than the analogous return estimated for purchase acquisitions. It is higher than the average 6.77 percent interest rate on Baa corporate bonds over the years 1965–70,[23] but considerably lower than the median 12 percent *after-tax* "hurdle rate" applied by sizable corporations in determining whether or not to go forward with investment prospects during the late 1960s.[24]

The analysis thus far relates 1975–77 returns to earlier acquisition investments. Because the profitability of acquired lines declined over time from quite high pre-merger levels, it is possible that merger investments were justified primarily on the basis of their early cash inflows. To explore this possibility, internal rates of return were computed for two pooling acquisition cash-flow scenarios consistent with the statistical findings of chapters 4 and 6. Since available hurdle rate benchmarks are in after-tax terms, we must also take into account income tax obligations. The following assumptions were made:

1. As worked out previously, the normal pre-tax operating income/ assets ratio was 13.69 percent. The average pooling acquisition target earned in its last pre-merger year a return exceeding that norm by 9.8 points, that is, a total return of 23.49 percent.

2. After acquisition, the acquired company's profitability declined linearly to the normal 13.69 percent level over ten years (somewhat longer than the average period identified in chapter 4's matched pre-

23. *Economic Report of the President, February 1985*, p. 310.

24. See Ronald B. Williams, Jr., "Industry Practice in Allocating Capital Resources," *Managerial Planning*, May-June 1970, p. 21, presenting results for 68 companies surveyed in April 1969. Only 4 of Williams's respondents had hurdle rates of 8 percent or lower. To be comparable with the pre-tax operating income/asset ratios examined at this stage, the hurdle rates found by Williams would have to be higher—by at least half, if a 60/40 equity/debt relationship was maintained and the marginal corporate income tax rate was 0.50.

For later and higher hurdle rate estimates reflecting the inflation that followed in the early and mid-1970s, see Lawrence J. Gitman and John R. Forrester, Jr., "A Survey of Capital Budgeting Techniques Used by Major U.S. Firms," *Financial Management*, vol. 6 (Fall 1977), pp. 66–71; and Samuel L. Hayes III, "Capital Commitments and the High Cost of Money," *Harvard Business Review*, vol. 55 (May-June 1977), p. 159.

versus post-merger analysis). Barring sell-off, it then remained at that level through year 25, after which the economic life of acquired assets was exhausted.

3. The company's financial structure was such that the effective income tax rate on operating income was 25 percent.

4. Cash flows associated with depreciation were 4.56 percent of assets (derived from the relationships between 1975–77 cash flow, operating income, and assets). They were fully shielded against income taxation.

5. From chapter 6, 33 percent of acquired lines were eventually sold off. Sell-off occurred linearly over post-merger years 1–20. The operating income returns of sold-off lines were identical to those of assumptions 1 and 2 until five years before sell-off, after which the full sell-off return pattern of table 6-2 took over. Depreciation continued at 4.56 percent of assets until sell-off. After sell-off, operating income and depreciation flows were zero.

6. All asset values in assumptions 1–5 were at undepreciated pre-merger book values consistent with pooling-of-interests accounting. However, a premium of 75 percent over book value was paid in making the acquisition; thus, the acquirer's initial investment was 1.75 times book asset values.

Given these assumptions, which were formulated to parallel our pooling acquisition and sell-off findings as closely as possible, internal rates of return were calculated. If assumption 5 is waived, that is, assuming no degradation of cash flows owing to sell-offs, the internal rate of return after taxes is found to be 8.27 percent—a good deal less than the after-tax hurdle rates used by U.S. corporations at the peak of the 1960s merger wave. If assumption 5 is included, letting sell-offs reduce average returns, the internal rate of return is 6.05 percent.

These findings indicate that the average acquisition, if not downright unprofitable, was not highly profitable. To press our data further along these lines would be to ask more of them than they can deliver.

Stock Market Performance

Our generally bearish evaluation of the profitability of merger to acquirers might appear at odds with our discovery in chapter 2 that 3 of the 13 most merger-intensive conglomerate corporations of the 1960s conferred spectacular returns upon early common stock investors, and a majority outperformed the Standard & Poor's industrials portfolio from 1965 through 1983.[25] The experience of the 13 merger-intensive conglomerates, encompassing about 16 percent of all the mergers (manufacturing and nonmanufacturing) made by Line of Business sample members, may not have been representative of the larger cross section. Or our profitability analyses, which put equal weight on each LB observation, may have underestimated the importance of the occasional merger that remained highly profitable and grew rapidly to dominate its parent's profit and stock price picture. Although this is conceivable, there is an equally plausible alternative explanation for the apparent divergence between the profit cross-section findings and the leading conglomerates' stock price records. The stock price conclusions are sensitive to the choice of a date at which investors are assumed to have bought their shares. When a mid-1968 date was selected, only 3 of the 13 were found to have outperformed the S&P portfolio.

To avoid making arbitrary buy-in date choices, we assume now that stockholders invested in the 13 leading conglomerates' stocks over time in proportion to the consideration paid by those companies in effecting acquisitions.[26] In this way, we take into account the fortunes not only of "early bird" investors, but also of those who bought stock to finance additional mergers and those who accepted the conglomerates' stock in mergers and then held it, rather than cashing it in immediately.[27] Concretely, we assume that investors invested a given sum,

$$\sum_{t=1962}^{1983} W_t,$$

in proportion to each of the 13 conglomerates' acquisition activity between 1962 and 1978, holding on to their shares (and reinvesting cash dividends) to June 30, 1983. The June 1983 terminal date coincides with a stock market peak, assuring relatively favorable returns. We compute the investment-weighted average internal rate of return:

25. It is important to recall that these 13 had more favorable stock market experiences than less acquisitive conglomerates. See chap. 2, note 19.

26. The consideration paid data, often approximate, were taken from the FTC's "all merger" historical data files, supplemented by research in *Moody's Industrial Manual* and similar sources.

27. The two actions are substitutes, since if one person receives stock as consideration for an acquisition and quickly sells it, the buyer of the stock in effect finances the acquisition.

(7-1)
$$\frac{\sum_{t=1962}^{1983} \left[W_t \, 100 \ln (P_{1983} / P_t) / (1983 - t) \right]}{\Sigma \, W_t},$$

where P_t is the value of a share of the company's stock on June 30 of year t and P_{1983} is the value of the same share, appropriately adjusted for splits, stock dividends, and reinvested cash dividends, in 1983. Tax liabilities are ignored.

For comparison, we assume that the same sum was invested in the Standard & Poor's industrials portfolio. How that investment was distributed over time is important. The scenario most neutral with respect to alternative temporary funds "parking" assumptions is one in which the funds were invested at a rate proportional to the summed consideration paid for mergers in each year by all 13 conglomerates. A less comparable but plausible scenario is to assume that the sum was invested in the S&P index in proportion to the current-dollar gross private investment component of U.S. gross national product. The latter assumption implies a more even rate of investment over time than the merger proportionality assumption, which had a pronounced bunching at the time of the 1966–70 merger wave, and thus required less temporary parking of funds.

Table 7-2 summarizes the results. Two conglomerates, Teledyne and Gulf & Western, continue to show high returns to investors. Compared to table 2-10, which assumes that all investments were made in 1965, Whittaker plunges, having consummated most of its mergers when its stock prices were unsustainably high, and W. R. Grace ascends, presumably on the strength of more favorable merger timing. Overall, only 4 of the 13 conglomerates outperformed S&P portfolio investments with comparable aggregate timing. Despite the high returns on Teledyne and Gulf & Western investments, the 7.57 percent mean rate of return for the 13 conglomerates together was somewhat below the acquisition-weighted return on the S&P portfolio. Only 2 conglomerates outperformed an investment in the S&P index at rates proportional to GNP investment flows. However, this comparison is supportable only on the questionable assumption that excess funds could be invested temporarily during the late 1960s at returns approximating the S&P's 10.2 percent. With either timing assumption, it is clear that merger-linked investments in the leading conglomerates were not abnormally profitable. This conclusion emerges all the more strongly when we recall from chapter 2

Table 7-2. *Internal Rates of Return as of 1983 from Investments Financing the Leading Conglomerates' Acquisition Activity, 1962–78*

Company	Acquisition-weighted return (percent)
Teledyne	15.78
Gulf & Western Industries	13.59
W. R. Grace & Co.	10.12
Kidde	9.43
Consolidated Foods Corp.	8.18
Textron	8.17
Beatrice Foods Co.	6.80
ITT Corp.	6.16
U.S. Industries	5.68
Genesco	5.61
Whittaker Corp.	4.04
Litton Industries	3.24
Chromalloy American Corp.	1.58
Mean	7.57
Median	6.80
S&P 425 industrials	
Acquisition-weighted return	8.24
GNP investment-weighted return	10.20[a]

a. The annualized inflation rate (from the GNP deflator) over the 1962–83 period was 5.31 percent.

that common stock investments in the leading conglomerates had extraordinarily high systematic risk, with β values averaging 1.49. Thus, investors got less return on average with more risk. In this respect, the stock market evidence for the 13 leading conglomerates is consistent with the profitability evidence for our much larger cross section of corporate acquirers.

Merger Performance and Merger Motives

There are surely more opinions on why mergers are made than there are economists who have written on the subject.[28] This may be inevitable, since merger motives are complex, and multiple motives may be at work in any given decision. Despite the difficulties, it is useful to see what light our research sheds on the question. Among other things, we

28. For references to the most important surveys and new contributions, see chap. 1, note 7.

must attempt to explain what motives led companies to make so many acquisitions that on average yielded such modest returns.

There are many broad (but not necessarily mutually exclusive) theories of merger motivation. The efficiency theory says that mergers occur because they improve the combined firms' operations—for example, by letting superior managers assume control, by exploiting cost-reducing "synergies" or complementarities in the partners' operations, or by taking fuller advantage of scale economies and risk-spreading opportunities, among other things in securing capital. The monopoly theory stresses the price-raising opportunities arising from consolidated market control, especially following horizontal mergers, or the possibility of buying inputs more cheaply owing to enhanced monopsony power. Undervalued-assets and bargain theories point to the opportunity for perceived mutual gain when a potential acquirer values a company's anticipated earnings stream more highly than current shareholders do. Empire-building theories propose that managers make acquisitions because they seek the power, prestige, and perquisites of controlling a large organization, even if shareholders' wealth is reduced in the process. Mergers can also be effected to secure tax advantages or to avoid investment strategy constraints imposed by the tax laws. And to round out what must necessarily be an incomplete list, we include the speculative or "bubble" theories, which imply that firms can persuade investors to support intensive merger activity through accounting manipulations, clever public relations, and the like.

None of these theories can be rejected flatly on the basis of our evidence. The most we can do is suggest degrees of plausibility and importance.

One that can be given low weight for our sample is the monopoly power theory. The bulk of U.S. manufacturing company acquisitions made in the 1950–76 period were conglomerate, for which it is hard (but not impossible) to concoct convincing monopoly power scenarios.[29] Most of the horizontal acquisitions involved market shares too small to confer much monopoly power, in part because larger horizontal acquisitions were under intense antitrust scrutiny. Exceptions existed, but they were not important enough to emphasize here.

Our finding that, on average, profitability declines and efficiency

29. See John T. Scott, "Multimarket Contact and Economic Performance," *Review of Economics and Statistics*, vol. 64 (August 1982), pp. 368–75; and Robert M. Feinberg, " 'Sales-at-Risk': A Test of the Mutual Forebearance Theory of Conglomerate Behavior," *Journal of Business*, vol. 58 (April 1985), pp. 225–41.

losses resulted from mergers of the 1960s and early 1970s casts doubt on the widespread applicability of an efficiency theory of merger motives. But we must be cautious in imputing motives from results.

It is clear from our case studies that some efficiencies did result from mergers, especially from the second round of mergers, mostly horizontal or into leveraged buyouts, that complemented sell-off by an earlier acquirer. The case studies also reveal that synergies anticipated from acquisition frequently did not materialize. Merger-makers tended to expect more than the circumstances proved to support, which is one reason why profitability was disappointing.

There is a broader implication in the same vein. Much more serious than the failure to achieve hoped-for synergies, our research indicates, was the failure to manage acquired companies as well as they were managed before acquisition. We have no reason to believe this was either intentional or fully anticipated. To the contrary, merger-makers of the 1960s and 1970s suffered from massive hubris. Successful in their main-line operations and perhaps in early diversification mergers, they over-estimated their ability to manage a sizable portfolio of acquisitions, large and small, related and unrelated. By the time they learned that they had erred, they had already overextended themselves and were unable to cope with the problems emerging from accumulated acquisitions. Or alternatively, they recognized their limitations but pursued a damage-limiting strategy, continuing (like Beatrice Foods) to make mergers but ruthlessly selling off acquisitions that showed signs of persistent difficulty.

What does not emerge from our research is strong support for the efficiency-through-management-displacement merger motive. At least in first-round acquisitions, acquirers sought well-managed companies and tried, not always successfully, to retain their managers. Indeed, in conglomerate acquisitions, there was often no alternative, for the acquirer lacked a pool of talent with the skills needed to lead a new and unfamiliar subsidiary successfully. Second-round acquisitions of sold-off units were an exception, especially when the acquirer had relevant skills and the divested unit's management ranks had been depleted during the crisis that led to sell-off.

Our research sheds relatively little light on what may be the most important synergy in conglomerate and related-business acquisitions—more elastic, or lower-cost, access to investable funds. There are definite and apparently persistent economies of scale in capital-raising. During the mid-1960s, for example, the average interest rate paid by U.S. corporations was reduced by approximately 0.46 percentage points with each tenfold increase in company size.[30] Because our quantitative analyses take operating income before the deduction of interest and other capital charges as the principal measure of company or LB profitability, they fail to account for possible merger-based capital cost savings. From the available evidence, such savings appear to have been too small to come anywhere near offsetting the operating inefficiencies stemming from merger-related organizational and motivational changes. Nevertheless, capital cost savings and the greater price elasticity of capital supplies under a large parent's umbrella were considered by case study interviewees to be one of the most important, if not the most important, advantage of being acquired. On the other hand, our asset growth analyses in chapter 4 yielded no evidence of growth retardation in small but profitable unmerged companies and only weak evidence of more rapid growth in acquired lines of business. Companies with profits approximating the average of our NYSE sample must have been attractive investment prospects, and it seems reasonable to suppose that many, if not all, could have attracted growth capital with or without merger.

A closely related advantage alleged for conglomerate mergers is the creation of an "internal capital market" within which the competition for investable funds is distorted minimally by transactions costs and tax considerations.[31] The tax connection is of special importance. Some companies, especially those at home in slowly growing industries, may have activities that generate more cash than they can reinvest profitably. If the surplus funds were distributed to shareholders as dividends, they would be taxed, often heavily, as ordinary personal income. At least during the period we analyzed, it often appeared preferable to retain the funds, use them to buy and build companies in fields with richer investment opportunities, and let the accumulated gains be realized by shareholders in the form of more lightly taxed capital gains. Such reasoning was clearly evident in some of the parent companies covered

30. See F. M. Scherer and others, *The Economics of Multi-Plant Operation: An International Comparisons Study* (Harvard University Press, 1975), pp. 284–88, which also summarizes the capital cost–company size literature.

31. See Oliver E. Williamson, *Corporate Control and Business Behavior: An Inquiry into the Effects of Organization Form on Enterprise Behavior* (Prentice-Hall, 1970), pp. 121–30, 163–64, and 176–77.

by our case studies—most notably, Chromalloy American. The literature on merger motives suggests that it is widespread, although our analysis in chapter 2 showed no strong tendency for conglomerates to diversify into industries markedly more profitable or more rapidly growing than the fields they originally occupied.

However important it may have been in practice, the internal capital market theory of merger motives is subject to some serious limitations. If the units acquired to absorb excess cash are managed poorly, the hoped-for capital gains will not materialize. Also, internal capital markets are often highly politicized, and it is not clear that they succeed better than "arms length" markets in generating the information and incentives needed to allocate funds into their most profitable uses. And there are alternative ways of solving the excess cash flow problem without unduly enriching the tax collector. Among others, a cash-rich company can buy noncontrolling stock interests in cash-absorbing enterprises without paying the stock price premiums, or creating the organizational complexities, associated with full merger. It may be significant that the two most successful conglomerates in terms of table 7-2's weighted average returns to shareholders—Teledyne and Gulf & Western—pursued the partial interest acquisition strategy extensively during the 1970s. Other merger-prone companies rejected it, despite its advantages, because their managers strongly preferred to have clear control over the units to which they were channeling their funds.

This leads us to consider the empire-building motive for mergers. It provides a plausible explanation of managers' strong desire for formal control and organizational integration, even when achieving them through merger means paying more for assets, raising bureaucratic costs, and increasing the likelihood of incentive failures. We are persuaded that empire-building motives were present in many of the acquisitions covered by our case studies. What is less certain is how clearly the acquiring companies' chief executives perceived the costs. The most charitable, and probably also the most accurate, interpretation is that empire-building motives interacted with hubris. Merger-makers seriously overestimated their ability to integrate, motivate, and effectively control the companies they acquired, and as a result they underestimated the costs that came with formal control. Whether they would have made the same trade-off had they foreseen the consequences more clearly is a question we cannot confidently answer.

The empire-building motive combines in turn with undervalued assets motivations to help explain much of what occurred in the conglomerate merger boom of the late 1960s. Most of the acquisitions comprising that wave were of small, private companies—those whose securities were not traded on organized markets. Determining what a company is "worth" over the long run is hard enough when its securities are openly traded. It is even more difficult for private firms. Uncertainties abound. As we have stressed repeatedly in this volume, conglomerate acquirers sought, and usually believed they were buying, well-managed companies with good future prospects. Although in hindsight it appears they may have bid too aggressively and suffered from the "winner's curse," they also believed they were striking good bargains. There would be mistakes, but there was also the potentiality, as Samuel Johnson recognized two centuries earlier in seeking a buyer for London's Thrale Brewery, of "growing rich beyond the dreams of avarice."[32]

In America, and probably also elsewhere, the most common fast path to great wealth has entailed buying and accumulating assets of uncertain value. Many fail at the game, but a few succeed spectacularly. The conglomerate merger wave of the 1960s was in many respects an "asset play" of vast dimensions. Some companies such as Teledyne and Gulf & Western did achieve impressive financial success. Others fared less well, but emerged from periods of poor earnings, equity-reducing sell-offs, and belt-tightening with much larger and stronger industrial empires than they possessed at the outset. For a while during the late 1960s, before the control loss problems became apparent, investors were entranced, providing funds (consistent with diverse speculative motives) at price-earnings multiples that encouraged continued, vigorous acquisition programs. Managers built their empires, some stockholders and managers became very rich, and most other investors spent an exciting time in the casino before returning home poorer. Who is to say that this constellation of motives was inappropriate—unless one emphasizes the extensive organizational wreckage and efficiency losses that lay in the wake of the many failed mergers?

32. James Boswell, *The Life of Samuel Johnson*, 6th rev. ed. (London: T. Cadell and W. Davies, 1811), vol. 4, p. 93.

CHAPTER EIGHT

Broader Implications

WHAT BROADER implications flow from our research? And in particular, what is their relevance to public policy?

The Importance of Understanding

We believe our research is more valuable as a contribution to knowledge than as a guide to specific policies, public or private. Serious errors were made by managers who engaged in wide-ranging merger activity and by the investors who financed them. It is important for business leaders to understand what went wrong and how to avoid making similar errors in the future. It is also important for policymakers to understand what happened. Good policy is unlikely to grow from the barren soil of misunderstanding.

This point is brought out well by the President's Council of Economic Advisers, even though in the end the council's interpretation seems quite wrong. To quote at length:

> Although extensive research has established that takeovers tend to be beneficial, not every takeover is successful in attaining its originally contemplated benefits, and there are many examples of takeovers that, in hindsight, appear to have been misguided. Takeovers should not, however, be singled out in this regard because investments in physical plant, research and development, petroleum exploration, and numerous other activities also often appear misguided in hindsight. However, because it is impossible to predict which takeovers will be unsuccessful, the takeover process must be evaluated in the aggregate, and cannot be assessed on the basis of isolated examples of failure or success.[1]

The council is correct in recognizing that mistakes are inevitable and are not per se evidence that something is systematically amiss. It is equally

---

1. *Economic Report of the President, February 1985*, p. 191.

right in insisting that the takeover process must be evaluated in the aggregate, not on the basis of isolated examples. Where it fails is in not undertaking such a balanced evaluation.

Preoccupied with evidence on the reactions of common stock investors during a few weeks surrounding merger "events," the council does not take a longer and broader view. It therefore fails to recognize that the merger wave of the 1960s—the last great merger wave before the one that captured the council's attention in 1985—led to efficiency losses substantially exceeding identifiable gains. When losses systematically outweigh gains, one is compelled to question whether the process itself, and the rules and mores that governed it, were at fault.

Nor does it suffice to laud, however accurately, sell-offs as an effective means of undoing the acquisitions "that did not work out as planned."[2] When the roads are strewn with wrecks, government officials cannot rest content because the tow trucks, ambulances, and hearses are doing a good job removing the remnants and clearing the right-of-way. They must also inquire whether there might be something wrong with driver training, traffic engineering, and the rules of the road.

We are convinced that the driver training does need significant improvement. Thousands of would-be managers and middle managers pour from the business administration schools each year imbued with naive views of merger-making as a quick, easy road to wealth creation. We do not propose this book as remedial reading, just as we would not suggest that automobile driver's license applicants be required to read the technical reports in the *Journal of Safety Research*. Instead, our message is addressed in part to the business school professors, who must understand the historical record themselves and find ways to impress upon their students that making mergers while drunk with power greatly increases the risk of mishap, that merger trips should be planned carefully, with adequate attention to the known hazards, and that double-bottom 18-wheeler conglomerates should be operated only by the extraordinarily skilled.

Managers have already begun to learn these and other relevant lessons. The dubious payoffs and appreciable risks of conglomerate merger-making have received prominent attention in the brochures of

2. Ibid., p. 195. See also Michael C. Jensen, "The Takeover Controversy: Analysis and Evidence," in John C. Coffee, Jr., Louis Lowenstein, and Susan Rose-Ackerman, eds., *Knights, Raiders, and Targets: The Impact of the Hostile Takeover* (Oxford University Press, 1987).

management consulting firms[3] and in popular "how to manage" tracts.[4] The consequences of this learning are evident in a diminution of purely conglomerate merger activity in comparison to horizontal and related-business acquisitions. The direction of movement is encouraging, the amount of movement less so. Conglomerate merger activity continues at substantial rates. New merger-making entrepreneurs appear continuously, eager to try their hand at the game and convinced that they will succeed even where others have stumbled.

Is History Irrelevant?

Our research has been avowedly historical, ending with 1976 acquisitions and 1981 sell-offs and focusing on the preponderantly conglomerate merger wave that peaked in 1968. It might be argued that our findings are less relevant, or even irrelevant, to the 1980s, because managers have learned the appropriate lessons and because 1980s mergers are different from those of the 1960s and 1970s. Although comparable data equal in quality to ours are not available, it is almost surely true that the merger mix of the 1980s *is* different. The typical 1980s acquisition has been larger on average in constant-dollar terms than its 1960s counterpart;[5] the 1980s have seen more hostile takeovers, especially of relatively large corporations; and the incidence of horizontal mergers has increased, in part because the tough antitrust prohibitions enforced during the 1960s and 1970s have been relaxed.

3. McKinsey & Company, "The Role of the Corporate Center" (October 1985), p. 14, finds that only 6 of the 58 companies it studied achieved returns on their merger-based diversification programs exceeding their cost of capital.

4. Thomas J. Peters and Robert H. Waterman, Jr., *In Search of Excellence: Lessons from America's Best-Run Companies* (Harper and Row, 1982), pp. 292–305. See also Robert H. Hayes and William J. Abernathy, "Managing Our Way to Economic Decline," *Harvard Business Review*, vol. 58 (July-August 1980), pp. 75–76; "Why Some Mergers Work and Many More Don't" (interview with Peter Drucker), *Forbes*, January 18, 1982, pp. 34–36; and Michael E. Porter, "From Competitive Advantage to Corporate Strategy," *Harvard Business Review*, vol. 65 (May-June 1987), pp. 43–59.

5. For the mergers on which W. T. Grimm & Co. had purchase price data, the median acquisition value (in constant 1982 dollars) rose from $6.5 million in 1972–76 to $14.7 million in 1981–85. The constant-dollar mean value (influenced more by a few very large mergers) rose from $22.0 million to $85.5 million. *Mergerstat Review, 1985* (Chicago: Grimm, 1986), p. 9. Median values were not reported by Grimm for years prior to 1972. However, the median 1982-dollar asset value for our chap. 3 New York Stock Exchange listing application sample, weighted heavily toward 1968 acquisitions, is $6.2 million.

We are persuaded that these changes have not made historical research on mergers irrelevant, and not only because of Santayana's warning to those who cannot remember the past.

For one, almost every form of merger distinctive during the 1980s was also present in our sample, though in different proportions. Pure conglomerate acquisitions were the least successful members of our sample, in terms of both subsequent sell-off rates and the profitability of the survivors. The movement away from such acquisitions is, as indicated already, a good sign. Our sample included 96 tender offer acquisitions or their "white knight" alternatives, so unless managers have become considerably more adept at making hostile unions turn out favorably, our findings continue to have relevance. They provide only faint reassurance. Although the baseline operating income of tender offer targets did not significantly deteriorate after takeover, it also did not improve, and the tenderers paid high premiums to effect a change of control with no evident efficiency advantages. The most successful mergers covered by our sample were the mergers of equals. They probably owe their relative success to the fact that their importance to top management of *both* partners mandated the most strenuous efforts to make them "work." Even though the performance of mergers of equals in raising profitability was mixed, the 1980s trend toward mergers whose managerial challenges the parties take seriously is on balance an improvement.

The shift toward large horizontal mergers is more difficult to evaluate solely on the basis of our research. Our mergers of equals provide little direct guidance. They were preponderantly nonhorizontal. Fewer than 15 percent of the Line of Business sample lines with merger of equals histories involved a joinder of merging company activities in the same four-digit industry category. Our sample does include a few relatively large horizontal mergers, but the vast majority entailed the acquisition of quite small targets—smaller on average than the companies absorbed in conglomerate acquisitions. The average (small) horizontal acquisition was more successful in avoiding full (but not partial) sell-off, and those that survived into 1977 were more profitable post-merger than purely conglomerate (but not related-business) acquisitions. In principle, both the pertinence of managerial expertise across merged operations and the possibilities for post-merger integration of complementary or competing operations suggest that horizontal mergers should offer richer cost reduction opportunities than conglomerates. Yet the differences between the horizontal acquisitions of the 1960s and those of the 1980s might make our findings less than fully generalizable.

For historical evidence on the outcome of large horizontal mergers, the European experience is more directly relevant. With weaker antitrust laws and government industrial policies that often actively encouraged major horizontal mergers, Europe provides a fertile area for comparative analysis. It has been analyzed thoroughly, even though line of business breakdowns similar to those used in this volume are not available, and accounting effects have received little attention.[6] The weight of the findings is that preponderantly horizontal, often large, European mergers have on average exhibited little or no tendency to raise profitability and/ or efficiency. To quote the conclusion of the most ambitious multinational study:

> No consistent pattern of either improved or deteriorated profitability can therefore be claimed across the seven countries. Mergers would appear to result in a slight improvement here, a slight worsening of performance there. If a generalization is to be drawn, it would have to be that mergers have but modest effects, up or down, on the profitability of the merging firms in the three to five years following merger. Any economic efficiency gains from the mergers would appear to be small, judging from these statistics, as would any market power increases.[7]

Thus, the European evidence is hardly positive on balance.

Our historical research is relevant in another respect. The view among corporate finance specialists and some economists that mergers are on average efficiency-increasing is based largely on "event" studies that show stock price gains in the weeks surrounding merger announcements. The event study research to date has demonstrated no important differ-

---

6. The exception on accounting methods is G. Meeks, *Disappointing Marriage: A Study of the Gains from Merger* (Cambridge University Press, 1977).

7. Dennis C. Mueller, "A Cross-National Comparison of the Results," in Mueller, ed., *The Determinants and Effects of Mergers: An International Comparison* (Cambridge, Mass.: Oelgeschlager, Gunn & Hain, 1980), p. 306. The seven nations studied were Belgium, West Germany, France, the Netherlands, Sweden, the United Kingdom, and the United States. See also Meeks, *Disappointing Marriage*; Gerald D. Newbould, *Management and Merger Activity* (Liverpool: Guthstead, 1970); Keith Cowling and others, *Mergers and Economic Performance* (Cambridge University Press, 1980); Manmohan S. Kumar, *Growth, Acquisition and Investment* (Cambridge University Press, 1984); and Paul A. Geroski and Alexis Jacquemin, "Large Firms in the European Corporate Economy and Industrial Policy in the 1980s," in Jacquemin, ed., *European Industry: Public Policy and Corporate Strategy* (Oxford: Clarendon Press, 1984), pp. 344–49.

ences in the stock market's reactions to mergers over the time interval covered by our sample, as compared to those of the 1980s. The only known study that attempted to make a distinction suggests that stock market "abnormal returns" accompanying 1957–75 acquisitions were if anything more favorable for conglomerate mergers than for non-conglomerates.[8] Yet "the market" was demonstrably and massively wrong in its enthusiastic reaction to conglomerate mergers at the peak of 1960s activity. The conclusion of event studies that mergers were on average efficiency-enhancing appears from our data, taking a longer-term perspective, to have been more wrong than right. Efficient markets axioms do not insist that the market is always or even usually right; they require only that investors act upon all the information available to them at any given time. If event studies gave a wrong answer for the 1960s, what assurance is there that, if one waits long enough for the actual merger consequences to unfold, they will not prove wrong again for the 1980s? Even if the necessary evidence becomes available, we will not know the answer until the 1990s. But at the very least, the experience from times past advises caution in using event study findings as an intellectual foundation for generalized merger policy.

The Policy Instruments

Our historical research suggests a skeptical public policy stance toward mergers. This is not to say that all mergers are bad, which is most assuredly not true. Some mergers are clearly efficiency-increasing. Prominent among them are the second-order mergers that move units being sold off by a previous acquirer to a new, more knowledgeable, less organizationally complex parent. Other mergers are so equivocal in their effects that there is little cause for tilting the instruments of policy one way or another to influence them. But that mergers *on average* can lead to efficiency losses is reason for concern. At minimum, policy should not be biased toward encouraging mergers willy-nilly. And to the extent that fine-tuning is possible, an attempt should be made to encourage the good mergers and discourage the unpromising ones.

8. Pieter T. Elgers and John J. Clark, "Merger Types and Shareholder Returns: Additional Evidence," *Financial Management*, vol. 9 (Summer 1980), pp. 66–72.

Tax Policy

Tax policy is not per se a primary cause of mergers. At most, it tips the balance in what might otherwise be close cases. It is also far too important to be formulated with much emphasis on how it influences merger activity. Merger considerations should play no more role than adding weight in favor of policies that have other compelling merits, resolving close calls, and illuminating the choice of special policies whose impact is confined to merger-making and its aftermath. Within this restrictive framework, two policy issues deserve attention.

One is the problem of companies whose internal investment opportunities are insufficient to utilize the lion's share of their internal cash flows. Until 1987, the U.S. federal income tax laws were not neutral with respect to such enterprises' decisions. By taxing corporate income once and then taxing dividend distributions to individual shareholders more steeply than capital gains, they encouraged retention and then reinvestment in acquisitions over dividend payout. The most comprehensive solution would be unifying the corporate and personal income tax structures so as to make shareholders indifferent on tax grounds between earnings payout and retention. This could be done by going to either of two extremes: abolishing the corporate income tax altogether, or taxing stockholders for earnings retained as well as for those distributed as dividends. Needless to say, issues of equity, investment stimulation, and the efficiency of corporations as tax collectors are much more important than merger effects. Although favoring unification to eliminate cash-flow use distortions, we cannot recommend it on that basis alone. If it were implemented, major changes would be required in accompanying tax provisions to achieve equity and other desired goals.

A second-best solution is the substantial tax reform approved by the U.S. Congress in 1986. By eliminating differential capital gains taxation rates for individuals, it will discourage the retention of earnings to make mergers yielding prospective returns worthwhile only if lightly taxed. In this respect, it is an improvement over past tax structures. And since "an old tax is a good tax," its newly achieved incumbency means that further substantial reforms are unlikely in the foreseeable future.

The tax law overhaul of 1986 also removed a distortion more directly associated with merger decisions. Under long-standing principles, corporations with depreciable assets could, through a merger on which a premium over tax book value was paid, "step up" their depreciable assets to a higher basis. Section 337 of the pre-1987 tax code, along with earlier Supreme Court interpretations,[9] minimized capital gains tax liabilities for corporations enjoying such asset basis step-ups through acquisition. The result was that depreciation-embodied tax shields could be increased almost at will through merger and re-merger. The Tax Act of 1981 strengthened the incentive even more, permitting depreciable assets whose basis was stepped up through merger to be subjected to accelerated cost recovery (ACR) depreciation schedules.[10] Thus, depreciation shields against tax were increased by shortening the lives of assets, and hence raising initial depreciation rates, as well as by enlarging the asset base to which the rates were applied. The 1986 tax reform repealed the provisions allowing tax-free step-ups of asset values through merger and also lengthened allowable depreciation lives for many types of business plant and equipment. Although the full consequences remain to be seen, the result will most likely be some reduction in merger activity and/or in the size of acquisition premiums driven by depreciation considerations.

Antitrust

More than half the acquisitions by dollar value in our main sample were purely conglomerate or of a diversifying related-business character. It is an interesting question whether the high incidence of diversifying mergers was induced by antitrust policy. For that to be true, two conditions must have been satisfied. There had to be an autonomous "urge to merge" which, when blocked in one direction by the restraints of the Celler-Kefauver Act against sizable horizontal and vertical mergers, spilled over in another. And second, the latent motives for conglomerate or diversifying merger had to be sufficiently weak that they would not have given rise to substantial activity without a biasing effect rooted in antitrust law.

To the extent that merger activity occurred because companies' cash flows exceeded profitable internal investment opportunities, the "urge

9. See U.S. Congress, Joint Committee on Taxation, *Federal Income Tax Aspects of Mergers and Acquisitions,* JCS-6-85, 99 Cong. 1 sess. (Government Printing Office, 1985), especially pp. 6–11 and 26–36. A key Supreme Court decision was *General Utilities and Operating Co.* v. *Helvering,* 296 U.S. 200 (1935).

10. A disadvantage of accelerated depreciation was that step-up gains, if taxable at all, were taxed as ordinary income rather than capital gains.

to merge" hypothesis receives support. However, our chapter 2 finding that the most active diversifiers started from relatively rapidly growing industries raises doubts. There is also reason to question whether diversification motives were weak. European companies facing few horizontal merger bars also turned increasingly toward conglomerate acquisitions during the 1960s and 1970s.[11] Still the characteristically smaller fraction of diversifying mergers abroad does suggest that the U.S. laws had some biasing effect. Tax reform that makes companies less reluctant to pay out surplus funds as dividends may solve the problem. Absent that, the relevant question is whether weakening the restrictions against horizontal mergers would be justified by the consequent reduction in incentives to make efficiency-reducing conglomerate acquisitions. We have no definite answer. We would prefer to see an improvement in the education of business managers so they avoid making poorly justified acquisitions for the right reasons, and not for reasons that ought to be irrelevant. And we believe policy toward horizontal mergers ought to be chosen primarily for its direct consequences, and not merely to minimize undesirable side effects.

The horizontal acquisitions in our main statistical sample had higher post-merger profitability than the pure conglomerate acquisitions. The small absolute sizes and market shares involved provide no reason to believe that this difference was the result of increased monopoly power. Our case studies uncovered clear examples of efficiencies when business units owned by a conglomerate parent were sold off into horizontal relationships. Yet the combination of evidence covering the horizontal subset of our 634-company pre-merger sample and our post-merger Line of Business sample suggests that on average horizontal acquisitions, like conglomerate mergers, were followed by deteriorating profit performance. The balance of cost-reducing and price-raising effects appears to have been negative on average.

Whether that balance would change substantially if U.S. antitrust laws were amended to permit horizontal mergers entailing much larger market shares is more difficult to predict. The experience with massive horizontal mergers around the turn of the century reveals clear and

11. See A. W. Goudie and G. Meeks, "Diversification by Merger," *Economica*, vol. 49 (November 1982), pp. 447–59 (on British trends) and (more broadly) Organisation for Economic Cooperation and Development, *Merger Policies and Recent Trends in Mergers* (Paris: OECD, 1984), especially p. 53.

important monopoly power consequences.[12] Equally clearly, both in principle and from our sell-off case studies, horizontal mergers *can* confer efficiencies. However, the research on European horizontal mergers, like our own evidence, provides no reason to believe that *on average* the efficiency gains have been appreciable.

Given a low-level balance of costs and benefits but the possibility of important exceptions, the best policy would combine a tough presumption against sizable horizontal mergers with a waiver of that presumption if the parties demonstrate the likelihood of substantial efficiencies unattainable except by merger. This would put the emphasis in merger policy where it belongs—on weighing benefits against costs.[13]

Favoring this approach is another more subtle but vital consideration. One reason why so many mergers yield disappointing results is that managers devote too little critical thought pre-merger to determining how the partners' operations can be integrated to achieve maximum efficiency and, equally important, what problems might interfere with attaining the desired results. All too often, the fusion is viewed only through rose-tinted glasses. Like the prospect of hanging in a fortnight, the prospect of having to explain to a skeptical judge precisely how a proposed merger will yield efficiencies could marvelously concentrate managers' minds on making their mergers work.

The principal drawback of this proposed policy is the limited competence of judges to carry out such complex business and economic weightings.[14] However, the task might be done tolerably well if the antitrust adjudication process were reformed (1) to ensure that the judges assigned to merger cases have had solid training in the relevant areas of economics, and (2) to have the judges retain clerks competent in

12. See Richard E. Caves, Michael Fortunato, and Pankaj Ghemawat, "The Decline of Dominant Firms, 1905–1929," *Quarterly Journal of Economics*, vol. 99 (August 1984), pp. 523–46; Donald O. Parsons and Edward John Ray, "The United States Steel Consolidation: The Creation of Market Control," *Journal of Law & Economics*, vol. 18 (April 1975), pp. 194–206; and Hideki Yamawaki, "Dominant Firm Pricing and Fringe Expansion: The Case of the U.S. Iron and Steel Industry, 1907–1930," *Review of Economics and Statistics*, vol. 67 (August 1985), pp. 429–37.

13. A pioneering theoretical contribution was Oliver E. Williamson, "Economies as an Antitrust Defense: The Welfare Tradeoffs," *American Economic Review*, vol. 58 (March 1968), pp. 18–36.

14. See Derek C. Bok, "Section 7 of the Clayton Act and the Merging of Law and Economics," *Harvard Law Review*, vol. 74 (December 1960), pp. 291–99.

economics. Such reforms would be desirable with or without merger policy revisions.

Securities Regulation

Merger activity is also affected by the securities laws administered by the Securities and Exchange Commission and the federal and state courts. Particularly controversial in recent years have been the complex rules (rooted at the federal level in the Williams Act of 1968 and later amendments) governing tender offer takeovers. Those who view such takeovers as efficiency-increasing on average have advocated minimizing the restraints placed on tenderers.[15] We believe the emphasis on efficiency (as distinguished, say, from achieving "equity" among managers, shareholders, and raiders) is appropriate. However, our evidence calls for much greater skepticism concerning the tendency of takeovers to increase operating efficiency. Substantial legal and financial intermediary costs are also incurred in the typical contested takeover case. And there remain unsettled but burning questions as to whether pervasive takeover threats induce managers to become more short-sighted in their pricing and investment decisions and to employ defensive tactics that increase operating costs and risks.[16]

If we are correct that the efficiency gains from hostile takeovers are small or even negative on average, then changes in the rules are warranted. A particularly important procedural problem is the tendency for shareholder choices to be structured as "prisoner's dilemma" games once a target company is put "in play."[17] That is, the representative

15. See, for example, Henry G. Manne, "Mergers and the Market for Corporate Control," *Journal of Political Economy*, vol. 73 (April 1965), pp. 110–20; Sanford J. Grossman and Oliver D. Hart, "Takeover Bids, the Free-Rider Problem, and the Theory of the Corporation," *Bell Journal of Economics*, vol. 11 (Spring 1980), pp. 42–64; Frank H. Easterbrook and Daniel R. Fischel, "The Proper Role of a Target's Management in Responding to a Tender Offer," *Harvard Law Review*, vol. 94 (April 1981), pp. 1161–1204; and Michael C. Jensen, "Takeovers: Folklore and Science," *Harvard Business Review*, vol. 62 (November-December 1984), pp. 109–21. For a more balanced debate on the issues, see Coffee and others, eds., *Knights, Raiders, and Targets*.

16. See F. M. Scherer, "Takeovers: Present and Future Dangers," *Brookings Review*, vol. 4 (Winter-Spring 1986), pp. 15–20; and Louis Lowenstein, "Pruning Deadwood in Hostile Takeovers: A Proposal for Legislation," *Columbia Law Review*, vol. 83 (March 1983), pp. 249–333.

17. Lucian A. Bebchuk, "A Model of the Outcome of Takeover Bids," Discussion Paper 11 (Harvard Law School, November 1985).

shareholder may prefer not to tender, but if he believes other shareholders will tender (because they go through the same reasoning process as he) and that by not tendering he will be "frozen out" on relatively unfavorable terms, the shareholder will feel compelled to tender despite his contrary innate preference. To correct these incentive biases, we favor Lucian Bebchuk's proposal that shareholders be permitted to tender conditionally to protect their interests, and at the same time to cast separate and binding votes indicating their innate preference for or against the proposed takeover.[18]

A more neglected area of securities regulation is the provision of information on merger transactions. We believe the SEC and the New York Stock Exchange do a good job in their requirements for information disclosure at the time a merger proposal, or the attending issuance of new securities, is before existing shareholders and potential investors for decision. Much less satisfactory is the documentation of what happens after merger. When a merger is consummated, the acquired firm usually disappears into the folds of the acquirer, and information on the acquired entity's performance vanishes. When there are very many mergers, as in the late 1960s and early 1980s, the information loss is great.[19] Substantial losses of financial performance information also occur when there are many "going private" transactions—for example, when whole companies or parts of companies are transformed into leveraged buyouts issuing no publicly traded securities. If the efficiency of the merger and sell-off process is to be evaluated on a continuing basis, these informational lacunae must be remedied. We recommend three information policy changes to redress the situation:

1. Acquiring companies with publicly traded securities should be required to file annually with the SEC a report detailing *all* acquisitions made during the prior year, the consideration paid, the book value of assets acquired, the method of accounting used, a description of each unit sold off during the year, and the loss or gain recorded in connection with each such divestiture.

2. When nonhorizontal acquisitions entailing consideration of $50 million or more, or 5 percent or more of acquiring company assets, are made, the SEC should insist that the parent corporation designate the

18. Ibid., pp. 22–25.
19. See U.S. Federal Trade Commission, Bureau of Economics, *Conglomerate Merger Performance: An Empirical Analysis of Nine Corporations* (FTC, 1972), pp. 87–126, for an early analysis of the information loss problem.

acquired entity as one or more new and distinct "industry segments" on which disaggregated sales, asset, and operating income information will be disclosed in subsequent annual reports or 10-K reports to the SEC.

3. The Census Bureau should tap its *Quarterly Financial Report* surveys to prepare regular analytic reports on the performance of private companies, including leveraged buyouts, by industry sector. The reports should include information on the incidence of going-private transactions and the magnitude of asset revaluations occurring as a consequence.

Absent such changes, companies that have made misguided merger decisions or mismanaged their acquisitions will be able to cloak their mistakes, while those who seek to understand the links between mergers and efficiency can only curse the darkness. Through the use of Line of Business data (whose collection has been discontinued by the Federal Trade Commission), we have attempted to light a candle. More, however, must be lit before important recent developments can be fully evaluated.

Predicting the Merger Accounting Method

COMPANIES IN THE United States have used two main merger accounting methods: pooling of interests and purchase. For our research on the profitability of mergers, it was important to distinguish the accounting method used, since the choice can significantly affect reported asset and depreciation values. An extensive search in company disclosure documents yielded accounting choice information on approximately 67 percent of the acquisitions in our basic merger sample by number, and 87 percent by value of acquired assets. To determine the choices made in the remaining cases, the prediction model described in this appendix was applied.[1]

Predictive Hypotheses

The choice of merger accounting methods has been affected by both regulatory suasion and company-specific economic considerations. The regulatory framework was provided by a series of guidelines beginning with Research Bulletin 40, issued by the American Institute of Certified

1. For earlier work in a similar tradition, see Jean-Marie Gagnon, "Purchase versus Pooling of Interests: The Search for a Predictor," Empirical Research in Accounting: Selected Studies, *Journal of Accounting Research*, vol. 5 supplement (1967), pp. 187–204; Gagnon, "The Purchase-Pooling Choice: Some Empirical Evidence," *Journal of Accounting Research*, vol. 9 (Spring 1971), pp. 52–72; Ronald M. Copeland and Joseph G. Wojdak, "Income Manipulation and the Purchase-Pooling Choice," *Journal of Accounting Research*, vol. 7 (Autumn 1969), pp. 189–95; John C. Anderson and Joseph G. Louderback III, "Income Manipulation and Purchase-Pooling: Some Additional Results," *Journal of Accounting Research*, vol. 14 (Autumn 1975), pp. 338–43; Robert Libby, "The Early Impact of APB Opinions No. 16 and 17—An Empirical Study," *CPA Journal*, vol. 42 (October 1972), pp. 837–42; and Frank R. Rayburn, "Another Look at the Impact of Accounting Principles Board Opinion No. 16—An Empirical Study," *Mergers & Acquisitions*, vol. 10 (Spring 1975), pp. 7–9.

Public Accountants in 1950, and evolving over time with additional pronouncements that culminated in November 1970 with the issuance of Accounting Principles Board (APB) Opinion No. 16 on "Business Combinations."[2]

One potentially important variable is the type of consideration paid in consummating the acquisition. Especially since APB 16, but even before, pooling was considered more appropriate for exchange-of-stock transactions than for cash acquisitions. The Federal Trade Commission's merger history files distinguish among acquisitions effected through an exchange of securities (including bonds), those made for cash, and those entailing a combination of cash and securities. Even after the FTC data were augmented with information from other sources, no evidence on the consideration form was available for some 15 percent of the sample acquisitions. Rather than omit an important explanatory variable or drop many observations from the sample, we "plugged" the missing observations at the all-sample average ratio of "securities only" transactions to total transactions. However, the acquisitions for which no data were available tended to be the smaller ones on which no New York Stock Exchange listing application was filed, and for them, the pure cash mode may have been favored. To offset any possible bias, we multiplied the plugged value by a separate 1–0 "plug" dummy variable to serve as an interactive correction to the plugged value if the mergers it characterized were in fact different from the all-sample average.

Early AICPA research bulletins placed considerable stress on the relative sizes of the merging firms, arguing that pooling was normally appropriate only when the acquired entity was not small relative to the acquirer. The threshold for "relative smallness" was set in various statements between 5 percent and 20 percent of the value of exchanged shares. This criterion disappeared from APB 16, although only after the Accounting Principles Board had provisionally accepted its continuation. Our prediction variable is the ratio of the acquired to the acquiring entity's estimated assets (or when asset data were unavailable, consideration paid). We expect that the larger the relative size of the acquired

2. For historical accounts on the development of policy, see Andrew Barr, "Accounting Aspects of Business Combinations," *Accounting Review*, vol. 34 (April 1959), pp. 175–81; Samuel R. Sapienza, "Distinguishing between Purchase and Pooling," *Journal of Accountancy*, vol. 111 (June 1961), pp. 35–40; and Richard Leftwich, "Evidence of the Impact of Mandatory Changes in Accounting Principles on Corporate Loan Agreements," *Journal of Accounting and Economics*, vol. 3 (March 1981), pp. 3–36.

entity was, the more likely a choice of pooling was, especially before 1970.

There is reason to believe that acquiring firms have tried to improve their post-merger accounting profit ratios by favoring pooling when the acquisition price substantially exceeded acquired firm book values. In such cases, the premium is treated as a reduction of stockholders' equity. Purchase accounting, on the other hand, was more apt to be used when acquisitions were made at consideration below book values. However, the implementation of this hypothesis must deal with two complications.

First, the reasoning above applies mainly for mergers accepted by the Internal Revenue Service as tax-free reorganizations, which usually meant those accomplished through an exchange of securities. On the other hand, when an acquisition was consummated for cash, capital gains realized by stockholders were usually taxable, but the acquiring firm could "step up" the value of depreciable assets acquired by the amount of premiums paid over book value, thereby securing a larger depreciation shield against future income taxation. To the extent acquisitions are made for cash, one might expect a stronger tendency toward the use of purchase accounting, the more the consideration paid exceeds pre-merger book values.

Data limitations make the implementation of these predictions difficult. We could determine the values of both consideration paid and acquired entity book value for only 1,409 of the 4,562 acquisitions in our main sample. To capture in the full-sample analysis the effect of market conditions conducive to the payment of premiums over book, we were forced to adopt a cruder, more aggregative approach. We introduce a variant of Tobin's Q index, measuring for any given year the average ratio of consideration paid to book value for *all* the mergers in that year for which both variables were available.[3] We then perform a separate analysis for the 1,409 merger subset on which complete individual consideration paid and book value data were available. In both instances, we expect a stronger tendency toward pooling for acquisitions consummated through an exchange of securities when the Tobin's Q index, aggregate or disaggregate, is high. For cash acquisitions, the opposite pattern is anticipated.

3. Values of the ratio ranged from 0.934 (for 1958) to 1.837 (for 1964) and 2.712 (for 1979). The ratio is biased downward relative to an ideal measure because the data for consideration paid normally do not include the value of debt and other liabilities assumed.

APB 16 requires the use of purchase accounting for acquisitions of only part of a company (that is, subsidiaries, divisions, or plants) and for acquisitions in which an early and substantial sell-off of acquired assets is contemplated. Earlier guidelines included similar criteria, but more permissively. An attempt was made to identify acquisitions followed by substantial sell-offs within the next three years. A separate variable identifies acquisitions of only a part of the selling entity's assets.

For industry-specific or idiosyncratic reasons, different companies may have manifested divergent preferences for one mode of accounting over another even when such "objective" variables as relative size and form of exchange were similar. Within a given company, accountants' desire for consistency may have imparted considerable stability to these choices. We therefore include in our analysis a company-specific policy variable denoting the fraction of all accounting choice-coded acquisitions (except the one being analyzed) treated as poolings, given that the company had at least five coded acquisitions over the 1950–79 time span. For companies with fewer than five coded acquisitions, a plug was inserted giving the fraction of coded poolings to *all* sample companies' coded acquisitions. Since companies with fewer than five coded acquisitions are not necessarily representative, a bias control dummy variable, multiplying 1 times the plug value for any plugged acquisition, is also introduced.

Finally, the rules governing accounting method choices, and perhaps also corporations' interpretations of those rules, have changed over time—presumably, toward extensive use of pooling up to 1970 and decreased use thereafter. We take this effect into account in two ways. First, we include a time variable to pick up possible trends. Second, we divide the sample into pre- and post-1970 acquisitions, testing for the homogeneity of coefficients between periods. Because APB 16 was issued in exposure draft form during February 1970 and may have had some preemptive influence, we delete that year from the split sample.

Summing up, the variables used in our prediction analysis, their mnemonic characterizations, and their full-sample means are as follows:[4]

4. For a 1–0 dummy variable, the mean indicates the relative frequency of the unit value's incidence. Thus, the mean for *ACCTG* reveals that 55.4 percent of the sample acquisitions were poolings. The Q ratios have a more complex interpretation. They must be divided by the relative frequency of securities-exchange or cash transactions to obtain the raw average Q ratio. The ratios calculated in this way are 1.510 for *Q-STOCK*, 1.501 for *Q-CASH*, 1.677 for *P-STOCK*, and 1.244 for *P-CASH*.

	Variable	*Mean value*
ACCTG	A dummy variable denoting the accounting method chosen: 1 if pooling, 0 if purchase.	0.554
STOCK	A dummy variable reflecting the consideration form: 1 if all securities, plugged at the all-sample mean if consideration form unknown, 0 otherwise.	0.701
STPLG	A dummy variable with a value of 1 if the STOCK variable was plugged at the all-sample mean.	0.152
MIXED	A dummy variable with value of 1 if the merger was made with a combination of securities and cash (plugged at the sample mean if the consideration form was unknown).	0.044
PARTIAL	A dummy variable with a value of 1 for acquisitions of only a part of the selling firm's assets.	0.059
DIVEST	A dummy variable with a value of 1 for acquisitions followed within three years by a substantial acquired asset sell-off.	0.019
RELSIZ	The ratio of the acquired to the acquiring entity's estimated assets at the time of acquisition.	0.049
Q-STOCK	Aggregate Tobin's Q index (consideration paid/book value of assets) for the year of acquisition if acquisition made through exchange of securities, 0 otherwise.	1.059
Q-CASH	Aggregate Tobin's Q index for cash acquisitions, 0 if not a cash acquisition.	0.382
P-STOCK	For subsample of 1,409, individual consideration paid/book value of acquired assets on stock acquisitions, 0 otherwise.	1.224
P-CASH	For subsample of 1,409, consideration paid/book value of acquired assets on cash acquisitions, 0 otherwise.	0.280
EXPER	Fraction of other coded mergers treated as poolings for individual companies with five or more coded mergers.	0.541
EXPLG	Dummy variable with value of 1 if a company had fewer than five coded mergers, so that the all-sample pooling ratio was plugged into EXPER.	0.062
YEAR	Time trend variable (1950 = 0, 1979 = 29).	17.60

Statistical Methodology

We approach the accounting method prediction problem using multiple regression analysis. Because the dependent variable ACCTG is always either 1 (for pooling) or 0 (for purchases), ordinary least squares estimates are inefficient. We therefore use the logit technique, which has superior error structure properties and which ensures that predicted values of the dependent variable lie in the range from 0 to 1. Specifically, we estimate nonlinearly the logistic transformation:

$$\text{(A-1)} \qquad \Pr(ACCTG = 1) = \frac{\exp\left(\sum_i b_i X_{ij}\right)}{1 + \exp\left(\sum_i b_i X_{ij}\right)},$$

where X_{ij} is the ith independent variable for acquisition j, and b_i is that variable's regression coefficient. When $\sum b_i X_{ij} = 0$, $\Pr(ACCTG = 1) = 0.5$, that is, pooling and purchase are equally likely. This feature lets the model predict the use of pooling when $\sum b_i X_{ij} > 0$.

The main sample consists of all manufacturing industry acquisitions between 1950 and 1979 for which the accounting method choice was known. It includes 4,562 observations. A secondary sample with 1,409 observations is limited to the cases in which both consideration paid and acquired entity asset values were known.

The Results

Table A-1 presents the coefficient estimates from logit regressions for the full sample period (1950–79) and for the pre- and post-1970 subperiods. Because the implications of the individual coefficients are difficult to fathom intuitively, the final column presents (for the full sample period results only) the change in the pooling-of-interests choice probability as dummy variable values move from 0 to 1, or as continuously scaled independent variables increase from two standard deviations below their means to two standard deviations above their means. For each such change, all other independent variables are held constant at their mean values.

Many but not all of the a priori hypotheses are confirmed. There are clear differences between the pre- and post-1970 periods, as shown inter alia by a highly significant likelihood ratio of 112.5 in a test for homogeneity of coefficients between the two subperiods.[5] Before 1970, there was a trend *toward* pooling; after 1970, a weaker reverse trend material-

5. With 12 degrees of freedom, the 0.05 significance level value of the likelihood ratio is 21.0.

Table A-1. *Logit Regressions Predicting the Probability of Pooling Accounting for All Manufacturing Acquisitions, 1950–79*[a]

Variable	1950–79	Pre-1970	Post-1970	Change in probability, 1950–79[b]
Constant	−2.96[c]	−2.68[c]	−4.19[c]	...
	(3.26)	(2.35)	(1.90)	
STOCK	1.27	0.75	5.85[c]	0.307
	(1.21)	(0.58)	(2.97)	
STOCK × STPLG	−1.59[c]	−1.03[c]	−2.38[c]	−0.335
	(8.65)	(4.68)	(5.81)	
MIXED	−0.30	−1.50	1.69	−0.075
	(0.32)	(1.28)	(0.92)	
PARTIAL	−1.22[c]	−1.00[c]	−1.65[c]	−0.289
	(5.01)	(3.12)	(3.47)	
DIVEST	−0.18	−0.64[d]	0.15	−0.044
	(0.57)	(1.52)	(0.26)	
RELSIZ	1.30[c]	1.70[c]	−1.02	0.196
	(4.22)	(4.62)	(0.87)	
YEAR	0.002	0.10[c]	−0.09[e]	0.009
	(0.19)	(7.53)	(2.11)	
EXPER	3.41[c]	3.09[c]	4.23[c]	0.719
	(19.14)	(14.30)	(11.08)	
EXPER × EXPLG	−0.39	−0.18	−0.22	−0.049
	(1.25)	(0.49)	(0.32)	
Q-STOCK	0.83[c]	0.15	−0.25	0.486
	(2.98)	(0.47)	(0.38)	
Q-CASH	−0.75	−1.73[e]	1.00	−0.417
	(1.25)	(2.24)	(0.90)	
Summary statistics				
Number of observations	4,562	2,850	1,380	...
Correct predictions (percent)	84.2	82.5	86.7	...

a. See definitions in text. Numbers in parentheses are t-ratios.
b. Change in probability moving from 0 to 1 for dummy variables and from two standard deviations below the mean to two standard deviations above for continuous variables.
c. Significant in a one-tailed test at 0.01 level of confidence.
d. Significant in a one-tailed test at 0.10 level of confidence.
e. Significant in a one-tailed test at 0.05 level of confidence.

ized. The *STOCK* consideration variable performs only weakly before 1970 but strongly and in the expected direction after 1970. The *STOCK × STPLG* correction term shows that acquisitions for which consideration form information was unavailable are wrongly characterized as typical of all transactions. Rather, they were more apt to be purchases, presumably because they were small and made with cash. Mixed consideration acquisitions had unpredictable accounting method choices, all else equal. Acquisitions of only parts of an enterprise were unlikely to be treated as poolings. Sell-offs within three years of a merger made little difference, even after the 1970 APB guidelines called for purchase accounting. The 1970 guidelines appear to have obliterated the role of relative size, which was previously an important predictor. The most powerful single predictor is general company policy, reflected in the *EXPER* variable. For all years together, a high Tobin's Q value was conducive to pooling accounting on exchange-of-securities acquisitions, as expected. However, the relationship deteriorates within time sub-periods, probably because Q values were relatively high before 1970 and relatively low thereafter, so that valuation effects at an aggregate level may have become confounded with time trend effects.

The line "correct predictions" tells what fraction of predictions turns out correctly when each acquisition's independent variables are entered into the estimated logit equation and pooling is predicted by equation values greater than, or equal to, 0.5. Using this discriminant technique, correct predictions are made in 84 percent of the cases without a time period breakdown. A higher degree of prediction accuracy is obtained after 1970, suggesting that APB 16 succeeded in reducing the amount of ambiguity in pooling versus purchase choices. In chapter 4, predictions based upon the separated time period equation(s) are used to designate the merger accounting method when no explicit information on the choice actually made was available.

Table A-2 provides further perspective on the interactions between time, consideration choice, and the ratio of consideration paid to book value for the acquisitions on which both the consideration paid and the acquired entity's book value were known. By accepting a smaller sample of 1,409 acquisitions, we can allow each merger to have its own Q index, now relabelled *P-STOCK* and *P-CASH*. For this richer data subset, stock acquisitions exhibit a stronger and more consistent tendency toward pooling. In addition, there is compelling evidence that for such acquisitions, as expected, pooling is more likely, the larger is the premium paid over book values. Somewhat surprisingly, the tendency to choose exchange-of-securities transaction accounting methods in a way that maximized post-merger accounting earnings was stronger in the post-1970 period. This casts some doubt on the effectiveness of APB 16 in discouraging the use of pooling to "pad" returns on stockholders' equity and assets following high-premium acquisitions. For the (mostly taxable) all-cash acquisitions, the predicted negative premium relationship failed

Table A-2. *Logit Regressions Predicting the Probability of Pooling Accounting for Acquisitions with Both Asset and Consideration Paid Data, 1950–79*[a]

Variable	1950–79	Pre-1970	Post-1970	Change in probability, 1950–79[b]
Constant	−3.49[c]	−4.75[c]	−0.30	. . .
	(7.85)	(7.21)	(0.19)	
STOCK	2.97[c]	3.41[c]	2.46[c]	0.626
	(8.29)	(6.37)	(4.43)	
STOCK × STPLG	0.10	0.74	−0.21	0.008
	(0.16)	(0.84)	(0.21)	
MIXED	−0.09	−0.01	−0.65	−0.018
	(0.16)	(0.01)	(0.58)	
PARTIAL	−0.80[d]	−0.10	−2.32[c]	−0.184
	(1.88)	(0.17)	(2.77)	
DIVEST	0.16	0.21	0.66	0.031
	(0.23)	(0.17)	(0.72)	
RELSIZ	0.89[d]	0.92[d]	−1.91	0.143
	(2.12)	(1.83)	(1.09)	
YEAR	−0.027[d]	0.07[c]	−0.16[c]	−0.130
	(1.94)	(2.61)	(2.50)	
EXPER	3.00[c]	2.69[c]	3.29[c]	0.581
	(8.63)	(5.81)	(5.75)	
EXPER × EXPLG	−0.58	−0.15	−1.29	−0.064
	(1.00)	(0.20)	(1.24)	
P-STOCK	0.79[c]	0.54[d]	1.02[c]	0.734
	(5.69)	(3.07)	(4.29)	
P-CASH	0.12	0.24	0.06	0.070
	(0.75)	(0.91)	(0.27)	
Summary statistics				
Number of observations	1,409	744	612	. . .
Correct predictions (percent)	86.7	86.0	88.1	. . .

a. See definitions in text. Numbers in parentheses are *t*-ratios.
b. Change in probability moving from 0 to 1 for dummy variable and from two standard deviations below the mean to two standard deviations above for continuous variables.
c. Significant in a one-tailed test at 0.01 level of confidence.
d. Significant in a one-tailed test at 0.05 level of confidence.

to materialize. Other relationships in table A-2 are similar to those of table A-1, except that the tendency toward purchase accounting on partial acquisitions is weaker, the dummy variable correcting for missing *STOCK* data cases is statistically insignificant (probably because there are only 33 plugged data cases), and general company experience plays a somewhat weaker explanatory role. The regressions of table A-2, like those of table A-1, show a trend toward increased pooling-of-interests accounting before 1970 and decreased use of that method thereafter. Further analysis reveals that the highest incidence of poolings (76 percent) was in 1968, with declines thereafter to 70 percent in 1969 and 65 percent in 1970. The declining trend then continued to a trough of 31 percent in 1975 and 1976.

Narrative Summary of the Case Studies

THIS APPENDIX summarizes the histories of the 15 companies whose acquisition and divestiture experiences are discussed in chapter 5.

American Safety Razor (ASR)

In 1960, as an early step in its effort to diversify around its tobacco products home base, the Philip Morris Company acquired the American Safety Razor Company, a producer of razor blades, surgical scalpels, home hair clippers, and other items. ASR's common stock, which was publicly traded, was exchanged for Philip Morris stock valued at approximately $23.5 million. It was expected that marketing complementarities would make ASR a more potent challenger to Gillette, which at the time controlled roughly 70 percent of the razor blade market. The retail outlets served were similar, and ASR television advertising could be "piggy-backed" on Philip Morris cigarette commercials to gain lower media rates and broader coverage.

The first significant marketing innovation of the merged company was the introduction in 1962 of a new injector razor designed by Henry Dreyfuss to use ASR's Pal single-edge blades, which up to that time had been sold for use in competitor Eversharp Schick's injectors. To complement ASR's blades, Philip Morris also acquired in 1963 the Burma-Vita Corporation, maker of Burma Shave shaving cream, whose roadside sign limericks enlivened many a trip through rural America.

A much more important event, however, was the introduction of stainless steel blades. Wilkinson led the way in 1962. ASR (along with Schick) followed suit ahead of Gillette in early 1963. An intensive television advertising campaign for ASR's Personna double-edge and Pal injector stainless blades achieved impressive first trial rates. However, ASR experienced very high stainless blade rejection rates in manufacturing, and of the blades that reached the market, so many were

239

defective that repeat purchases were disappointing. Gillette meanwhile had delayed its stainless blade introduction date to the fall of 1963, when quality control problems had been solved.[1] Subsequent analysis revealed that ASR's blade design was inferior, that its machinery was not up to the task of producing uniformly high quality stainless blades, and that ASR lagged Gillette in production know-how. A management shakeup followed, bringing in production personnel from outside the razor industry, and Philip Morris supported a research and retooling program that brought ASR close to Gillette's quality standards. However, by that time momentum had been ceded to market leaders Gillette and Wilkinson. A consulting firm study concluded that there was simply no way for ASR profitably to catch up. As a result, Philip Morris–ASR contented itself with being the leading supplier in the limited but profitable market for private label blades and with branded blade sales which, because of sizable advertising costs at low volumes, yielded at best modest profits. The principal success of subsequent years was ASR's introduction of the Flicker women's razor. With a highly innovative design, it captured a leading position despite only modest advertising support. Several million dollars were also invested in a new double-edge razor introduced in 1973.

Although disappointed with the ASR venture, Philip Morris kept it going. ASR's share of company sales shrank to 1 percent as PM's cigarette and Miller beer sales grew rapidly. Sell-off was first considered seriously in 1976, when Bic Pen Corporation contracted with ASR to produce blades for its newly introduced low-price disposable razors and then offered to buy the company. A purchase price of $20 million was negotiated. However, the Federal Trade Commission opposed the merger on antitrust grounds and Bic withdrew its offer. Philip Morris threatened to close ASR's Staunton, Virginia, plant and initiated a two-year phaseout program focused initially on the least profitable branded blades. Political interest, stirred in part by ASR workers' picketing at the Federal Trade Commission, led to the provision of a $6 million low-interest economic development loan through the federal government and the state of Virginia. Meanwhile, ASR's management was aided by a West Coast investment banking firm in organizing a highly leveraged buyout and obtaining additional short-term loan financing from a Virginia bank. The May 1977 purchase price of nearly $17 million was said to be

1. See "Razor's Edge," *Barron's*, January 28, 1963, p. 21.

almost equivalent in present value to Bic's offer, involving some delayed payments, of $20 million.

In part from its dealings with Bic, ASR management perceived opportunities for substantial cost savings through tighter production line and inventory control. These were implemented after the buyout, as were a shift of marketing headquarters from New York City to Virginia, the use of a less expensive computer system, reduced advertising, and many other belt-tightening measures. Profitability improved significantly despite the burden of soaring interest charges on the prime-plus adjustable bank loan. A program of productivity-increasing plant investment was sustained, and in the early 1980s ASR's financial position had improved to the point where a private label soap manufacturer and a shuttered candy maker could be acquired. ASR union representatives reported widespread satisfaction with the results of the buyout, which was believed to have preserved more jobs and greater job satisfaction than had been expected under Bic, which planned to specialize the Virginia plant in producing blades for assembly at a New York plant. Employment reductions resulting from productivity gains and the phaseout of branded razor blade sales were accomplished largely through attrition.

Robert Bruce

Robert Bruce was a well-established, family-controlled company whose common stock was first listed on the American Stock Exchange in 1969. It specialized in producing and marketing men's and boys' sweaters and other knit sportswear, aimed mainly at the middle segments of the market. In 1973 Bruce was acquired by the Consolidated Foods Corporation, originally a food products wholesaler which had diversified aggressively, first into food retailing and manufacturing and then, beginning in the later 1960s, into a wide range of product lines. The acquisition was made through an exchange of shares valued at $26 million.

Bruce continued to thrive under Consolidated Foods' ownership. Managerial continuity was maintained, and in the late 1970s several million dollars were invested to modernize the company's principal North Philadelphia factory.

Consolidated's experience on other garment manufacturing lines was much less favorable. Its corporate management lacked the experience and "feel" needed to operate successfully in fashion-sensitive lines with substantial inventory obsolescence risks, and when operating division management faltered, there was little it could do to improve matters. In 1976, with its stock trading at one-half early 1970s share values, Consolidated commenced a program of divesting divisions, in apparel and other lines, that failed to satisfy "fit" and return-on-investment criteria. During the next five years, approximately 50 such units were sold off. The first to go were those in the greatest financial difficulty. Divestiture of Bruce, a particularly healthy subsidiary, was deferred, and in 1979 Consolidated greatly expanded its apparel operations by acquiring the Hanes Company (of L'Eggs hosiery fame). Bruce was put under the supervision of Hanes management, but the two operations were quite different, with Hanes selling packaged items through the supermarket outlets used also by Consolidated's food products while Bruce moved its line through more conventional garment distribution channels. Thus, Bruce remained on the "for sale" block, awaiting an offer that recognized the lack of pressure on Consolidated's top management to make the "fire sale" deals accepted for losing operations.

That offer came in 1980 from Savoy Industries, a leveraged buyout holding company controlled by a group of New York City investors. The total purchase price, divided for financing reasons into separate plant and other operating asset elements, was $27 million. Bruce's top two executives remained in place, acquired modest common stock interests immediately, and were offered substantial stock purchase options exercisable over a five-year period. Except for the much closer cash-flow controls necessitated by the parent's high leveraging, there was little change in the way Bruce was managed, and the company continued to perform well through 1984 despite recession (which affected branded sportswear much less than durable goods) and unexpectedly high interest rates. In 1984 a public issue of common stock in Bruce was floated, reducing Savoy's ownership interest to 53.5 percent and permitting a reduction in borrowings.

Bendix Home Systems

During the late 1960s, the Bendix Corporation embarked upon a program to lessen its dependence upon automobile and (especially) volatile and declining defense business. One such diversification move was the acquisition of a timber company, American Forest Products, in 1969. Further mergers complementary to AFP were then sought. In the early 1970s the Boise Cascade Corporation experienced a financial crisis owing to the failure of its recreational community and other on-site homebuilding ventures. To raise cash, it offered for sale several of its more viable businesses. In 1972 William Agee left Boise to become executive vice president of Bendix. At his suggestion, Bendix evaluated various Boise purchase options, the most ambitious of which was a bid to take over all of Boise. Talks converged on the acquisition of Boise's mobile home and recreational vehicle division, part of which had been purchased from Divco-Wayne Corporation for $47 million only five years before. The operation had been expanded to 36 plants in the United States, Canada, and Europe. As negotiations progressed in late 1972, it became clear to Bendix management that the Boise operation was more problematic than originally believed, and the initially agreed-upon purchase price was reduced from $68 million to $63.4 million. Bendix came close to dropping out altogether, and when the purchase contract was sealed, it was considered a sufficiently close call that the new Bendix Home Systems division was implicitly "up for sale" from the moment the ink was dry.

Further disappointments followed. The "synergies" expected with American Forest Products proved to be minimal. Among other things, Home Systems purchased little Forest Products lumber. Although mobile home designs were altered by Bendix to exceed industry strength codes, some Bendix leaders were unhappy because the quality standards were so much lower than in the company's traditional product lines. And with the rise in gasoline prices and shortages following OPEC's pricing moves of late 1973 and early 1974, recreational vehicle (RV) sales, accounting for 43 percent of total division sales in 1972, plummeted.

The European plants were sold off relatively early, and the most unprofitable North American plants were closed. In October of 1978, 18 remaining U.S. and Canadian plants were sold for approximately $25 million to the Commodore Corporation, a small mobile home specialist that had recently emerged from a Chapter XI (bankruptcy) reorganization. Commodore approached Bendix and proposed the purchase, which was leveraged, among other things, by a Bendix loan. Commodore closed the former Bendix divisional headquarters in Atlanta and consolidated central office operations in Syracuse, Indiana. It also effected marketing strategy changes, altering the Bendix mobile home designs from the high to the low end of the market, where demand was much stronger. Viewing the remaining recreational vehicle operations as an unprofitable diversion from its main mobile home focus, Commodore at first encouraged the plant managers to organize an employee buyout. When the necessary financing could not be arranged, the RV business was sold in November 1982 to Thor Industries, a holding company with no other activities.

Commodore was hit hard by the 1980 and 1982 recessions. Although it managed to report modest profits in 1981 and 1983 and to reduce its debt by a third, it suffered massive operating losses in 1984 and early 1985. Closing several more plants with the most serious problems was insufficient to stem the tide, and in June 1985 the company again filed for bankruptcy.[2] By that time, it had through sale and closure consolidated its operations to its 4 most profitable plants—down from 20 at the time of its Bendix buyout. Two of those 4 remaining plants had come from the Bendix purchase and 2 were operated by Commodore before the purchase.

Caradco

During 1979, in a continuing effort to complement its American Forest Products operation, Bendix purchased from Scovill Inc. the Caradco Company, whose experience as a producer of wooden windows and doors dated back to 1865.

Scovill had acquired Caradco in 1968. At the time Caradco was the nation's second-largest maker of preassembled wooden windows. Scovill hoped to achieve complementarities with the lighting fixture, bathroom cabinet, exhaust fan, and other products of its Nu-Tone Division, purchased in 1967. The synergies achieved were in fact modest, and Caradco was gradually falling behind its more aggressive competitor, Andersen. In part to strengthen its competitive posture, and partly in anticipation of growth induced by energy conservation efforts, Caradco management persuaded Scovill that operations should be moved from an old, multistory plant in Dubuque, Iowa, to a much larger new plant in Rantoul, Illinois. The move, carried out in 1976, was replete with problems. Working with wood requires a "feel" that can only be

2. "Commodore Corp. Unit To File Today for Chapter 11 Aid," *Wall Street Journal*, June 10, 1985.

developed through experience, and with a completely new work force at Rantoul, Caradco experienced low productivity and high rates of unsalvageable waste. The original plant layouts proved unsatisfactory, and costly production line redesign was necessary. These problems occurred just as a boom developed in the market, but Caradco was unable to meet the demand. Facing three-month order backlogs, its distributors took on competing lines to remain in business. Losses mounted, and management changes were made. The major production problems were gradually solved, but then housing starts declined and the market for windows contracted. Caradco's position in this less favorable market was aggravated by the earlier loss of distributor goodwill. Finding Caradco's profit returns below expectations and anticipating continuing softness in housing, Scovill management decided to sell out to Bendix. At the time it wrote off disposition losses of $2.7 million.

Bendix considered Caradco attractive because of complementarities with American Forest Products. Caradco's lumber-cutting plant in Sacramento, California, was underutilized. It was closed, and its supply functions were merged into a Bendix plant at Stockton, California. Almost concurrently with the Caradco acquisition, Bendix purchased Bass and Company, a chain of 15 builders' supply outlets in the Southwest. This strengthened Caradco's channels of distribution at a time when it was scrambling for outlets.

Despite these advantages, the purchase was a disappointment to Bendix. With interest rates soaring, the 1979 housing start decline accelerated in 1980, leaving considerable excess capacity at Rantoul. There was further turnover in Caradco's management, and production problems continued. Heavy warranty expenses were incurred when many windows experienced post-sale paint peeling. Most important, the raison d'être for Caradco's acquisition vanished when Bendix sold off American Forest Products at a price of $425 million (with a capital gain of nearly $300 million) in late 1980, just before lumber prices began falling sharply. Both Caradco and Bass were sold soon thereafter, engendering disposition losses much smaller than the large profit made in selling American Forest Products. For Caradco, the September 1981 sale price was $13.3 million, compared to the purchase price two years earlier of $21.1 million.

Caradco's new owner was the Kusan Division of Bethlehem Steel Corporation. The attraction again, in addition to a fire sale price, was complementarity. An important part of Kusan's product line consisted of vinyl siding and shutters, with distribution channels potentially similar to Caradco's. At the time our field research was concluded, Kusan was working hard to correct Caradco's quality problems, improve production efficiency by increasing the number of interchangeable parts, strengthen sales of lower-priced wood windows, and build Caradco's previously weak sales position in the remodeling market, where most of Kusan's vinyl siding sales occurred. By 1985 the unit had become profitable, although Bethlehem management considered it unlikely that Caradco could overtake industry leaders Andersen and Pella.

Chromalloy Sintercast

The Chromalloy American Corporation was founded in 1951 to commercialize new technologies for coating and repairing turbojet engine parts and other components subjected to high temperatures and considerable abrasion. This "chromizing" venture prospered and grew, eventually throwing off such large amounts of cash that acquisition candidates were sought. Presiding over the acquisition program was the company's cofounder and chairman, "Joe" Friedman. Friedman was a charismatic patriarchal leader who inspired the affection of virtually everyone with whom he did business.

One of his first acquisitions, in 1959, involved the Sintercast Company. Founded in 1947 by two scientists and a financier, it too worked on new technologies for making jet engine blades. The effort was unsuccessful, but two by-products showed commercial promise. One was an aluminum-boron alloy for making nuclear reactor control rods, the other a sintered, machinable titanium carbide with high abrasion resistance. The sales of these products grew slowly during the 1950s, and profits were negligible. When the company's financial backer died in 1959, a merger with Chromalloy was arranged. Sintercast's growth accelerated, and the division began making handsome returns on invested capital. However, the market for Sintercast's products remained relatively small, and some Chromalloy veterans believed the unit had not lived up to its possibilities fully. But because Sintercast was an early member of the Chromalloy family and was doing well on a small scale, no special corrective measures were taken, nor was there any thought of sell-off.

During the 1960s Chromalloy's acquisition program took new turns.

Its pace and scope exploded, and the company moved outside familiar metallurgical lines into farm machinery, textiles, furniture, pharmaceuticals, glass, trucking, barge operation, hotels, and much else. Sales rose from $34 million in 1965 to $372 million in 1970 and $541 million in 1972. As the company became larger and more complex, Friedman was forced by other stockholders to deemphasize his patriarchal approach to management, implement formal planning and control systems, and organize the operating units into more tightly structured groups. Friedman's power to influence events waned and decisionmaking slowed, but he remained in control until his death in late 1977. With it, a vacuum was created, and a power struggle ensued.

His successor as chairman for the next two years, who had headed Chromalloy's barge line, brought a new orientation and inaugurated an extensive divestiture program. In 1979 the Sun Chemical Company began an attempt to take over the company. Chromalloy's top management was divided over how to react. After the company's president was toppled by an internal cabal, a decision to resist the takeover was made, but the defense was unsuccessful. In August 1980 Sun Chemical's chairman became chairman of Chromalloy, exercising control of Chromalloy's St. Louis headquarters operations from New York. Further top management purges followed. Through the period of rapid managerial turnover between 1977 and 1982, the principal constants were dominance of financial control executives over those stressing technical operations, greater emphasis on short-run results, and a continuation of the divestiture program, aimed both at simplifying control and raising cash. By early 1982, 53 businesses had been sold off and 25 more were scheduled for sale.

With Joe Friedman's death, Sintercast lost its protected status. Its image at corporate headquarters was also tarnished by a decline in profits resulting from start-up costs at a French plant opened in 1977 and from rising overhead costs (attributed by some interviewees to more elaborate controls). Following considerable argument, those favoring divestiture prevailed in 1981. A buyout attempt by one of Chromalloy's cofounders and the previous Sintercast president (who had fallen victim to the infighting) failed to win corporate approval. After further competitive negotiations, Sintercast was taken over in a leveraged buyout headed by the unit's controller and its marketing manager. A new name, Alloy Technology International, was adopted. The new owner-managers changed marketing methods, pruned the field sales force, hired a new technical director from outside, and intensified work on new applications of Sintercast's titanium carbide products. As of 1986, no dramatic changes had occurred, although the company was seeking financial support to introduce an expanded array of product sizes and forms.

Chromalloy Glass

Chromalloy Glass, principal component of a more diverse Building Products group, came together during the peak period of Chromalloy American's conglomerate acquisition phase. The key acquisitions were made by the Water Treatment Company, in which Chromalloy owned a sizable minority interest, and were brought fully into the corporate fold with Water Treatment's absorption in 1971. Brought together were Perilstein and Hires-Turner, two of the East Coast's leading wholesale and contract glass installation firms, with more than 20 branches spread out from Alexandria, Virginia, to Tulsa, Oklahoma; another Miami, Florida, contracting firm; a Houston mirror manufacturer; Safetee of Philadelphia, a pioneer in tempered and bullet-proof glass; and Sentinel of Hatboro, Pennsylvania, a specialist in glass tubing and other fabricated glassware. Heading the group, which in 1972 established a new plant and headquarters at Valley Forge, Pennsylvania, was the president of Sentinel, Sidney Traurig, who through the mergers had become an important stockholder of Chromalloy. Under Traurig, who enjoyed close relationships with Joe Friedman and other St. Louis headquarters executives, the group integrated its operations, closed some of the smallest branches, and generally thrived. Among other things, it met the exacting filter safety glass requirements of the National Gallery of Art's East Building, opened in 1978.

When Friedman's successor initiated a divestiture program in 1978, Chromalloy Glass was spared, in part because of Traurig's position as stockholder, board of directors member, and later candidate for the corporate presidency considered capable of reconciling the warring factions. Indeed, while most segments of Chromalloy American were retrenching, the glass products group was allowed in 1980 to begin constructing a new $5 million plant in Lewistown, Pennsylvania. However, Traurig's health deteriorated, triggering a divisional management succession power struggle won by the financial control faction—the "bean counters," in the words of one operating manager. The "double-dip" building recessions of 1980–82 also hit hard. Small branches were sold off simply because they were small, even though profitable. In early 1982 the entire Glass division (along with its aluminum anodizing and lumber siblings) was added to the general "sell" list. Branch units were for the most part sold off singly. Little or no help was provided by corporate headquarters in financing larger purchases, and when no ready buyer appeared, the units were simply shut down. Operating-level management morale plummeted. Plans for the new Lewistown plant were changed in midstream by persons lacking production know-how so that, for example, a new tempering line proved inoperable. The entire plant was sold off in 1984 to a New York State glass products specialist, a year after its full-scale start-up and a transfer of production and headquarters operations to Lewistown from Valley Forge. By May of 1984, all but two of the Glass division's units had been sold or closed. While the division was being dismantled during 1982 and 1983, Chromalloy American operations selected for continuation experienced pretax losses totaling 12 percent of end-of-1981 stockholders' equity. Only the metal-working operations that had been the basis of Chromalloy's formation in 1951 reported sustained profitability through 1985.

ESB

ESB (for Electric Storage Battery) Inc., with headquarters in Philadelphia, was one of the world's largest battery manufacturers in 1974. Beginning from its strong base in "wet" (that is, lead-acid) automobile and industrial batteries bearing the Exide and Willard brand names, it moved into the dry cell business in 1957 by acquiring Ray-O-Vac of Madison, Wisconsin. Further diversification efforts carried it into the production of electric motors and electronic and safety products (for example, emergency lighting and uninterruptible power systems, respirators, and cardiac pacemakers).

In 1974 ESB was subjected to a hostile takeover attempt by International Nickel Company of Canada (later INCO), the world's largest nickel producer. Seeking diversification from its cyclical nickel business, INCO identified storage batteries (some of which use nickel electrodes) as its best prospect. It tried first to acquire Chloride, the leading British battery maker, but was rebuffed. It then commenced a tender offer for ESB that was viewed as precedent-setting, since hostile tender offers in the United States had previously been made mainly by less well established companies, and since INCO was aided by the traditionally conservative Morgan-Stanley and Company banking house.[3] ESB resisted vigorously, among other things supporting United Technologies Corporation (then called United Aircraft Corporation) as a "white knight." But INCO bid ESB's stock up from $19.50 to $41 per share and won the contest, paying a total takeover price of $234 million. All interviewees agreed that the price paid was excessive relative to ESB's intrinsic value. A Department of Justice antimerger suit required INCO to "hold separate" ESB's operations until the suit was settled through a patent licensing decree in early 1978. Until that time, when INCO installed one of its own people as president, ESB operated nearly autonomously, subject to broad financial controls and consultation over policy.

During this period, ESB made two serious mistakes. First, it backed a new three-piece automotive battery design when the other leading members were moving into the so-called (but not strictly accurate) "no maintenance" design using new lead-calcium grids. Once the error of this commitment became evident, retooling for the lead-calcium process was found to be financially infeasible. Second, it failed to anticipate the wide consumer acceptance of longer-lived but more expensive alkaline dry cells, introduced first by Duracell (P. R. Mallory and Company) and imitated aggressively by Eveready (Union Carbide Corporation). When Ray-O-Vac belatedly offered its own alkaline cells, its traditional rivals enjoyed formidable first-mover advantages. Even before the alkaline battery revolution, Ray-O-Vac's market share had been declining because of unaggressive marketing and a shift in consumer battery purchase habits from such outlets as hardware stores, where Ray-O-Vac was relatively strong, to food and drug outlets, where it was weak.

From this inauspicious start, the situation deteriorated as INCO assumed direct managerial control in April 1978. ESB's incumbent president was mortally ill and could consult only briefly with the new head. Health problems also sidelined other key management members at a critical time. Automobile battery sales declined because of greatly extended existing battery lives, rising imports and declining new car sales, and mild winters. This general problem was aggravated by ESB's design disadvantage. INCO was in no position to help out because of

3. See "Aiding Hostile Takeover Bids," *New York Times*, December 28, 1981.

depressed earnings in 1977 and 1978 and huge financial obligations for new nickel facilities in Guatemala (later shut down) and Indonesia. Following a brief recovery, INCO's financial position became even worse as world nickel prices fell sharply in 1981 and 1982, nickel inventories soared, and nickel operations began losing money for the first time in 50 years. ESB's situation deteriorated further. It incurred operating losses of $15 million in 1980 and $25 million in 1981. In an atmosphere of crisis, INCO announced in December 1981 that it would sell off the entire ESB operation, projecting cash proceeds of $220 million and a loss on the dispositions of $245 million after tax offsets.

The divestiture was carried out in numerous separate pieces, mostly to leveraged buyout groups. The electric motor and safety products groups went first. International Ray-O-Vac operations were separated from domestic activity and sold to a management group. The domestic dry cell company was sold to an investor group organized by an outside marketing consultant, who became its new president. A Swedish battery maker acquired during INCO's ownership period was sold to a Finnish concern. In anticipation of divestiture, several Exide storage battery plants were closed. ESB managers were outbid by an outside consortium for the purchase of the remaining domestic storage battery operations. ESB's central research staff, considered to have been one of the world's best battery technology groups, had already been dispersed following an INCO decision to move it to INCO's central R&D facility in New York State. The development and product engineering staffs, which were decentralized to the operating divisions, were cut back as ESB's financial crisis mounted.

The largest domestic fragments, Exide and Ray-O-Vac, were heavily leveraged and entered the world of independent firms burdened by appreciable strategic handicaps. The new Rayovac Company (with altered spelling) focused special attention on solving marketing problems—for example, modernizing its battery display packages, reorganizing the sales force, and attempting to build its presence in outlets such as food and drug stores, where Duracell and Eveready were strongly entrenched. Those two rivals controlled 48 percent and 42 percent, respectively, of overall U.S. dry cell sales, well ahead of Rayovac's 10 percent market share. Rayovac's remaining product development resources were reallocated to serve marketing goals more closely. Several innovations followed: a series of "Workhorse" flashlights, ranging from purse to lantern size; an easily opened "Smart Pack" package containing six to eight batteries, aimed at high-volume users; and an extended-life hearing aid battery.[4] In the difficult months preceding sell-off, Rayovac had undertaken strenuous cost reduction measures, so its new management was spared the problem of further morale-impairing cutbacks. Within a year, it had turned the corner to profitability. In 1985 its advertising budget was increased to $15 million, with a stated goal of eventually reaching levels competitive with those of Duracell and Eveready (with 1985 outlays of $28 and $22 million, respectively).[5]

The domestic wet battery business was sold to the Spectrum Group, an investment consortium. A consultant who had advised INCO on sell-off strategy became its new president. The new management refused to be interviewed, and there were sharply conflicting views of Exide's fortunes after sell-off. A knowledgeable competitor saw Exide as severely distressed: reduced to a 5 percent auto battery market share (down from 16 percent in the early 1970s), losing the West Coast segment of its important Montgomery Ward account in 1983 and the remainder later, and suffering profitability and cash-flow problems that led it to sell off its polyethylene and rubber case molding facilities.[6] According to the competitor, its greatest remaining strengths were in heavy-duty industrial batteries, in which it had long been the U.S. market leader but dropped to second place, and its original equipment sales to a booming Chrysler Corporation, which remained loyal in gratitude for the credit ESB had extended when Chrysler was on the verge of bankruptcy in 1979. In a July 1984 letter commenting on an earlier draft of this summary, an Exide representative painted a more optimistic picture, observing that two automotive battery plants were reopened in 1983, that two new West Coast accounts had been gained, that Exide's automobile battery market share had risen to 7.5 percent after declining to 5.5 percent, and that its industrial battery share continued to exceed 20 percent. He claimed also that following the buyout, Exide's product development and engineering staff had been strengthened. Among other things, Exide

4. See "Marketing Innovative at Rayovac," *Chain Drug Review*, June 17, 1985; and "The Comeback at Rayovac," *Corporate Report Wisconsin*, vol. 1 (September 1985), pp. 52–53.

5. Laurie Freeman, "Rayovac Back on Beam in Battery Market," *Advertising Age*, September 16, 1985, p. 47. In 1986, Eveready was sold by Union Carbide to the Ralston Purina Company, and Eastman Kodak entered the alkaline battery business de novo with a new, longer-life design.

6. "Stokes To Sell Assets of Only Plant to Witco," *Rubber & Plastics News*, February 11, 1985, p. 1.

had moved into the production of lead-calcium "no maintenance" batteries.

Subsequent developments reveal that the optimistic view was not fully warranted. The initial management team was discharged, and a new team headed by an executive with experience in auto parts marketing was brought in. A policy of competing aggressively on a price basis for private-label replacement battery business was adopted. The company's West Coast operations were strengthened by the acquisition of a Canadian firm's plant. Important new accounts were won, and Exide's market share rose. However, the profit margins on which new business was gained were sufficiently slender that Exide's long-run viability remained in doubt.

In 1987, with loans of $180 million arranged by Citicorp of New York, Exide acquired the General Battery Corporation, another important U.S. wet battery maker.

Great Lakes Screw

Great Lakes Screw's principal product was engineered industrial fasteners—that is, fasteners made to the specification of customers such as the automobile and appliance manufacturers. Located in south Chicago, it was founded in 1945 by the Crawford brothers (Robert and Jennings). It grew to operate more than 100 machines (mostly cold-heading forges and screw threaders) and employ as many as 400 people. The Crawfords ran it paternalistically, with few rules, flexible working hours, and casual, friendly interpersonal relations. In 1967, possibly because of disillusion over recent unionization and an unfair labor practices suit, the Crawfords decided to sell out to U.S. Industries.

U.S.I. was founded around the turn of the century by "Diamond Jim" Brady to manufacture railroad cars. It gradually moved into other fields of heavy industrial equipment and then, in the second half of the 1960s, began a torrent of conglomerate acquisitions, mostly small, that made it the operator of some 132 separate divisions with activities ranging from tool and die fabrication to the purchase and resale of retailers' overstocked tennis shoes. Many of these, including Great Lakes Screw, were so-called "contingency buyouts," under which the owner-manager of the acquired firm received part of the purchase price in U.S.I. stock immediately and was to be paid the remainder over a five-year period, the exact magnitude and schedule depending upon how well dollar profit goals were exceeded. At first the divisions were overseen by regional vice presidents, but in 1974, as profits went into a steep decline and U.S.I.'s stock fell from a 1967 high of $44 to as little as $2 per share, the units were reorganized into four more coherent groups directed by group vice presidents supported by an augmented corporate staff. There was much discontent and a "rebellion" among divisional "owner-managers" over the depreciation of the stock they had received and their loss of autonomy to "accountant types." Corporate management retaliated with firings and lawsuits.[7]

The Crawford brothers of Great Lakes Screw were no longer with U.S.I. when these problems came to a head. Soon after the merger, division president Robert Crawford began clashing with U.S.I. management over operating styles, and in 1971 he resigned. From 1969 to 1979, Great Lakes had six different chief operating executives and considerable turnover in key divisional staff positions. As the parent corporation's profitability deteriorated, great pressure was brought to bear by group vice presidents to improve cash flow. The situation at Great Lakes was aggravated by a sharp recession of automobile industry demand in 1975. The need to meet corporate cash-flow demands led to less maintenance of equipment, strong pressure on foremen to improve on-line productivity, and the neglect of formal training for new workers. Header machines are subjected to considerable wear and tear, and when they are not maintained to high standards, downtime increases (exacerbating the productivity problem) and product tolerances deteriorate. Meanwhile, the auto makers, pressed by import competition and moving toward smaller cars, were demanding closer tolerances and threatened Great Lakes during the late 1970s with cancellation of orders unless it raised its quality standards. The combination of these problems, falling demand for U.S. autos, and sharp price competition from smaller, lower-overhead fastener shops plunged Great Lakes into unprofitability. In October 1979, Great Lakes was sold at a $6 million price close to its book value. For U.S. Industries, the sale was a small part of a larger pattern. By 1983 it had reduced its scope, mostly through the sell-off or closure of small units, from the 132 divisions of its heyday to roughly 30.

Great Lakes' buyer was Allied Products Corporation, a less diversified conglomerate with a significant complementary position in nuts, bolts,

7. See "Trying To Put the Profit Back into U.S. Industries," *Business Week*, July 7, 1975, pp. 38–39.

and specialized industrial fasteners. Less than a year after the acquisition, Allied began phasing out the Great Lakes plant and moving its equipment to a related Allied plant in Michigan. By 1981, the plant was closed. Because Allied management would not grant an interview, its reasons for buying an enterprise and then shutting it down remain unclear. Great Lakes alumni believed that the acquisition was made to obtain Great Lakes' customers, the patent rights to an exclusive hose clamp product, and Great Lakes' machinery (which, although under-maintained, was said to be in better condition than that of the Allied plants to which it was moved). Since Allied acted to renegotiate Great Lakes' labor union contract only six months before the phaseout began, it was also suggested that Allied hoped to use its bargain with the Great Lakes boilermakers' union as a lever to extract concessions from the different unions in other Allied fastener plants.

Harley Davidson

Harley Davidson is the only surviving native American manufacturer of motorcycles, with operations dating back to 1903. Its specialty has long been large twin-cylinder motorcycles (with total cylinder displacement in the 1,000–1,340 cubic-centimeter range), known as "Hogs." After the company went public as an over-the-counter traded stock, roughly 65 percent of its shares remained in the hands of Harley and Davidson family members during 1966. In 1968 the Bangor Punta Company commenced a takeover attempt considered hostile by the Harley management. The AMF Corporation entered the picture as a "white knight," and in late 1968 Harley agreed to be acquired by AMF in an exchange of common stock valued at roughly $26 million.

For AMF, the acquisition, which included Harley's golf cart operations as well as motorcycles, was considered a natural extension of its effort to diversify into sporting goods and recreational businesses. Beginning from a base in bowling equipment, AMF had previously expanded by merger into golfing products. Subsequent acquisitions added Head skis and tennis racquets, Tyrolia ski bindings, and Hatteras yachts. Retaining members of the Davidson family in key positions but installing some of its own lower-level managers, AMF embarked upon a program of raising Harley's output. Sales rose from approximately 14,000 cycles per year in 1969 to 50,000 units in 1979. The main impetus for this sales expansion came from population growth plus the general growth of interest in motorcycling, spurred largely by Japanese stimulation of the market for smaller, lower-price cycles. Harley did not change its large cycle designs significantly during the 1970s, and its advertising expenditure (for example, $255,000 in 1971) was much lower than that of Honda ($2.4 million) or Suzuki ($805,000).[8] But Harley's dominant position in the large cycle market and its unique image made it a beneficiary of some consumers' desire to "trade up" from the smaller Japanese machines, of which nearly a million units were sold in the peak year 1973.

The increase in output was accommodated by specializing Harley's Milwaukee home plant in the production of engines, transmissions, and other components, transferring assembly operations to an AMF plant in York, Pennsylvania, that had previously been used to produce munitions and (later) bowling pin-setters. This solution was a compromise, entailing some increase in transportation and coordination costs and perhaps also a loss of know-how, and consequently lessened quality control. However, it seemed the best alternative, given the inability of the Milwaukee plant to handle the rising demand and the fact that nearly all of Harley's production was concentrated in a narrow range of designs, making the establishment of two integrated machining-to-assembly lines infeasible.

Another facet of AMF's expansion program was the purchase of an Italian firm, Aermacchi, which had previously entered a joint venture to supply Harley with lightweight cycles. The original hope was that, in addition to rounding out Harley distributors' lines, the small cycles would be bought by consumers who would later trade up to Hogs. However, the Italian models sold poorly against better-known Japanese cycles, and the size gap between lines was too large to permit much trading up. As a result, U.S. assembly of Italian cycles was discontinued in 1976, and in 1978 the Italian subsidiary was sold off.

The third main thrust of AMF's strategy was the development of new Harley models for domestic production. New designs were conceived using the basic Harley drive train. Then an effort was mounted to develop completely new drive trains. The traditional Harley V-twin engine was in this respect both a problem and an asset. It was a problem because it ran much rougher and (for equal displacement) with less performance than its four-cylinder Japanese counterparts. But it was an asset because

8. Kathleen Crighton, "Cycle Market Revs Up Again After Slump," *Advertising Age*, September 4, 1972, p. 57.

its distinctive roughness differentiated it from the Japanese models and gave it a macho image important to Hog aficionados. AMF therefore proceeded along two tracks. It undertook a thorough but evolutionary redesign of the V-twin engine, and it contracted with Porsche of Germany, providing several million dollars of support annually, for the development of a completely new engine that could be produced in two-, four-, and six-cylinder configurations. The upgraded V-twin was introduced, eliciting laudatory reviews, in 1983.[9]

As the more ambitious Porsche program neared completion, AMF faced a difficult decision. Implementing the program was expected to require an investment of $50 million–$100 million, depending upon the number of new medium-size and large models introduced. AMF's capital investment in Harley during the late 1970s had been averaging approximately $10 million per year, and during the 1970s Harley had been consistently (though far from spectacularly) profitable. However, import competition was growing. The Japanese in particular, with a cost advantage of $1,500 to $2,000 against the average $6,000 Harley cycle price, were moving up the size spectrum, and Harley's share of the 1,000 cc and above cycle segment had declined from nearly 100 percent in 1974 to 40 percent in 1979. Overall market growth appeared to be slowing, and sales of the new Porsche engine models would to some extent cannibalize V-twin Hog sales. AMF had alternative investment opportunities—most notably, in its booming Tuboscope oil well pipe inspection and coating equipment line. Although it could have financed all of its programs by borrowing heavily, its management had a conservative policy toward debt structure. AMF decided not to finance the Porsche retooling program and to focus its resources instead on Tuboscope—a choice that later proved embarrassing, as oil well drilling fell sharply during the early 1980s and Tuboscope turned unprofitable. In view of Harley's declining prospects, a further decision was made to sell the division off.

Buyers were sought among the array of established corporations, but none appeared. An internal management group including Davidson family members stepped forward to offer a highly leveraged buyout at a purchase price of $82 million. AMF provided $19 million of debt and stock financing (redeemed in 1984) and took a net write-off on the sale

9. See "Harley-Davidson FXRT Sport Glide," and Kevin Cameron, "Evolution on Trial," *Cycle*, November 1983; and David Friedman, "The Hog Takes It on the Chin," *Philadelphia*, October 1983, pp. 167 ff.

of $26 million. At the time a letter of intent was signed in February 1981, neither of the two parties foresaw how difficult subsequent business conditions would be. In 1980 pre-tax profits of $12.3 million had been recorded. But high interest rates raised debt service costs and depressed cycle sales. Japanese producers maintained their production of large cycles in the face of the slump and doubled their U.S. inventories, precipitating a fall in prices. Harley cut back employment sharply but incurred substantial losses in 1981 and 1982. The company's cash flow was maintained from depreciation, tax rebates, inventory liquidation, and the proceeds (shared with AMF) of the golf cart operation's sale. A sufficient level of investment was sustained to introduce a new line with the redesigned V-twin engine in July 1983, but some productivity-raising investments and implementation of the Porsche engine program had to be deferred. In March 1983, Harley's plea for protection from Japanese imports was accepted by the U.S. government, with tariff rates on large cycles being raised 45 percentage points from 4.4 percent to 49.4 percent, declining over five years back to 4.4 percent. Because Japanese inventories in the United States were so high, the full effects of the tariff were not expected to take hold until 1984. Harley recorded slim profits in 1983 and 1984, among other things filling out the workload at its York plant by resuming the production of bomb casings.[10] A return to substantial profitability was not expected before 1987. Meanwhile, the company's new motorcycles, the quality increases it had achieved, and the cost-cutting programs it carried out to reach "minimal" profitability despite depressed demand were praised by outsiders as "a model for any company."[11] In 1986 Harley went public with a $16 million common stock issue that reduced incumbent management's controlling share to 54 percent.[12]

While Harley's fortunes gradually improved, AMF's declined. The energy sector investments favored at the time of Harley's sell-off proved unprofitable, and in 1985 a hostile takeover attempt succeeded. AMF's headquarters staff (said to be laden with "fat") was cut to one-third of earlier levels, and 13 divisions accounting for more than half of the

10. "Old Harley-Davidson Rides Out of the Red," *Philadelphia Inquirer*, July 1, 1984.

11. "Harley-Davidson Roars Back," *New York Times*, October 3, 1985.

12. "Report to SEC Details How Harley Roared Back under Tariff Protection," *American Metal Market*, June 2, 1986, p. 23; and "Harley-Davidson: Ready To Hit the Road Again," *Business Week*, July 21, 1986, p. 70.

company's sales were targeted for divestiture.[13] Tuboscope was originally included on the sell-off list, but in 1986 the decision was reversed.[14]

Harman International

Harman-Kardon was founded in 1953 to develop an AM-FM tuner-amplifier with all the key electronic components in one package, rather than in the three boxes customary at the time. In 1961 the high fidelity operations were sold to the Jerrold Corporation, maker of community antenna systems. Jerrold resold them in 1967 to the Jervis Corporation, an automobile mirror and metals producer whose presidency had been assumed by Harman-Kardon cofounder Sidney Harman. Subsequent acquisitions added J. B. Lansing loudspeakers (in 1969), Rabco turntables (1972), and diverse European high fidelity specialist firms. The name Harman International Industries was adopted in 1974. In December 1976, Harman's common stock moved from the American to the New York Stock Exchange. Shortly thereafter, company chairman Harman, who owned 11.7 percent of the outstanding shares, was asked by newly elected President Carter to become Under Secretary of Commerce. After consulting with other management members, he decided to offer the company for sale. The buyer, for stock valued at $103 million, was the Beatrice Foods Company.

Beatrice was the most acquisition-prone corporation in modern American industrial history.[15] Through hundreds of acquisitions, it had expanded by 1977 to control nearly 400 widely diversified profit centers, overseen by a corporate headquarters staff of 200 in Chicago. A senior Beatrice executive saw high fidelity equipment as a booming field Beatrice should enter. His first approach to Harman was turned down, but when Harman's chairman decided to sell the company, Beatrice was approached and proved a willing buyer. The transaction was consummated in July 1977. The high fidelity and auto mirror activities were set up as separate profit centers reporting to group management. Following

13. "Behind the AMF Takeover: From Highflier to Sitting Duck," *Business Week*, August 12, 1985, pp. 50–51; and "Jacobs Loses No Time at AMF," *Business Week*, September 16, 1985, p. 38.

14. See "Irv the Liquidator Is Now Irv the Oilman," *Business Week*, February 24, 1986, p. 34; and "Minstar Sells Off Another AMF Unit," *Business Week*, May 26, 1986, p. 50.

15. See table 2-8.

standard Beatrice practice, the existing company management (except-ing Dr. Harman) was kept in place.

Shortly after the merger, problems began to appear. According to one participant, Beatrice paid far too much for the acquisition. Its negotiators received segmental profit information and knew that some parts of the business were unprofitable, but these were perceived as necessary to maintaining a full line. However, the Beatrice officials apparently failed to discern the depth of problems in the FM receiver business, which had fallen behind in design and was experiencing mounting losses. At about the time of the merger, demand for high fidelity equipment, which had been growing steadily in the past, peaked and then began to decline. Just before the merger, a threefold expansion of the profitable J. B. Lansing loudspeaker plant near Los Angeles was initiated. With the drop in demand, its augmented capacity was excessive and a drain on profits. The JBL speaker magnets contained important quantities of cobalt. In 1978 a cutoff of supplies from Zaire led to a quadrupling of cobalt prices, squeezing profits even more. Harman was apparently slower than its rivals in redesigning its equipment to avoid the problem. It also failed to maintain its status as a pacesetter in introducing new products. Beatrice's insistence on steadily increasing quarterly profits added to the demor-alization of Harman executives. Results at the European high fidelity branches were also disappointing. Only the auto mirror operation lived up to expectations, at least until the 1980 auto sales slump.

With its small corporate staff, Beatrice considered itself unable to move in and correct problems in ailing divisions. Its standard reaction to the emergence of problems like those of Harman was to sell off, or if need be close down, the unit. The first to go, in June of 1979, was the money-losing Harman-Kardon receiver operation. It was sold to the Shin Shirasuna Corporation, an offspring of the Japanese concern that manufactured most of Harman-Kardon's receivers, tuners, and ampli-fiers. The remaining U.S. production was ended, products were rede-signed, and, according to a high fidelity equipment retailer, quality was substantially improved. The British and Danish divisions were sold to European interests. The J. B. Lansing operation and its Los Angeles plant were sold at book value (including goodwill) to a group led by former chairman Sidney Harman. Included in that sale were Harman's high fidelity equipment distribution operations in France, Great Britain, Japan, Germany, and several other nations. According to chairman-again Harman, the problems of restoring the company to profitability were solved for most of the units soon after the purchase from Beatrice. Contributing factors included a general recovery of audio equipment demand beginning in 1983 and Ford Motor Company's choice of Harman to supply JBL high fidelity systems (with as many as 12 loudspeakers) as original equipment in its cars.[16] In 1985 the new Harman International Company reacquired the Harman-Kardon line from Shin Shirasuna. Plans were made to reverse the tides toward off-shore manufacture and resume tuner production in the United States.[17]

The sell-off of Harman high fidelity lines was a reaction to specific perceived problems, and apparently not a forerunner of a more general program announced by Beatrice in 1983 to divest 50 more units. One of these was the profitable auto mirror line, which Beatrice had previously chosen to retain, and on which the new Harman Company was outbid by another enterprise, Harvard Industries. Write-offs of $127 million were taken by Beatrice at the 1983 divestiture program's inception. Apparently disappointed by the reaction of its common stock investors, Beatrice management said it was shifting its emphasis from acquisition to marketing and reorganizing its 250 remaining units into some 50 to 100 (later revised to 27) divisional groups.[18] However, in May 1984 it returned to its acquisitive ways by offering $2.8 billion for Esmark. To pay for the deal, Beatrice announced that it would embark upon a further program of aggressively divesting business units that did not fit its new strategy of concentrating on food products and similar consumer goods. Severe management style clashes ensued in the attempt to integrate Beatrice and Esmark, leading in August 1985 to the removal of the merged company's chairman.[19] In 1986 the company was taken over in a tender offer by Kohlberg, Kravis Roberts & Company, specialists in leveraged buyouts.

16. See "The Consumer Rush Is on for Anything Electronic," *Business Week*, February 27, 1984, p. 149; and "Autosound Aftermarket Digs in for Imminent Battle with Detroit," *Merchandising*, vol. 10 (July 1985), p. 12.

17. See "Sidney Harman Loves the Sound of 'Made in the U.S.A.,' " *Business Week*, June 2, 1986, p. 102.

18. "Beatrice Foods vs. Inflation," *New York Times*, March 3, 1982; "Beatrice Foods in Shift," *New York Times*, February 17, 1983; and "Beatrice Changes Course," *Dun's Business Month*, April 1983, p. 34.

19. "Beatrice: 'An Acquisition Junkie' Gets the Shakes," *Business Week*, June 3, 1985, pp. 91–92; and "Why Beatrice Had To Dump Dutt," *Business Week*, August 19, 1985, pp. 34–35.

Letisse

Letisse designed and produced moderately priced women's fashion leather handbags. Its founder, Nicholas Braun, had been hospitalized while a student at the Harvard Law School during the 1940s and began making leather billfolds as a diversion. Seeing potential in the field, he entered the handbag business and built Letisse into one of the largest and most profitable U.S. leather handbag producers, with 400 employees and sales of $3.8 million at its peak in 1967. Tax and estate considerations led him to sell out in 1969 to the W. R. Grace Company for stock valued at 2.7 times Letisse's net worth.

Grace, originally an ocean shipping company, had diversified into chemicals during the 1950s and in the 1960s continued an aggressive diversification program. The executives of its consumer products group were given what amounted to an "open pocketbook" and made numerous small acquisitions, including shoe and clothing manufacturers, the F.A.O. Schwartz toy store, the Herman's World of Sporting Goods retail chain, the Berman Buckskin retail chain, and diverse restaurant and home repair supply chains. The consumer goods manufacturing acquisitions were for the most part unsuccessful. Grace lacked the talent at its corporate headquarters to understand their operations and correct emerging problems. As a result, when problems appeared, the units were simply sold off. Also, divisions like Letisse were considered too small to be manageable in an organization as large as Grace. Consequently, although Letisse had been relatively successful, it was divested with several other consumer goods units in 1977. A small profit was made by Grace on the sale of Letisse, unlike the other members of its sell-off cohort. Grace continued to operate various retail store and restaurant chains, although it was moving away from those lines too.[20]

The character of Letisse's operations changed markedly with the shift from private to Grace ownership. Founder Braun ran his company in the "old world" manner, with paternalistic concern for his Reading, Pennsylvania, factory employees and, as Thoreau would say, "keeping his accounts on his thumbnail." After selling out to Grace, he remained

20. "J. Peter Grace Is Swallowing His Pride and Shifting Course—Well, Sort Of," *Business Week*, December 10, 1984, pp. 98–99; "Grace To Buy Back 26% of Its Stock," *New York Times*, December 11, 1985; and "Inside the Troubled Empire of Peter Grace," *Business Week*, June 16, 1986, pp. 68–71.

with the company only long enough to effect a transition. A new chief executive was brought in from a plastics company acquired by Grace. Executive offices were opened in New York City. The Reading factory was modernized, and accounting functions were computerized. Five-year forecasts were made (despite the enormous volatility of the fashion-sensitive handbag business). Aggressive sales expansion efforts were mounted. Sales in fact grew at a constant-dollar rate of 4.6 percent per year between 1968 and 1977. But for a business with from 300 to 450 employees during the period of Grace ownership, the overhead cost burden increased disproportionately, and Letisse, though successful, was not as profitable as it had been under private ownership.

Buying Letisse from Grace was the Lane Wood Company, which previously operated in the self-service store fixture, mobile home, and insurance businesses. The purchase, like Lane Wood's acquisitions of another handbag maker and a ladies' belt specialist, was financed entirely through debt. In 1983 handbag operations were expanded further by obtaining exclusive rights to design and sell high-fashion handbags under the Evan-Picone name. Lane Wood's intention was to build a fashion accessories division with sales of approximately $50 million and then to spin the operation off to Lane Wood shareholders as a separate corporation. However, beginning in 1982 and escalating in 1983 and 1984, the sharp fall in the value of the U.S. dollar attracted a flood of reasonably priced handbag imports from Europe and the Far East. Lane Wood management reacted too slowly in cutting costs and contracting for off-shore production, sales fell, and losses were incurred. The shock was accentuated by the fashion division's high leverage and lack of an equity cushion. In 1985 a substantial write-off was taken on the sale of Lane Wood's higher-priced handbag manufacturer, and in 1986 Letisse was forced to close its doors and be liquidated.

After nine years of retirement in Majorca, the founder of Letisse returned to Reading and founded, with his wife and daughter, a new leather handbag firm, Juliette Originals. It was reported in 1985 to be profitable and expanding rapidly.

Marquette Cement

Marquette Cement Company was established in Illinois in 1902. Mainly through acquisitions, it grew to operate 12 cement plants on and east of the Mississippi River by the early 1970s. After a period of declining vigor and profitability, new management was installed in 1973. A turnaround followed, improving profits and causing Marquette to gain a reputation, despite its relatively old and small plants, as one of the best-managed U.S. cement makers. In 1976 plans were laid for the construction of a new million-ton annual capacity state-of-the-art plant at the site of its existing plant and limestone quarry at Cape Girardeau, Missouri. At the time, the investment cost anticipated was $75 million, to be spread over a three-year period. The Cape Girardeau program alone would require twice as much capital spending as Marquette had achieved in any previous year, and other more modest modernization projects were also contemplated. Although a cash hoard of $20 million had been accumulated, it was unclear whether the program could be accomplished without scrimping on maintenance and/or selling off some plants. Also, the cash hoard, combined with the fact that a depressed market for capital goods company stocks had valued Marquette's shares at less than a third their book value, made Marquette a likely takeover candidate. Consequently, Marquette's management sought a friendly suitor and agreed in May of 1976 to be acquired by Gulf & Western Industries for approximately $50 million in preferred stock—somewhat less than half Marquette's equity book value.

Building from a base in auto parts, Gulf & Western had, through more than 100 acquisitions during the 1950s and 1960s, become a leading conglomerate, with activity in motion picture production (Paramount and Desilu), sugar, zinc, paper, clothing, cigars, consumer finance, book publishing, and much else. Its interest in Marquette reflected the belief of its chairman, Charles Bluhdorn, that Marquette was both a bargain and an attractive "shortage play." That is, at the time the U.S. cement industry had large amounts of obsolete capacity that was gradually being closed down. With building activity still slack as a result of the 1974–75 recession, cement company profits were weak, and the addition of modern cement-making capacity was not expected to keep pace with shutdowns. Sooner or later, Bluhdorn believed, demand would outrun supply and cement would become a bonanza industry. With its new Cape Girardeau plant and a fleet of barges to serve the entire Mississippi River Valley, Marquette would be especially well poised to take advantage. Even if the expected boom was delayed, Marquette was well-hedged by being able to shut down higher-cost plants in the South Central states when the low-cost Cape Girardeau facility came on stream. Gulf

& Western therefore acquired Marquette and provided both the $105 million (with inflation) eventually needed at Cape Girardeau and enough to maintain the company's other long-run-viable plants to high standards. Marquette's incumbent chairman was subsequently promoted to head Gulf & Western's entire Natural Resources group, but other than that, Marquette's management was kept intact. Gulf & Western functioned mainly as a holding company, with little headquarters intervention in operating unit affairs except in the realm of financing and key personnel choices.

Gulf & Western's hopes for Marquette were, however, disappointed. After a brief recovery, the cement industry was hit hard by the monetary policy crunch of late 1979 and the severe capital goods recession that followed. Bluhdorn's optimism turned to pessimism. He foresaw a protracted period of tight money and unacceptably low returns in capital-intensive industries. In 1981 he decided to sell off not only Marquette, but also New Jersey Zinc, Brown Paper, and other subsidiaries requiring substantial continuing investments. The proceeds of those divestitures were applied to purchase minority stock interests in a portfolio of companies whose shares Bluhdorn considered undervalued. After Bluhdorn's death in early 1983, a new top management took advantage of booming stock market prices to sell many of those holdings, mostly at substantial gains.[21]

Marquette was purchased by Lone Star Industries in April of 1982, a year after the new Cape Girardeau kiln came on stream, for cash and securities valued at $267 million. The purchase made Lone Star the largest North American cement producer, with 6 plants acquired from Marquette (6 others having been closed) and 12 of its own. Underlying the transaction was a classic disparity of expectations: Gulf & Western's chairman was pessimistic about cement's prospects; Lone Star's chairman was optimistic for reasons similar to those that motivated Gulf & Western's earlier purchase of Marquette. Indeed, to concentrate the company's efforts on cement and concrete products, which he considered more promising, Lone Star chairman James Stewart had in 1979 sold off the chain of home improvement stores that brought him into Lone Star's management. In addition, the largely horizontal merger offered unusually attractive efficiency increase potential. Prior to the merger, Lone Star's New Orleans and Houston plants each produced

21. "Portfolio Sale Lifts G&W," *New York Times*, May 13, 1983; and "A Round of Applause for G&W," *Business Week*, December 19, 1983, p. 101.

regular and oil well cement. With the shipment of low-cost clinker (unground cement) to those plants from Cape Girardeau, New Orleans could produce oil well cement for both markets and Houston (whose clinker operation was shut down) could specialize in grinding regular cement. Marquette's Nashville headquarters office, accounting for 6 percent of total company employment, was closed and its operations were transferred to Greenwich, Connecticut, without any augmentation of the Greenwich staff. Savings also resulted temporarily from operating Lone Star's Roanoke, Virginia, and Nazareth, Pennsylvania, plants in tandem with Marquette's Catskill, New York, and Hagerstown, Maryland, plants, permitting high-cost kilns to be shut down and meeting (slack) demands by cross-shipping from the lowest-cost sources.[22]

Despite these "synergies," the post-merger period was not an easy one for Lone Star. A heavy debt burden was assumed at a time of high interest rates and the worst capital goods recession since the 1930s. Severance and reorganization costs were incurred. Lone Star's profits (before gains on asset dispositions) were minimal in 1982 and negative in 1983. To raise cash and ease its debt burden, Lone Star sold off Marquette's Catskill plant in late 1983 and the Hagerstown plant in mid-1985. Although sizable capital gains were recorded, one source of multi-plant coordination economies was sacrificed. Whether its purchase of Marquette will turn out well over the longer run will depend upon macroeconomic events beyond Lone Star's control.

Talon

In America, Talon has traditionally meant zippers and vice versa. Its predecessor companies were formed to exploit the rudimentary pre-zipper technology, and its own employee invented in 1913 a device with all the features of modern metal zippers. It also developed and patented high-speed machines to produce them, and at first it enjoyed a virtual domestic monopoly. As its patents expired, new rivals entered, but in the late 1960s, Talon continued to make approximately 42 percent of U.S. zipper sales, including 30 percent of all metal zippers and 65 percent

22. See F. M. Scherer and others, *The Economics of Multi-Plant Operation: An International Comparisons Study* (Harvard University Press, 1975), pp. 275–76, in which U.S. firms' cement plants were found to be too far apart in most instances to benefit from such rationalization and cross-shipping.

of the newer nonmetal types. At that time, the company was still controlled by descendants of the founding Walker family. However, the family lacked a chain of managerial succession and were anxious to make their assets more liquid. As a result, in April of 1968 they agreed to sell out to Textron for securities valued then at $204 million. In the preceding year, Talon had experienced record after-tax profits of $9.9 million on sales of $114 million. Returns on investment were considerably higher in zippers (accounting for sales of $82 million) than in the other lines into which Talon had diversified beginning in 1955.

Textron is widely regarded as the prototype of the modern American conglomerate. Under its chairman Royal Little, it began during the 1950s acquiring companies in a variety of fields to diversify away from its historical base, the cyclical and ailing textile industry. Under Little it moved successfully into auto parts, fasteners, power tools, watches, machinery, helicopters, fountain pens, and much else. When it bought Talon, the U.S. conglomerate merger wave was at its peak, but Textron was already a relatively mature conglomerate destined, as events later revealed, to make few additional acquisitions. Announcing the Talon purchase, Textron president G. William Miller (later Federal Reserve Board chairman and secretary of the treasury) said that the acquisition brought Textron into an entirely new field with continued growth potential.[23] He was half right.

Textron tried hard to make Talon grow. It soon made several complementary acquisitions: of Donahue Sales Corporation, the firm that distributed Talon zippers to retail home sewing outlets throughout the United States; Ri-Ri (selling zippers in Switzerland, the Benelux countries, Italy, and Germany); and Aero Zipp (with operations in the United Kingdom and Australia). Several small new plants were built in low-wage areas of the United States.

However, signs of trouble were already evident to insiders at the time Textron acquired Talon. Indeed, several interviewees suggested that Textron bought at the peak and paid far too much. The home sewing center market, which (with extremely high markups) accounted for 14 percent of unit sales but 35 percent of profits, peaked in 1967 and then began declining, at first slowly and then rapidly, as increasing numbers of women joined the work force and ceased making their own clothes and as high schools cut back sewing instruction. Clothing imports were

23. *Wall Street Journal*, April 3, 1968.

starting to rise rapidly, often displacing U.S.-made zippers. After introducing nylon filament zippers during the early 1960s, Talon tended to rest on its technological oars, and there was little progress in its zipper-making machine design. Meanwhile YKK, the leading Japanese zipper manufacturer, was beginning to move. It took the Talon and European nylon filament zipper and machinery designs, allegedly infringing some patents, and improved upon them. The machinery Talon installed in its new plants during the early 1970s was, in hindsight, already obsolescent relative to YKK standards. Perceiving that it lacked the skills to set up its own operations, Talon entered into joint ventures in Hong Kong and the West Indies and licensed other producers in Argentina and the Philippines. YKK was more aggressive and captured the lion's share of zippers sewn into garments imported into the United States. Talon later had to back off from a law suit seeking to impound imported garments with patent-infringing YKK zippers because the importers—large American manufacturers and retailers—were among Talon's best domestic customers. In 1960 YKK began importing zipper parts for assembly in the United States. Its efforts accelerated noticeably in 1968—the year Talon was acquired.[24] In the early 1970s it introduced a completely new molded Delrin zipper for which Talon had no U.S. counterpart, and which appealed to outerwear manufacturers. Talon failed to take advantage of Ri-Ri's comparable product, and Talon's own countervailing Omni zipper design came much too late (1978) and was of inferior quality. YKK's intentions became increasingly clear when it invited buyers from Levi Strauss and other large U.S. zipper users to be its guests at the 1972 Winter Olympics in Sapporo and escorted them through its previously secretive plants, urging them to compare Talon's machinery with its own more advanced equipment. Claiming injury, Talon reacted to rapidly rising YKK imports with an eventually unsuccessful plea for sharply increased tariffs. But YKK hedged against possible import barriers by opening in March 1974 an ultramodern integrated zipper factory in Macon, Georgia.

How Talon responded to this perceived and growing threat is partly disputed. Lewis Walker, president and heir of the founding family, retired shortly after the merger. During the next decade there was considerable turnover of Talon top managers, some brought in from other Textron divisions and some emerging from the Talon ranks, and

24. U.S. International Trade Commission, *Slide Fasteners and Parts Thereof*, Report to the President (ITC, 1976), p. A-46.

different interviewees had quite divergent perspectives. Claims of certain interviewees that Talon was starved of investible funds were denied by others. The truth seems to converge on five points. First, Textron expected and obtained from Talon substantial cash-flow returns. In the early post-merger years, zipper income plus depreciation consistently exceeded capital outlays by two to five times. Second, Textron imposed upon Talon the same return on new capital investment criteria as for its other subsidiaries: 25 percent before taxes, implying for a 15-year constant payoff point investment a 3.91-year payback period. This was not out of line with the capital budgeting "hurdle rates" applied by many U.S. corporations in the mid-1970s.[25] Third, Textron did fund numerous Talon investment proposals, and in fact it supported record capital outlays in 1972 and 1973. There is no evidence that it turned down an unusual number of *formal* proposals. Fourth, Talon management was at times unaggressive in its requests for funds. Its R&D program suffered from a deficiency of good internal ideas and from a "not invented here" syndrome, and the plant expenditures it formally proposed were for marginal changes rather than the thoroughgoing modernization required to achieve parity with YKK. But fifth, the executives who did approach Textron's top management with informal proposals for major modernization were led to believe that they were inconsistent with Textron's financial objectives. Indeed, it is unlikely that any such program could have yielded the required 25 percent, given YKK's technical lead and lower cost of capital.

There were also difficulties on the pricing front. Excepting its innovative molded nylon zipper, YKK at first focused its sales efforts on the best-selling zipper types, ignoring the special colors and designs whose prices failed to reflect the higher costs of low-volume production. After experimenting with price changes and observing the YKK reaction, Talon management concluded during the early 1970s that to repel YKK, it would be necessary to conduct a product-by-product price war that would at least in the short run reduce profits sharply. Two Talon alumni claimed in separate interviews that such a strategy was proposed to Textron management. The person to whom the proposals were allegedly made could not recall them. What is clear is that there was disagreement within both Talon and Textron over the desirability of price warfare.

25. See Samuel L. Hayes III, "Capital Commitments and the High Cost of Money," *Harvard Business Review*, vol. 55 (May-June 1977), pp. 155–61. See also chap. 7, note 24.

The consensus seemed to be that it would be very costly and would at best have retarded but not stopped the YKK inroads. In any event, the strategy was not pursued. In 1980, Talon tried to restore disappearing profit margins through a 25 percent price *increase*, but YKK refused to follow and captured major chunks of Talon's best accounts (including Levi Strauss).

With these reverses, Talon was reeling. U.S. zipper consumption was down, YKK had a cost advantage on most models along with first-mover advantages on molded zippers, and it was rapidly gaining market share. Talon was forced to retrench. It closed three plants before 1975 and six more between 1976 and 1980. In 1979, Talon had an outright loss. In 1980 it lost $8 million. Early in 1981, when a decision to divest was taken by Textron, Talon's loss rate mounted to nearly 10 percent of sales. The main corpus of Talon and two other Textron divisions were sold in April 1981 to Nucon Holdings for $66 million—a third of what Textron had paid for Talon alone 13 years earlier. Textron's pre-tax write-off against net worth on the three units' divestiture was $125 million.

Nucon Holdings was a holding company set up by a complex assortment of financial interests to purchase Talon and the other Textron sell-offs. Nucon's principal organizer had past experience liquidating other business operations, and that experience was quickly put to use. Donahue Sales, a Talon button and trouser clasp subsidiary, and two other domestic Textron divisions were sold off as separate pieces. All but one of the European zipper units were sold individually to their previous managers. Because of a legal snag, Talon's Canadian operation (acquired in 1947) reverted to Textron and was closed. Closures and sell-offs (or in one case, donation to a state redevelopment agency) contracted the company's core domestic manufacturing activity to 5 main plants, down from 15 in 1974. Talon's two headquarters in Meadville, Pennsylvania, and New York City were consolidated at a low-rent Jersey City, New Jersey, site. Thirteen regional sales offices were closed and replaced by a smaller computerized central order processing facility. Talon's product line, which had included vast numbers of low-volume, high-cost specialties, was pruned to a much smaller set of generally high-volume profitable items. Inventories were liquidated. Sufficient cash was raised through the sale of divisions, subsidiaries, plants, and inventories that Nucon's investors were fully repaid with profit within two years of the divestiture action.[26] In late 1983, Nucon's interest in Talon's continuing

26. In its 1984 Annual Report, p. 3, Semicon, a major participant in Nucon Holdings,

operations was purchased in a highly leveraged transaction spearheaded by Sidney Merians, a former textile industry executive brought in by Nucon to manage Talon's reorganization.

Most outside interviewees predicted that under Nucon, Talon would be completely liquidated. In a 1984 interview, Merians said that his original assignment was to reduce the company to a viable core that could be resold, but in the process, he "fell in love" with the business, and his decision (with other Talon operating executives) to buy Nucon out reflected their intent to remain in for the long pull. With a rationalized product line and plant structure, Talon had been restored to profitability, and its U.S. market share had been stabilized at roughly 30 percent. YKK meanwhile had taken over industry leadership with a market share of close to 50 percent.

S. S. White

S. S. White was a century-old firm that had grown to be one of the largest dental equipment and supplies manufacturers in the United States. Its common stock was listed on the New York Stock Exchange. It produced a full line, including chairs, dental units (holding the dentist's tools and patient rinse bowls), X-ray equipment, hand instruments, burs (drills), and amalgams. It also maintained a nationwide chain of 42 "retail" dental supply stores that "detailed" and sold to dentists. It had been a pioneer during the early 1950s in introducing carbide dental burs, which permitted drilling at much higher speeds and took much of the pain out of routine dental work. It also led in the development of "panoramic" dental X-ray units.

In 1966 White's management recommended that the company be acquired by another Philadelphia concern, the Pennwalt Corporation (at the time called Pennsalt Chemicals Corporation) for preferred stock convertible into Pennwalt common stock valued at $34 million. White's annual sales at the time were $51 million. Pennwalt was an old-line industrial chemicals house that sought diversification during the 1960s by acquiring companies in fields that bore some relationship to its home base—for example, in specialty chemicals, pharmaceuticals, chemical processing machinery, and instrumentation. In approving the merger,

---

reported that from its original 1981 investment of $980,000 in Nucon, it had received $7 million in cash, $2.1 million in notes, and a small equity position in one sold-off company.

White's management stressed the advantages of a broader financial base, greater diversification, access to Pennwalt's research and development facilities, and managerial depth. Pennwalt installed its own top managers to complement and replace retiring senior White executives. It also began pruning White's product line of numerous unprofitable items. In 1968 it augmented its dental products position by acquiring the Jelenko Company, which was the leading supplier of dental gold alloys. White and Jelenko were operated as separate divisions.

An early problem was that White's manufacturing was spread over three locations, the largest of which was an antiquated, multistory facility on Staten Island with high materials handling costs and difficult labor relations. Pennwalt's solution was to consolidate operations at a newly acquired and then expanded plant in Holmdel, New Jersey. Dislocation costs of the move, whose principal phase was completed in 1972, pulled down profits in 1971 and 1972, but sales and profits rose to record levels in 1973 and 1974. Among other things, the move made White the low-cost producer of dental burs and helped strengthen its dominant position in that field.

Problems persisted, however. Because of a design error, inadequate testing, the loss of production know-how through the move, or (most likely) some combination of the three, the arm of a newly introduced X-ray machine developed a tendency to break, sometimes, to White's great embarrassment, while in use above patients. Correcting the problem was costly, and White's sales suffered from the reputation blow. White also fell behind technologically in some important areas. Traditionally, dentists worked standing (or bending) at the side of a seated patient. This was hard on the dentist's back. In 1958 a U.S. dentist developed the idea of a dental chair in which the patient lies supine while the dentist works more comfortably from a seated position. The company he founded, Den-Tal-Ez, took over the leading position in the supply of dental chairs.[27] Established dental equipment manufacturers such as White, Ritter, and Weber adopted the new concept only slowly and lost ground. Another newcomer to the dental supply business, Johnson & Johnson, introduced in 1969 a new tooth-colored ceramic-resin composite filler and restorative for rebuilding chipped, gapped, and otherwise unsightly teeth. White's belated answer to the innovation proved to have

27. A Japanese company, J. Morita, carried the concept further at its Human Performance Institute established in collaboration with an American dentist, Dr. D. R. Beach.

been inadequately field-tested, again causing embarrassment and a loss of market position. Sales were also lost to competitors with dental units that combined the best instruments from several manufacturers rather than insisting that all components be produced by the assembler.

As a consequence of innovative entry by newcomers and mistakes by incumbents, the dental equipment business became increasingly fragmented. For White this aggravated a further problem. The leading dental equipment manufacturers distributed their wares through their own vertically integrated "retail" stores.[28] Among other things, the stores helped young dentists and those who were expanding their practices finance their major equipment purchases, thereby building goodwill for the continuing sale of more profitable expendable products. But as White fell behind in chairs, X-ray equipment, and dental units, its captive retailers had an increasingly difficult time competing with independent retailers who picked and chose the most-favored equipment available anywhere on the market. Also, some of White's best retailers were independents, and they were irritated by the fact that members of the White family competed directly at retail with them. This hurt the sale of the products where White remained technologically strong. White's disadvantage in this respect was worse than that of its largest rival, Ritter, since White's retailers bore the name S. S. White Retail Division, whereas Ritter maintained some psychological distance from its Patterson retail division. Adding insult to injury, a new group of low-overhead mail order retailers sprang up during the 1970s, undercutting the expendable supply prices of the vertically integrated outlets. Because of these interacting developments, White's retail chain began losing money. In 1979 four retail outlets were closed, and in early 1982 all remaining U.S. outlets plus those in France were sold off to a private group. The buyer closed the units east of the Mississippi River, liquidated their inventories, and continued to operate only a few western outlets.

An important source of demand for major dental equipment during the 1970s came from dentists adding a second chair and an assistant so that two patients could be served simultaneously. By 1980 this demand stagnated, partly from saturation and partly because of high interest

28. A flurry of retail outlet acquisitions during the 1960s by White, Ritter, and Dentsply (the leading false teeth supplier) was challenged in 1966 by the Department of Justice. White agreed in a consent settlement to divest stores with sales of $4.4 million. *U.S.* v. *Pennsalt Chemicals Corp.,* 1967 Trade Cases (CCH) para. 72,322, and *U.S.* v. *Sybron Corp.,* 1971 Trade Cases (CCH) para. 73,633.

rates. Dental school graduations, which had grown at 4.2 percent annually in the 1970s, also peaked. And Japanese companies were beginning to make significant inroads into the U.S. dental equipment market, especially on the West Coast. Seeing little future growth in the market and discouraged over its past mistakes and declining market position, Pennwalt decided in December 1981 to divest its dental equipment manufacturing business (excluding Jelenko and an industrial precision cutting tool offshoot of White) as well as its retailing operations. After-tax write-offs of approximately $10 million were taken.

However, partly because the manufacturing business had slumped into unprofitability and in part because manufacturing (at Holmdel), headquarters (downtown Philadelphia), and R&D (divided between a Philadelphia suburb and Sunnyvale, California) were only loosely integrated, Pennwalt had trouble finding a buyer. White reposed for more than two years in the limbo of "discontinued operations," with a marked adverse impact on staff morale. A prospective West German buyer would probably have closed the Holmdel plant altogether and consolidated activities elsewhere—an outcome Pennwalt wished to avoid. Finally, in early 1984, the U.S. manufacturing operation along with a sizable production venture in Brazil and smaller units in France, Australia, and England were conditionally sold to a group headed by the former president of a smaller dental equipment company. The financial arrangements were unusual. Because of White's losses, financial intermediaries were wary. Pennwalt therefore continued to finance the White operations for a two-year period during which the new group, working under a management contract, sought to rebuild White's profitability and simultaneously arrange permanent financing.

Intermediate-level staff interviewed before the change in control were enthusiastic that for the first time in recent memory, their organization would be headed by someone who knew the dental supply business well. The new president assumed control in April 1984 and began a vigorous program to consolidate domestic operations, integrate previously autonomous overseas branches with them, trim organizational fat, reorganize selling activities, revamp union relations and wage and salary structures, and rebuild employee morale. White's product line was cut back sharply to emphasize "expendable" supplies, especially those used in preventive dentistry, rather than the durable equipment whose demand had sagged. The X-ray apparatus operations were closed. A decision was provisionally taken to move the remaining, potentially profitable U.S. production operations to the South. However, the required financing proved difficult to secure. Parent Pennwalt was insistent that the financial arrangements be completed, and its connection severed, by early 1986. White's problems were complicated by the loss of key staff as uncertainty over its future mounted. The new group's equity partner dropped out, and no new capital source was found by Pennwalt's March 1986 deadline. The new president therefore stepped out, and White was left in the hands of a caretaker management. The Holmdel plant was sold, and in April 1986 it was expected that White's remaining dental supply manufacturing operations would be liquidated piecemeal.

In 1986 the Jelenko dental alloys division was also sold off because its operating income had deteriorated into the negative range and because its growth–return-on-investment profile was deemed incompatible with Pennwalt's corporate strategy.[29]

Youngstown Sheet & Tube

The Youngstown Sheet & Tube Company was the United States' eighth-largest steel producer during the 1970s. It had three main steel-making works: two at its headquarters city, Youngstown, Ohio, and one at the south end of Lake Michigan in Indiana Harbor, Indiana. It also owned coal mines, iron ore mining interests, and a subsidiary that manufactured and distributed oil well drilling equipment. In 1956 Youngstown sought to merge with Bethlehem Steel but was blocked under a precedent-setting 1958 antitrust judgment. Having lost momentum in anticipation of the merger, Youngstown's management resolved during the mid-1960s to modernize its operations in two stages, first at Indiana Harbor and then at the older Youngstown works. Through a half-billion-dollar investment program, new basic oxygen furnaces, a blast furnace, a cold strip mill, and what was still in 1984 one of the nation's most modern 84-inch hot strip mills were installed during the late 1960s. In the meantime, however, Youngstown lagged other industry members technologically, experiencing somewhat lower profits. Breaking-in problems on the new rolling mills combined with rising imports and lagging sales to depress profits even more. The stock market reacted unfavorably, driving the value of Youngstown's outstanding common stock to as

29. See Pennwalt Corporation, Annual Report, 1985, pp. 4–6.

little as $308 million—less than half the book value of the company's net worth. Youngstown became a prime takeover candidate. After a failed takeover attempt by the Signal Companies, two offers from the Lykes Corporation rejected by Youngstown management, and the unsuccessful cultivation of a "white knight," Youngstown agreed in February of 1969 to be acquired by Lykes in a complex securities swap valued at the time of announcement at $540 million.

Lykes was a Johnny-come-lately to the conglomerate merger business and remained one of the least diversified of our sample parent companies. It had a long-established position in ocean shipping. Prior to the Youngstown takeover, it had moved into insurance and (on a minor scale) into banking and electronics. It was much smaller than Youngstown at the time of the takeover. To finance the acquisition of Youngstown's common stock, it added $237 million to its debt and roughly $225 million of preferred stock. Their servicing obligations were $32 million per year. In the years before the merger, Youngstown had been paying dividends of $19 million per year.

In the years following the merger, Youngstown yielded almost consistently poor profits, averaging in 1970–73 no more before taxes than Lykes's acquisition finance servicing needs. There were several reasons for the poor performance. Following the merger, Youngstown experienced massive senior management turnover, partly because of age and partly because of disaffection lubricated by Lykes-approved "golden parachute" contracts. By 1974 only 2 of 1968's top 15 Youngstown executives remained on duty. Those who replaced them were said by interviewees, including some of the replacements, to be less experienced and able. Second, Lykes appointed as chief executive officer of Youngstown its own person who, except for a two-year period, attempted to run the company from Lykes's headquarters in New Orleans. The arrangement did not work well. Third, in part for these reasons, Youngstown's profits continued to be modest, but Lykes's financial demands were strenuous. Youngstown was forced to scrimp on capital expenditures. In the seven calendar years following the merger, Lykes paid to itself 80 percent of Youngstown's net income in dividends. Among other things, the previously planned modernization of the two Youngstown, Ohio, plants was never started. Finally and most importantly, as both effect and cause of these developments, Youngstown's operating efficiency deteriorated. The plant capital expenditure squeeze was so severe that, among other things, Youngstown was not allowed to maintain an inventory of major spare parts adequate to cope with the repair problems of its complex new rolling mills at Indiana Harbor. When something broke down, the mill would be shut down until the part was repaired or replaced. This disrupted the operations of other upstream and down-stream units. According to operating-level interviewees, such problems plus a top-down managerial philosophy instilled among production management and workers the attitude, "Top management doesn't give a damn how we run this thing, so why should we care?"[30] As a result, the hot strip mill at Indiana Harbor—pacesetter for most of the plant's other activities—operated in its best year at only 68 percent of rated capacity. A similar but older mill at Inland Steel's adjacent plant averaged 21 percent more output per shift.

A weakened Youngstown was ill-prepared to cope with the continued sluggishness of steel demand after the 1975 recession and the resurgence of import competition. In 1976 the Youngstown operations lost $7.3 million before-tax offsets. In 1977 they lost $224 million on sales of $1.5 billion. In September 1977 Lykes-Youngstown reacted by closing down most of one plant at Youngstown, Ohio, and laying off 5,000 workers—an action that precipitated the emergence of a powerful "steel caucus" in the U.S. Congress, whose demands led to the "trigger price" import control system. Two months later, Lykes announced its intention to merge with the LTV Corporation for common and preferred stock valued at $188 million. LTV owned the Jones & Laughlin (J&L) Steel Company, the seventh-largest U.S. steel producer. After an antitrust review conducted personally by the attorney general, the merger was authorized, and it was consummated in December 1978.

LTV was a prominent actor in the late 1960s conglomerate merger wave. From a base in aerospace and electronics, it had diversified by making several large acquisitions, but antitrust and financial difficulties forced it to divest its holdings in airlines (Braniff), insulated wire and cable, sporting goods, and pharmaceuticals, among others. By 1978, it had largely concentrated its focus to aerospace, meat packing, and steel. The steel product lines of LTV's J&L and Lykes's Youngstown were similar, and the geographic locations of the two firms' steel-making plants corresponded sufficiently closely that operating and raw materials procurement economies might be achieved through integration.

Even before the merger was formally consummated, J&L manage-

30. This contention was denied by one senior management alumnus but not by two others.

ment began a drive to improve Youngstown's operations and maximize integration economies. Youngstown's corporate headquarters and ancillary offices were closed, and the two firms' sales forces were combined and pruned by a third. J&L assigned some of its best operating executives to lead the Youngstown plants. A $20 million–30 million commitment was made for rolling mill spare parts and other needed equipment. This plus managerial improvements (partly effected before the merger through the transfer of particularly able Youngstown executives from closed Ohio operations) plus an active program to bolster labor-management cooperation broke the capacity bottlenecks at Indiana Harbor. Youngstown's antiquated Ohio furnaces were closed down, and seamless tube production was specialized. Small diameter tubes were rolled at J&L's Aliquippa, Pennsylvania, works (later closed), and large-diameter tubes were rolled at Youngstown from tube rounds made with Aliquippa's more efficient basic oxygen furnaces. The output of iron ore mines was rerouted to minimize costs, and a pollution problem was solved by shipping coke from Pittsburgh to Indiana Harbor.

These and other changes moved the combined J&L-Youngstown operation from having steel output per manhour below the all-industry average in 1979 to 8 percent higher productivity in 1983. Counting only basic steel operations, that is, ignoring the oil well supply business Youngstown brought into the merger (which had remained profitable in 1977), combined operating profits were $171 million in 1979, $69 million in the 1980 recession year, and a record $336 million in 1981. After this honeymoon, however, the company was hit by a series of severe shocks: the recession of 1982–83, intensified import competition, and the virtual collapse of demand for high-priced seamless oil well tube, which in 1981 accounted for 15 percent of the J&L-Youngstown steel tonnage but 30 percent of revenues. Steel segment operating losses were $299 million in 1982, $200 million in 1983, and $217 million in 1984. The high profits of 1981 were attributable much more to strong demand for high-margin products than to operating efficiencies. Yet without the efficiencies achieved following the merger, the post-1981 picture would have been even worse.

Unlike Lykes, LTV also made major investments to improve the Youngstown remnants' operating efficiency. To enhance productivity and quality at the Youngstown, Ohio, large seamless tube mill, $60 million was spent. A continuous slab caster costing $190 million was completed at Indiana Harbor in late 1983. These and other investments were financed by selling back the Lykes Brothers Steamship Company at a $34 million pre-tax profit to a group including its original owners, selling off a coal mine (one of the few major steel-related investments made by Lykes), and issuing new common and preferred stock.

In 1984, LTV moved from third to second rank among U.S. steel producers by acquiring another large but ailing steel company, fourth-ranked Republic Steel. Although further cost-cutting measures like those that followed the Youngstown acquisition were undertaken, there were also serious post-merger indigestion problems.[31] These plus the additional debt obligations assumed in the Republic merger plus the continued depression of steel demand put LTV in a precarious financial position despite stringent cash conservation measures, including cutbacks in capital investment for steel operations. In July 1986 LTV filed a Chapter XI bankruptcy petition, and in subsequent weeks it closed significant parts of its steel-making facilities, including the modernized seamless tube mill at Youngstown and its bar-rolling operations at Indiana Harbor.

31. "Why LTV Is Stymied in Steel," *Business Week*, April 1, 1985, pp. 65–68; "LTV's Steel-Industry Gamble," *New York Times*, November 22, 1985; and "LTV, Dragged Down by Steel Subsidiary, Struggles To Survive," *Wall Street Journal*, January 6, 1986.

Mnemonics Used in the Principal Statistical Analyses

VARIABLE	DESCRIPTION
ACQUI	Dummy for companies with acquisitions valued at $50 million or more in year.
ADV/S	Ratio of media advertising outlays to sales.
CAP/S	Ratio of industry assets to industry sales.
CAPINT	Ratio of 1977 industry assets to industry sales.
CONGLOM	Fraction of acquired assets from "pure" conglomerate acquisitions.
COPROF	Ratio of company-level operating income to assets.
CR4	Four-firm industry seller concentration ratio.
DM	Dummy variable identifying matched pre- versus post-merger lines of business.
Δ *CEO*	0-1-2 variable identifying company chief executive officer changes.
Δ *OUTPUT*	Industry real output growth, 1972–77.
EQUALS	Dummy variable for lines of business in mergers of equals.
EQUITY	Ratio of book value of company stockholders' equity to debt.
EXPORT	Ratio of 1972 industry exports to industry sales.
EXPT	Ratio of 1977 industry exports to industry sales.
FLOW:S	Cash flow/sales (in percent).
GROWTH	Average annual growth rate of industry assets, in current dollars, 1957–76.
IGROWTH	Average annual real output growth rate of industry, 1974–81.
HORIZ	Fraction of acquired assets from essentially horizontal mergers.

VARIABLE	DESCRIPTION
HOSTILE	Dummy variable identifying lines of business involved in tender offers opposed by management.
ICOUNT	Fraction of industry lines of business that entered their parents' control through merger.
IMERGROW	Acquired industry assets, inflated by post-acquisition industry growth rate, divided by total 1975 industry assets.
IMERGSHR	Fraction of 1975 industry assets stemming from prior acquisitions.
IMPORT	Ratio of relevant 1972 U.S. imports to industry sales.
IMPT	1975 imports/industry production for domestic use.
LBPROF	Ratio of line of business operating income to assets.
LIFO	Fraction of line of business inventory assets covered by LIFO accounting.
MACRO	Ratio of year's *QFR* manufacturing universe operating income/assets percentage to 1974–77 benchmark percentage.
MERGSHR	Fraction of line of business assets originating from acquisitions.
MERGSHR:G	Fraction of line of business assets originating from acquisition, with acquired asset values inflated by a post-acquisition industry growth factor.
MES	Estimate of minimum efficient plant scale as percentage of industry employment.
NATRES	Dummy variable denoting natural resource-based industries.
NEW	Dummy variable identifying post-1950 lines without mergers.
NEWMERG	Dummy variable identifying lines of business that entered parent company after 1950 through acquisition.
NUMM	Count of nonequals acquisitions made by a line of business.
ORIG	Dummy variable identifying lines of business operated by parent in 1950 and without subsequent acquisitions.
ORIGMERG	Dummy variable identifying lines of business operated by parent in 1950 and with subsequent acquisitions.
OSELL/S	Ratio of selling costs (other than media advertising) to sales.

VARIABLE	DESCRIPTION
OTHER	Dummy variable for lines of business subjected to tender offer acquisitions other than hostile and white knight cases.
OWNGRO	Annual growth rate of assets from last pre-merger year (or 1965) to 1974–77.
PART	Fraction of assets acquired by a line of business from other firms' sell-offs.
PCM	Average 1963–67 industry price-cost margin.
POOL	Fraction of acquired assets covered by pooling of interests accounting.
POSTPI	1974–77 average operating income/assets (in percent) minus 12.5 percent.
PREPI	For matched pre-merger sample, pre-merger operating income/assets (in percent) minus 12.5 percent.
PROF:A	Operating income/assets (in percent).
PROF:S	Operating income/sales (in percent).
PURCH	Fraction of acquired assets covered by purchase accounting.
Q	Modified Tobin's *Q* ratio for all acquisitions in weighted average year of acquisition.
RD/S	Ratio of company-financed research and development outlays to sales.
RD:S	Company-financed R&D as a percentage of line of business sales.
RELAT	Fraction of acquired assets from "related business" mergers.
SHR	Market share of line of business relative to its industry category sales (ratio).
STLNE	Fraction of line of business depreciable assets subjected to straight-line depreciation.
SUPRA	Operating income/assets percentage minus corresponding percentage for the company's home industry sector.
TENDER	Dummy variable for lines of business involved in tender offer acquisitions.
VERT	Fraction of acquired assets from essentially vertical mergers.

VARIABLE	DESCRIPTION
WHITE	Dummy variable identifying lines of business involved in white knight acquisitions.
WORKAP	Ratio of company working capital to total assets.
YEAR	Asset-weighted year of acquisition.
YLAG	Weighted average year of merger minus 1950.

Index

Accelerated cost recovery (ACR) depreciation schedules, 223
Accounting: of acquiring firms, 13–14; of acquisitions, 13–14, 78–79; and FIFO inventory method, 15; and LIFO inventory method, 15–16, 104–05; merger, 13–14; and merger analysis, 12–17; and profits, measure of, 13–16; in sell-offs, 147–49, 173, 183. *See also* Pooling-of-interests accounting; Prediction model of accounting methods; Purchase accounting
Acquired firms. *See* Acquisitions
Acquiring firms: accounting of, 13–14; assets of, 13, 230; and cash-flow timing patterns, 10–12; financial data of, 12–13; industries favored by, 52–54; motives of, 3, 5, 211–15; and pooling-of-interests accounting, 13–14; stock prices of, 6–7, 40–45, 208–10; and tender offer mechanism, 68–70; and undervalued targets, 7–10
Acquisitions: accounting of, 13–14; assets of, 13, 59, 71, 80–82, 98; and divestitures, 2; financial data of, 12–13, 58; and NYSE listing application, 58–59; pooling-of-interests, 205–07; problems with, 1–2; purchase, 204–05; stock prices of, 6–7; and tender offer mechanism, 68–70. *See also* Mergers; Pooling-of-interest acquisitions; Purchase acquisitions; Post-merger financial performance; Pre-merger profitability; Targets
ACQUI variable, 171, 176, 182
Advertising, 47, 84, 171, 179
ADV/S variable, 47, 84, 179
Agee, William, 243
Allied Products, 151, 254–55
Alternative controls for industry effect, 88–89, 92
Altman, Edward I., 170
American Safety Razor (ASR), 131; narrative summary of, 239–41; and

Philip Morris, 131, 134, 141, 145–46
AMF, 130, 140, 145n, 255–59
Antitrust policy, 7, 211, 223–26
ASR. *See* American Safety Razor
Assets: of acquiring firms, 13, 230; of acquisitions, 13, 59, 71, 80–82, 98; and pooling-of-interests accounting, 13–14; and purchase accounting, 14; of uncertain value, 215
Austin, Douglas V., 68

Beatrice Foods, 37, 38, 134, 139, 144, 259–61
Bebchuk, Lucian, 227
Bendix Home Systems: and Caradco, 130–31, 134, 152; and Commodore Corporation, 151–52; and leveraged buyouts, 145n, 156; narrative summary of, 242–44
Benston, George J., 16–17, 187
Berry, Charles H., 28
Bethlehem Steel, 149–50, 152, 245
Bluhdorn, Charles, 145, 264–65
Boise Cascade, 130–31, 243
Borden, 125
Boston Consulting Group, 10
Boyle, Stanley E., 57, 59, 67–68, 73
Bradley, Michael, 9
Braun, Nicholas, 262
Bubble theories, 211
Build strategies, 10–11, 140
Buyers, 3, 100, 149–50. *See also* Acquiring firms

CAPINT variable, 84
Capital intensity, 46–47, 49, 84
Capital investment, 112–13, 139–41, 155, 187–88, 212–13
CAP/S, 46–47, 49
Caradco: and Bendix Home Systems, 130–31, 134, 152; and Bethlehem Steel, 149–50, 152; narrative summary of, 244–46; and Scovill, 131
Carleton, Willard T., 58, 62

285

Case study evidence of economics of sell-offs: and accounting valuation consequences, 147–49; conclusion of, 157–58; and decision to sell off, 144–46; developments after sell-off, 149–50; and emerging problems, 134–35; and failures of merger, 132–33; and financial objectives, corporate, 139–41; and horizontal merger efficiencies, 150–52; and inspection problems, 133; and "lemons" problem, 146–47; and leveraged buyouts, 152–56; methodology of studying, 123–27; and NYSE listing applications, 131; and reasons for merger, 128–32; sample in studying, 127, 129; and stock market valuation consequences, 147–49; and successes of merger, 141–44; and transitional behavior after sell-off, 156–57

Cash cow strategies, 10–11, 111–12, 115, 139–41, 187–90

Cash-flow timing patterns, 10–12, 103–05, 206–07

Celler-Kefauver Act, 223

Chemical Investors Inc., 125

Chromalloy American, 127, 140, 144, 210, 214, 246–49

Chromalloy Glass, 131; financial objectives of, 140; narrative summary of, 248–49

Chromalloy Sintercast, 140, 246–48

Clark, Darral G., 171

Clark, John J., 221

Commodore Corporation, 151–52, 156, 243–44

Conglomerates: and diversification, 22, 23–24, 43–44, 124; and stock market reaction, 38–39, 41–45; stock prices of, 41–45, 208–10. See also Mergers

CONGLOM variable, 98, 172, 183

COPROF variable, 169–70, 176, 185

Corporate patterns, 25–26, 76, 174

Coyne, John, 152, 154, 155

CR4 variable, 46, 51, 84

Cross-sectional analysis of merger profitability: alternative controls, 88–89, 92; core model results, 87–88; description of, 85, 87; differences, among years, 92–93; explanatory variables in, other, 95, 98–103; preliminary interpretation of, 93–95; sensitivity analyses, 103, 105–08; time structure of profit effects, 108–11

Δ CEO variable, 170, 176, 182, 187

Δ OUTPUT variable, 84

Depreciation schedules, accelerated, 105, 223

Desai, Arnand, 68

Dewey, Donald, 56

Dirty pooling, 78n

Discount rates, 11, 206, 207

Diversification: comparison of, between 1950 and 1975, 27–33; of conglomerates, 43–44, 124; hypotheses, 44–48; paths of, 33–36; and profits, 46; and R&D, 47; trajectories of, 48–49, 51

Divestitures: and acquisitions, 2; behavior before, 187–90

Drucker, Peter, 1, 136

Duhaime, Irene M., 144

Eckbo, B. Espen, 7

Efficiency theory of mergers, 3, 6–7, 10, 192–93, 211–12, 217

Efficient stock markets, 8–9, 221

Electric Storage Battery (ESB) Inc.: and INCO, 129–30, 133, 141; narrative summary of, 249–53

Elgers, Pieter T., 221

Empire-building theories, 211, 214–15

EQUALS variable, 85, 94–95, 173

ESB (Electric Storage Battery) Inc.: and INCO, 129–30, 133, 141; narrative summary of, 249–53

Event studies, 5–7, 220–21

Federal Trade Commission (FTC): and corporate patterns, 25–26, 174; and LB data, 17–18, 82, 162, 175, 228; merger series of, 22–24, 57, 67–68, 76–77. See also Quarterly Financial Report

Financial accounting data, 12–17

Financial objectives, corporate, 139–41

Financial performance. See Post-merger financial performance; Pre-merger profitability

Fisher, Franklin, 17, 187

FLOW:S variable, 83, 94, 102

Friedman, "Joe," 246–47, 248

FTC. See Federal Trade Commission.

Galtonian regression, 51n, 113, 115–17, 198–99

Georgia-Pacific Corporation, 38–39

Grace, W. R., 144, 209, 262–63

Grant, John H., 144

Great Lakes Screw: and Allied Products, 135, 144, 151–52; financial objectives of, 140; and leveraged buyouts, 156; narrative summary of, 253–55

Grimm, W. T., & Co., 2, 20, 159–61, 205n, 218n

GROWTH variable, 46, 49, 53, 106–07, 118–19
Gulf & Western: and capital investment, 141, 214; divestitures of, 144, 145; and Marquette Cement, 264–66; problems of, 134; and returns to investors, 43, 209
Harley Davidson: and AMF, 130, 141; narrative summary of, 255–59
Harman, Sidney, 255, 260
Harmon International, 130, 134, 259–61
Harris, Robert S., 58, 62
Harvest strategies, 10–11. *See also* Cash cow strategies
Horizontal acquisitions. *See* Horizontal mergers
Horizontal mergers: description of, 22–24, 98; efficiencies of, 150–52; and efficiency theory, 211–12; and monopoly, 6–7, 21, 99n, 219; in Europe, 220, 224; between *1962* and *1972*, 57–58
HORIZ variable, 98, 172
Hostile takeovers, 70, 101–02, 129–30, 133
HOSTILE variable, 101
Hurdle rate, 206

IGROWTH variable, 173
IMERGROW variable, 53
IMERGSHR variable, 52–53
INCO (International Nickel), 129–30, 133, 141, 249–53
Inspection problem, 133
Internal capital market, 3, 140, 213–14
International Nickel (INCO), 129–30, 133, 141, 249–53

Johnson, Samuel, 215
Jones & Laughlin Steel Company, 151–52, 277–79

Klein, April, 148–49
Kohlberg, Kravis, Roberts & Co., 261

LB. *See* Line of Business
LBPROF variable, 169, 177–79
Lemons problem, 146–47
Letisse, 141, 150, 156, 262–63
Leveraged buyouts: consequences of, 152–56, 212, 227
LIFO inventory method, 15–16, 105
LIFO variable, 105
Line of Business (LB): and comparison of sample companies between *1950* and *1975*, 27–33; conglomerate samples in,

36–39; creation of, 16; and diversification hypotheses, 45–48; and joinder of merging company activities, 219; and mergers of equals, 71; and nontraceable costs and assets, 105; and paths of diversification of sample companies for *1975*, 33–36; reporting program, 25, 228; and SIC four-digit industries, 26; and tender offer targets, 68–70; and trajectories of diversification of sample companies, 48–49, 51; and types of sample companies for *1975*, 25–27. *See also* Line of Business data
Line of Business (LB) data: advantages of, 16–17, 75, 187; and mergers, 17–18; and post-merger financial performance, 75–78; and R&D, 119–22; and securities regulation, 228; on sell-offs, 162–66, 177–78; and tender offer targets, 101–03
Little, Royal, 267
Lone Star Cement, 151–52, 265–66
Long, William, 16, 105
Lykes, 130, 139, 145n, 275–79
Lynch, Harry H., 38–39, 42, 132

McConnell, Joseph L., 62
McGowan, John J., 17, 187
MACRO variable, and adjustment of profitability, 65–67, 71, 72, 94–95, 114, 129, 195–96
Magenheim, Ellen, 8, 9
Managerial control, loss of, 98, 111–12, 135–39, 172, 183–84, 193, 217–18
Mandelker, Gershon, 1
Manne, Henry G., 2, 56
Manufacturing and mineral industries: and comparison of diversification in sample companies of, 27–33; and path of diversification in sample companies of, 33–36; and stock market reaction to conglomerates in, 38–39, 41–45; and structural correlates of merger activity in, 45–49, 51–54; trends in, between *1895* and *1985*, 20–24; and types of sample companies of, 24–27
Market extension mergers, 23, 150
Markham, Jesse W., 106, 132
Marquette Cement: acquisition of, 134, 141; and Lone Star Cement, 151–52; narrative summary of, 263–66
Matched merger analysis, 113–17
Meeks, Geoffrey, 14, 87, 220
Merged unit growth, 106–07, 114–15, 117–19

Merger activity: and antitrust policy, 22, 223–26; categorical measures, 89, 92; and comparison of diversification of sample companies, 27–33; historical perspective, 20–24; measuring, 85, 87; and paths to diversification of sample companies, 33–36; and securities regulation, 226–28; and stock market reaction to conglomerates in, 38–39, 41–45, 207–10, 215; structural correlates of, 45–54; and tax policy, 222–23; types of sample companies, 24–27. *See also* Cross-sectional analysis of merger profitability; Mergers

Mergers: bubble theories of, 211; and combined efficiency consequences, 195–203; conglomerate, in *1960*s, 1, 58–59; and diversification hypotheses, 45–48; efficiency theory of, 3–10, 211–12; emerging problems in, 134–35; empire-building theories of, 211, 214–15; European experience of, 220, 224; and event studies, 5–7, 220–221; failures of, 132–33; and financial accounting data, 12–17; financial objectives in, corporate, 139–41; history of, 218–21; and industries favored by acquirers, 52–54; inspection problems in, 133; interaction effects in, 135–39; and internal market, 213–14; market extension, 23; monopoly theory of, 7, 211; motives of, 210–15; performance of, 210–15; of petroleum companies, 37; and pooling-of-interests acquisitions, 205–07; product extension, 23; of publishing companies, 37; and purchase acquisitions, 204–05; pure conglomerate, 23; and R&D, 34–35, 119–22; related business, 23; securities regulation in, 226–28; and sell-offs, 192–93; and stock market, 38–39, 41–45, 207–10; and stock prices, 1, 5–7; successes of, 141–44; and synergies, 3; tax advantages of, 211, 213–14; tax policy in, 222–23; and trajectories of diversification, 48–49, 51; trends of, in manufacturing and mining industries, 20–24; undervalued-assets and bargain theories of, 7–10, 211; vertical, 22–23, 98–99, 172, 183; waves of, 21–22. *See also* Acquisitions; Merger activity; Post-merger financial performance

Mergers of equals, 71, 76–77, 94–95, 173, 182, 200, 219–20

MERGSHR:G variable, 53, 107, 118–19

MERGSHR variable: and alternative controls, 89, 92; and merged unit growth, 118–19; and model specification, 52, 83–85; and R&D, 120–21; and sell-offs, 173, 183; and sensitivity analyses, 105–07

Merians, Sidney, 271

Miller, G. William, 267

Mineral industries. *See* Manufacturing and mineral industries

Mnemonics for statistical analyses, list of, 280–83

Monopoly theory of mergers, 3, 7, 211

Morale: executive, 136–37; staff, 156

Morgan-Stanley, 250

Mueller, Dennis, 3, 8, 9, 58, 88, 113, 116, 194, 220

Multiyear profit dynamics, 70–73

Murphy's Law, 135

Mystik Tape, 125, 156

Narrative summary of case studies: ASR, 239–41; Bendix Home Systems, 242–44; Caradco, 244–46; Chromalloy Glass, 248–49; Chromalloy Sintercast, 246–48; ESB, 249–53; Great Lakes Screw, 253–55; Harley Davidson, 255–59; Harmon International, 259–61; Letisse, 262–63; Marquette Cement, 263–66; Robert Bruce, 241–42; S. S. White, 271–75; Talon, 266–71; Youngstown Sheet & Tube, 275–79

NE. *See* Numbers-equivalent index

NEWMERG lines, 48–49, 51, 81–82, 89, 114n, 120–21, 174, 182–84

NEWMERG variable: and explanation of sell-offs, 172; in full sell-offs, 182–85; in partial sell-offs, 185–86; and profit model specification, 83; and R&D, 120–21, 203

NEW variable, 34–35, 85, 88, 95, 182, 186, 204; and R&D, 35, 122

New York Stock Exchange (NYSE), 227

New York Stock Exchange (NYSE) listing applications: and acquisitions, 58–59; evidence showing profitability, 61–64, 71, 127; and executive retention, 131

Numbers-equivalent index (NE), 28–29

NUMM variable, 77, 99–100

ORIG lines, 48–49, 51, 81, 184

ORIGMERG lines, 81, 89, 184–86; and R&D, 120–21, 203

ORIGMERG variable: and explanation of sell-offs, 172; in full sell-offs, 182; in partial sell-offs, 185–86

PART variable, 100–01, 147n, 201
Pennwalt, 131, 134, 145n, 156, 271–75
Philip Morris, 131, 134, 141, 145–46, 239–41
Pooling-of-interests accounting, 13–14; choice of, 78–80, 229–38
Pooling-of-interests acquisitions: and mergers of equals, 76; and post-merger profitability, 78–80, 87–92, 93–94, 106, 108–10, 113, 195–99, 205–07; and pre-merger profitability, 61–64, 65n; and sell-offs, 183
Porter, Michael E., 165
Portfolio strategy, 140, 213–14, 222
Post-merger financial performance: and accounting methods, choice of, 78–80; and alternative controls for industry effects, 88–89, 92; and assets, estimation of, 80–82; and differences of, among years, 92–93; and matched pre- versus post-merger analysis, 113–17; and merged unit growth, 117–19; and R&D expenditures, 119–22; sample companies in, 82–83; sensitivity analyses, 103, 105–08; and tender offer targets, 101–03; and time structure of profit effects, 108–11
Post-merger growth, 114–15, 117–19
POSTPI variable, 115–17
Prediction model of accounting methods: methodology of, statistical, 233–24; predictive hypotheses, 229–33; results of, 70, 79, 106, 234–38
Pre-merger profitability: analysis of, 56–74; and failure of mergers, 111–13, 195–98; and macroeconomic variations, 65–67; and multiyear dynamics, 70–73; research in, prior, 56–58; and sold-off lines, 64–65; and tender offer targets, 68–70; and time trends, 67–68, 71, 73
PREPI variable, 115–17, 198–99
President's Council of Economic Advisers, 1, 57, 216–17
Prisoner's dilemma, 226–27
Product extension mergers, 23
PROF:A variable, 83
PROF:S variable, 83
Profitability. *See* Pre-merger profitability; Profits; Supranormal profitability
Profits: and accounting methods, 13–16; and cash-flow timing patterns, 10–12; decline in, 111–12; and financial

accounting data, 12–17; measures of, 12–17, 60, 83; and pooling-of-interests acquisitions, 61–64; and purchase acquisitions, 61–64; and sell-offs, 166–69, 147n, 191; time structure of effects, 108–11, 114
Purchase accounting, choice of, 78–80, 229–38
Purchase acquisitions: and post-merger profitability, 78–80, 87–92, 93–94, 100, 106, 109, 111, 195–99, 204–05; and pre-merger profitability, 61–64, 65n; and sell-offs, 183
Pure conglomerate mergers, 23, 98–99, 183

Q variable. *See* Tobin's *Q* index
Quarterly Financial Report, 57, 60–61, 65–66, 69, 78n, 114

Ravenscraft, David J., 16
R&D. *See* Research and development
RD:S variable, 120–22
RD/S variable, 47, 84
Related business mergers, 23
RELAT variable, 98, 172
Republic Corporation, 38
Research and development (R&D): and diversification, 34–35, 47; expenditures on, post-merger, 119–22; in leveraged buyouts, 155; and productivity growth, 203; and sell-offs, 157, 171–72, 179, 184, 186–87, 187–90
Robert Bruce, 141, 149–50, 241–42

Scherer, F. M., 20, 21
Scovill, 131, 152, 244–45
Securities and Exchange Commission (SEC), 226–28
Securities regulation, 226–28
Selling costs, 47, 51, 53–54
Sell-offs: and accounting valuation consequences, 147–49; behavior before, 156–57, 187–90; decision for, 144–46; developments after, 149–56; frequency of, 159–66; as frequent result of mergers, 2, 161–62; full, explanations of, 178–85; Grimm data on, 2, 159–61; and horizontal merger efficiencies, 150–52; LB data on, 162–66, 177–78; and "lemons" problem, 146–47; and leveraged buyouts, 152–56; and mergers, 192–93; partial, explanation of, 185–87; profit aftermath of, 100–01, 147n, 151–52, 155–56, 191; profit antecedents, 132, 166–69; sample

selection of, 177–78; and stock market valuation consequences, 147–49; transitional behavior after, 156–57; variables explaining, 169–73. *See also* Case study evidence of economics of sell-offs

Shrieves, Ronald E., 44

SHR variable, 85, 88, 121–22, 171, 179

Smith, Keith V., 44

Spearman correlation, 31

Standard Industrial Classification (SIC) four-digit industries, 26

Standard & Poor's *425* industrials portfolio, 41–44, 209–10

Stewart, James, 265

Stewart, John F., 58, 62

Stigler, George J., 22, 62

Stillman, Robert, 7

Stock market: and conglomerates, reaction to, 38–39, 41–45, 215; efficient, 7–10, 221; event studies, 5–7, 220–21; and mergers, 38–39, 41–45, 207–10; and sell-offs, 147–49. *See also* Stock prices

Stock prices: acquiring firm's, 6–7; acquisition's, 6–7; analyses of, 5–7; competitors', 7; of conglomerates, 41–45; and mergers, 1, 5–7; target's, 5–6; of Teledyne, 42–43; undervalued, 7–10. *See also* Stock market

Supranormal profitability, 61–63, 69

Synergies, 3, 7, 47, 51, 98–99, 131, 212–13, 239, 243, 244, 245, 246, 248, 267, 272

Talon, 125n, 134–35, 139, 157; narrative summary of, 266–71

Tax Act of *1981*, 223

Tax policy: and mergers, 222–23; and motives for mergers, 3, 211, 213–14

Teledyne: reasons for success of, 140–44; and returns to investors, 42–43, 209

Tender offer targets: and post-merger financial performance, 101–03; and pre-tender profits, 68–70; and reasons for selection, 129–30; and sell-off experience, 173, 182, 185

10-K reports, 228

Textron, 134–35, 139, 144, 267–71

Tobin's *Q* index, 80, 100, 231, 236–38

Undervalued-assets and bargain theories, 7–10, 211

Vertical mergers, 22–23, 98–99, 172, 183, 243, 245

Weiss, Leonard W., 2, 47, 166, 201

Weston, J. Fred, 44

White, S. S., 131, 134, 141, 150, 156; narrative summary of, 271–75

Whittaker Corp., 209

Williams, Ronald B. Jr., 206

Williamson, Oliver E., 213, 225

Wrapp, H. Edward, 136

Wright, Mike, 152, 154, 155

YKK, 134, 139

Youngstown Sheet & Tube, 125n, 130, 139, 144, 151, 152; narrative summary of, 275–79